THE LOEB CLASSICAL LIBRARY

FOUNDED BY JAMES LOEB, LL.D.

EDITED BY

E. H. WARMINGTON, M.A., F.R.HIST.SOC.

PREVIOUS EDITORS

† T. E. PAGE, C.H., LITT.D.   † E. CAPPS, PH.D., LL.D.

† W. H. D. ROUSE, LITT.D.   L. A. POST, L.H.D

SENECA

I

MORAL ESSAYS

I

214

SENECA

IN TEN VOLUMES

I

MORAL ESSAYS

WITH AN ENGLISH TRANSLATION BY

JOHN W. BASORE, Ph.D.

PRINCETON UNIVERSITY

IN THREE VOLUMES

I

CAMBRIDGE, MASSACHUSETTS

HARVARD UNIVERSITY PRESS

LONDON

WILLIAM HEINEMANN LTD

MCMLXX

American
ISBN 0-674-99236-9

British
ISBN 0 434 99214 3

First printed 1928
Reprinted 1958, 1963, 1970

CONTENTS OF VOLUME I

INTRODUCTION

Sprung from the rich and talented Spanish family
of the *Annaei*, Lucius Annaeus Seneca, second son of
Seneca the rhetorician, became the most important
public and literary figure at Rome in the age of Nero.
His mother was Helvia, a lady of native intelligence,
some culture, and many virtues.   An elder brother,
Novatus, known after his adoption as Gallio, was
governor of Achaia under Claudius, and survives in
Christian annals (Acts xviii. 12-17) with undeserved
odium as the Roman official before whom the apostle
Paul was arraigned.   Mela, the younger brother, of
more retiring disposition, but rated by his father
as the ablest of the three, lives only as the father
of a famous son—the epic poet Lucan, whose
precocious and flamboyant powers marked him out
as the prodigy of his distinguished, but ill-fated,
family, of which no chief member survived the
catastrophe of the Pisonian conspiracy.   Lucan, his
father, and both his uncles were all objects of
Nero's vengeance.

The career of Seneca himself was marked by
spectacular shifts of fortune, amid which he appears
a puzzling and at times a pathetic figure—the
victim alike of imperial hostility and favour.   Born

at Corduba about 4 B.C., he was brought to Rome
while still a child in arms. There, carefully nurtured
and broadly trained in rhetoric and philosophy,
he entered upon the senatorial career and gained
the quaestorship probably under Tiberius. By his
eloquence in the Senate, he is said to have aroused
the jealousy of Caligula and to have escaped death
only because, it was averred, he was already doomed
by ill-health to die. Of his ill-health we hear much
in his writings, but he outlived Caligula and missed
no opportunity to take pitiless revenge upon him
with his pen. Under Claudius he fell upon actual
disaster. Through the agency of the empress Mes-
salina, Seneca, now established as a man of letters
and, apparently, of fashion, was accused of an intrigue
with the notorious Julia Livilla, sister of Caligula,
whom her uncle promptly upon his accession had
recalled from exile, and both were banished. After
he had spent eight weary and fretful years in dismal
Corsica, during which, however, he found some solace
in writing and study, Agrippina, now the wife of
Claudius, secured his recall in A.D. 49, and raised him
to the post of tutor to her young son, the future
emperor Nero. A year later he was praetor. From
this time Seneca's fortunes were linked with those
of Nero. He grew in honour, wealth,[a] and power, and
for five years after Nero's accession was, along with
Burrus, the virtuous old praetorian, the emperor's
acknowledged confidant and guide. But gradually
his influence weakened, and after the death of
Burrus in A.D. 62 he sought unavailingly for obscurity

[a] There are many references to the lordly wealth which
Seneca amassed. *Cf.* Tac. *Ann.* xiii. 42. 6: Juv. x. 16;
Dio, lxi. 10. 2.

INTRODUCTION

in retirement. Three years later, charged with complicity in the conspiracy of Piso, he was forced to commit suicide, and met death with dignity and Stoic fortitude.

The special significance of Seneca is, in brief, that he revived the subject of philosophy in Latin literature, spiritualized and humanized Stoicism, and became the exponent of a new style, that exploited the short sentence, rhetoric, and declamation. The artificialities of his pointed style have found many critics, both early and late. Caligula[a] called his speeches—not now extant—" prize declamations, sand without lime," the archaist Gellius[b] condemns his influence, and Fronto[c] censures his literary affectations. Quintilian[d] with truer discernment indicts more severely his taste than his methods, for it is in the excesses of rhetoric that he most often offends.[e] That he was the most brilliant writer, as well as the most independent thinker, of his day few will now deny.

In philosophy Seneca's interests were purely ethical. He was a bold, but inconsistent, moralist—a preacher rather than an exemplar of Stoic virtue. His discourses are, in the end, Stoic sermons, informal in structure, lacking too often the marks of ordered presentation, but usually effective in the quickness of their appeal. While ostensibly an adherent of Stoic materialism, he shows the independence of an eclectic and becomes particularly noteworthy in his

---

[a] Suet. *Calig.* 53. [b] xii. 2.
[c] *Epist.* p. 156 (Naber). [d] x. 1. 130.
[e] An admirable analysis and discussion of Seneca's style will be found in the Introductions A and B of Mr. Summers's edition of *Select Letters.*

conception of deity and the kindred doctrine of the brotherhood of man, in both of which he went far beyond his times. Although, utilizing the Stoic doctrine of a Unity out of a plurality of gods (as, while there are many virtues, Virtue is one), he causes confusion by his terminology, yet he verges constantly toward the representation of God as a moral and spiritual being, a beneficent Providence, instinct with fatherly regard for the human race. Closely linked with this conception is a bitter condemnation of gladiatorial contests, slavery, and any form of cruelty of man to fellow man.

Seneca was a voluminous writer of both prose and poetry. Besides some epigrams, ten extant tragedies are associated with his name, though one, the *Octavia*, appears from internal evidence to be unmistakably the work of a later poet. The other nine plays are unique and notable specimens of Roman tragedy adapted from Greek originals, of which, however, they appear to be little more than rhetorical travesties. But their influence upon the dramatic literature of Italy, France, and England, though distorting, was profound. His extant prose works comprise a significant group of writings that are moral in purpose, a quasi-scientific treatise—the *Naturales Quaestiones* in seven books —and the *Apocolocyntosis*, a satirical skit on the apotheosis of the emperor Claudius. To the group of moral writings belong the twenty books of the *Epistulae Morales*, a unit by reason of their form, and a series of more formal compositions, which, developed with vague consciousness of an argumentative second person, are likewise united by a similarity of form. These quasi-dialogues are the twelve treatises grouped together in the

INTRODUCTION

Ambrosian manuscript under the title *Dialogi* [a] and traditionally known as *Dialogues*, the *De Clementia*, originally in three books, and the seven books of the *De Beneficiis*, all of which it has been convenient for the purpose in hand to combine under the comprehensive title of *Moral Essays*.

The chronology of Seneca's writings is in most cases doubtful. Of the essays included in this volume, the *De Providentia* and the *De Constantia* are associated by Waltz [b] with the early years of the exile (A.D. 41–42), but equally wise conjecture will place them later. When Seneca wrote the *De Ira*, Caligula was undoubtedly dead, and Novatus, to whom it was dedicated, had not yet been adopted by Junius Gallio. It shows bitter hostility to Caligula, and may well have been written when the memory of his excesses was fresh. By reason of the allusion to the age of Nero (i. 9. 1), the *De Clementia* may be definitely assigned to the year A.D. 55 or 56.

Concerning Lucilius, to whom the *De Providentia*, the *Naturales Quaestiones*, and the *Epistulae* are addressed, Seneca himself supplies incidental information. A native, probably, of Naples or Pompeii, by his own energy he attained equestrian rank and was appointed procurator of Sicily. He was a student of philosophy, with a leaning toward Epicureanism, and a writer of both prose and poetry. His name has gained some importance in literary history as the conjectural author of the *Aetna*, a philosophical poem ascribed in the manuscripts to

[a] Quintilian used the term (x. 1. 129), but that he applied it only to the treatises of the Ambrosian corpus may be doubted.

[b] *Vie de Sénèque*, p. 7, note.

INTRODUCTION

Virgil. Younger than Seneca, he seems to have maintained with him a long friendship of peculiar loyalty. If, as Waltz supposes, the *De Providentia* belongs to the early years of the exile, Seneca's own fortunes may well have called forth the questioning of Lucilius concerning the ways of Providence which gave excuse for the essay. In treating his subject Seneca elaborates the thesis that no evils can befall the good man, by interpreting adversities, not as evils, but as wholesome opportunities provided by a beneficent deity for the testing of virtue. The discourse closes with a passage of restrained rhetoric, giving Stoic approval of suicide as a reasonable departure from trials too great.

Annaeus Serenus, the young friend, or relative, of Seneca to whom are addressed the *De Constantia* and two other treatises, is said to have been prefect of Nero's nightwatchmen (*praefectus Neronis vigilum*). He is mentioned by Tacitus [a] as an intimate friend of Seneca, who with a show of loyalty screened the indiscretions of Nero in his affair with Acte. Seneca had for him the deepest affection and counselled him in philosophy with fatherly solicitude. He apparently was an Epicurean. Though much younger than Seneca, he died first, probably in A.D. 62. Seneca descants upon his premature death in one of his *Letters* (lxiii. 14), and refers feelingly to the bitterness of his grief.

The essay itself is exceptional in its orderly arrangement. After affirming the superiority of the Stoics over other schools of philosophy, the author takes as his text the Stoic paradox that the wise man can receive no injury. This he proceeds to relieve

[a] *Ann.* xiii. 13.

INTRODUCTION

by an exposition of the true inwardness of the wise man's fortunes. Setting up a distinction between "injury" and "insult," he shows *seriatim* the invulnerability of the wise man to both, and after conditioned praise of Epicurus's view, closes the discussion with a justification of the Stoic position.

Of Seneca's brother Novatus, to whom the *De Ira* is addressed, something has already been said. He was much beloved for his amiability, was an eminent declaimer, if we are to trust Jerome,[a] and at an unknown date was adopted by the rhetorician Junius Gallio. He reached the consulship, was governor of Achaia in A.D. 52, and died by his own hand in 66.

Seneca used authorities assiduously, and for the elaborate disquisition *On Anger* had several available; Sotion, his master in philosophy, had written περὶ ὀργῆς, and may well have been one. Though the arrangement of the essay is noticeably faulty,[b] and its style is fervid with rhetoric, the wealth of its illustrative matter gives it unusual interest. Book I. deals with the outward aspects, the harm, and the various definitions of anger; Book II. discusses its origin, its nature, and its remedies; Book III. repeats much that has been said before, and continues with the new topic of how to check the anger of others.

The *De Clementia*, addressed to the emperor Nero, was written just after the young prince had finished his eighteenth year, and was intended to guide him toward the ideal of a merciful and popular ruler. It gives interesting evidence of Seneca's own public

[a] In the statement of Jerome (*ad a. Abr.* 2080) the son may be confused with his adoptive father.

[b] Compare the similarity of the topical divisions in ii. 18. 1 and iii. 5. 2.

INTRODUCTION

wisdom, of his tendency to flattery, and of his method in dealing with his difficult pupil. Unfortunately, more than half of the work has been lost.

The most important manuscript of the *Dialogues* is the *Codex Ambrosianus*, at Milan, belonging to the tenth or the eleventh century. This has been designated A, and the readings of its later correctors, A [1-6]. An additional manuscript available for the *De Ira* is the *Codex Laurentianus* (designated L) of the twelfth or thirteenth century. The best manuscript of the *De Clementia* is the *Codex Nazarianus* (designated N) in the Palatine collection of the Vatican. This belongs to the eighth or ninth century. Two others of the twelfth century are the *Codex Amplonianus* at Erfurt (designated A), which is not complete, and the *Codex Parisinus* 8542 (designated T). In the critical notes O is used to designate a consensus of N, A, and other principal manuscripts. For the complete apparatus the editions of Hermes and Hosius may be consulted.

The texts adopted for translation are, for the *Dialogues*, that of Hermes, Leipzig, 1905, for the *De Clementia*, that of Hosius, Leipzig, 1900. Except minor changes in punctuation and orthography, divergencies from these have been duly recorded in the critical notes.

J. W. B.

SELECT BIBLIOGRAPHY

EDITIONS AND TRANSLATIONS

THE *editio princeps* was published at Naples in 1475. This omitted the *Apocolocyntosis*, but contained some spurious works along with some of the works of the elder Seneca. Famous editions of the sixteenth and seventeenth centuries were those of Erasmus, Justus Lipsius, and J. F. Gronovius.

Noteworthy are the more recent editions of:

F. E. Ruhkopf, Leipzig, 1797–1811.

C. R. Fickert, Leipzig, 1842–1845.

F. Haase, Leipzig (Teubner), 1852.

M. C. Gertz, *De Beneficiis* and *De Clementia*, Berlin, 1876 ; *Dialogi XII.*, Copenhagen, 1886.

C. Hosius, *De Beneficiis* and *De Clementia*, Leipzig (Teubner), 1900.

E. Hermes, *Dialogi XII.*, Leipzig (Teubner), 1905.

Select essays, with commentary, appear in the editions of Hurst and Whiting (New York, 1884), A. P. Ball (New York, 1908), and J. D. Duff (Cambridge, 1915).

Well known are the older translations of Thomas Lodge (London, 1614) and Roger L'Estrange (London, 1673).

WORKS FOR REFERENCE

E. V. Arnold, *Roman Stoicism*, Cambridge, 1911.

A. Bourgery, *Sénèque prosateur*, Paris, 1922, pp. 1-205 (a discussion of Seneca's art and influence).

S. Dill, *Roman Society from Nero to Marcus Aurelius,*

BIBLIOGRAPHY

London, 1904 (particularly the chapter on the " Philosophic Director ").

F. W. Farrar, *Seekers after God* (Seneca, Epictetus, and Marcus Aurelius), London, 1874.

R. M. Gummere, *Seneca the Philosopher and his Modern Message*, Boston, 1922.

F. L. Lucas, *Seneca and Elizabethan Tragedy*, Cambridge, 1922, pp. 25-52 (" Seneca the Man ").

C. Martha, *Les Moralistes sous l'Empire Romain*, Paris, 1907.

W. C. Summers, *The Silver Age of Latin Literature*, London, 1920, pp. 175 ff.

René Waltz, *Vie de Sénèque*, Paris, 1909 (the best life of Seneca).

In the Budé series we now have :

Sénèque, *Dialogues* I, A. Bourgery, 1953 ; II, A. Bourgery, 1955 ; III, R. Waltz, 1923 ; IV, R. Waltz, 1927 ; *De la Clémence*, F. Préchac, 1961 ; *Des Bienfaits* I, 1926 : II, 1927, F. Préchac.

Note also :

J. Duff, ed. of *Dialogorum* 10, 11, 12, Cambridge, 1915

P. Grimal, *De Constantia Sapientis*, commentary, Paris. 1953 ; ed. of *De Brevitate Vitae*, Paris, 1959.

H. Dahlmann, *De Brevitate Vitae*, ed. with German translation, Munich, 1949.

H. Lenzen, *Dialog de Brev. Vit.*, Leipzig, 1937.

C. Favez, *Dialogorum Liber 6 ad Marciam de Consolatione*, Paris, 1928.

O. Apelt, ed. of *Die Dialoge*, German translation and notes, Leipzig, 1923.

K. Abel, *Bauformen in Senecas Dialogen*, Heidelberg, 1967.

P. Grimal, ed. of *Operum Moralium Concordantia*, Paris, 1965-1969.

SENECA
MORAL ESSAYS

L. ANNAEI SENECAE DIALOGORVM

LIBER I

AD LVCILIVM

QVARE ALIQVA INCOMMODA BONIS VIRIS ACCIDANT, CVM PROVIDENTIA SIT

(*De Providentia*)

1 1. Quaesisti a me, Lucili, quid ita, si providentia
mundus regeretur, multa bonis viris mala acciderent.
Hoc commodius in contextu operis redderetur, cum
praeesse universis providentiam probaremus et interesse nobis deum ; sed quoniam a toto particulam
revelli placet et unam contradictionem manente lite
integra solvere, faciam rem non difficilem, causam
deorum agam.

2 Supervacuum est in praesentia ostendere non sine
aliquo custode tantum opus stare nec hunc siderum
coetum discursumque fortuiti impetus esse, et quae
casus incitat saepe turbari et cito arietare, hanc in-
offensam velocitatem procedere aeternae legis imperio

2

THE DIALOGUES OF
LUCIUS ANNAEUS SENECA

BOOK I

TO LUCILIUS ON PROVIDENCE

*Why, though there is a Providence, some Misfortunes
befall Good Men.*

You have asked me, Lucilius, why, if a Providence
rules the world, it still happens that many evils befall
good men. This would be more fittingly answered
in a coherent work designed to prove that a Providence does preside over the universe, and that God
concerns himself with us. But since it is your wish
that a part be severed from the whole, and that I
refute a single objection while the main question is
left untouched, I shall do so ; the task is not difficult,
—I shall be pleading the cause of the gods.

For the present purpose it is unnecessary to show
that this mighty structure of the world does not
endure without some one to guard it, and that the
assembling and the separate flight of the stars above
are not due to the workings of chance ; that while
bodies which owe their motion to accident often fall
into disorder and quickly collide, this swift revolution of the heavens, being ruled by eternal law, goes

3

tantum rerum terra marique gestantem, tantum
clarissimorum luminum et ex disposito relucentium ;
non esse materiae errantis hunc ordinem nec quae
temere coierunt tanta arte pendere, ut terrarum
gravissimum pondus sedeat immotum et circa se
properantis caeli fugam spectet, ut infusa vallibus
maria molliant terras nec ullum incrementum flumi-
num sentiant, ut ex minimis seminibus nascantur
3 ingentia. Ne illa quidem quae videntur confusa et
incerta, pluvias dico nubesque et elisorum fulminum
iactus et incendia ruptis montium verticibus effusa,
tremores labantis soli aliaque quae tumultuosa pars
rerum circa terras movet, sine ratione, quamvis subita
sint, accidunt, sed suas et illa causas habent non
minus quam quae alienis locis conspecta miraculo
sunt, ut in mediis fluctibus calentes aquae et nova
4 insularum in vasto exsilientium mari spatia. Iam
vero si quis observaverit nudari litora pelago in se
recedente eademque intra exiguum tempus operiri,
credet caeca quadam volutatione modo contrahi undas
et introrsum agi, modo erumpere et magno cursu
repetere sedem suam, cum interim illae portionibus
crescunt et ad horam ac diem subeunt ampliores

---

^a Seneca's rhetoric omits the intermediate step of the
transformation into rain.

on unhindered, producing so many things on land and sea, so many brilliant lights in the sky all shining in fixed array ; that this regularity does not belong to matter moving at random, and that whatever combinations result from chance do not adjust themselves with that artistry whereby the earth, the heaviest in weight, abides immovable and beholds the flight of the sky as it whirls around it, and the seas, flooding ^a the valleys, soften the land, and feel no increase from the rivers, and whereby huge growths spring up from the tiniest seeds. Even those phenomena which seem irregular and undetermined —I mean showers and clouds, the stroke of crashing thunderbolts and the fires that belch from the riven peaks of mountains, tremors of the quaking ground, and the other disturbances which the turbulent element in nature sets in motion about the earth, these, no matter how suddenly they occur, do not happen without a reason ; nay, they also are the result of special causes, and so, in like manner, are those things which seem miraculous by reason of the incongruous situations in which they are beheld, such as warm waters in the midst of the sea-waves, and the expanses of new islands that spring up in the wide ocean. Moreover, if any one observes how the shore is laid bare as the sea withdraws into itself, and how within a short time the same stretch is covered over again, he will suppose that it is some blind fluctuation which causes the waves now to shrink and flow inwards, now to burst forth and in mighty sweep seek their former resting - place, whereas in fact they increase by degrees, and true to the hour and the day they approach in propor-

minoresque, prout illas lunare sidus elicuit, ad cuius
arbitrium oceanus exundat. Suo ista tempori re-
serventur, eo quidem magis quod tu non dubitas de
5 providentia sed quereris. In gratiam te reducam cum
diis adversus optimos optimis. Neque enim rerum
natura patitur ut umquam bona bonis noceant; inter
bonos viros ac deos amicitia est conciliante virtute.

Amicitiam dico? Immo etiam necessitudo et similitudo, quoniam quidem bonus tempore tantum a deo
differt, discipulus eius aemulatorque et vera progenies,
quam parens ille magnificus, virtutum non lenis
6 exactor, sicut severi patres, durius educat. Itaque
cum videris bonos viros acceptosque diis laborare,
sudare, per arduum escendere, malos autem lascivire
et voluptatibus fluere, cogita filiorum nos modestia
delectari, vernularum licentia, illos disciplina tristiori
contineri, horum ali audaciam. Idem tibi de deo
liqueat. Bonum virum in deliciis non habet, experitur,
indurat, sibi illum parat.

1 2. " Quare multa bonis viris adversa eveniunt ? "
Nihil accidere bono viro mali potest; non miscentur
contraria. Quemadmodum tot amnes, tantum superne
deiectorum imbrium, tanta medicatorum vis fontium
non mutant saporem maris, ne remittunt quidem, ita
adversarum impetus rerum viri fortis non vertit ani-

6

tionately larger or smaller volume according as they are attracted by the star we call the moon, at whose bidding the ocean surges. But let such matters be kept for their fitting time,—all the more so, indeed, because you do not lack faith in Providence, but complain of it. I shall reconcile you with the gods, who are ever best to those who are best. For Nature never permits good to be injured by good; between good men and the gods there exists a friendship brought about by virtue.

Friendship, do I say? Nay, rather there is a tie of relationship and a likeness, since, in truth, a good man differs from God in the element of time only; he is God's pupil, his imitator, and true offspring, whom his all-glorious parent, being no mild taskmaster of virtues, rears, as strict fathers do, with much severity. And so, when you see that men who are good and acceptable to the gods labour and sweat and have a difficult road to climb, that the wicked, on the other hand, make merry and abound in pleasures, reflect that our children please us by their modesty, but slave-boys by their forwardness; that we hold in check the former by sterner discipline, while we encourage the latter to be bold. Be assured that the same is true of God. He does not make a spoiled pet of a good man; he tests him, hardens him, and fits him for his own service.

You ask, " Why do many adversities come to good men ? " No evil *can* befall a good man; opposites do not mingle. Just as the countless rivers, the vast fall of rain from the sky, and the huge volume of mineral springs do not change the taste of the sea, do not even modify it, so the assaults of adversity do not weaken the spirit of a brave man. It always

7

mum. Manet in statu et quicquid evenit in suum
colorem trahit; est enim omnibus externis potentior.
2 Nec hoc dico: non sentit illa, sed vincit et alioqui
quietus placidusque contra incurrentia attollitur.
Omnia adversa exercitationes putat. Quis autem, vir
modo et erectus ad honesta, non est laboris adpetens
iusti et ad officia cum periculo promptus? Cui non
3 industrio otium poena est? Athletas videmus, quibus
virium cura est, cum fortissimis quibusque confligere
et exigere ab is per quos certamini praeparantur, ut
totis contra ipsos viribus utantur; caedi se vexarique
patiuntur et si non inveniunt singulos pares, pluribus
4 simul obiciuntur. Marcet sine adversario virtus;
tunc apparet quanta sit quantumque polleat, cum
quid possit patientia ostendit. Scias licet idem viris
bonis esse faciendum, ut dura ac difficilia non refor-
mident nec de fato querantur, quicquid accidit boni
consulant, in bonum vertant. Non quid sed quemadmodum feras interest.
5 Non vides quanto aliter patres, aliter matres indul-
geant? Illi excitari iubent liberos ad studia obeunda
mature, feriatis quoque diebus non patiuntur esse
otiosos et sudorem illis et interdum lacrimas ex-
cutiunt; at matres fovere in sinu, continere in umbra
volunt, numquam contristari, numquam flere, num-
6 quam laborare. Patrium deus habet adversus bonos

8

maintains its poise, and it gives its own colour to everything that happens ; for it is mightier than all external things. And yet I do not mean to say that the brave man is insensible to these, but that he overcomes them, and being in all else unmoved and calm rises to meet whatever assails him. All his adversities he counts mere training. Who, moreover, if he is a man and intent upon the right, is not eager for reasonable toil and ready for duties accompanied by danger ? To what energetic man is not idleness a punishment ? Wrestlers, who make strength of body their chief concern, we see pitting themselves against none but the strongest, and they require of those who are preparing them for the arena that they use against them all their strength ; they submit to blows and hurts, and if they do not find their match in single opponents, they engage with several at a time. Without an adversary, prowess shrivels. We see how great and how efficient it really is, only when it shows by endurance what it is capable of. Be assured that good men ought to act likewise ; they should not shrink from hardships and difficulties, nor complain against fate ; they should take in good part whatever happens, and should turn it to good. Not what you endure, but how you endure, is important.

Do you not see how fathers show their love in one way, and mothers in another ? The father orders his children to be aroused from sleep in order that they may start early upon their pursuits,—even on holidays he does not permit them to be idle, and he draws from them sweat and sometimes tears. But the mother fondles them in her lap, wishes to keep them out of the sun, wishes them never to be unhappy, never to cry, never to toil. Toward good

9

viros animum et illos fortiter amat et " Operibus,"
inquit, " doloribus, damnis exagitentur, ut verum
colligant robur." Languent per inertiam saginata nec
labore tantum sed motu et ipso sui onere deficiunt.
Non fert ullum ictum inlaesa felicitas ; at cui assidua
fuit cum incommodis suis rixa, callum per iniurias
duxit nec ulli malo cedit sed etiam si cecidit de
7 genu pugnat. Miraris tu, si deus ille bonorum
amantissimus, qui illos quam optimos esse atque ex-
cellentissimos vult, fortunam illis cum qua exerceantur
adsignat ? Ego vero non miror, si aliquando impetum
capiunt spectandi magnos viros conluctantis cum
8 aliqua calamitate. Nobis interdum voluptati est, si
adulescens constantis animi irruentem feram vena-
bulo excepit, si leonis incursum interritus pertulit,
tantoque hoc spectaculum est gratius, quanto id
honestior fecit. Non sunt ista, quae possint deorum
in se vultum convertere, puerilia et humanae oblecta-
9 menta levitatis. Ecce spectaculum dignum ad quod
respiciat intentus operi suo deus, ecce par deo
dignum, vir fortis cum fortuna mala compositus,
utique si et provocavit. Non video, inquam, quid
habeat in terris Iuppiter pulchrius, si eo[1] convertere
animum velit, quam ut spectet Catonem iam partibus
non semel fractis stantem nihilo minus inter ruinas
10 publicas rectum. " Licet," inquit, " omnia in unius

---

[1] eo *added by Goerenz.*

men God has the mind of a father, he cherishes for
them a manly love, and he says, " Let them be
harassed by toil, by suffering, by losses, in order that
they may gather true strength." Bodies grown fat
through sloth are weak, and not only labour, but
even movement and their very weight cause them
to break down. Unimpaired prosperity cannot withstand a single blow; but he who has struggled
constantly with his ills becomes hardened through
suffering, and yields to no misfortune ; nay, even if
he falls, he still fights upon his knees. Do you wonder
if that God, who most dearly loves the good, who
wishes them to become supremely good and virtuous,
allots to them a fortune that will make them struggle ?
For my part, I do not wonder if sometimes the gods
are moved by the desire to behold great men wrestle
with some calamity. We men at times are stirred
with pleasure if a youth of steady courage meets
with his spear an onrushing wild beast, if unterrified
he sustains the charge of a lion. And the more
honourable the youth who does this, the more pleasing this spectacle becomes. But these are not the
things to draw down the gaze of the gods upon us
—they are childish, the pastimes of man's frivolity.
But lo ! here is a spectacle worthy of the regard of
God as he contemplates his works ; lo ! here a contest worthy of God,—a brave man matched against
ill-fortune, and doubly so if his also was the challenge.
I do not know, I say, what nobler sight the Lord
of Heaven could find on earth, should he wish to
turn his attention there, than the spectacle of Cato,
after his cause had already been shattered more
than once, nevertheless standing erect amid the
ruins of the commonwealth. " Although," said he,

dicionem concesserint, custodiantur legionibus terrae,
classibus maria, Caesarianus portas miles obsideat;
Cato qua exeat habet; una manu latam libertati
viam faciet. Ferrum istud, etiam civili bello purum
et innoxium, bonas tandem ac nobiles edet operas:
libertatem, quam patriae non potuit, Catoni dabit.
Aggredere, anime, diu meditatum opus, eripe te
rebus humanis. Iam Petreius et Iuba concucur-
rerunt iacentque alter alterius manu caesi. Fortis
et egregia fati conventio, sed quae non deceat magnitudinem nostram; tam turpe est Catoni mortem ab
11 ullo petere quam vitam." Liquet mihi cum magno
spectasse gaudio deos, dum ille vir, acerrimus sui vin-
dex, alienae saluti consulit et instruit discedentium
fugam, dum studia etiam nocte ultima tractat, dum
gladium sacro pectori infigit, dum viscera spargit et
illam sanctissimam animam indignamque quae ferro
12 contaminaretur manu educit. Inde crediderim fuisse
parum certum et efficax vulnus; non fuit diis immor-
talibus satis spectare Catonem semel. Retenta ac
revocata virtus est, ut in difficiliore parte se ostenderet; non enim tam magno animo mors initur quam
repetitur. Quidni libenter spectarent alumnum suum
tam claro ac memorabili exitu evadentem? Mors illos
consecrat, quorum exitum et qui timent laudant.
1 3. Sed iam procedente oratione ostendam, quam

---

^a After Caesar's victory at Thapsus (46 b.c.), these two
supporters of the opposition, despairing of pardon, sought
death in hand-to-hand combat. Seneca accords with
Cassius Dio (xliii. 8. 4) in placing the incident before the
suicide of Cato at Utica.

^b Cato stabbed himself, but accomplished death by
tearing open the hideous wound which his physician had
attempted to dress (Plutarch, *Cato the Younger*, lxx.;
Cassius Dio, xliii. 11. 5).

" all the world has fallen under one man's sway, although Caesar's legions guard the land, his fleets the sea, and Caesar's troops beset the city gates, yet Cato has a way of escape; with one single hand he will open a wide path to freedom. This sword, unstained and blameless even in civil war, shall at last do good and noble service : the freedom which it could not give to his country it shall give to Cato! Essay, my soul, the task long planned; deliver yourself from human affairs. Already Petreius and Juba have met and lie fallen, each slain by the other's hand.[a] Their compact with Fate was brave and noble, but for my greatness such would be unfit. For Cato it were as ignoble to beg death from any man as to beg life." I am sure that the gods looked on with exceeding joy while that hero, most ruthless in avenging himself, took thought for the safety of others and arranged the escape of his departing followers ; while even on his last night he pursued his studies ; while he drove the sword into his sacred breast ; while he scattered his vitals, and drew forth by his hand that holiest spirit, too noble to be defiled by the steel.[b] I should like to believe that this is why the wound was not well-aimed and efficacious— it was not enough for the immortal gods to look but once on Cato. His virtue was held in check and called back that it might display itself in a harder rôle ; for to seek death needs not so great a soul as to reseek it. Surely the gods looked with pleasure upon their pupil as he made his escape by so glorious and memorable an end! Death con-secrates those whose end even those who fear must praise.

But as the discussion progresses, I shall show how

non sint quae videntur mala. Nunc illud dico, ista
quae tu vocas aspera, quae adversa et abominanda,
primum pro ipsis esse quibus accidunt, deinde pro universis, quorum maior diis cura quam singulorum est,
post hoc volentibus accidere ac dignos malo esse, si
nolint. His adiciam fato ista sic et recte[1] eadem lege
bonis evenire qua sunt boni. Persuadebo deinde tibi,
ne umquam boni viri miserearis; potest enim miser
dici, non potest esse.

2 Difficillimum ex omnibus quae proposui videtur
quod primum dixi, pro ipsis esse quibus eveniunt
ista quae horremus ac tremimus. "Pro ipsis est,"
inquis, "in exilium proici, in egestatem deduci, liberos coniugem ecferre, ignominia affici, debilitari?"
Si miraris haec pro aliquo esse, miraberis quosdam
ferro et igne curari nec minus fame ac siti. Sed si
cogitaveris tecum remedii causa quibusdam et radi
ossa et legi et extrahi venas et quaedam amputari
membra quae sine totius pernicie corporis haerere non
poterant, hoc quoque patieris probari tibi, quaedam
incommoda pro is esse quibus accidunt, tam me

---

[1] et recte *Petschenig from A* : ire et *Madvig.*

14

the things that seem to be evils are not really so. This much I now say,—that those things which you call hardships, which you call adversities and accursed, are, in the first place, for the good of the persons themselves to whom they come ; in the second place, that they are for the good of the whole human family, for which the gods have a greater concern than for single persons ; again, I say that good men are willing that these things should happen and, if they are unwilling, that they deserve misfortune. I shall add, further, that these things happen thus by destiny, and that they rightly befall good men by the same law which makes them good. I shall induce you, in fine, never to commiserate a good man. For he can be called miserable, but he cannot be so.

Of all the propositions which I have advanced, the most difficult seems to be the one stated first,— that those things which we all shudder and tremble at are for the good of the persons themselves to whom they come. " Is it," you ask, " for their own good that men are driven into exile, reduced to want, that they bear to the grave wife or children, that they suffer public disgrace, and are broken in health ? " If you are surprised that these things are for any man's good, you must also be surprised that by means of surgery and cautery, and also by fasting and thirst, the sick are sometimes made well. But if you will reflect that for the sake of being cured the sick sometimes have their bones scraped and removed, and their veins pulled out, and that some- times members are amputated which could not be left without causing destruction to the whole body, you will allow yourself to be convinced of this as well,— that ills are sometimes for the good of those to whom

15

hercules quam quaedam quae laudantur atque ap-
petuntur contra eos esse quos delectaverunt, simillima
cruditatibus ebrietatibusque et ceteris quae necant
3 per voluptatem. Inter multa magnifica Demetri
nostri et haec vox est, a qua recens sum; sonat
adhuc et vibrat in auribus meis: "Nihil," inquit,
"mihi videtur infelicius eo, cui nihil umquam evenit
adversi." Non licuit enim illi se experiri. Ut ex
voto illi fluxerint omnia, ut ante votum, male tamen
de illo dii iudicaverunt. Indignus visus est a quo
vinceretur aliquando fortuna, quae ignavissimum
quemque refugit, quasi dicat: "Quid ego istum mihi
adversarium adsumam? Statim arma submittet; non
opus est in illum tota potentia mea, levi comminatione
pelletur, non potest sustinere vultum meum. Alius
circumspiciatur cum quo conferre possimus manum;
4 pudet congredi cum homine vinci parato." Ignominiam iudicat gladiator cum inferiore componi et scit
eum sine gloria vinci, qui sine periculo vincitur. Idem
facit fortuna: fortissimos sibi pares quaerit, quosdam
fastidio transit. Contumacissimum quemque et rectis-
simum aggreditur, adversus quem vim suam intendat:
ignem experitur in Mucio, paupertatem in Fabricio,
exilium in Rutilio, tormenta in Regulo, venenum in
Socrate, mortem in Catone. Magnum exemplum nisi
mala fortuna non invenit.

---

a A catalogue of stock types of virtue; see Index under
the names.

16

they come ; just as much so, my word for it, as that things which are lauded and sought after are sometimes to the hurt of those who delight in them, being very much like over-eating, drunkenness, and the other indulgences which kill by giving pleasure. Among the many fine sayings of our friend Demetrius there is this one, which I have just heard ; it still rings and sings in my ears. " No man," said he, " seems to me more unhappy than one who has never met with adversity." For such a man has never had an opportunity to test himself. Though all things have flowed to him according to his prayer, though even before his prayer, nevertheless the gods have passed an adverse judgement upon him. He was deemed unworthy ever to gain the victory over Fortune, who draws back from all cowards, as if she said, " Why should I choose that fellow as my adversary ? He will straightway drop his weapons ; against him I have no need of all my power—he will be routed by a paltry threat ; he cannot bear even the sight of my face. Let me look around for another with whom to join in combat. I am ashamed to meet a man who is ready to be beaten." A gladiator counts it a disgrace to be matched with an inferior, and knows that to win without danger is to win without glory. The same is true of Fortune. She seeks out the bravest men to match with her ; some she passes by in disdain. Those that are most stubborn and unbending she assails, men against whom she may exert all her strength. Mucius she tries by fire, Fabricius by poverty, Rutilius by exile, Regulus by torture, Socrates by poison, Cato [a] by death. It is only evil fortune that discovers a great exemplar.

5 Infelix est Mucius, quod dextra ignes hostium premit et ipse a se exigit erroris sui poenas ? Quod regem, quem armata manu non potuit, exusta fugat ? Quid ergo ? Felicior esset, si in sinu amicae foveret manum ?

6 Infelix est Fabricius, quod rus suum, quantum a re publica vacavit, fodit ? Quod bellum tam cum Pyrrho quam cum divitiis gerit ? Quod ad focum cenat illas ipsas radices et herbas quas in repurgando agro triumphalis senex vulsit ? Quid ergo ? Felicior esset, si in ventrem suum longinqui litoris pisces et peregrina aucupia congereret, si conchylis superi atque inferi maris pigritiam stomachi nausiantis erigeret, si ingenti pomorum strue cingeret primae formae feras, captas multa caede venantium ?

7 Infelix est Rutilius, quod qui illum damnaverunt causam dicent omnibus saeculis ? Quod aequiore animo passus est se patriae eripi quam sibi exilium ? Quod Sullae dictatori solus aliquid negavit et revocatus tantum non retro cessit et longius fugit ? " Viderint," inquit, " isti quos Romae deprehendit felicitas tua. Videant largum in foro sanguinem et supra Servilianum lacum (id enim proscriptionis Sullanae spoliarium est)

---

a An ironical allusion to Sulla's assumption of the title of Felix.

Is Mucius unfortunate because he grasps the flames of the enemy with his right hand and forces himself to pay the penalty of his mistake? because with his charred hand he routs the king whom with his armed hand he could not rout? Tell me, then, would he be happier if he were warming his hand in his mistress's bosom?

Is Fabricius unfortunate because, whenever he has leisure from affairs of state, he tills his fields? because he wages war not less on riches than on Pyrrhus? because the roots and herbs on which he dines beside his hearth are those that he himself, an old man and honoured by a triumph, grubbed up in cleaning off his land? Tell me, then, would he be happier if he loaded his belly with fish from a distant shore and with birds from foreign parts? if he aroused the sluggishness of his loathing stomach with shell-fish from the eastern and the western sea? if he had game of the first order, which had been captured at the cost of many a hunter's life, served with fruit piled high around?

Is Rutilius unfortunate because those who condemned him will have to plead their cause through all the ages? because he was more content to endure that his country should be robbed of him than that he should be robbed of exile? because he was the only one who refused anything to the dictator Sulla, and when recalled from exile all but drew back and fled farther away? " Let those," says he, " whom your ' happy ' era[a] has caught at Rome, behold it. Let them see the forum streaming with blood, and the heads of senators placed above the pool of Servilius—for there the victims of Sulla's proscriptions are stripped,—and bands of assassins

19

senatorum capita et passim vagantis per urbem per-
cussorum greges et multa milia civium Romanorum
uno loco post fidem, immo per ipsam fidem trucidata ;
8 videant ista qui exulare non possunt." Quid ergo ?
Felix est L. Sulla, quod illi descendenti ad forum gladio
summovetur, quod capita sibi consularium virorum
patitur ostendi et pretium caedis per quaestorem ac
tabulas publicas numerat ? Et haec omnia facit ille,
ille qui legem Corneliam tulit !

9   Veniamus ad Regulum : quid illi fortuna nocuit,
quod illum documentum fidei, documentum patientiae
fecit ? Figunt cutem clavi et quocumque fatigatum
corpus reclinavit, vulneri incumbit, in perpetuam
vigiliam suspensa sunt lumina. Quanto plus tormenti
tanto plus erit gloriae. Vis scire quam non paeniteat
hoc pretio aestimasse virtutem ? Refice illum et mitte
10 in senatum ; eandem sententiam dicet. Feliciorem
ergo tu Maecenatem putas, cui amoribus anxio et
morosae uxoris cotidiana repudia deflenti somnus per
symphoniarum cantum ex longinquo lene resonan-
tium quaeritur ? Mero se licet sopiat et aquarum
fragoribus avocet et mille voluptatibus mentem
anxiam fallat, tam vigilabit in pluma quam ille in
cruce ; sed illi solacium est pro honesto dura tolerare
et ad causam a patientia respicit, hunc voluptatibus
marcidum et felicitate nimia laborantem magis his

---

a The *lex Cornelia de sicariis et veneficis*, which was
passed under Sulla and provided severe punishment for
murder, gives point to Seneca's sneer.

roaming at large throughout the city, and many thousands of Roman citizens butchered in one spot after, nay, by reason of, a promise of security,—let those who cannot go into exile behold these things ! " Is Lucius Sulla happy because his way is cleared by the sword when he descends to the forum ? because he suffers the heads of consulars to be shown him and has the treasurer pay the price of their assassination out of the public funds ? And these all are the deeds of that man—that man who proposed the Cornelian Law ! [a]

Let us come now to Regulus : what injury did Fortune do to him because she made him a pattern of loyalty, a pattern of endurance ? Nails pierce his skin, and wherever he rests his wearied body he lies upon a wound ; his eyes are stark in eternal sleeplessness. But the greater his torture is, the greater shall be his glory. Would you like to know how little he regrets that he rated virtue at such a price ? Make him whole again and send him back to the senate ; he will express the same opinion. Do you, then, think Maecenas a happier man, who, distressed by love and grieving over the daily repulses of his wayward wife, courted slumber by means of harmonious music, echoing faintly from a distance ? Although he drugs himself with wine, and diverts his worried mind with the sound of rippling waters, and beguiles it with a thousand pleasures, yet he, upon his bed of down, will no more close his eyes than that other upon his cross. But while the one, consoled by the thought that he is suffering hardship for the sake of right, turns his eyes from his suffering to its cause, the other, jaded with pleasures and struggling with too much good fortune,

SENECA

11 quae patitur vexat causa patiendi. Non usque eo in
possessionem generis humani vitia venerunt, ut
dubium sit an electione fati data plures nasci Reguli
quam Maecenates velint; aut si quis fuerit, qui audeat
dicere Maecenatem se quam Regulum nasci maluisse,
idem iste, taceat licet, nasci se Terentiam maluit!

12 Male tractatum Socratem iudicas, quod illam potionem publice mixtam non aliter quam medicamentum
immortalitatis obduxit et de morte disputavit usque
ad ipsam? Male cum illo actum est, quod gelatus est
est sanguis ac paulatim frigore inducto venarum vigor

13 constitit? Quanto magis huic invidendum est quam
illis quibus gemma ministratur, quibus exoletus omnia
pati doctus exsectae virilitatis aut dubiae suspensam
auro nivem diluit! Hi quicquid biberunt vomitu
remetientur tristes et bilem suam regustantes, at ille
venenum laetus et libens hauriet.

14 Quod ad Catonem pertinet, satis dictum est sum-
mamque illi felicitatem contigisse consensus hominum
fatebitur, quem sibi rerum natura delegit cum quo
metuenda conlideret. "Inimicitiae potentium graves
sunt; opponatur simul Pompeio, Caesari, Crasso.
Grave est a deterioribus honore anteiri; Vatinio

---

a The difficult and none too admirable wife of Maecenas.
Seneca (*Epist.* cxiv. 6) remarks caustically upon their
relations that "Maecenas married his wife a thousand
times though he never had but one." Here the rhetorical
types are in descending scale: the heroic Regulus, the
effeminate Maecenas, the contemptible Terentia!

b The cup of hemlock which Socrates drained with good
cheer after discoursing on the immortality of the soul.
See the account in Plato's *Phaedo*.

c As the political tool of Caesar he defeated Cato in the
candidature for the praetorship in 55 B.C.

is harassed less by what he suffers than by the reason for his suffering. Surely the human race has not come so completely under the sway of vice as to cause a doubt whether, if Fate should give the choice, more men would rather be born a Regulus than a Maecenas ; or if there should be one bold enough to say that he would rather have been born a Maecenas than a Regulus, the fellow, although he may not admit it, would rather have been born a Terentia [a] !

Do you consider that Socrates was ill-used because he drank down that draught [b] which the state had brewed as if it were an elixir of immortal life, and up to the point of death discoursed on death ? Was he ill-treated because his blood grew cold, and, as the chill spread, gradually the beating of his pulses stopped ? How much more should we envy him than those who are served in cups of precious stone, whose wine a catamite—a tool for anything, an unsexed or sexless creature—dilutes with snow held above in a golden vessel ! *They* will measure out afresh all their drink in vomit, with wry faces tasting in its stead their own bile ; but *he* will quaff the poison gladly and with good cheer.

Touching Cato, enough has been said, and it will be granted by the consensus of mankind that that great man reached the pinnacle of happiness,—he whom Nature chose to be the one with whom her dread power should clash. " The enmity of the powerful," said she, " is a hardship ; then let him match himself at one and the same time against Pompey, Caesar, and Crassus. It is a hardship to be outstripped by an inferior in the candidacy for office ; then let him be defeated by Vatinius. [c] It is

postferatur. Grave est civilibus bellis interesse;
toto terrarum orbe pro causa bona tam infeliciter
quam pertinaciter militet. Grave est manus sibi
afferre; faciat. Quid per haec consequar? Ut
omnes sciant non esse haec mala quibus ego dignum
Catonem putavi."

1 4. Prosperae res et in plebem ac vilia ingenia
deveniunt; at calamitates terroresque mortalium sub
iugum mittere proprium magni viri est. Semper vero
esse felicem et sine morsu animi transire vitam igno-
2 rare est rerum naturae alteram partem. Magnus vir
es; sed unde scio, si tibi fortuna non dat facultatem
exhibendae virtutis? Descendisti ad Olympia, sed
nemo praeter te; coronam habes, victoriam non
habes Non gratulor tamquam viro forti, sed tanquam consulatum praeturamve adepto; honore
3 auctus es. Item dicere et bono viro possum, si illi
nullam occasionem difficilior casus dedit in qua una[1]
vim animi sui ostenderet: "Miserum te iudico, quod
numquam fuisti miser. Transisti sine adversario
vitam; nemo sciet quid potueris, ne tu quidem ipse."
Opus est enim ad notitiam sui experimento; quid
quisque posset nisi temptando non didicit. Itaque
quidam ipsi ultro se cessantibus malis obtulerunt et
virtuti iturae in obscurum occasionem per quam
4 enitesceret quaesierunt. Gaudent, inquam, magni
viri aliquando rebus adversis, non aliter quam fortes

---

[1] una *Gertz and Hermes omit.*

a hardship to engage in civil war ; then let him fight the whole world over for a just cause, ever with ill success but with equal stubbornness. It is a hardship to lay hand upon oneself ; then let him do it. And what shall I gain thereby ? that all may know that these things of which I have deemed Cato worthy are not real ills."

Success comes to the common man, and even to commonplace ability ; but to triumph over the calamities and terrors of mortal life is the part of a great man only. Truly, to be always happy and to pass through life without a mental pang is to be ignorant of one half of nature. You are a great man ; but how do I know it if Fortune gives you no opportunity of showing your worth ? You have entered as a contestant at the Olympic games, but none other besides you ; you gain the crown, the victory you do not gain. You have my congratulations—not as a brave man, but as if you had obtained the consulship or praetorship ; you have enhanced your prestige. In like manner, also, I may say to a good man, if no harder circumstance has given him the opportunity whereby alone he might show the strength of his mind, " I judge you unfortunate because you have never been unfortunate ; you have passed through life without an antagonist ; no one will know what you can do,—not even yourself." For if a man is to know himself, he must be tested ; no one finds out what he can do except by trying. And so some men have presented themselves voluntarily to laggard misfortune, and have sought an opportunity to blazon forth their worth when it was about to pass into obscurity. Great men, I say, rejoice oft-times in adversity, as do brave soldiers in

milites bello. Triumphum ego murmillonem sub
Tib. Caesare de raritate munerum audivi querentem :
" Quam bella," inquit, " aetas perit ! "

Avida est periculi virtus et quo tendat, non quid
passura sit cogitat, quoniam etiam quod passura est
gloriae pars est.   Militares viri gloriantur vulneribus,
laeti fluentem meliori casu sanguinem ostentant ;
idem licet fecerint qui integri revertuntur ex acie,
5 magis spectatur qui saucius redit.   Ipsis, inquam,
deus consulit, quos esse quam honestissimos cupit,
quotiens illis materiam praebet aliquid animose
fortiterque faciendi, ad quam rem opus est aliqua
rerum difficultate.   Gubernatorem in tempestate, in
acie militem intellegas.   Unde possum scire quantum
adversus paupertatem tibi animi sit, si divitiis diffluis ?
Unde possum scire quantum adversus ignominiam et
infamiam odiumque populare constantiae habeas, si
inter plausus senescis, si te inexpugnabilis et in-
clinatione quadam mentium pronus favor sequitur ?
Unde scio quam aequo animo laturus sis orbitatem,
si quoscumque sustulisti vides ?   Audivi te, cum alios
consolareris : tunc conspexissem, si te ipse consolatus
6 esses, si te ipse dolere vetuisses.   Nolite, obsecro vos,
expavescere ista, quae dii immortales velut stimulos
admovent animis : calamitas virtutis occasio est.
Illos merito quis dixerit miseros qui nimia felicitate

warfare. I once heard Triumphus, a gladiator in the time of Tiberius Caesar, complaining of the scarcity of shows : " How fair an age," he said, " has passed away ! "

True worth is eager for danger and thinks rather of its goal than of what it may have to suffer, since even what it will have to suffer is a part of its glory. Warriors glory in their wounds and rejoice to display the blood spilled with luckier fortune. Those who return from the battle unhurt may have fought as well, but the man who returns with a wound wins the greater regard. God, I say, is showing favour to those whom he desires to achieve the highest possible virtue whenever he gives them the means of doing a courageous and brave deed, and to this end they must encounter some difficulty in life. You learn to know a pilot in a storm, a soldier in the battle-line. How can I know with what spirit you will face poverty, if you wallow in wealth ? How can I know with what firmness you will face disgrace, ill fame, and public hatred, if you attain to old age amidst rounds of applause,—if a popularity attends you that is irresistible, and flows to you from a certain leaning of men's minds ? How do I know with what equanimity you would bear the loss of children, if you see around you all that you have fathered ? I have heard you offering consolation to others. If you had been offering it to yourself, if you had been telling yourself not to grieve, then I might have seen your true character. Do not, I beg of you, shrink in fear from those things which the immortal gods apply like spurs, as it were, to our souls. Disaster is Virtue's opportunity. Justly may those be termed unhappy who are dulled by

torpescunt, quos velut in mari lento tranquillitas
iners detinet ; quicquid illis inciderit, novum veniet.

7 Magis urgent saeva inexpertos, grave est tenerae
cervici iugum.   Ad suspicionem vulneris tiro pallescit,
audacter veteranus cruorem suum spectat, qui scit se
saepe vicisse post sanguinem.   Hos itaque deus quos
probat, quos amat, indurat, recognoscit, exercet ;
eos autem quibus indulgere videtur, quibus parcere,
molles venturis malis servat.   Erratis enim, si quem
iudicatis exceptum.   Veniet et[1] ad illum diu felicem
sua portio ; quisquis videtur dimissus esse, dilatus

8 est.   Quare deus optimum quemque aut mala vali-
tudine aut luctu aut aliis incommodis afficit ?   Quia
in castris quoque periculosa fortissimis imperantur ;
dux lectissimos mittit, qui nocturnis hostes aggredian-
tur insidiis aut explorent iter aut praesidium loco
deiciant.   Nemo eorum qui exeunt dicit : " Male de
me imperator meruit," sed " bene iudicavit."   Item
dicant quicumque iubentur pati timidis ignavisque
flebilia : " Digni visi sumus deo in quibus experiretur
quantum humana natura posset pati."

9   Fugite delicias, fugite enervantem felicitatem, qua
animi permadescunt et nisi aliquid intervenit quod
humanae sortis admoneat, manent[2] velut perpetua
ebrietate sopiti.   Quem specularia semper ab afflatu

---

[1] et *Gruter inserts.*   [2] manent *Hermes inserts.*

an excess of good fortune, who rest, as it were, in dead calm upon a quiet sea ; whatever happens will come to them as a change. Cruel fortune bears hardest upon the inexperienced ; to the tender neck the yoke is heavy. The raw recruit turns pale at the thought of a wound, but the veteran looks undaunted upon his own gore, knowing that blood has often been the price of his victory. In like manner God hardens, reviews, and disciplines those whom he approves, whom he loves. Those, however, whom he seems to favour, whom he seems to spare, he is really keeping soft against ills to come. For you are wrong if you suppose that any one is exempt from ill. Even the man who has prospered long will have his share some day ; whoever seems to have been released has only been reprieved. Why is it that God afflicts the best men with ill health, or sorrow, or some other misfortune ? For the same reason that in the army the bravest men are assigned to the hazardous tasks ; it is the picked soldier that a general sends to surprise the enemy by a night attack, or to reconnoitre the road, or to dislodge a garrison. Not a man of these will say as he goes, " My commander has done me an ill turn," but instead, " He has paid me a compliment." In like manner, all those who are called to suffer what would make cowards and poltroons weep may say, " God has deemed us worthy instruments of his purpose to discover how much human nature can endure."

Flee luxury, flee enfeebling good fortune, from which men's minds grow sodden, and if nothing intervenes to remind them of the common lot, they sink, as it were, into the stupor of unending drunkenness. The man who has always had glazed

vindicaverunt, cuius pedes inter fomenta subinde
mutata tepuerunt, cuius cenationes subditus et parietibus circumfusus calor temperavit, hunc levis aura non
10 sine periculo stringet. Cum omnia quae excesserunt
modum noceant, periculosissima felicitatis intemperantia est : movet cerebrum, in vanas mentes imagines
evocat, multum inter falsum ac verum mediae cali-
ginis fundit. Quidni satius sit perpetuam infelici-
tatem advocata virtute sustinere quam infinitis atque
immodicis bonis rumpi ? Lenior ieiunio mors est,
cruditate dissiliunt.

11   Hanc itaque rationem dii sequuntur in bonis viris
quam in discipulis suis praeceptores, qui plus laboris
ab is exigunt, in quibus certior spes est. Numquid
tu invisos esse Lacedaemoniis liberos suos credis,
quorum experiuntur indolem publice verberibus ad-
motis ? Ipsi illos patres adhortantur, ut ictus
flagellorum fortiter perferant, et laceros ac semianimes rogant, perseverent vulnera praebere vulne-
12 ribus. Quid mirum, si dure generosos spiritus deus
temptat ? Numquam virtutis molle documentum est.
Verberat nos et lacerat fortuna ; patiamur ! Non
est saevitia, certamen est, quod quo[1] saepius ad-
ierimus, fortiores erimus. Solidissima corporis pars est
quam frequens usus agitavit. Praebendi fortunae
sumus, ut contra illam ab ipsa duremur ; paulatim
nos sibi pares faciet, contemptum periculorum ad-
13 siduitas periclitandi dabit. Sic sunt nauticis corpora

___

[1] quod quo *Hermes, after Thomas* : quo id *Gertz* : quod
A^1 : quod si A^5.

windows to shield him from a draught, whose feet have been kept warm by hot applications renewed from time to time, whose dining-halls have been tempered by hot air passing beneath the floor and circulating round the walls,—this man will run great risk if he is brushed by a gentle breeze. While all excesses are hurtful, the most dangerous is unlimited good fortune. It excites the brain, it evokes vain fancies in the mind, and clouds in deep fog the boundary between falsehood and truth. Would it not be better, summoning virtue's help, to endure everlasting ill fortune than to be bursting with unlimited and immoderate blessings? Death from starvation comes very gently, but from gorging men explode.

And so, in the case of good men the gods follow the same rule that teachers follow with their pupils; they require most effort from those of whom they have the surest hopes. Do you imagine that the Lacedaemonians hate their children when they test their mettle by lashing them in public? Their own fathers call upon them to endure bravely the blows of the whip, and ask them, though mangled and half-dead, to keep offering their wounded bodies to further wounds. Why, then, is it strange if God tries noble spirits with severity? No proof of virtue is ever mild. If we are lashed and torn by Fortune, let us bear it; it is not cruelty but a struggle, and the oftener we engage in it, the stronger we shall be. The staunchest member of the body is the one that is kept in constant use. We should offer ourselves to Fortune in order that, struggling with her, we may be hardened by her. Gradually she will make us a match for herself. Familiarity with exposure to danger will give contempt for danger. So the

31

ferendo mari dura, agricolis manus tritae, ad ex-
cutienda tela militares lacerti valent, agilia sunt
membra cursoribus ; id in quoque solidissimum est
quod exercuit. Ad contemnendam patientiam malorum animus patientia pervenit ; quae quid in nobis
efficere possit scies, si aspexeris quantum nationibus
14 nudis et inopia fortioribus labor praestet. Omnes
considera gentes in quibus Romana pax desinit,
Germanos dico et quicquid circa Histrum vagarum
gentium occursat. Perpetua illos hiemps, triste
caelum premit, maligne solum sterile sustentat ;
imbrem culmo aut fronde defendunt, super durata
glacie stagna persultant, in alimentum feras captant.
15 Miseri tibi videntur ? Nihil miserum est quod in
naturam consuetudo perduxit ; paulatim enim
voluptati sunt quae necessitate coeperunt. Nulla
illis domicilia nullaeque sedes sunt nisi quas lassitudo
in diem posuit ; vilis et hic quaerendus manu victus,
horrenda iniquitas caeli, intecta corpora ; hoc quod
tibi calamitas videtur tot gentium vita est ! Quid
16 miraris bonos viros, ut confirmentur, concuti ? Non
est arbor solida nec fortis nisi in quam frequens
ventus incursat ; ipsa enim vexatione constringitur
et radices certius figit ; fragiles sunt quae in aprica
valle creverunt. Pro ipsis ergo bonis viris est, ut
esse interriti possint, multum inter formidolosa

---

a Submission to the course of nature was a fundamental
Stoic doctrine.

bodies of sailors are hardy from buffeting the sea,
the hands of farmers are callous, the soldier's muscles
have the strength to hurl weapons, and the legs of
a runner are nimble. In each, his staunchest member
is the one that he has exercised. By enduring ills
the mind attains contempt for the endurance of
them; you will know what this can accomplish in
our own case, if you will observe how much the
peoples that are destitute and, by reason of their
want, more sturdy, secure by toil. Consider all the
tribes whom Roman civilization does not reach—I
mean the Germans and all the nomad tribes that
assail us along the Danube. They are oppressed by
eternal winter and a gloomy sky, the barren soil
grudges them support, they keep off the rain with
thatch or leaves, they range over ice-bound marshes,
and hunt wild beasts for food. Are they unhappy,
do you think? There is no unhappiness for those
whom habit has brought back to nature.[a] For what
they begin from necessity becomes gradually a
pleasure. They have no homes and no resting-
places except those which weariness allots for the
day; their food is mean and must be got by the
hand; terrible harshness of climate, bodies un-
clothed,—such for countless tribes is the life which
seems to you so calamitous! Why, then, do you
wonder that good men are shaken in order that they
may grow strong? No tree becomes rooted and
sturdy unless many a wind assails it. For by its
very tossing it tightens its grip and plants its roots
more securely; the fragile trees are those that have
grown in a sunny valley. It is, therefore, to the
advantage even of good men, to the end that they
may be unafraid, to live constantly amidst alarms

versari et aequo animo ferre quae non sunt mala
nisi male sustinenti.

1 5. Adice nunc, quod pro omnibus est optimum
quemque, ut ita dicam, militare et edere operas.
Hoc est propositum deo quod sapienti viro, ostendere
haec quae vulgus appetit, quae reformidat, nec bona
esse nec mala ; apparebit autem bona esse, si illa
non nisi bonis viris tribuerit, et mala esse, si tantum
2 malis irrogaverit. Detestabilis erit caecitas, si nemo
oculos perdiderit, nisi cui eruendi sunt : itaque
careant luce Appius et Metellus. Non sunt divitiae
bonum ; itaque habeat illas et Elius leno, ut homines
pecuniam, cum in templis consecraverint, videant et
in fornice. Nullo modo magis potest deus concupita
traducere, quam si illa ad turpissimos defert, ab
3 optimis abigit. "At iniquum est virum bonum
debilitari aut configi aut alligari, malos integris corporibus solutos ac delicatos incedere." Quid porro ?
Non est iniquum fortes viros arma sumere et in castris
pernoctare et pro vallo obligatis stare vulneribus,
interim in urbe securos esse percisos et professos
impudicitiam ? Quid porro ? Non est iniquum no-
bilissimas virgines ad sacra facienda noctibus excitari,
4 altissimo somno inquinatas frui ? Labor optimos
citat. Senatus per totum diem saepe consulitur,
cum illo tempore vilissimus quisque aut in campo

---

a In Stoic dogma *virtus* was the sole good and *dedecus*
the sole evil. All things not related to these standards
were considered neither good nor evil, and, consequently,
negligible (ἀδιάφορα).

b The Vestal Virgins, who maintained the public
worship of Vesta.

and to bear with patience the happenings which are ills to him only who ill supports them.

Consider, too, that it is for the common good to have the best men become soldiers, so to speak, and do service. It is God's purpose, and the wise man's as well, to show that those things which the ordinary man desires and those which he dreads are really neither goods nor evils.[a] It will appear, however, that there *are* goods, if these are bestowed only on good men, and that there *are* evils, if these are inflicted only on the evil. Blindness will be a curse if no one loses his eyes but the man who deserves to have them torn out ; therefore let an Appius and a Metellus be deprived of the light. Riches are not a good ; therefore let even the panderer Elius possess them in order that men, though they hallow wealth in temples, may see it also in a brothel. In no better way can God discredit what we covet than by bestowing those things on the basest men while withholding them from the best. "But," you say, "it is unjust that a good man be broken in health or transfixed or fettered, while the wicked are pampered and stalk at large with whole skins." What then ? Is it not unjust that brave men should take up arms, and stay all night in camp, and stand with bandaged wounds before the rampart, while perverts and professional profligates rest secure within the city ? What then ? Is it not unjust that the noblest maidens[b] should be aroused from sleep to perform sacrifices at night, while others stained with sin enjoy soundest slumber ? Toil summons the best men. The senate is often kept in session the whole day long, though all the while every worthless fellow is either amusing himself at the recreation-

otium suum oblectet aut in popina lateat aut tempus
in aliquo circulo terat. Idem in hac magna re publica
fit ; boni viri laborant, impendunt, impenduntur et
volentes quidem ; non trahuntur a fortuna, sequuntur
illam et aequant gradus. Si scissent, antecessissent.
5 Hanc quoque animosam Demetri fortissimi viri vocem
audisse me memini : " Hoc unum," inquit, " de vobis,
di immortales, queri possum, quod non ante mihi
notam voluntatem vestram fecistis ; prior enim ad
ista venissem, ad quae nunc vocatus adsum. Vultis
liberos sumere ? vobis illos sustuli. Vultis aliquam
partem corporis ? sumite ; non magnam rem pro-
mitto, cito totum relinquam. Vultis spiritum? quidni?
nullam moram faciam, quo minus recipiatis quod
6 dedistis. A volente feretis quicquid petieritis. Quid
ergo est ? Maluissem offerre quam tradere. Quid
opus fuit auferre ? Accipere potuistis ; sed ne nunc
quidem auferetis, quia nihil eripitur nisi retinenti."

Nihil cogor, nihil patior invitus nec servio deo sed
assentior, eo quidem magis, quod scio omnia certa et
7 in aeternum dicta lege decurrere. Fata nos ducunt
et quantum cuique temporis restat prima nascentium
hora disposuit. Causa pendet ex causa, privata ac

ground, or lurking in an eating-house, or wasting his time in some gathering. The same is true in this great commonwealth of the world. Good men labour, spend, and are spent, and withal willingly. Fortune does not drag them—they follow her, and match her pace. If they had known how, they would have outstripped her. Here is another spirited utterance which, I remember, I heard that most valiant man, Demetrius, make : " Immortal gods," he said, " I have this one complaint to make against you, that you did not earlier make known your will to me ; for I should have reached the sooner that condition in which, after being summoned, I now am. Do you wish to take my children ?—it was for you that I fathered them. Do you wish to take some member of my body ?—take it ; no great thing am I offering you ; very soon I shall leave the whole. Do you wish to take my life ?—why not ? I shall make no protest against your taking back what once you gave. With my free consent you shall have whatever you may ask of me. What, then, is my trouble ? I should have preferred to offer than to relinquish. What was the need to take by force ? You might have had it as a gift. Yet even now you will not take it by force, because nothing can be wrenched away from a man unless he withholds it."

I am under no compulsion, I suffer nothing against my will, and I am not God's slave but his follower, and the more so, indeed, because I know that everything proceeds according to law that is fixed and enacted for all time. Fate guides us, and it was settled at the first hour of birth what length of time remains for each. Cause is linked with cause, and all public and private issues are directed

publica longus ordo rerum trahit. Ideo fortiter omne patiendum est, quia non, ut putamus, incidunt cuncta sed veniunt. Olim constitutum est quid gaudeas, quid fleas, et quamvis magna videatur varietate singulorum vita distingui, summa in unum venit;

8 accipimus peritura perituri. Quid itaque indignamur? Quid querimur? Ad hoc parti[1] sumus. Utatur ut vult suis natura corporibus; nos laeti ad omnia et fortes cogitemus nihil perire de nostro.

Quid est boni viri? Praebere se fato. Grande solacium est cum universo rapi; quicquid est quod nos sic vivere, sic mori iussit, eadem necessitate et deos alligat. Irrevocabilis humana pariter ac divina cursus vehit. Ille ipse omnium conditor et rector scripsit quidem fata, sed sequitur; semper paret,

9 semel iussit. "Quare tamen deus tam iniquus in distributione fati fuit, ut bonis viris paupertatem et vulnera et acerba funera ascriberet?" Non potest artifex mutare materiam; hoc passa est. Quaedam separari a quibusdam non possunt, cohaerent, individua sunt. Languida ingenia et in somnum itura aut in vigiliam somno simillimam inertibus nectuntur elementis; ut efficiatur vir cum cura dicendus, fortiore fato opus est. Non erit illi planum iter; sursum

---

[1] parti *Hermes* : parati *A*.

by a long sequence of events. Therefore everything should be endured with fortitude, since things do not, as we suppose, simply happen—they all come. Long ago it was determined what would make you rejoice, what would make you weep, and although the lives of individuals seem to be marked by great dissimilarity, yet is the end one—we receive what is perishable and shall ourselves perish. Why, therefore, do we chafe? why complain? For this were we born. Let Nature deal with matter, which is her own, as she pleases; let us be cheerful and brave in the face of everything, reflecting that it is nothing of our own that perishes.

What, then, is the part of a good man? To offer himself to Fate. It is a great consolation that it is together with the universe we are swept along; whatever it is that has ordained us so to live, so to die, by the same necessity it binds also the gods. One unchangeable course bears along the affairs of men and gods alike. Although the great creator and ruler of the universe himself wrote the decrees of Fate, yet he follows them. He obeys for ever, he decreed but once. "Why, however," do you ask, "was God so unjust in his allotment of destiny as to assign to good men poverty, wounds, and painful death?" It is impossible for the moulder to alter matter; to this law it has submitted. Certain qualities cannot be separated from certain others; they cling together, are indivisible. Natures that are listless, that are prone to sleep, or to a kind of wakefulness that closely resembles sleep, are composed of sluggish elements. It takes sterner stuff to make a man who deserves to be mentioned with consideration. His course will not be the level way;

oportet ac deorsum eat, fluctuetur ac navigium in
turbido regat. Contra fortunam illi tenendus est
cursus ; multa accident dura, aspera, sed quae molliat
10 et complanet ipse. Ignis aurum probat, miseria fortes
viros. Vide quam alte escendere debeat virtus ; scies
illi non per secura vadendum :

> Ardua prima via est et quam vix mane recentes
> enituntur equi ; medio est altissima caelo,
> unde mare et terras ipsi mihi saepe videre
> sit timor et pavida trepidet formidine pectus.
> ultima prona via est et eget moderamine certo ;
> tunc etiam quae me subiectis excipit undis,
> ne ferar in praeceps, Tethys solet ima vereri.

11 Haec cum audisset ille generosus adulescens :
" Placet," inquit, " via ; escendo. Est tanti per ista
ire casuro." Non desinit acrem animum metu
territare :

> Utque viam teneas nulloque errore traharis,
> per tamen adversi gradieris cornua tauri
> Haemoniosque arcus violentique ora leonis.

Post haec ait : " Iunge datos currus ! His quibus
deterreri me putas incitor. Libet illic stare ubi ipse
Sol trepidat." Humilis et inertis est tuta sectari ;
per alta virtus it.
1   6. " Quare tamen bonis viris patitur aliquid mali
deus fieri ? " Ille vero non patitur. Omnia mala

---

[a] Ovid, *Met.* ii. 63 *sqq.* The speaker is Phoebus, the
Sun-god, who seeks to dissuade the youthful Phaëthon
from his desire to drive the chariot of the Sun.
[b] Ovid, *Met.* ii. 79 *sqq.*

uphill and downhill must he go, be tossed about, and guide his bark through stormy waters; he must keep his course in spite of fortune. Much that is hard, much that is rough will befall him, but he himself will soften the one, and make the other smooth. Fire tests gold, misfortune brave men. See to what a height virtue must climb! you will find that it has no safe road to tread:

> The way is steep at first, and the coursers strain
> To climb it, fresh in the early morn. They gain
> The crest of heaven at noon; from here I gaze
> Adown on land and sea with dread amaze,
> And oft my heart will beat in panic fear.
> The roadway ends in sharp descent—keep here
> A sure control; 'twill happen even so
> That Tethys, stretching out her waves below,
> Will often, while she welcomes, be affright
> To see me speeding downward from the height.[a]

Having heard the words, that noble youth replied, " I like the road, I shall mount; even though I fall, it will be worth while to travel through such sights." But the other did not cease from trying to strike his bold heart with fear:

> And though you may not miss the beaten track,
> Nor, led to wander, leave the zodiac,
> Yet through the Bull's fierce horns, the Centaur's bow
> And raging Lion's jaws you still must go.[b]

In reply to this he said, " Harness the chariot you offered; the very things that you think affright me urge me on. I long to stand aloft where even the Sun-god quakes with fear." The groveller and the coward will follow the safe path: virtue seeks the heights.

" But why," you ask, " does God sometimes allow evil to befall good men?" Assuredly he does not.

41

ab illis removit, scelera et flagitia et cogitationes improbas et avida consilia et libidinem caecam et alieno
imminentem avaritiam ; ipsos tuetur ac vindicat :
numquid hoc quoque aliquis a deo exigit, ut bonorum
virorum etiam sarcinas servet ? Remittunt ipsi hanc
2 deo curam : externa contemnunt. Democritus divitias
proiecit onus illas bonae mentis existimans. Quid
ergo miraris, si id deus bono viro accidere patitur
quod vir bonus aliquando vult sibi accidere ? Filios
amittunt viri boni ; quidni, cum aliquando et occi-
dant ? In exilium mittuntur ; quidni, cum aliquando
ipsi patriam non repetituri relinquant ? Occiduntur ;
quidni, cum aliquando ipsi sibi manus afferant ? Quare
3 quaedam dura patiuntur ? Ut alios pati doceant ;
nati sunt in exemplar. Puta itaque deum dicere :
" Quid habetis quod de me queri possitis, vos,
quibus recta placuerunt ? Aliis bona falsa circumdedi
et animos inanes velut longo fallacique somnio
lusi. Auro illos et argento et ebore adornavi, intus
4 boni nihil est. Isti quos pro felicibus aspicis, si non
qua occurrunt sed qua latent videris, miseri sunt,
sordidi, turpes, ad similitudinem parietum suorum
extrinsecus culti ; non est ista solida et sincera
felicitas ; crusta est et quidem tenuis. Itaque dum
illis licet stare et ad arbitrium suum ostendi, nitent

---

^a As, notably, did Lucius Junius Brutus and Manlius
Torquatus, exalting public duty.
^b Cato is the favourite exemplar.

Evil of every sort he keeps far from them—sin and crime, evil counsel and schemes for greed, blind lust and avarice intent upon another's goods. The good man himself he protects and delivers: does any one require of God that he should also guard the good man's luggage? Nay, the good man himself relieves God of this concern; he despises externals. Democritus, considering riches to be a burden to the virtuous mind, renounced them. Why, then, do you wonder if God suffers that to be the good man's lot which the good man himself sometimes chooses should be his lot? Good men lose their sons; why not, since sometimes they even slay them? [a] They are sent into exile; why not, since sometimes they voluntarily leave their native land, never to return? They are slain; why not, since sometimes they voluntarily lay hand upon themselves? [b] Why do they suffer certain hardships? It is that they may teach others to endure them; they were born to be a pattern. Think, then, of God as saying: " What possible reason have you to complain of me, you who have chosen righteousness? Others I have surrounded with unreal goods, and have mocked their empty minds, as it were, with a long, deceptive dream. I have bedecked them with gold, and silver, and ivory, but within there is nothing good. The creatures whom you regard as fortunate, if you could see them, not as they appear to the eye, but as they are in their hearts, are wretched, filthy, base—like their own house-walls, adorned only on the outside. Sound and genuine such good fortune is not; it is a veneer, and that a thin one. So long, therefore, as they can stand firm and make the show that they desire, they glitter and deceive;

et imponunt; cum aliquid incidit quod disturbet ac
detegat, tunc apparet quantum altae ac verae
5 foeditatis alienus splendor absconderit. Vobis dedi
bona certa, mansura, quanto magis versaverit aliquis
et undique inspexerit, meliora maioraque : permisi
vobis metuenda contemnere, cupiditates fastidire ;
non fulgetis extrinsecus, bona vestra introrsus obversa
sunt. Sic mundus exteriora contempsit spectaculo
sui laetus. Intus omne posui bonum ; non egere
felicitate felicitas vestra est.

6 ' At multa incidunt tristia, horrenda, dura toleratu.'
Quia non poteram vos istis subducere, animos vestros
adversus omnia armavi ; ferte fortiter. Hoc est quo
deum antecedatis ; ille extra patientiam malorum est,
vos supra patientiam. Contemnite paupertatem ;
nemo tam pauper vivit quam natus est. Contemnite
dolorem ; aut solvetur aut solvet. Contemnite mortem ;
quae vos aut finit aut transfert. Contemnite fortunam ; nullum illi telum quo feriret animum dedi.
7 Ante omnia cavi, ne quid vos teneret invitos ; patet
exitus. Si pugnare non vultis, licet fugere. Ideo ex
omnibus rebus quas esse vobis necessarias volui nihil
feci facilius quam mori. Prono animam loco posui ;
trahitur, adtendite modo et videbitis quam brevis ad
libertatem et quam expedita ducat via. Non tam
longas in exitu vobis quam intrantibus moras posui ;
alioqui magnum in vos regnum fortuna tenuisset,

when, however, something occurs to overthrow and
uncover them, then you see what deep-set and
genuine ugliness their borrowed splendour hid. But
to you I have given the true and enduring goods,
which are greater and better the more any one turns
them over and views them from every side. I have
permitted you to scorn all that dismays and to disdain desires. Outwardly you do not shine ; your
goods are directed inward. Even so the cosmos, rejoicing in the spectacle of itself, scorns everything
outside. Within I have bestowed upon you every
good ; your good fortune is not to need good fortune.

' Yet,' you say, ' many sorrows, things dreadful
and hard to bear, do befall us.' Yes, because I could
not withdraw you from their path, I have armed
your minds to withstand them all ; endure with
fortitude. In this you may outstrip God ; he is
exempt from enduring evil, while you are superior
to it. Scorn poverty ; no one lives as poor as he
was born. Scorn pain ; it will either be relieved or
relieve you. Scorn death, which either ends you or
transfers you. Scorn Fortune ; I have given her no
weapon with which she may strike your soul. Above
all, I have taken pains that nothing should keep you
here against your will ; the way out lies open. If
you do not choose to fight, you may run away.
Therefore of all things that I have deemed necessary
for you, I have made nothing easier than dying. I
have set life on a downward slope : if it is prolonged,
only observe and you will see what a short and easy
path leads to liberty. I have not imposed upon you
at your exit the wearisome delay you had at entrance. Otherwise, if death came to a man as
slowly as his birth, Fortune would have kept her

8 si homo tam tarde moreretur quam nascitur. Omne tempus, omnis vos locus doceat quam facile sit renuntiare naturae et munus illi suum impingere ; inter ipsa altaria et sollemnes sacrificantium ritus, dum optatur vita, mortem condiscite. Corpora opima taurorum exiguo concidunt vulnere et magnarum virium animalia humanae manus ictus impellit ; tenui ferro commissura cervicis abrumpitur, et cum articulus ille qui caput collumque committit incisus est, tanta 9 illa moles corruit. Non in alto latet spiritus nec utique ferro eruendus est ; non sunt vulnere penitus impresso scrutanda praecordia : in proximo mors est. Non certum ad hos ictus destinavi locum ; quacumque vis pervium est. Ipsum illud quod vocatur mori, quo anima discedit a corpore, brevius est quam ut sentiri tanta velocitas possit. Sive fauces nodus elisit, sive spiramentum aqua praeclusit, sive in caput lapsos subiacentis soli duritia comminuit, sive haustus ignis cursum animae remeantis interscidit ; quicquid est, properat. Ecquid erubescitis ? Quod tam cito fit, timetis diu ! "

great dominion over you. Let every season, every place, teach you how easy it is to renounce Nature and fling her gift back in her face. In the very presence of the altars and the solemn rites of sacrifice, while you pray for life, learn well concerning death. The fatted bodies of bulls fall from a paltry wound, and creatures of mighty strength are felled by one stroke of a man's hand; a tiny blade will sever the sutures of the neck, and when that joint, which binds together head and neck, is cut, the body's mighty mass crumples in a heap. No deep retreat conceals the soul, you need no knife at all to root it out, no deeply driven wound to find the vital parts; death lies near at hand. For these mortal strokes I have set no definite spot; anywhere you wish, the way is open. Even that which we call dying, the moment when the breath forsakes the body, is so brief that its fleetness cannot come within the ken. Whether the throat is strangled by a knot, or water stops the breathing, or the hard ground crushes in the skull of one falling headlong to its surface, or flame inhaled cuts off the course of respiration,—be it what it may, the end is swift. Do you not blush for shame? You dread so long what comes so quickly!"

LIBER II

NEC INIVRIAM NEC CONTVMELIAM ACCIPERE SAPIENTEM

(*De Constantia Sapientis*)

1   1. Tantum inter Stoicos, Serene, et ceteros sapientiam professos interesse quantum inter feminas et
mares non immerito dixerim, cum utraque turba ad
vitae societatem tantundem conferat, sed altera pars
ad obsequendum, altera imperio nata sit. Ceteri
sapientes molliter et blande, ut fere domestici et
familiares medici aegris corporibus, non qua optimum
et celerrimum est medentur sed qua licet ; Stoici
virilem ingressi viam non ut amoena ineuntibus
videatur curae habent, sed ut quam primum nos
eripiat et in illum editum verticem educat, qui adeo
extra omnem teli iactum surrexit, ut supra fortunam
2 emineat. " At ardua per quae vocamur et confragosa
sunt." Quid enim ? Plano aditur excelsum ? Sed
ne tam abrupta quidem sunt quam quidam putant.
Prima tantum pars saxa rupesque habet et invii
speciem, sicut pleraque ex longinquo speculantibus
48

BOOK II

TO SERENUS ON THE FIRMNESS
OF THE WISE MAN

The Wise Man can receive neither Injury nor Insult.

I MIGHT say with good reason, Serenus, that there is
as great a difference between the Stoics and the other
schools of philosophy as there is between males and
females, since while each set contributes equally to
human society, the one class is born to obey, the
other to command. Other philosophers, using gentle
and persuasive measures, are like the intimate family
physician, who, commonly, tries to cure his patients,
not by the best and the quickest method, but as he
is allowed. The Stoics, having adopted the heroic
course, are not so much concerned in making it
attractive to us who enter upon it, as in having it
rescue us as soon as possible and guide us to that
lofty summit which rises so far beyond the reach
of any missile as to tower high above all fortune.
" But," you say, " the path by which we are called
to go is steep and rugged." What of it ? Can the
heights be reached by a level path ? But the way is
not so sheer as some suppose. The first part only
has rocks and cliffs, and appears impassable, just as
many places, when viewed from afar, seem often to

abscisa et conexa videri solent, cum aciem longin-
quitas fallat, deinde propius adeuntibus eadem illa,
quae in unum congesserat error oculorum, paulatim
adaperiuntur, tum illis quae praecipitia ex intervallo
apparebant redit lene fastigium.

3   Nuper cum incidisset mentio M. Catonis, indigne
ferebas, sicut es iniquitatis impatiens, quod Catonem
aetas sua parum intellexisset, quod supra Pompeios
et Caesares surgentem infra Vatinios posuisset, et
tibi indignum videbatur, quod illi dissuasuro legem
toga in foro esset erepta quodque a rostris usque
ad arcum Fabianum per seditiosae factionis manus
traditus voces improbas et sputa et omnis alias
insanae multitudinis contumelias pertulisset.

1   2. Tum ego respondi habere te, quod rei publicae
nomine movereris, quam hinc P. Clodius, hinc
Vatinius ac pessimus quisque venundabat et caeca
cupiditate correpti non intellegebant se dum vendunt
et venire.   Pro ipso quidem Catone securum te esse
iussi ; nullam enim sapientem nec iniuriam accipere
nec contumeliam posse, Catonem autem certius exemplar sapientis viri nobis deos immortalis dedisse
quam Ulixen et Herculem prioribus saeculis.   Hos
enim Stoici nostri sapientes pronuntiaverunt, invictos
laboribus et contemptores voluptatis et victores
2 omnium terrorum.   Cato non cum feris manus contulit, quas consectari venatoris agrestisque est, nec

be an unbroken steep since the distance deceives the eye ; then, as you draw nearer, these same places, which by a trick of the eyes had merged into one, open up gradually, and what seemed from a distance precipitous is now reduced to a gentle slope.

Recently, when there happened to be some mention of Marcus Cato, you, with your impatience of injustice, grew indignant because Cato's own age had failed to understand him, because it had rated him lower than any Vatinius though he towered above any Pompey and Caesar ; and it seemed to you shameful that when he was about to speak against some law in the forum, his toga was torn from his shoulders, and that, after he had been hustled by a lawless mob all the way from the rostrum to the Arch of Fabius, he had to endure vile language, and spittle, and all the other insults of a maddened crowd.

And then I made answer that on behalf of the state you had good reason to be stirred—the state which Publius Clodius on the one hand, Vatinius and all the greatest rascals on the other, were putting up for sale, and, carried away by blind cupidity, did not realize that, while they were selling, they too were being sold. For Cato himself I bade you have no concern, for no wise man can receive either injury or insult. I said, too, that in Cato the immortal gods had given to us a truer exemplar of the wise man than earlier ages had in Ulysses and Hercules. For we Stoics have declared that these were wise men, because they were unconquered by struggles, were despisers of pleasure, and victors over all terrors. Cato did not grapple with wild beasts— the pursuit of these is for the huntsman and the

51

monstra igne ac ferro persecutus est nec in ea
tempora incidit quibus credi posset caelum umeris
unius inniti. Excussa iam antiqua credulitate et
saeculo ad summam perducto sollertiam cum ambitu
congressus, multiformi malo, et cum potentiae immensa cupiditate, quam totus orbis in tres divisus
satiare non poterat, adversus vitia civitatis degene-
rantis et pessum sua mole sidentis stetit solus et
cadentem rem publicam, quantum modo una retrahi
manu poterat, tenuit, donec abstractus comitem se
diu sustentatae ruinae dedit simulque exstincta sunt
quae nefas erat dividi ; neque enim Cato post
3 libertatem vixit nec libertas post Catonem. Huic tu
putas iniuriam fieri potuisse a populo, quod aut
praeturam illi detraxit aut togam ? Quod sacrum
illud caput purgamentis oris adspersit ? Tutus est
sapiens nec ulla affici aut iniuria aut contumelia
potest.

1 3. Videor mihi intueri animum tuum incensum et
effervescentem ; paras adclamare : " Haec sunt quae
auctoritatem praeceptis vestris detrahant. Magna
promittitis et quae ne optari quidem, nedum credi
possint ; deinde ingentia locuti cum pauperem
negastis esse sapientem, non negatis solere illi et
servum et tectum et cibum deesse, cum sapientem negastis insanire, non negatis et alienari et

---

peasant; he did not hunt down monsters with fire and sword, nor did he chance to live in the times when it was possible to believe that the heavens rested on one man's shoulders. In an age when the old credulity had long been thrown aside, and knowledge had by time attained its highest development, he came into conflict with ambition, a monster of many shapes, with the boundless greed for power which the division of the whole world among three men [a] could not satisfy. He stood alone against the vices of a degenerate state that was sinking to destruction beneath its very weight, and he stayed the fall of the republic to the utmost that one man's hand could do to draw it back, until at last he was himself withdrawn and shared the downfall which he had so long averted, and the two whom heaven willed should never part were blotted out together. For Cato did not survive freedom, nor freedom Cato. Think you that what the people did to such a man could have been an injury, even if they tore from him either his praetorship or his toga ? even if they bespattered his sacred head with filth from their mouths ? The wise man is safe, and no injury or insult can touch him.

I imagine that I see you flaring up in a temper and about to boil over ; you are getting ready to exclaim : " This is the sort of thing that detracts from the weight of the teachings of you Stoics. You make great promises, promises which are not even to be desired, still less believed ; then after all your big words, while you deny that a wise man is poor, you do not deny that he usually possesses neither slave nor house nor food ; while you deny that a wise man is mad, you do not deny that he does lose

parum sana verba emittere et quicquid vis morbi
cogit audere, cum sapientem negastis servum esse,
idem non itis infitias et veniturum et imperata
facturum et domino suo servilia praestaturum ministeria. Ita sublato alte supercilio in eadem quae
2 ceteri descenditis mutatis rerum nominibus. Tale
itaque aliquid et in hoc esse suspicor, quod prima
specie pulchrum atque magnificum est, nec iniuriam
nec contumeliam accepturum esse sapientem. Multum autem interest, utrum sapientem extra indig-
nationem an extra iniuriam ponas. Nam si dicis
illum aequo animo laturum, nullum habet privilegium,
contigit illi res vulgaris et quae discitur ipsa iniuriarum assiduitate, patientia ; si negas accepturum
iniuriam, id est neminem illi temptaturum facere,
omnibus relictis negotiis Stoicus fio."
3 Ego vero sapientem non imaginario honore verborum exornare constitui, sed eo loco ponere quo
nulla permittatur iniuria. " Quid ergo ? Nemo erit
qui lacessat, qui temptet ? " Nihil in rerum natura
tam sacrum est, quod sacrilegum non inveniat, sed
non ideo divina minus in sublimi sunt, si exsistunt
qui magnitudinem multum ultra se positam non
tacturi appetant ; invulnerabile est non quod non
feritur, sed quod non laeditur ; ex hac tibi nota
4 sapientem exhibebo. Numquid dubium est, quin
certius robur sit quod non vincitur quam quod non

---

a While the Stoics preached, and sometimes practised,
the doctrine of participation in public affairs, they emphasized
the desirability of peaceful retirement as a means to the
higher activity of intellectual research. See Seneca, *De
Otio*, 5. 8 ; 6. 4.

his reason, that he babbles crazy words, that he will venture to do whatever his violent disorder impels him to do ; while you deny that a wise man is ever a slave, you do not likewise go on to deny that he will be sold, that he will do what he is ordered to do, and render to his master the services of a slave. So, for all your lofty assumption, you reach the same level as the other schools—only the names of things are changed. And so I suspect that something of this sort lurks behind this maxim also, ' A wise man will receive neither injury nor insult '—a maxim which, at first sight, appears noble and splendid. But it makes a great difference whether you place the wise man beyond feeling injured or beyond being injured. For if you say that he will bear injury calmly, he has no peculiar advantage ; he is fortunate in possessing a common quality, one which is acquired from the very repetition of injuries—namely, endurance. If you say that he will not receive injury, that is, that no one will attempt to injure him, then, abandoning all other business, I am for becoming a Stoic." [a]

I assuredly did not intend to deck up the wise man with the fanciful honour of words, but to place him in the position where no injury may reach him. " What then ? " you say ; " will there be no one to assail him, no one to attempt it ? " Nothing in the world is so sacred that it will not find some one to profane it, but holy things are none the less exalted, even if those do exist who strike at a greatness that is set far beyond them, and which they will never damage. The invulnerable thing is not that which is not struck, but that which is not hurt ; by this mark I will show you the wise man. Is there any doubt that the strength that cannot be overcome is a truer

lacessitur, cum dubiae sint vires inexpertae, at merito
certissima firmitas habeatur, quae omnis incursus
respuit ? Sic tu sapientem melioris scito esse
naturae, si nulla illi iniuria nocet, quam si nulla fit.
Et illum fortem virum dicam, quem bella non subi-
gunt nec admota vis hostilis exterret, non cui pingue
5 otium est inter desides populos. Hoc igitur dico,
sapientem nulli esse iniuriae obnoxium ; itaque non
refert, quam multa in illum coiciantur tela, cum sit
nulli penetrabilis. Quomodo quorundam lapidum
inexpugnabilis ferro duritia est nec secari adamas
aut caedi vel deteri potest sed incurrentia ultro
retundit, quemadmodum quaedam non possunt igne
consumi sed flamma circumfusa rigorem suum habitumque conservant, quemadmodum proiecti quidam
in altum scopuli mare frangunt nec ipsi ulla saevitiae
vestigia tot verberati saeculis ostentant ; ita sapientis
animus solidus est et id roboris collegit, ut tam tutus
sit ab iniuria quam illa quae rettuli.

1 4. " Quid ergo ? Non erit aliquis qui sapienti
facere temptet iniuriam ? " Temptabit, sed non
perventuram ad eum ; maiore enim intervallo a
contactu inferiorum abductus est, quam ut ulla vis
noxia usque ad illum vires suas perferat. Etiam
cum potentes et imperio editi et consensu servientium
validi nocere intendent, tam citra sapientiam omnes
eorum impetus deficient, quam quae nervo tormentis-

sort than that which is unassailed, seeing that un-
tested powers are dubious, whereas the stability that
repels all assaults is rightly deemed most genuine?
So you must know that the wise man, if no injury
hurts him, will be of a higher type than if none is
offered to him, and the brave man, I should say, is he
whom war cannot subdue, whom the onset of a hostile
force cannot terrify, not he who battens at ease
among the idle populace. Consequently I will assert
this—that the wise man is not subject to any injury.
It does not matter, therefore, how many darts are
hurled against him, since none can pierce him. As
the hardness of certain stones is impervious to steel,
and adamant cannot be cut or hewed or ground, but
in turn blunts whatever comes into contact with it; as
certain substances cannot be consumed by fire, but,
though encompassed by flame, retain their hardness
and their shape; as certain cliffs, projecting into
the deep, break the force of the sea, and, though
lashed for countless ages, show no traces of its
wrath, just so the spirit of the wise man is impregnable, and has gathered such a measure of
strength as to be no less safe from injury than those
things which I have mentioned.

"What then?" you say; "will there be no one
who will attempt to do the wise man injury?"
Yes, the attempt will be made, but the injury will
not reach him. For the distance which separates
him from contact with his inferiors is so great that
no baneful force can extend its power all the way to
him. Even when the mighty, exalted by authority
and powerful in the support of their servitors, strive
to injure him, all their assaults on wisdom will fall as
short of their mark as do the missiles shot on high by

ve in altum exprimuntur, cum extra visum exsilierint,
2 citra caelum tamen flectuntur. Quid ? Tu putas
tum, cum stolidus ille rex multitudine telorum diem
obscuraret, ullam sagittam in solem incidisse aut
demissis in profundum catenis Neptunum potuisse
contingi ? Ut caelestia humanas manus effugiunt
et ab his qui templa diruunt ac simulacra conflant
nihil divinitati nocetur, ita quicquid fit in sapientem
proterve, petulanter, superbe, frustra temptatur.
" At satius erat neminem esse qui facere vellet."
3 Rem difficilem optas humano generi, innocentiam ;
et non fieri eorum interest qui facturi sunt, non
eius qui pati ne si fiat quidem potest. Immo nescio
an magis vires sapientiae ostendat tranquillitas inter
lacessentia, sicut maximum argumentum est imperatoris armis virisque pollentis tuta securitas in
hostium terra.

1   5. Dividamus, si tibi videtur, Serene, iniuriam a
contumelia. Prior illa natura gravior est, haec levior
et tantum delicatis gravis, qua non laeduntur homines
sed offenduntur. Tanta est tamen animorum dissolutio
et vanitas, ut quidam nihil acerbius putent. Sic invenies servum qui flagellis quam colaphis caedi malit
et qui mortem ac verbera tolerabiliora credat quam
2 contumeliosa verba. Ad tantas ineptias perventum
est, ut non dolore tantum sed doloris opinione

---

[a] *i.e.,* Xerxes. The incidents mentioned are associated
respectively with his prowess before Thermopylae and his
wrath expended upon the Hellespont ; *cf.* Herodotus, vii. 226
and 35.

bowstring or catapult, which though they leap beyond our vision, yet curve downwards this side of heaven. Tell me, do you suppose that when that stupid king *a* darkened the day with the shower of his darts, any arrow fell upon the sun, or that he was able to reach Neptune when he lowered his chains into the deep ? As heavenly things escape the hands of man and divinity suffers no harm from those who demolish temples and melt down images, so every wanton, insolent, or haughty act directed against the wise man is essayed in vain. " But it would be better," you say, " if no one cared to do such things." You are praying for what is a hard matter—that human beings should do no wrong. And that such acts be not done is profitable to those who are prone to do them, not to him who cannot be affected by them even if they are done. No, I am inclined to think that the power of wisdom is better shown by a display of calmness in the midst of provocation, just as the greatest proof that a general is mighty in his arms and men is his quiet unconcern in the country of the enemy.

Let us make a distinction, Serenus, if you like, between injury and insult. The former is by its nature more serious ; the latter, a slighter matter— serious only to the thin-skinned—for men are not harmed, but angered by it. Yet such is the weakness and vanity of some men's minds, there are those who think that nothing is more bitter. And so you will find the slave who would rather be struck with the lash than the fist, who considers stripes and death more endurable than insulting words. To such a pitch of absurdity have we come that we are harrowed not merely by pain but by the idea of pain, like

vexemur more puerorum, quibus metum incutit
umbra et personarum deformitas et depravata facies,
lacrimas vero evocant nomina parum grata auribus et
digitorum motus et alia quae impetu quodam erroris
3 improvidi refugiunt. Iniuria propositum hoc habet
aliquem malo adficere ; malo autem sapientia non
relinquit locum, unum enim illi malum est turpitudo,
quae intrare eo ubi iam virtus honestumque est non
potest. Ergo, si iniuria sine malo nulla est, malum
nisi turpe nullum est, turpe autem ad honestis
occupatum pervenire non potest, iniuria ad sapientem
non pervenit. Nam si iniuria alicuius mali patientia
est, sapiens autem nullius mali est patiens, nulla ad
4 sapientem iniuria pertinet. Omnis iniuria deminutio
eius est in quem incurrit, nec potest quisquam iniuriam accipere sine aliquo detrimento vel dignitatis
vel corporis vel rerum extra nos positarum. Sapiens
autem nihil perdere potest ; omnia in se reposuit,
nihil fortunae credit, bona sua in solido habet contentus virtute, quae fortuitis non indiget ideoque
nec augeri nec minui potest ; nam et in summum
perducta incrementi non habent locum et nihil eripit
fortuna nisi quod dedit ; virtutem autem non dat,
ideo nec detrahit ; libera est, inviolabilis, immota,
inconcussa, sic contra casus indurat, ut ne inclinari
5 quidem, nedum vinci possit ; adversus adparatus
terribilium rectos oculos tenet, nihil ex vultu mutat,
sive illi dura sive secunda ostentantur. Itaque nihil

---

a Perhaps the superstitious gesture described by Persius, ii.
31 *sqq.*, as a charm against the evil eye.

children who are terror-stricken by darkness and the
ugliness of masks and a distorted countenance ; who
are provoked even to tears by names that are unpleasant to their ears, by gesticulation of the fingers,[a]
and other things which in their ignorance they shrink
from in a kind of blundering panic. Injury has as its
aim to visit evil upon a person. But wisdom leaves no
room for evil, for the only evil it knows is baseness,
which cannot enter where virtue and uprightness
already abide. Consequently, if there can be no
injury without evil, no evil without baseness, and if,
moreover, baseness cannot reach a man already
possessed by uprightness, then injury does not reach
the wise man. For if injury is the experiencing of
some evil, if, moreover, the wise man can experience
no evil, no injury affects a wise man. All injury is
damaging to him who encounters it, and no man can
receive injury without some loss either in respect to
his position or his person or things external to us.
But the wise man can lose nothing. He has everything invested in himself, he trusts nothing to fortune,
his own goods are secure, since he is content with
virtue, which needs no gift from chance, and which,
therefore, can neither be increased nor diminished.
For that which has come to the full has no room for
further growth, and Fortune can snatch away only
what she herself has given. But virtue she does
not give ; therefore she cannot take it away.
Virtue is free, inviolable, unmoved, unshaken, so
steeled against the blows of chance that she cannot
be bent, much less broken. Facing the instruments
of torture she holds her gaze unflinching, her expression changes not at all, whether a hard or a happy
lot is shown her. Therefore the wise man will lose

perdet quod perire sensurus sit ; unius enim in possessione virtutis est, ex qua depelli numquam potest, ceteris precario utitur ; quis autem iactura movetur alieni ? Quodsi iniuria nihil laedere potest ex his quae propria sapientis sunt, quia virtute salva[1] sua salva sunt, iniuria sapienti non potest fieri.

6 Megaram Demetrius ceperat, cui cognomen Poliorcetes fuit. Ab hoc Stilbon philosophus interrogatus, num aliquid perdidisset : " Nihil," inquit, " omnia mea mecum sunt." Atqui et patrimonium eius in praedam cesserat et filias rapuerat hostis et patria in alienam dicionem pervenerat et ipsum rex circumfusus victoris exercitus armis ex superiore loco rogitabat.

7 At ille victoriam illi excussit et se urbe capta non invictum tantum sed indemnem esse testatus est. Habebat enim vera secum bona, in quae non est manus iniectio, at quae dissipata et direpta ferebantur, non iudicabat sua sed adventicia et nutum fortunae sequentia. Ideo ut non propria dilexerat ; omnium enim extrinsecus adfluentium lubrica et incerta possessio est.

1 6. Cogita nunc, an huic fur aut calumniator aut vicinus impotens aut dives aliquis regnum orbae senectutis exercens facere iniuriam possit, cui bellum et hostis et ille egregiam artem quassandarum urbium

2 professus eripere nihil potuit. Inter micantis ubique

---

[1] salva *added by Madvig.*

nothing which he will be able to regard as loss ; for the only possession he has is virtue, and of this he can never be robbed. Of all else he has merely the use on sufferance. Who, however, is moved by the loss of that which is not his own ? But if injury can do no harm to anything that a wise man owns, since if his virtue is safe his possessions are safe, then no injury can happen to the wise man.

When Demetrius, the one who had the appellation of Poliorcetes, had captured Megara, he questioned Stilbo, a philosopher, to find out whether he had lost anything, and his answer was, " Nothing ; I have all that is mine with me." Yet his estate had been given up to plunder, his daughters had been out-raged by the enemy, his native city had passed under foreign sway, and the man himself was being questioned by a king on his throne, ensconced amid the arms of his victorious army. But he wrested the victory from the conqueror, and bore witness that, though his city had been captured, he himself was not only unconquered but unharmed. For he had with him his true possessions, upon which no hand can be laid, while the property that was being scattered and pillaged and plundered he counted not his own, but the adventitious things that follow the beck of Fortune. Therefore he had esteemed them as not really his own ; for all that flows to us from without is a slippery and insecure possession.

Consider now, can any thief or traducer or violent neighbour, or any rich man who wields the power conferred by a childless old age, do injury to this man, from whom war and the enemy and that exponent of the illustrious art of wrecking cities could snatch away nothing ? Amid swords flashing

gladios et militarem in rapina tumultum, inter
flammas et sanguinem stragemque impulsae civitatis,
inter fragorem templorum super deos suos cadentium
uni homini pax fuit. Non est itaque, quod audax
iudices promissum, cuius tibi, si parum fidei habeo,
sponsorem dabo. Vix enim credis tantum firmitatis
in hominem aut tantam animi magnitudinem cadere ;
3 sed is prodit in medium qui dicat : " Non est quod
dubites, an attollere se homo natus supra humana
possit, an dolores, damna, ulcerationes, vulnera,
magnos motus rerum circa se frementium securus
aspiciat et dura placide ferat et secunda moderate, nec
illis cedens nec his fretus, unus idemque inter diversa
sit nec quicquam suum nisi se putet, et se quoque
4 ea parte qua melior est. En adsum hoc vobis pro-
baturus, sub isto tot civitatium eversore munimenta
incussu arietis labefieri et turrium altitudinem cuniculis
ac latentibus fossis repente desidere et aequaturum
editissimas arces aggerem crescere, at nulla machina-
menta posse reperiri, quae bene fundatum animum
5 agitent. Erepsi modo e ruinis domus et incendis undique relucentibus flammas per sanguinem fugi ; filias
meas quis casus habeat, an peior publico, nescio ; solus
et senior et hostilia circa me omnia videns tamen integrum incolumemque esse censum meum profiteor.

---

a i.e., that the wise man can lose nothing, receive no
injury.

on every side and the uproar of soldiers bent on pillage, amid flames and blood and the havoc of the smitten city, amid the crash of temples falling upon their gods, one man alone had peace. It is not for you, therefore, to call reckless this boast of mine [a]; and if you do not give me credence, I shall adduce a voucher for it. For you can hardly believe that so much steadfastness, that such greatness of soul falls to the lot of any man. But here is one [b] who comes into our midst and says : " There is no reason why you should doubt that a mortal man can raise himself above his human lot, that he can view with unconcern pains and losses, sores and wounds, and nature's great commotions as she rages all around him, can bear hardship calmly and prosperity soberly, neither yielding to the one nor trusting to the other ; that he can remain wholly unchanged amid the diversities of fortune and count nothing but himself his own, and of this self, even, only its better part. See, here am I to prove to you this—that, though beneath the hand of that destroyer of so many cities fortifications shaken by the battering-ram may totter, and high towers undermined by tunnels and secret saps may sink in sudden downfall, and earthworks rise to match the loftiest citadel, yet no war-engines can be devised that will shake the firm-fixed soul. I crept just now from the ruins of my house, and while the conflagration blazed on every side, I fled from the flames through blood ; what fate befalls my daughters, whether a worse one than their country's own, I know not. Alone and old, and seeing the enemy in possession of everything around me, I, nevertheless, declare that my holdings are all intact

[b] *i.e.*, Stilbo.

6 Teneo, habeo quicquid mei habui. Non est quod me victum victoremque te credas. Vicit fortuna tua fortunam meam. Caduca illa et dominum mutantia ubi sint nescio ; quod ad res meas pertinet, mecum 7 sunt, mecum erunt. Perdiderunt isti divites patrimonia, libidinosi amores suos et magno pudoris impendio dilecta scorta, ambitiosi curiam et forum et loca exercendis in publico vitiis destinata ; feneratores perdiderunt tabellas, quibus avaritia falso laeta divitias imaginatur. Ego quidem omnia integra illibataque habeo. Proinde istos interroga qui flent, lamentantur, qui strictis gladiis nuda pro pecunia corpora opponunt, qui hostem onerato sinu fugiunt."
8 Ergo ita habe, Serene, perfectum illum virum, humanis divinisque virtutibus plenum, nihil perdere. Bona eius solidis et inexsuperabilibus munimentis praecincta sunt. Non Babylonios illis muros contuleris, quos Alexander intravit, non Carthaginis aut Numantiae moenia una manu capta, non Capitolium arcemve, habent ista hostile vestigium. Illa, quae sapientem tuentur, et a flamma et ab incursu tuta sunt, nullum introitum praebent, excelsa, inexpugnabilia, diis aequa.
1 7. Non est quod dicas, ita ut soles, hunc sapientem nostrum nusquam inveniri. Non fingimus istud

---

^a Scipio Africanus the younger reduced Carthage in 146 B.C., Numantia in 133 B.C.

and unharmed. I still possess them; whatever I have
had as my own, I have. There is no reason for you
to suppose me vanquished and yourself the victor;
your fortune has vanquished my fortune. Where
those things are that pass and change their owners,
I know not; so far as my possessions are concerned,
they are with me, and ever will be with me. The
losers are yonder rich men who have lost their estates
—the libertines who have lost their loves—the prosti-
tutes whom they cherished at a great expenditure
of shame—politicians who have lost the senate-house,
the forum, and the places appointed for the public
exercise of their failings; the usurers have lost their
records on which their avarice, rejoicing without
warrant, based its dream of wealth. But I have
still my all, untouched and undiminished. Do you,
accordingly, put your question to those who weep
and wail, who, in defence of their money, present
their naked bodies to the point of the sword, who,
when their pockets are loaded, flee from the enemy."
Know, therefore, Serenus, that this perfect man, full
of virtues human and divine, can lose nothing. His
goods are girt about by strong and insurmountable
defences. Not Babylon's walls, which an Alexander
entered, are to be compared with these, not the
ramparts of Carthage or Numantia, both captured by
one man's hand,[a] not the Capitol or citadel of Rome,
—upon them the enemy has left his marks. The
walls which guard the wise man are safe from both
flame and assault, they provide no means of entrance,
—are lofty, impregnable, godlike.

There is no reason for you to say, Serenus, as your
habit is, that this wise man of ours is nowhere to be
found. He is not a fiction of us Stoics, a sort of

humani ingenii vanum decus nec ingentem imagi-
nem falsae rei concipimus, sed qualem conformamus,
exhibuimus, exhibebimus, raro forsitan magnisque
aetatium intervallis unum; neque enim magna et
excedentia solitum ac vulgarem modum crebro gig-
nuntur. Ceterum hic ipse M. Cato, a cuius mentione
haec disputatio processit, vereor ne supra nostrum
exemplar sit.

2 Denique validius debet esse quod laedit eo quod
laeditur; non est autem fortior nequitia virtute;
non potest ergo laedi sapiens. Iniuria in bonos nisi
a malis non temptatur; bonis inter se pax est, mali
tam bonis perniciosi quam inter se. Quodsi laedi
nisi infirmior non potest, malus autem bono infirmior
est, nec iniuria bonis nisi a dispari verenda est;
iniuria in sapientem virum non cadit. Illud enim
iam non es admonendus neminem bonum esse nisi
3 sapientem. "Si iniuste," inquit, "Socrates damnatus est, iniuriam accepit." Hoc loco intellegere
nos oportet posse evenire, ut faciat aliquis iniuriam
mihi et ego non accipiam. Tamquam si quis rem,
quam e villa mea subripuit, in domo mea ponat, ille
4 furtum fecerit, ego nihil perdiderim. Potest aliquis
nocens fieri, quamvis non nocuerit. Si quis cum
uxore sua tamquam cum aliena concumbat, adulter

---

^a *Cf.* 1. 3.

phantom glory of human nature, nor is he a mere conception, the mighty semblance of a thing unreal, but we have shown him in the flesh just as we delineate him, and shall show him—though perchance not often, and after a long lapse of years only one. For greatness which transcends the limit of the ordinary and common type is produced but rarely. But this self-same Marcus Cato, the mention of whom started this discussion,[a] I almost think surpasses even our exemplar.

Again, that which injures must be more powerful than that which is injured; but wickedness is not stronger than righteousness; therefore it is impossible for the wise man to be injured. Only the bad attempt to injure the good; the good are at peace with each other, the bad are no less harmful to the good than they are to each other. But if only the weaker man can be injured, and if the bad man is weaker than the good man, and the good have to fear no injury except from one who is no match for them, then injury cannot befall the wise man. For by this time you do not need to be reminded of the fact that there is no good man except the wise man. " But," some one says, " if Socrates was condemned unjustly, he received an injury." At this point it is needful for us to understand that it is possible for some one to do me an injury and for me not to receive the injury. For example, if a man should steal something from my country-house and leave it in my town-house, he would have committed a theft, but I should have lost nothing. It is possible for one to become a wrong-doer, although he may not have done a wrong. If a man lies with his wife as if she were another

erit, quamvis illa adultera non sit. Aliquis mihi
venenum dedit, sed vim suam remixtum cibo perdidit ;
venenum ille dando sceleri se obligavit, etiam si non
nocuit ; non minus latro est, cuius telum obposita
veste elusum est. Omnia scelera etiam ante effectum
operis, quantum culpae satis est, perfecta sunt.
5 Quaedam eius condicionis sunt et hac vice copulantur,
ut alterum sine altero esse possit, alterum sine altero
non possit. Quod dico conabor facere manifestum.
Possum pedes movere, ut non curram ; currere non
possum, ut pedes non moveam. Possum, quamvis
in aqua sim, non natare ; si nato, non possum in
6 aqua non esse. Ex hac sorte et hoc est de quo
agitur. Si iniuriam accepi, necesse est factam esse ;
si est facta, non est necesse accepisse me ; multa
enim incidere possunt quae submoveant iniuriam.
Ut intentatam manum deicere aliquis casus potest
et emissa tela declinare, ita iniurias qualescumque
potest aliqua res repellere et in medio intercipere,
ut et factae sint nec acceptae.

1   8. Praeterea iustitia nihil iniustum pati potest,
quia non coeunt contraria. Iniuria autem non potest
fieri nisi iniuste ; ergo sapienti iniuria non potest
fieri. Nec est quod mireris ; si nemo illi potest
iniuriam facere, ne prodesse quidem quisquam potest.
Et sapienti nihil deest quod accipere possit loco

man's wife, he will be an adulterer, though she will not be an adulteress. Some one gave me poison, but the poison lost its efficacy by being mixed with food; the man, by giving the poison, became guilty of a crime, even if he did me no injury. A man is no less a murderer because his blow was foiled, intercepted by the victim's dress. All crimes, so far as guilt is concerned, are completed even before the accomplishment of the deed. Certain acts are of such a character, and are linked together in such a relation, that while the first can take place without the second, the second cannot take place without the first. I shall endeavour to make clear what I mean. I can move my feet without running, but I cannot run without moving my feet. It is possible for me, though being in the water, not to swim; but if I swim, it is impossible for me not to be in the water. To the same category belongs the matter under discussion. If I have received an injury, it must necessarily have been done. If an injury was done, I have not necessarily received it; for many things can happen to avert the injury. Just as, for example, some chance may strike down the hand while it takes aim and turn the speeding missile aside, so it is possible that some circumstance may ward off injuries of any sort and intercept them in mid-course, with the result that they may have been done, yet not received.

Moreover, justice can suffer no injustice, because opposites do not meet. But no injury can be done without injustice; therefore no injury can be done to the wise man. And you need not be surprised; if no one can do him an injury, no one can do him a service either. The wise man, on the one hand, lacks nothing that he can receive as a gift; the evil

muneris, et malus nihil potest dignum tribuere sapiente ; habere enim prius debet quam dare, nihil autem habet quod ad se transferri sapiens gavisurus

2 sit. Non potest ergo quisquam aut nocere sapienti aut prodesse, quoniam divina nec iuvari desiderant nec laedi possunt, sapiens autem vicinus proximusque dis consistit, excepta mortalitate similis deo. Ad illa nitens pergensque excelsa, ordinata, intrepida, aequali et concordi cursu fluentia, secura, benigna, bono publico nata, et sibi et aliis salutaria nihil

3 humile concupiscet, nihil flebit. Qui rationi innixus per humanos casus divino incedit animo, non habet ubi accipiat iniuriam—ab homine me tantum dicere putas ? Ne a fortuna quidem, quae quotiens cum virtute congressa est, numquam par recessit. Si maximum illud ultra quod nihil habent iratae leges ac saevissimi domini quod[1] minentur, in quo imperium suum fortuna consumit, aequo placidoque animo accipimus et scimus mortem malum non esse, ob hoc ne iniuriam quidem, multo facilius alia tolerabimus, damna et dolores, ignominias, locorum commutationes, orbitates, discidia, quae sapientem, etiam si universa circumveniant, non mergunt, nedum ut ad singulorum impulsus maereat. Et si fortunae iniurias moderate fert, quanto magis

---

[1] *So inferior MSS. and Pincianus: A omits.*

man, on the other, can bestow nothing good enough for the wise man to have. For a man must have before he can give ; the evil man, however, has nothing that the wise man would be glad to have transferred to himself. It is impossible, therefore, for any one either to injure or to benefit the wise man, since that which is divine does not need to be helped, and cannot be hurt ; and the wise man is next-door neighbour to the gods and like a god in all save his mortality. As he struggles and presses on towards those things that are lofty, well-ordered, undaunted, that flow on with even and harmonious current, that are untroubled, kindly, adapted to the public good, beneficial both to himself and to others, the wise man will covet nothing low, will never repine. The man who, relying on reason, marches through mortal vicissitudes with the spirit of a god, has no vulnerable spot where he can receive an injury. From man only do you think I mean ? No, not even from Fortune, who, whenever she has encountered virtue, has always left the field outmatched. If that supreme event, beyond which outraged laws and the most cruel masters have nothing with which to threaten us, and in which Fortune uses up all her power, is met with calm and unruffled mind, and if it is realized that death is not an evil and therefore not an injury either, we shall much more easily bear all other things—losses and pains, disgrace, changes of abode, bereavements, and separations. These things cannot overwhelm the wise man, even though they all encompass him at once ; still less does he grieve when they assault him singly. And if he bears composedly the injuries of Fortune, how much

hominum potentium quos scit fortunae manus
esse !

1 9. Omnia itaque sic patitur ut hiemis rigorem et
intemperantiam caeli, ut fervores morbosque et
cetera forte accidentia, nec de quoquam tam bene
iudicat, ut illum quicquam putet consilio fecisse, quod
in uno sapiente est. Aliorum omnium non consilia,
sed fraudes et insidiae et motus animorum inconditi
sunt, quos casibus adnumerat ; omne autem fortuitum circa nos saevit et in vilia.[1]

2 Illud quoque cogita, iniuriarum latissime patere
materiam in[2] illis per quae periculum nobis quaesitum est, ut accusatore submisso aut criminatione
falsa aut irritatis in nos potentiorum odiis quaeque
alia inter togatos latrocinia sunt. Est et illa iniuria
frequens, si lucrum alicui excussum est aut praemium
diu captatum, si magno labore adfectata hereditas
aversa est et quaestuosae domus gratia erepta. Haec
effugit sapiens qui nescit nec in spem nec in metum
3 vivere. Adice nunc quod iniuriam nemo inmota
mente accipit, sed ad sensum eius perturbatur, caret
autem perturbatione vir ereptus erroribus, moderator
sui, altae quietis et placidae. Nam si tangit illum

---

[1] in vilia *Madvig*: invitia *A*.
[2] in *added by Madvig*.

---

the more will he bear those of powerful men, whom he knows to be merely the instruments of Fortune!

All such things, therefore, he endures in the same way that he submits to the rigours of winter and to inclement weather, to fevers and disease, and the other accidents of chance; nor does he form so high an estimate of any man as to think that he has done anything with the good judgement that is found only in the wise man.[a] All others are actuated, not by judgement, but by delusions and deceptions and ill-formed impulses of the mind, which the wise men sets down to the account of chance; but every power of Fortune rages round about us and strikes what counts for naught!

Consider, further, that the most extensive opportunity for injury is found in those things through which some danger is contrived for us, as, for example, the suborning of an accuser, or the bringing of a false accusation, or the stirring up of the hatred of the powerful against us, and all the other forms of robbery that exist among civilians. Another common type of injury arises when a man has his profits or a long-chased prize torn from his grasp, as when a legacy which he has made great effort to secure is turned aside, or the goodwill of a lucrative house is withdrawn. All this the wise man escapes, for he knows nothing of directing his life either towards hope or towards fear. Add, further, that no man receives an injury without some mental disturbance, yea more, he is perturbed even by the thought of it; but the man who has been saved from error, who is self-controlled and has deep and calm repose, is free from such perturbation. For if an

iniuria, et movet et impellit,[1] caret autem ira sapiens,
quam excitat iniuriae species, nec aliter careret ira
nisi et iniuria, quam scit sibi non posse fieri. Inde
tam erectus laetusque est, inde continuo gaudio
elatus ; adeo autem ad offensiones rerum hominumque non contrahitur, ut ipsa illi iniuria usui sit, per
quam experimentum sui capit et virtutem temptat.
4 Faveamus, obsecro vos, huic proposito aequisque et
animis et auribus adsimus, dum sapiens iniuriae
excipitur ! Nec quicquam ideo petulantiae vestrae
aut rapacissimis cupiditatibus aut caecae temeritati
superbiaeque detrahitur. Salvis vitiis vestris haec
sapienti libertas quaeritur. Non ut vobis facere non
liceat iniuriam, agimus, sed ut ille omnes iniurias in
altum demittat patientiaque se ac magnitudine animi
5 defendat. Sic in certaminibus sacris plerique vicerunt
caedentium manus obstinata patientia fatigando. Ex
hoc puta genere sapientem eorum, qui exercitatione
longa ac fideli robur perpetiendi lassandique omnem
inimicam vim consecuti sunt.

1 10. Quoniam priorem partem percucurrimus, ad
alteram transeamus, qua quibusdam propriis, pleris-
que vero communibus contumeliam refutabimus.

---

[1] impellit *Bentley* : impedit *A*.

---

[a] In the Latin the language is priestly. That the wise
man can suffer no wrong is presented as a sort of divine
utterance which is to be received in solemn silence.

injury reaches him, it does stir and incite him ; yet, if he is a wise man, he is free from that anger which is aroused by the mere appearance of injury, and in no other way could he be free from the anger than by being free also from the injury, knowing that an injury can never be done to him. For this reason he is so resolute and cheerful, for this reason he is elate with constant joy. So far, moreover, is he from shrinking from the buffetings of circumstances or of men, that he counts even injury profitable, for through it he finds a means of putting himself to the proof and makes trial of his virtue. Let us, I beseech you, be silent *a* in the presence of this proposition, and with impartial minds and ears give heed while the wise man is made exempt from injury ! Nor because of it is aught diminished from your wantonness, or from your greediest lusts, or from your blind presumption and pride ! You may keep your vices—it is the wise man for whom this liberty is being sought. Our aim is not that you may be prevented from doing injury, but that the wise man may cast all injuries far from him, and by his endurance and his greatness of soul protect himself from them. Just so in the sacred games many have won the victory by wearing out the hands of their assailants through stubborn endurance. Do you, then, reckon the wise man in this class of men—the men who by long and faithful training have attained the strength to endure and tire out any assault of the enemy.

Having touched upon the first part of the discussion, let us now pass to the second, in which by arguments—some of them our own, most of them, however, common to our school—we shall disprove the possibility of insult. It is a slighter offence than

Est minor iniuria, quam queri magis quam exsequi possumus, quam leges quoque nulla dignam vindicta

2 putaverunt. Hunc affectum movet humilitas animi contrahentis se ob dictum factumve[1] inhonorificum : " Ille me hodie non admisit, cum alios admitteret," et " sermonem meum aut superbe aversatus est aut palam risit," et " non in medio me lecto sed in imo collocavit," et alia huius notae, quae quid vocem nisi querellas nausiantis animi ? In quae fere delicati et felices incidunt ; non vacat enim haec notare cui

3 peiora instant. Nimio otio ingenia natura infirma et muliebria et inopia verae iniuriae lascivientia his commoventur, quorum pars maior constat vitio interpretantis. Itaque nec prudentiae quicquam in se esse nec fiduciae ostendit qui contumelia afficitur ; non dubie enim contemptum se iudicat, et hic morsus non sine quadam humilitate animi evenit supprimentis se ac descendentis. Sapiens autem a nullo contemnitur, magnitudinem suam novit nullique tantum de se licere renuntiat sibi et omnis has, quas non miserias animorum sed molestias dixerim, non vincit sed ne sentit quidem.

4 Alia sunt quae sapientem feriunt, etiam si non pervertunt, ut dolor corporis et debilitas aut amicorum

------

[1] factumve *Gertz* : factumque *A*.

injury, something to be complained of rather than avenged, something which even the laws have not deemed worthy of punishment. This feeling is stirred by a sense of humiliation as the spirit shrinks before an uncomplimentary word or act. " So-and-so did not give me an audience to-day, though he gave it to others " ; " he haughtily repulsed or openly laughed at my conversation " ; " he did not give me the seat of honour, but placed me at the foot of the table." These and similar reproaches—what shall I call them but the complainings of a squeamish temper ? And it is generally the pampered and prosperous who indulge in them ; for if a man is pressed by worse ills, he has not time to notice such things. By reason of too much leisure natures which are naturally weak and effeminate and, from the dearth of real injury, have grown spoiled, are disturbed by these slights, the greater number of which are due to some fault in the one who so interprets them. Therefore any man who is troubled by an insult shows himself lacking in both insight and belief in himself ; for he decides without hesitation that he has been slighted, and the accompanying sting is the inevitable result of a certain abjectness of spirit, a spirit which depreciates itself and bows down to another. But no one can slight the wise man, for he knows his own greatness and assures himself that no one is accorded so much power over him, and all these feelings, which I prefer to call rather annoyances than distresses of the mind, he does not have to overcome—nay, he does not even have them.

Quite different are the things that do buffet the wise man, even though they do not overthrow him, such as bodily pain and infirmity, or the loss of friends

liberorumque amissio et patriae bello flagrantis
calamitas. Haec non nego sentire sapientem ; nec
enim lapidis illi duritiam ferrive adserimus. Nulla
virtus est, quae non sentiat se perpeti. Quid ergo
est ? Quosdam ictus recipit, sed receptos evincit
et sanat et comprimit, haec vero minora ne sentit
quidem nec adversus ea solita illa virtute utitur dura
tolerandi, sed aut non adnotat aut digna risu putat.

1   11. Praeterea cum magnam partem contumeliarum superbi insolentesque faciant et male felicitatem ferentes, habet quo istum affectum inflatum
respuat, pulcherrimam virtutem omnium,[1] magnani-
mitatem.   Illa, quicquid eiusmodi est, transcurrit ut
vanas species somniorum visusque nocturnos nihil
2 habentis solidi atque veri.   Simul illud cogitat omnes
inferiores esse, quam ut illis audacia sit tanto ex-
celsiora despicere. Contumelia a contemptu dicta est,
quia nemo nisi quem contempsit tali iniuria notat ;
nemo autem maiorem melioremque contemnit, etiam
si facit aliquid, quod contemnentes solent.   Nam et
pueri os parentium feriunt et crines matris turbavit
laceravitque infans et sputo adspersit aut nudavit in
conspectu suorum tegenda et verbis obscenioribus
non pepercit, et nihil horum contumeliam dicimus.

---

[1] *followed by* animi *in A.*

and children, and the ruin that befalls his country amid the flames of war. I do not deny that the wise man feels these things ; for we do not claim for him the hardness of stone or of steel. There is no virtue that fails to realize that it does endure. What, then, is the case ? The wise man does receive some wounds, but those that he receives he overcomes, arrests, and heals ; these lesser things he does not even feel, nor does he employ against them his accustomed virtue of bearing hardship, but he either fails to notice them, or counts them worthy of a smile.

Moreover, since, in large measure, insults come from the proud and arrogant and from those who bear prosperity ill, the wise man possesses that which enables him to scorn their puffed-up attitude— the noblest of all the virtues, magnanimity. This passes over everything of that sort as of no more consequence than the delusive shapes of dreams and the apparitions of the night, which have nothing in them that is substantial and real. At the same time he remembers this,—that all others are so much his own inferiors that they would not presume to despise what is so far above them. The word " contumely " is derived from the word " contempt," for no one outrages another by so grave a wrong unless he has contempt for him ; but no man can be contemptuous of one who is greater and better than himself, even if his action is of a kind to which the contemptuous are prone. For children will strike their parents in the face, and the infant tumbles and tears his mother's hair and slobbers upon her, or exposes to the gaze of the family parts that were better covered over, and a child does not shrink from foul language Yet we do not count any of these things an insult.

Quare ? Quia qui facit contemnere non potest.
3 Eadem causa est, cur nos mancipiorum nostrorum
urbanitas in dominos contumeliosa delectet, quorum
audacia ita demum sibi in convivas ius facit, si coepit
a domino ; et ut quisque contemptissimus et vel ludi-
brium est, ita solutissimae linguae est. Pueros quidam
in hoc mercantur procaces et illorum impudentiam
acuunt ac sub magistro habent, qui probra meditate
effundant, nec has contumelias vocamus, sed argutias.
Quanta autem dementia est isdem modo delectari,
modo offendi, et rem ab amico dictam maledictum
vocare, a servulo ioculare convicium !
1   12. Quem animum nos adversus pueros habemus,
hunc sapiens adversus omnes, quibus etiam post iu-
ventam canosque puerilitas est. An quicquam isti
profecerunt, quibus puerilis[1] animi mala sunt auctique
in maius errores, qui a pueris magnitudine tantum
formaque corporum differunt, ceterum non minus vagi
incertique, voluptatium sine dilectu adpetentes,
2 trepidi et non ingenio sed formidine quieti ? Non
ideo quicquam inter illos puerosque interesse quis
dixerit, quod illis talorum nucumve et aeris minuti
avaritia est, his auri argentique et urbium, quod illi
inter ipsos magistratus gerunt et praetextam
fascesque ac tribunal imitantur, hi eadem in campo

---

[1] puerilis *added by Gertz.*

And why ? because he who does them is incapable
of being contemptuous. For the same reason the
waggery of slaves, insulting to their masters, amuses
us, and their boldness at the expense of guests has
licence only because they begin with their master
himself; and the more contemptible and even
ridiculous any slave is, the more freedom of tongue
he has. For this purpose some people buy young
slaves because they are pert, and they whet their
impudence and keep them under an instructor in
order that they may be practised in pouring forth
streams of abuse ; and yet we call this smartness,
not insult. But what madness it is at one time to
be amused, at another to be affronted, by the same
things, and to call something, if spoken by a friend,
a slander ; if spoken by a slave, a playful taunt !

The same attitude that we have toward young
slaves, the wise man has toward all men whose childhood endures even beyond middle age and the
period of grey hairs. Or has age brought any profit
at all to men of this sort, who have the faults of
a childish mind with its defects augmented, who
differ from children only in the size and shape of
their bodies, but are not less wayward and unsteady,
who are undiscriminating in their passion for pleasure,
timorous, and peaceable, not from inclination, but
from fear ? Therefore no one may say that they
differ in any way from children. For while children
are greedy for knuckle-bones, nuts, and coppers,
these are greedy for gold and silver, and cities ;
while children play among themselves at being
magistrates, and in make-believe have their bordered
toga, lictors' rods and tribunal, these play in earnest
at the same things in the Campus Martius and the

foroque et in curia serio ludunt, illi in litoribus
harenae congestu simulacra domuum excitant, hi ut
magnum aliquid agentes in lapidibus ac parietibus et
tectis moliendis occupati tutelae corporum inventa
in periculum verterunt. Ergo par pueris longiusque
3 progressis, sed in alia maioraque error est. Non immerito itaque horum contumelias sapiens ut iocos
accipit, et aliquando illos tanquam pueros malo
poenaque admonet, adficit, non quia accepit iniuriam,
sed quia fecerunt et ut desinant facere ; sic enim
et pecora verbere domantur, nec irascimur illis, cum
sessorem recusaverunt, sed compescimus, ut dolor
contumaciam vincat. Ergo et illud solutum scies,
quod nobis opponitur : " Quare, si non accepit
iniuriam sapiens nec contumeliam, punit eos qui
fecerunt?" Non enim se ulciscitur, sed illos emendat.

1 13. Quid est autem, quare hanc animi firmitatem
non credas in virum sapientem cadere, cum tibi in
aliis idem notare sed non ex eadem causa liceat ?
Quis enim phrenetico medicus irascitur ? Quis
febricitantis et a frigida prohibiti maledicta in malam
2 partem accipit ? Hunc affectum adversus omnis
habet sapiens, quem adversus aegros suos medicus,
quorum nec obscena, si remedio egent, contrectare
nec reliquias et effusa intueri dedignatur nec per
furorem saevientium excipere convicia. Scit sapiens

---

a Horace's " celsae graviore casu decidunt turres " (*Carm.*
ii. 10. 10 *sq.*) points the trend of the thought. According
to a Stoic commonplace wisdom lay in the observance of
the " Golden Mean."

forum and the senate ; while children rear their toy houses on the sea-shore with heaps of sand, these, as though engaged in a mighty enterprise, are busied in piling up stones and walls and roofs, and convert what was intended as a protection to the body into a menace.[a] Therefore children and those who are farther advanced in life are alike deceived, but the latter in different and more serious things. And so the wise man not improperly considers insult from such men as a farce, and sometimes, just as if they were children, he will admonish them and inflict suffering and punishment, not because he has received an injury, but because they have committed one, and in order that they may desist from so doing. For thus also we break in animals by using the lash, and we do not get angry at them when they will not submit to a rider, but we curb them in order that by pain we may overcome their obstinacy. Now, therefore, you will know the answer to the question with which we are confronted : " Why, if the wise man cannot receive either injury or insult, does he punish those who have offered them?" For he is not avenging himself, but correcting them.

But why is it that you refuse to believe that the wise man is granted such firmness of mind, when you may observe that others have the same, although for a different reason ? What physician gets angry with a lunatic ? Who takes in ill part the abuse of a man stricken with fever and yet denied cold water ? The wise man's feeling towards all men is that of the physician towards his patients : he does not scorn to touch their privy parts if they need treatment, or to view the body's refuse and discharges, or to endure violent words from those who rage in delirium.

omnis hos, qui togati purpuratique incedunt ut[1]
valentes, coloratos male sanos esse, quos non aliter
videt quam aegros intemperantis. Itaque ne succen-
set quidem, si quid in morbo petulantius ausi sunt
adversus medentem, et quo animo honores eorum
nihilo aestimat, eodem parum honorifice facta.
3 Quemadmodum non placebit sibi, si illum mendicus
coluerit, nec contumeliam iudicabit, si illi homo
plebis ultimae salutanti mutuam salutationem non
reddiderit, sic ne suspiciet quidem, si illum multi
divites suspexerint—scit enim illos nihil a mendicis
differre, immo miseriores esse, illi enim exiguo, hi
multo egent—et rursus non tangetur, si illum rex
Medorum Attalusve Asiae salutantem silentio ac
vultu arroganti transierit. Scit statum eius non magis
habere quicquam invidendum quam eius, cui in magna
familia cura optigit aegros insanosque compescere.
4 Num moleste feram, si mihi non reddiderit nomen
aliquis ex his, qui ad Castoris negotiantur nequam
mancipia ementes vendentesque, quorum tabernae
pessimorum servorum turba refertae sunt ? Non, ut
puto ; quid enim is boni habet, sub quo nemo nisi
malus est ? Ergo ut huius humanitatem inhumani-
tatemque neglegit, ita et regis : " Habes sub te
Parthos et Medos et Bactrianos, sed quos metu
contines, sed propter quos remittere arcum tibi non

---

[1] ut *added by Weidner.*

The wise man knows that all who strut about in togas and in purple, as if they were well and strong, are, for all their bright colour, quite unsound, and in his eyes they differ in no way from the sick who are bereft of self-control. And so he is not even irritated if in their sick condition they venture to be somewhat impertinent to their physician, and in the same spirit in which he sets no value on the honours they have, he sets no value on the lack of honour they show. Just as he will not be flattered if a beggar shows him respect, nor count it an insult if a man from the dregs of the people, on being greeted, fails to return his greeting, so, too, he will not even look up if many rich men look up at him. For he knows that they differ not a whit from beggars—yea, that they are even more wretched ; since the beggar wants little, the rich man much. And, on the other hand, he will not be disturbed if the King of the Medes or King Attalus of Asia, ignoring his greeting, passes him by in silence and with a look of disdain. He knows that the position of such a man is no more to be envied than that of the slave in a large household whose duty it is to keep under constraint the sick and the insane. The men who traffic in wretched human chattels, buying and selling near the temple of Castor, whose shops are packed with a throng of the meanest slaves—if some one of these does not call me by name, shall I take umbrage ? No, I think not. For of what good is a man who has under him none but the bad ? Therefore, just as the wise man disregards this one's courtesy or discourtesy, so will he likewise disregard the king's : " You, O king, have under you Parthians and Medes and Bactrians, but you hold them in check by fear ; they never allow

contigit, sed hostes teterrimos, sed venales, sed novum
5 aucupantes dominum." Nullius ergo movebitur
contumelia. Omnes enim inter se differant, sapiens
quidem pares illos ob aequalem stultitiam omnis
putat ; nam si semel se demiserit eo, ut aut iniuria
moveatur aut contumelia, non poterit umquam esse
securus. Securitas autem proprium bonum sapientis
est ; nec committet, ut iudicando contumeliam sibi
factam honorem habeat ei qui fecit ; necesse est
enim, a quo quisque contemni moleste ferat, suspici
gaudeat.

1   14. Tanta quosdam dementia tenet, ut sibi contumeliam fieri putent posse a muliere. Quid refert
quam habeant, quot lecticarios habentem, quam one-
ratas aures, quam laxam sellam ? Aeque inprudens
animal est et, nisi scientia accessit ac multa eruditio,
ferum, cupiditatium incontinens. Quidam se a cine-
rario impulsos moleste ferunt et contumeliam vocant
ostiari difficultatem, nomenculatoris superbiam, cu-
biculari supercilium. O quantus risus inter ista
tollendus est ! quanta voluptate implendus animus ex
alienorum errorum tumultu contemplanti quietem
2 suam ! " Quid ergo ? Sapiens non accedet ad fores,
quas durus ianitor obsidet ? " Ille vero, si res
necessaria vocabit, experietur et illum, quisquis erit,
tanquam canem acrem obiecto cibo leniet nec
indignabitur aliquid impendere, ut limen transeat,

you to relax your bow; they are your bitterest
enemies, open to bribes, and eager for a new master."
Consequently the wise man will not be moved by any
man's insult. For men may all differ one from
another, yet the wise man regards them as all alike
because they are all equally foolish; since if he should
once so far condescend as to be moved either by
insult or injury, he could never be unconcerned.
Unconcern, however, is the peculiar blessing of the
wise man, and he will never allow himself to pay to
the one who offered him an insult the compliment of
admitting that it was offered. For, necessarily,
whoever is troubled by another's scorn, is pleased by
his admiration.

Some men are mad enough to suppose that even
a woman can offer them an insult. What matters
it how they regard her, how many lackeys she has
for her litter, how heavily weighted her ears, how
roomy her sedan? She is just the same unthinking
creature—wild, and unrestrained in her passions—
unless she has gained knowledge and had much
instruction. Some are affronted if a hairdresser
jostles them, and some call the rudeness of a house-
porter, an usher's arrogance, or a valet's loftiness an
insult. O what laughter should such things draw!
With what satisfaction should a man's mind be filled
when he contrasts his own repose with the unrest
into which others blunder! " What then ? " you say,
" will the wise man not approach a door that is
guarded by a surly keeper?" Assuredly, if some
necessary business summons him he will make the
venture, and placate the keeper, be he what he may,
as one quiets a dog by tossing him food, and he will
not deem it improper to pay something in order that

cogitans et in pontibus quibusdam pro transitu dari.
Itaque illi quoque, quisquis erit, qui hoc salutationum
publicum exerceat, donabit ; scit emi aere venalia.
Ille pusilli animi est, qui sibi placet, quod ostiario
libere respondit, quod virgam eius fregit, quod ad
dominum accessit et petît corium. Facit se adver-
3 sarium qui contendit, et ut vincat, par fuit. " At
sapiens colapho percussus quid faciet ? " Quod Cato,
cum illi os percussum esset ; non excanduit, non
vindicavit iniuriam, ne remisit quidem, sed factam
negavit ; maiore animo non agnovit quam ignovisset.
Non diu in hoc haerebimus ; quis enim nescit nihil
ex his, quae creduntur mala aut bona, ita videri
4 sapienti ut omnibus ? Non respicit, quid homines
turpe iudicent aut miserum, non it qua populus, sed
ut sidera contrarium mundo iter intendunt, ita hic
adversus opinionem omnium vadit.

1   15. Desinite itaque dicere : " Non accipiet ergo
sapiens iniuriam, si caedetur, si oculus illi eruetur ?
Non accipiet contumeliam, si obscenorum vocibus
improbis per forum agetur ? Si in convivio regis
recumbere infra mensam vescique cum servis igno-
miniosa officia sortitis iubebitur ? Si quid aliud ferre
cogetur eorum quae excogitari pudori ingenuo
2 molesta possunt ? " In quantumcumque ista vel

<a> It was supposed that the sphere of heaven revolved
about the earth from east to west, and that while the sun,
moon, and planets were swept along in this revolution,
they also moved in their own courses in the opposite
direction.

he may pass the threshold, remembering that even on
some bridges one has to pay to cross. And so to the
fellow, be he what he may, who plies this source of
revenue at receptions, he will pay his fee ; he knows
that money will buy whatever is for sale. The man
has a small mind who is pleased with himself because
he spoke his mind to a porter, because he broke his
staff on him, made his way to his master and demanded
the fellow's hide. Whoever enters a contest becomes
the antagonist of another, and, for the sake of victory,
is on the same level. " But," you ask, " if a wise
man receives a blow, what shall he do ? " What
Cato did when he was struck in the face. He did
not flare up, he did not avenge the wrong, he did not
even forgive it, but he said that no wrong had been
done. He showed finer spirit in not acknowledging it
than if he had pardoned it. But we shall not linger
long upon this point. For who is not aware that
none of the things reputed to be goods or ills appear
to the wise man as they do to men at large ? He does
not regard what men consider base or wretched ; he
does not walk with the crowd, but as the planets
make their way against the whirl of heaven,[a] so he
proceeds contrary to the opinion of the world.

Therefore leave off saying : " Will the wise man,
then, receive no injury if he is given a lashing, if he
has an eye gouged out ? Will he receive no insult
if he is hooted through the forum by the vile words
of a foul-mouthed crowd ? If at a king's banquet he
is ordered to take a place beneath the table and to
eat with the slaves assigned to the most disreputable
service ? If he is forced to bear whatever else can
be thought of that will offend his freeborn pride ? "
No matter how great these things may come to be,

numero vel magnitudine creverint, eiusdem naturae
erunt. Si non tangent illum parva, ne maiora quidem ; si non tangent pauca, ne plura quidem. Sed
ex imbecillitate vestra coniecturam capitis ingentis
animi, et cum cogitastis quantum putetis vos pati
posse, sapientis patientiae paulo ulteriorem terminum
ponitis. At illum in aliis mundi finibus sua virtus
3 collocavit nihil vobiscum commune habentem. Quaere
et aspera et quaecumque toleratu gravia sunt
audituque et visu refugienda. Non obruetur eorum
coetu et qualis singulis, talis universis obsistet. Qui
dicit illud tolerabile sapienti, illud intolerabile, et
animi magnitudinem intra certos fines tenet, male
agit ; vincit nos fortuna, nisi tota vincitur.
4   Ne putes istam Stoicam esse duritiam, Epicurus,
quem vos patronum inertiae vestrae assumitis puta-
tisque mollia ac desidiosa praecipere et ad voluptates
ducentia, " Raro," inquit, " sapienti fortuna intervenit." Quam paene emisit viri vocem ! Vis tu
5 fortius loqui et illam ex toto summovere ! Domus
haec sapientis angusta, sine cultu, sine strepitu, sine
apparatu, nullis adservatur ianitoribus turbam venali
fastidio digerentibus, sed per hoc limen vacuum et
ab ostiaris liberum fortuna non transit. Scit non esse
illic sibi locum, ubi sui nihil est.

ᵃ Epicurus's doctrine that the highest pleasure was peace
of mind (ἀταραξία) fostered naturally inaction and aloofness
from affairs ; λάθε βιώσας was the watchword of his
followers. *Cf.* Seneca, *De Beneficiis*, iv. 4. 1 : " deus aversus
a mundo aliud agit aut, quae maxima Epicuro felicitas
videtur, nihil agit."
ᵇ *Epicurea*, p. 74, xvi (Usener).

whether in number or in size, their nature will remain the same. If small things do not move him, neither will the greater ones ; if a few do not move him, neither will more. But from the measure of your own weakness you form your idea of an heroic spirit, and, having pictured how much you think that you can endure, you set the limit of the wise man's endurance a little farther on. But his virtue has placed him in another region of the universe ; he has nothing in common with you. Therefore search out the hard things and whatever is grievous to bear—things from which the ear and the eye must shrink. The whole mass of them will not crush him, and as he withstands them singly, so will he withstand them united. He who says that one thing is tolerable for the wise man, another intolerable, and restricts the greatness of his soul to definite bounds, does him wrong ; Fortune conquers us, unless we wholly conquer her.

Do not suppose that such austerity is Stoic only. Epicurus, whom you claim as the advocate of your policy of inaction,[a] who, as you think, enjoins the course that is soft and indolent and conducive to pleasure, has said, " Rarely does Fortune block the path of the wise man."[b] How near he came to uttering a manly sentiment ! Will you speak more heroically and clear Fortune from his path altogether? This house of the wise man is cramped, without adornment, without bustle, without pomp, is guarded by no doormen who, with venal fastidiousness, discriminate between the visitors ; but over its threshold, empty and devoid of keepers, Fortune does not pass. She knows that she has no place there, where nothing is her own.

1   16. Quodsi Epicurus quoque, qui corpori plurimum indulsit, adversus iniurias exsurgit, qui id apud nos incredibile videri potest aut supra humanae naturae mensuram ? Ille ait iniurias tolerabiles esse sapienti, nos iniurias non esse. Nec enim est, quod dicas hoc

2 naturae repugnare. Non negamus rem incommodam esse verberari et impelli et aliquo membro carere, sed omnia ista negamus iniurias esse ; non sensum illis doloris detrahimus, sed nomen iniuriae, quod non potest recipi virtute salva. Uter verius dicat videbimus ; ad contemptum quidem iniuriae uterque consentit. Quaeris quid inter duos intersit ? Quod inter gladiatores fortissimos, quorum alter premit vulnus et stat in gradu, alter respiciens ad clamantem populum significat nihil esse et intercedi non patitur.

3 Non est, quod putes magnum, quo dissidemus ; illud quo de agitur, quod unum ad vos pertinet, utraque exempla hortantur, contemnere iniurias et, quas iniuriarum umbras ac suspiciones dixerim, contumelias, ad quas despiciendas non sapiente opus est viro, sed tantum consipiente, qui sibi possit dicere : " Utrum merito mihi ista accidunt an inmerito ? Si merito, non est contumelia, iudicium est ; si inmerito,

4 illi qui iniusta facit erubescendum est." Et quid est illud quod contumelia dicitur ? In capitis mei levitatem iocatus est et in oculorum valitudinem et in crurum gracilitatem et in staturam. Quae contumelia est quod apparet audire ? Coram uno ali-

But if even Epicurus, who most of all indulged the flesh, is up in arms against injury, how can such an attitude on our part seem incredible or to be beyond the bounds of human nature ? He says that injuries are tolerable for the wise man ; we say that injuries do not exist for him. Nor, indeed, is there any reason why you should claim that this wars against nature. We do not deny that it is an unpleasant thing to be beaten and hit, to lose some bodily member, but we deny that all such things are injuries. We do not divest them of the sensation of pain, but of the name of injury, which is not allowable so long as virtue is unharmed. Which of the two speaks more truly we will consider : as to contempt, at any rate, for injury both think alike. Do you ask, then, what is the difference between the two ? The same difference that distinguishes two gladiators, both very brave, one of whom stops his wound and stands his ground, the other, turning to the shouting crowd, makes a sign that he has no wound, and permits no interference. There is no need for you to suppose that our difference is great ; as to the point, and it is the only one that concerns you, both schools urge you to scorn injuries and, what I may call the shadows and suggestions of injuries, insults. And one does not need to be a wise man to despise these, but merely a man of sense—one who can say to himself : " Do I, or do I not, deserve that these things befall me ? If I do deserve them, there is no insult—it is justice ; if I do not deserve them, he who does the injustice is the one to blush." And this insult, so called, what is it ? Some jest at the baldness of my head, the weakness of my eyes, the thinness of my legs, my build. But why is it an insult to be told what is self-evident ?

quid dictum ridemus, coram pluribus indignamur, et
eorum aliis libertatem non relinquimus, quae ipsi in
nos dicere adsuevimus ; iocis temperatis delectamur,
immodicis irascimur.

1   17. Chrysippus ait quendam indignatum, quod
illum aliquis vervecem marinum dixerat. In senatu
flentem vidimus Fidum Cornelium, Nasonis Ovidii
generum, cum illum Corbulo struthocamelum de-
pilatum dixisset ; adversus alia maledicta mores et
vitam convulnerantia frontis illi firmitas constitit,
adversus hoc tam absurdum lacrimae prociderunt ;
tanta animorum inbecillitas est, ubi ratio discessit.
2 Quid, quod offendimur, si quis sermonem nostrum
imitatur, si quis incessum, si quis vitium aliquod
corporis aut linguae exprimit ? Quasi notiora illa
fiant alio imitante quam nobis facientibus ! Senectutem quidam inviti audiunt et canos et alia ad quae
voto pervenitur ; paupertatis maledictum quosdam
perussit, quam sibi obiecit quisquis abscondit. Itaque
materia petulantibus et per contumeliam urbanis
detrahitur, si ultro illam et prior occupes ; nemo
3 risum praebuit qui ex se cepit. Vatinium, hominem
natum et ad risum et ad odium, scurram fuisse et
venustum ac dicacem memoriae proditum est. In
pedes suos ipse plurima dicebat et in fauces concisas ;
sic inimicorum, quos plures habebat quam morbos,
et in primis Ciceronis urbanitatem effugerat. Si hoc
potuit ille duritia oris, qui assiduis conviciis pudere

---

^a Pliny, *Nat. Hist.* ix. 44, describes a sea-monster, called
a "ram" (*aries*), which was not a nice creature. The
shift to "wether" coarsens the insult.

^b According to Plutarch, *Cicero*, 9 and 26, his neck was
covered with wens. He suffered also from some deformity
or disease of the feet : *cf.* Quintilian, vi. 3. 75.

Something is said in the presence of only one person and we laugh; if several are present, we become indignant, and we do not allow others the liberty of saying the very things that we are in the habit of saying about ourselves. Jests, if restrained, amuse us; if unrestrained, they make us angry.

Chrysippus says that a certain man grew indignant because some one had called him "a sea-wether."[a] We saw Fidus Cornelius, the son-in-law of Ovidius Naso, shed tears in the senate, when Corbulo called him a plucked ostrich. In the face of other charges, damaging to his character and standing, the composure of his countenance was unruffled, but at one thus absurd out burst his tears! Such is the weakness of the mind when reason flees. Why are we offended if any one imitates our talk or walk, or mimics some defect of body or speech? Just as if these would become more notorious by another's imitating them than by our doing them! Some dislike to hear old age spoken of and grey hairs and other things which men pray to come to. The curse of poverty galls some, but a man makes it a reproach to himself if he tries to hide it. And so sneerers and those who point their wit with insult are robbed of an excuse if you anticipate it with a move on your part. No one becomes a laughing-stock who laughs at himself. It is common knowledge that Vatinius, a man born to be a butt for ridicule and hate, was a graceful and witty jester. He uttered many a jest at the expense of his own feet and his scarred jowls.[b] So he escaped the wit of his enemies—they outnumbered his afflictions—and, above all, Cicero's. If the man who, through constant abuse, had forgotten how to blush, was able, by reason of his brazen face, to do this, why

97

dedidicerat, cur is non possit, qui studiis liberalibus
et sapientiae cultu ad aliquem profectum pervenerit ?
4 Adice quod genus ultionis est eripere ei, qui fecit,
factae contumeliae voluptatem ; solent dicere : " O
miserum me ! Puto, non intellexit." Adeo fructus
contumeliae in sensu et indignatione patientis est.
Deinde non deerit illi aliquando par ; invenietur qui
te quoque vindicet.

1   18. C. Caesar inter cetera vitia, quibus abundabat,
contumeliosus mira libidine ferebatur omnis aliqua
nota feriendi, ipse materia risus benignissima : tanta
illi palloris insaniam testantis foeditas erat, tanta
oculorum sub fronte anili latentium torvitas, tanta
capitis destituti et emendicaticiis capillis aspersi deformitas ; adice obsessam saetis cervicem et exili-
tatem crurum et enormitatem pedum. Immensum
est, si velim singula referre, per quae in parentes
avosque suos contumeliosus fuit, per quae in uni-
versos ordines ; ea referam, quae illum exitio
dederunt.

2   Asiaticum Valerium in primis amicis habebat,
ferocem virum et vix aequo animo alienas contumelias laturum ; huic in convivio, id est in contione,
voce clarissima, qualis in concubitu esset uxor eius,
obiecit. Di boni, hoc virum audire, principem scire et
usque eo licentiam pervenisse, ut, non dico consulari,

should any one be unable to do so, who, thanks to the liberal studies and the training of philosophy, has attained to some growth? Besides, it is a sort of revenge to rob the man who has sought to inflict an insult of the pleasure of having done so. " Oh dear me ! " he will say, " I suppose he didn't understand." Thus the success of an insult depends upon the sensitiveness and the indignation of the victim. The offender, too, will one day meet his match; some one will be found who will avenge you also.

Gaius Caesar, who amid the multitude of his other vices had a bent for insult, was moved by the strange desire to brand every one with some stigma, while he himself was a most fruitful source of ridicule ; such was the ugliness of his pale face bespeaking his madness, such the wildness of his eyes lurking beneath the brow of an old hag, such the hideousness of his bald head with its sprinkling of beggarly hairs. And he had, besides, a neck overgrown with bristles, spindle shanks, and enormous feet. It would be an endless task were I to attempt to mention the separate acts by which he cast insult upon his parents and grandparents and upon men of every class ; I shall, therefore, mention only those which brought him to his destruction.

Among his especial friends there was a certain Asiaticus Valerius, a proud-spirited man who was hardly to be expected to bear with equanimity another's insults. At a banquet, that is at a public gathering, using his loudest voice, Gaius taunted this man with the way his wife behaved in sexual intercourse. Ye gods ! what a tale for the ears of a husband ! what a fact for an emperor to know ! and what indecency that an emperor should go so far as to

non dico amico, sed tantum marito princeps et
3 adulterium suum narret et fastidium! Chaereae
contra, tribuno militum, sermo non pro manu erat,
languidus sono et, ni facta nosses, suspectior. Huic
Gaius signum petenti modo Veneris, modo Priapi
dabat aliter atque aliter exprobrans armato mollitiam;
haec ipse perlucidus, crepidatus, auratus. Coegit itaque illum uti ferro, ne saepius signum peteret! Ille
primus inter coniuratos manum sustulit, ille cervicem
mediam uno ictu decidit; plurimum deinde undique
publicas ac privatas iniurias ulciscentium gladiorum
ingestum est, sed primus vir fuit, qui minime visus
4 est. At idem Gaius omnia contumelias putabat, ut
sunt ferendarum impatientes faciendarum cupidis-
simi; iratus fuit Herennio Macro, quod illum Gaium
salutaverat, nec impune cessit primipilari, quod
Caligulam dixerat; hoc enim in castris natus et
alumnus legionum vocari solebat, nullo nomine militibus familiarior umquam factus, sed iam Caligulam
5 convicium et probrum iudicabat cothurnatus.[1] Ergo
hoc ipsum solacio erit, etiam si nostra facilitas
ultionem omiserit, futurum aliquem qui poenas
exigat a procace et superbo et iniurioso, quae vitia

[1] cothurnatus *Pincianus, cf. Suetonius,* Cal. 52 : contur-
batus *A.*

---

[a] *i.e.,* in Greek fashion. Gaius was given to eccentric
ostentation in dress (Suet. *Cal.* 52).
  [b] *i.e.,* a commander of the first company of the third-line
reserves of a Roman legion.
  [c] Reared in camp, he had been nicknamed " Caligula "
by the troops because he wore the soldier's low boot (*caliga*).

report his adultery and his dissatisfaction in it to the woman's very husband—to say nothing of his being a consular, to say nothing of his being a friend ! On the other hand, Chaerea, a tribune of the soldiers, had a way of talking that ill-accorded with his prowess ; his voice was feeble and, unless you knew his deeds, was apt to stir distrust. When he asked for the watchword, Gaius would give him sometimes "Venus," sometimes " Priapus," seeking to taunt the man of arms, in one way or another, with wantonness. He himself, all the while, was in gauzy apparel, shod with sandals,[a] and decked with gold. And so Chaerea was driven to use the sword in order to avoid having to ask for the watchword any more ! Among the conspirators he was the first to lift his hand ; it was he who with one blow severed the emperor's neck. After that from all sides blades showered upon him, avenging public and private wrongs, but the first hero was Chaerea, who least appeared one. Yet this same Gaius would interpret everything as an insult, as is the way of those who, being most eager to offer an affront, are least able to endure one. He became angry at Herennius Macer because he addressed him as Gaius, while a centurion of the first maniple[b] got into trouble because he said "Caligula." For in the camp, where he was born and had been the pet of the troops, this was the name by which he was commonly called, nor was there ever any other by which he was so well known to the soldiers. But now, having attained to boots, he considered " Little Boots "[c] a reproach and disgrace. This, then, will be our comfort : even if by reason of tolerance we omit revenge, some one will arise to bring the impertinent, arrogant, and injurious man to punish-

numquam in uno homine et in una contumelia consumuntur.

Respiciamus eorum exempla, quorum laudamus patientiam, ut Socratis, qui comoediarum publicatos in se et spectatos sales in partem bonam accepit risitque non minus quam cum ab uxore Xanthippe immunda aqua perfunderetur. Antistheni mater barbara et Thraessa obiciebatur ; respondit et deorum matrem Idaeam esse.

1 19. Non est in rixam conluctationemque veniendum. Procul auferendi pedes sunt et quicquid horum ab imprudentibus fiet (fieri autem nisi ab imprudentibus non potest) neglegendum et honores iniuriaeque vulgi in promiscuo habendae. Nec his dolendum nec illis 2 gaudendum ; alioqui multa timore contumeliarum aut taedio necessaria omittemus publicisque et privatis officiis, aliquando etiam salutaribus non occurremus, dum muliebris nos cura angit aliquid contra animum audiendi. Aliquando etiam obirati potentibus detegemus hunc affectum intemperanti libertate. Non est autem libertas nihil pati, fallimur ; libertas est animum superponere iniuriis et eum facere se, ex quo solo sibi gaudenda veniant, exteriora diducere a se, ne inquieta agenda sit vita omnium risus, omnium linguas timenti. Quis enim est, qui non possit con-3 tumeliam facere, si quisquam potest ? Diverso autem

---

[a] As notably the *Clouds* of Aristophanes.
[b] Since the worship of Rhea (or Cybele), " Mother of the Gods," was associated with Cretan (or Trojan) Mt. Ida, the Athenian might call her irreverently a " barbarian."

ment ; for his offences are never exhausted upon one individual or in one insult.

Let us turn now to the examples of those whose endurance we commend—for instance to that of Socrates, who took in good part the published and acted gibes directed against him in comedies,[a] and laughed as heartily as when his wife Xanthippe drenched him with foul water. Antisthenes was taunted with having a barbarian, a Thracian woman, for his mother ; his retort was that even the mother of the gods was from Mount Ida.[b]

Strife and wrangling we must not come near. We should flee far from these things, and all the provocations thereto of unthinking people—which only the unthinking can give—should be ignored, and the honours and the injuries of the common herd be valued both alike. We must neither grieve over the one, nor rejoice over the other. Otherwise, from the fear of insults or from weariness of them, we shall fall short in the doing of many needful things, and, suffering from a womanish distaste for hearing anything not to our mind, we shall refuse to face both public and private duties, sometimes even when they are for our well-being. At times, also, enraged against powerful men, we shall reveal our feelings with unrestrained liberty. But not to put up with anything is not liberty ; we deceive ourselves. Liberty is having a mind that rises superior to injury, that makes itself the only source from which its pleasures spring, that separates itself from all external things in order that man may not have to live his life in disquietude, fearing everybody's laughter, everybody's tongue. For if any man can offer insult, who is there who cannot ? But the truly wise man and the aspirant to wisdom

remedio utetur sapiens affectatorque sapientiae.
Imperfectis enim et adhuc ad publicum se iudicium
derigentibus hoc proponendum est inter iniurias ipsos
contumeliasque debere versari ; omnia leviora accident
expectantibus. Quo quisque honestior genere, fama,
patrimonio est, hoc se fortius gerat, memor in prima
acie altos ordines stare. Contumelias et verba pro-
brosa et ignominias et cetera dehonestamenta velut
clamorem hostium ferat et longinqua tela et saxa
sine vulnere circa galeas crepitantia ; iniurias vero ut
vulnera, alia armis, alia pectori infixa, non deiectus,
ne motus quidem gradu sustineat. Etiam si premeris
et infesta vi urgere, cedere tamen turpe est ; ad-
signatum a natura locum tuere. Quaeris quis hic
4 sit locus ? Viri. Sapienti aliud auxilium est huic
contrarium ; vos enim rem geritis, illi parta victoria
est. Ne repugnate vestro bono et hanc spem, dum ad
verum pervenistis, alite in animis libentesque meliora
excipite et opinione ac voto iuvate. Esse aliquid invictum, esse aliquem, in quem nihil fortuna possit, e
re publica est generis humani.

will use different remedies. For those who are not perfected and still conduct themselves in accordance with public opinion must bear in mind that they have to dwell in the midst of injury and insult; all misfortune will fall more lightly on those who expect it. The more honourable a man is by birth, reputation, and patrimony, the more heroically he should bear himself, remembering that the tallest ranks stand in the front battle-line. Let him bear insults, shameful words, civil disgrace, and all other degradation as he would the enemy's war-cry, and the darts and stones from afar that rattle around a soldier's helmet but cause no wound. Let him endure injuries, in sooth, as he would wounds— though some blows pierce his armour, others his breast, never overthrown, nor even moved from his ground. Even if you are hard pressed and beset with fierce violence, yet it is a disgrace to retreat; maintain the post that Nature assigned you. Do you ask what this may be? The post of a hero. The wise man's succour is of another sort, the opposite of this; for while you are in the heat of action, he has won the victory. Do not war against your own good; keep alive this hope in your breasts until you arrive at truth, and gladly give ear to the better doctrine and help it on by your belief and prayer. That there should be something unconquerable, some man against whom Fortune has no power, works for the good of the commonwealth of mankind.

LIBER III

AD NOVATVM

DE IRA

LIBER I

1   1. Exegisti a me, Novate, ut scriberem quemadmodum posset ira leniri, nec immerito mihi videris
hunc praecipue affectum pertimuisse maxime ex omnibus taetrum ac rabidum.   Ceteris enim aliquid quieti
placidique inest, hic totus concitatus et in impetu
doloris est, armorum sanguinis suppliciorum minime
humana furens cupiditate, dum alteri noceat sui neg-
legens, in ipsa irruens tela et ultionis secum ultorem
2 tracturae avidus.   Quidam itaque e sapientibus viris
iram dixerunt brevem insaniam; aeque enim impotens
sui est, decoris oblita, necessitudinum immemor, in
quod coepit pertinax et intenta, rationi consiliisque
praeclusa, vanis agitata causis, ad dispectum aequi
verique inhabilis, ruinis simillima, quae super id quod
3 oppressere franguntur.   Ut scias autem non esse sanos
quos ira possedit, ipsum illorum habitum intuere ;
nam ut furentium certa indicia sunt audax et minax
106

BOOK III

TO NOVATUS ON ANGER

BOOK I

You have importuned me, Novatus, to write on the subject of how anger may be allayed, and it seems to me that you had good reason to fear in an especial degree this, the most hideous and frenzied of all the emotions. For the other emotions have in them some element of peace and calm, while this one is wholly violent and has its being in an onrush of resentment, raging with a most inhuman lust for weapons, blood, and punishment, giving no thought to itself if only it can hurt another, hurling itself upon the very point of the dagger, and eager for revenge though it may drag down the avenger along with it. Certain wise men, therefore, have claimed that anger is temporary madness. For it is equally devoid of self-control, forgetful of decency, unmindful of ties, persistent and diligent in whatever it begins, closed to reason and counsel, excited by trifling causes, unfit to discern the right and true—the very counterpart of a ruin that is shattered in pieces where it overwhelms. But you have only to behold the aspect of those possessed by anger to know that they are insane. For as the marks of a madman are unmistakable—a bold and threatening mien, a gloomy

vultus, tristis frons, torva facies, citatus gradus,
inquietae manus, color versus, crebra et vehementius
acta suspiria, ita irascentium eadem signa sunt :
4 flagrant ac micant oculi, multus ore toto rubor ex-
aestuante ab imis praecordiis sanguine, labra quatiuntur, dentes comprimuntur, horrent ac surriguntur
capilli, spiritus coactus ac stridens, articulorum se
ipsos torquentium sonus, gemitus mugitusque et
parum explanatis vocibus sermo praeruptus et con
plosae saepius manus et pulsata humus pedibus et
totum concitum corpus "magnasque irae minas agens,"
foeda visu et horrenda facies depravantium se atque
5 intumescentium—nescias utrum magis detestabile
vitium sit an deforme. Cetera licet abscondere et
in abdito alere ; ira se profert et in faciem exit,
quantoque maior, hoc effervescit manifestius. Non
vides ut omnium animalium, simul ad nocendum
insurrexerunt, praecurrant notae ac tota corpora
solitum quietumque egrediantur habitum et feritatem
6 suam exasperent ? Spumant apris ora, dentes acu-
untur attritu, taurorum cornua iactantur in vacuum
et harena pulsu pedum spargitur, leones fremunt,
inflantur irritatis colla serpentibus, rabidarum canum
tristis aspectus est. Nullum est animal tam horren-
dum tam perniciosumque natura, ut non appareat in
7 illo, simul ira invasit, novae feritatis accessio. Nec
ignoro ceteros quoque affectus vix occultari, libidinem
metumque et audaciam dare sui signa et posse
praenosci ; neque enim ulla vehementior intrat

---

^a Conjecturally an iambic fragment.

brow, a fierce expression, a hurried step, restless
hands, an altered colour, a quick and more violent
breathing—so likewise are the marks of the angry
man ; his eyes blaze and sparkle, his whole face is
crimson with the blood that surges from the lowest
depths of the heart, his lips quiver, his teeth are
clenched, his hair bristles and stands on end, his
breathing is forced and harsh, his joints crack from
writhing, he groans and bellows, bursts out into
speech with scarcely intelligible words, strikes his
hands together continually, and stamps the ground
with his feet ; his whole body is excited and " performs great angry threats "[a]; it is an ugly and
horrible picture of distorted and swollen frenzy—you
cannot tell whether this vice is more execrable or
more hideous. Other vices may be concealed and
cherished in secret ; anger shows itself openly and
appears in the countenance, and the greater it is,
the more visibly it boils forth. Do you not see how
animals of every sort, as soon as they bestir themselves for mischief, show premonitory signs, and how
their whole body, forsaking its natural state of repose,
accentuates their ferocity ? Wild boars foam at the
mouth and sharpen their tusks by friction, bulls
toss their horns in the air and scatter the sand by
pawing, lions roar, snakes puff up their necks when
they are angry, and mad dogs have a sullen look.
No animal is so hateful and so deadly by nature as
not to show a fresh access of fierceness as soon as it
is assailed by anger. And yet I am aware that the
other emotions as well are not easily concealed ; that
lust and fear and boldness all show their marks and
can be recognized beforehand. For no violent agita-
tion can take hold of the mind without affecting in

concitatio, quae nihil moveat in vultu. Quid ergo
interest ? Quod alii affectus apparent, hic eminet.

1 2. Iam vero si effectus eius damnaque intueri velis,
nulla pestis humano generi pluris stetit. Videbis
caedes ac venena et reorum mutuas sordes et urbium
clades et totarum exitia gentium et principum sub
civili hasta capita venalia et subiectas tectis faces nec
intra moenia coercitos ignes sed ingentia spatia regio-
2 num hostili flamma relucentia. Aspice nobilissimarum
civitatum fundamenta vix notabilia ; has ira deiecit.
Aspice solitudines per multa milia sine habitatore
desertas ; has ira exhausit. Aspice tot memoriae
proditos duces mali exempla fati ; alium ira in cubili
suo confodit, alium intra sacra mensae iura percussit,
alium intra leges celebrisque spectaculum fori lan-
cinavit, alium filii parricidio dare sanguinem iussit,
alium servili manu regalem aperire iugulum, alium
3 in cruce membra distendere. Et adhuc singulorum
supplicia narro ; quid, si tibi libuerit relictis in quos
ira viritim exarsit aspicere caesas gladio contiones et
plebem immisso milite contrucidatam et in perniciem
promiscuam totos populos capitis damnatos¹

* * * * * * *

¹ damnatos *restored by Madvig, after which a leaf or
more of the* MS. *has been lost.*

ᵃ *i.e.*, base defendants bring countercharges of baseness.
ᵇ The proscriptions of Sulla, Marius, and the triumvirs,
and the destruction of such cities as Carthage, Corinth, and
Numantia give point to the rhetoric.
ᶜ *Cf.* the fate of Clitus, *De Ira*, iii. 17. 1.
ᵈ Perhaps a reference to the murder of Tiberius Gracchus.
ᵉ In the lost portion of the text Seneca seems to have
discussed the reason of anger, citing ancient definitions of

some way the countenance. Where, then, lies the difference ? In this—the other emotions show, anger stands out.

Moreover, if you choose to view its results and the harm of it, no plague has cost the human race more dear. You will see bloodshed and poisoning, the vile countercharges of criminals,[a] the downfall of cities and whole nations given to destruction, princely persons sold at public auction, houses put to the torch, and conflagration that halts not within the city-walls, but makes great stretches of the country glow with hostile flame.[b] Behold the most glorious cities whose foundations can scarcely be traced—anger cast them down. Behold solitudes stretching lonely for many miles without a single dweller—anger laid them waste. Behold all the leaders who have been handed down to posterity as instances of an evil fate—anger stabbed this one in his bed, struck down this one amid the sanctities of the feast,[c] tore this one to pieces in the very home of the law and in full view of the crowded forum,[d] forced this one to have his blood spilled by the murderous act of his son, another to have his royal throat cut by the hand of a slave, another to have his limbs stretched upon the cross. And hitherto I have mentioned the sufferings of individual persons only ; what if, leaving aside these who singly felt the force of anger's flame, you should choose to view the gatherings cut down by the sword, the populace butchered by soldiery let loose upon them, and whole peoples condemned to death in common ruin[e]

*   *   *   *   *   *   *

the passion and giving his own. Lactantius, *De Ira Dei*, 17, supplies significant evidence for the context.

4 tamquam aut curam nostram deserentibus aut
auctoritatem contemnentibus. Quid ? Gladiatoribus
quare populus irascitur et tam inique, ut iniuriam
putet, quod non libenter pereunt ? Contemni se
iudicat et vultu, gestu, ardore a spectatore in ad-
5 versarium vertitur. Quicquid est tale, non est ira,
sed quasi ira, sicut puerorum, qui si ceciderunt,
terram verberari volunt et saepe ne sciunt quidem,
cur irascantur, sed tantum irascuntur, sine causa et
sine iniuria, non tamen sine aliqua iniuriae specie
nec sine aliqua poenae cupiditate. Deluduntur itaque
imitatione plagarum et simulatis deprecantium
lacrimis placantur et falsa ultione falsus dolor tollitur.
1 3. " Irascimur," inquit, " saepe non illis qui laeserunt, sed iis qui laesuri sunt ; ut scias iram non ex
iniuria nasci." Verum est irasci nos laesuris, sed
ipsa cogitatione nos laedunt, et iniuriam qui facturus
2 est iam facit. " Ut scias," inquit, " non esse iram
poenae cupiditatem, infirmissimi saepe potentissimis
irascuntur nec poenam concupiscunt quam non
sperant." Primum diximus cupiditatem esse poenae
exigendae, non facultatem ; concupiscunt autem
homines et quae non possunt. Deinde nemo tam
humilis est, qui poenam vel summi hominis sperare
non possit ; ad nocendum potentes sumus. Aristo-

---

a The speaker here criticizes Seneca's definition of anger,
drawn from Posidonius, which has been preserved by
Lactantius (*l.c.*): " ira est cupiditas ulciscendae iniuriae."

as if either forsaking our protection, or despising our authority. Tell me, why do we see the people grow angry with gladiators, and so unjustly as to deem it an offence that they are not glad to die? They consider themselves affronted, and from mere spectators transform themselves into enemies, in looks, in gesture, and in violence. Whatever this may be, it is not anger, but mock anger, like that of children who, if they fall down, want the earth to be thrashed, and who often do not even know why they are angry—they are merely angry, without any reason and without being injured, though not without some semblance of injury and not without some desire of exacting punishment. And so they are deceived by imaginary blows and are pacified by the pretended tears of those who beg forgiveness, and mock resentment is removed by a mock revenge.

" We often get angry," some one rejoins, " not at those who have hurt us, but at those who intend to hurt us; you may, therefore, be sure that anger is not born of injury."[a] It is true that we do get angry at those who intend to hurt us, but by the very intention they do hurt us; the man who intends to do injury has already done it. " But," our friend replies, " that you may know that anger is not the desire to exact punishment, the weakest men are often angry at the most powerful, and if they have no hope of inflicting punishment, they have not the desire." In the first place, I spoke of the desire to exact punishment, not of the power to do so; moreover, men do desire even what they cannot attain. In the second place, no one is so lowly that he cannot hope to punish even the loftiest of men; we all have power to do harm. Aristotle's

3 telis finitio non multum a nostra abest ; ait enim
iram esse cupiditatem doloris reponendi. Quid inter
nostram et hanc finitionem intersit, exsequi longum
est. Contra utramque dicitur feras irasci nec iniuria
irritatas nec poenae dolorisve alieni causa ; nam
4 etiam si haec efficiunt, non haec petunt. Sed dicendum est feras ira carere et omnia animalia[1] praeter
hominem ; nam cum sit inimica rationi, nusquam
tamen nascitur, nisi ubi rationi locus est. Impetus
habent ferae, rabiem, feritatem, incursum ; iram
quidem non magis quam luxuriam, et in quasdam
5 voluptates intemperantiores homine sunt. Non est
quod credas illi qui dicit :

> Non aper irasci meminit, non fidere cursu
> cerva nec armentis incurrere fortibus ursi.

Irasci dicit incitari, impingi ; irasci quidem non magis
6 sciunt quam ignoscere. Muta animalia humanis
affectibus carent, habent autem similes illis quosdam
impulsus. Alioquin si amor in illis esset et odium,
esset amicitia et simultas, dissensio et concordia ;
quorum aliqua in illis quoque exstant vestigia, ceterum
humanorum pectorum propria bona malaque sunt.
7 Nulli nisi homini concessa prudentia est, providentia,
diligentia, cogitatio, nec tantum virtutibus humanis
animalia sed etiam vitiis prohibita sunt. Tota illorum
ut extra ita intra forma humanae dissimilis est ;

---

[1] animalia *added by Vahlen.*

---

[a] *De Anima*, 403 a 30 : διαφερόντως δ' ἂν ὁρίσαιντο φυσικός
τε καὶ διαλεκτικὸς ἕκαστον αὐτῶν, οἷον ὀργὴ τί ἐστίν · ὁ μὲν γὰρ
ὄρεξιν ἀντιλυπήσεως ἤ τι τοιοῦτον, ὁ δὲ ζέσιν τοῦ περὶ καρδίαν
αἵματος ἢ θερμοῦ. *Cf. Rhetor.* ii. 2.
[b] Ovid, *Met.* vii. 545 *sq.*, where he describes the effect
of a plague.

definition [a] differs little from mine ; for he says that
anger is the desire to repay suffering. To trace the
difference between his definition and mine would take
too long. In criticism of both it may be said that
wild beasts become angry though they are neither
stirred by injury nor bent on the punishment or the
suffering of another ; for even if they accomplish
these ends, they do not seek them. But our reply
must be that wild beasts and all animals, except man,
are not subject to anger; for while it is the foe of
reason, it is, nevertheless, born only where reason
dwells. Wild beasts have impulses, madness, fierceness, aggressiveness ; but they no more have anger
than they have luxuriousness. Yet in regard to
certain pleasures they are less self-restrained than
man. You are not to believe the words of the
poet :

> The boar his wrath forgets, the hind her trust in flight,
> Nor bears will now essay the sturdy kine to fight.[b]

Their being aroused and spurred to action he calls
their " wrath " ; but they know no more how to be
wroth than to pardon. Dumb animals lack the
emotions of man, but they have certain impulses
similar to these emotions. Otherwise, if they were
capable of love and hate, they would also be capable
of friendship and enmity, discord and harmony ; and
some traces of these qualities do appear in them also,
but the qualities of good and bad are peculiar to the
human breast. Wisdom, foresight, diligence, and
reflection have been granted to no creature but man,
and not only his virtues but also his faults have been
withheld from the animals. As their outward form
is wholly different from that of man, so is their inner

regium est illud et principale aliter ductum. Ut vox
est quidem, sed non explanabilis et perturbata et
verborum inefficax, ut lingua, sed devincta nec in
motus varios soluta, ita ipsum principale parum
subtile, parum exactum. Capit ergo visus speciesque
rerum quibus ad impetus evocetur, sed turbidas et
8 confusas. Ex eo procursus illorum tumultusque
vehementes sunt, metus autem sollicitudinesque et
tristitia et ira non sunt, sed his quaedam similia.
Ideo cito cadunt et mutantur in contrarium et, cum
acerrime saevierunt expaveruntque, pascuntur et ex
fremitu discursuque vesano statim quies soporque
sequitur.

1   4. Quid esset ira satis explicitum est. Quo distet
ab iracundia apparet ; quo ebrius ab ebrioso et
timens a timido. Iratus potest non esse iracundus ;
2 iracundus potest aliquando iratus non esse. Cetera,
quae pluribus apud Graecos nominibus in species
iram distinguunt, quia apud nos vocabula sua non
habent, praeteribo, etiam si amarum nos acerbumque
dicimus, nec minus stomachosum, rabiosum, cla-
mosum, difficilem, asperum, quae omnia irarum
differentiae sunt ; inter hos morosum ponas licet,
3 delicatum iracundiae genus. Quaedam enim sunt
irae, quae intra clamorem considant, quaedam non
minus pertinaces quam frequentes, quaedam saevae
manu verbis parciores, quaedam in verborum male-

nature ; its guiding and directing principle is cast
in a different mould. They have a voice, it is true,
but it is unintelligible, uncontrolled, and incapable
of speech ; they have a tongue, but it is shackled and
not free to make many different movements. So
likewise in them the ruling principle itself is lacking
in fineness and precision. Consequently, while it
forms impressions and notions of the things that
arouse it to action, they are clouded and indistinct.
It follows, accordingly, that while they have violent
outbreaks and mental disturbances, they do not have
fear and anxiety, sorrow and anger, but certain
states similar to them. These, therefore, quickly
pass and change to the exact reverse, and animals,
after showing the sharpest frenzy and fear, will begin
to feed, and their frantic bellowing and plunging is
immediately followed by repose and sleep.

What anger is has now been sufficiently explained.
The difference between it and irascibility is evident ;
it is like the difference between a drunken man and
a drunkard, between a frightened man and a coward.
An angry man may not be an irascible man ; an
irascible man may, at times, not be an angry man.
The other categories which the Greeks, using a
multiplicity of terms, establish for the different kinds
of anger I shall pass over, since we have no distinctive words for them ; and yet we call men bitter and
harsh, and, just as often, choleric, rabid, clamorous,
captious, and fierce—all of which designate different
aspects of anger. Here, too, you may place the
peevish man, whose state is a mild sort of irascibility.
Now there are certain kinds of anger which subside
in noise ; some are as persistent as they are common ;
some are fierce in deed but inclined to be frugal of

dictorumque amaritudinem effusae ; quaedam ultra
querellas et aversationes non exeunt, quaedam altae
gravesque sunt et introrsus versae. Mille aliae species
sunt mali multiplicis.

1   5. Quid esset ira quaesitum est, an in ullum aliud
animal quam in hominem caderet, quo ab iracundia
distaret, quot eius species essent ; nunc quaeramus
an ira secundum naturam sit et an utilis atque ex
aliqua parte retinenda.

2   An secundum naturam sit manifestum erit, si
hominem inspexerimus. Quo quid est mitius, dum
in recto animi habitus est ? Quid autem ira crudelius
est ? Quid homine aliorum amantius ? Quid ira
infestius ? Homo in adiutorium mutuum genitus est,
ira in exitium ; hic congregari vult, illa discedere ;
hic prodesse, illa nocere ; hic etiam ignotis succurrere,
illa etiam carissimos petere ; hic aliorum commodis
vel impendere se paratus est, illa in periculum,

3 dummodo deducat, descendere. Quis ergo magis
naturam rerum ignorat quam qui optimo eius operi
et emendatissimo hoc ferum ac perniciosum vitium
adsignat ? Ira, ut diximus, avida poenae est, cuius
cupidinem inesse pacatissimo hominis pectori minime
secundum eius naturam est. Beneficiis enim humana
vita constat et concordia, nec terrore sed mutuo
amore in foedus auxiliumque commune constringitur.

1   6. " Quid ergo ? Non aliquando castigatio necessaria est ? " Quidni ? Sed haec sine ira, cum ratione ;

---

a *i.e.*, not entirely discarded by the wise man.

words ; some are vented in bitterness of speech and curses ; certain kinds do not go beyond a word of complaint and a show of coolness, others are deep-seated and weighty and brood in a man. There are a thousand different shapes of the multiform evil.

Hitherto we have inquired what anger is, whether it belongs to any other creature than man, how it differs from irascibility, and in how many aspects it appears ; let us now inquire whether anger is in accordance with nature ; whether it is expedient and ought, therefore, in some measure to be kept.[a]

Whether it is in accordance with nature will become clear if we turn our eyes to man. What is more gentle than he while he is in a right state of mind ? But what is more cruel than anger ? What is more loving to others than man ? What more hostile than anger ? Man is born for mutual help ; anger for mutual destruction. The one desires union, the other disunion ; the one to help, the other to harm ; one would succour even strangers, the other attack its best beloved ; the one is ready even to expend himself for the good of others, the other to plunge into peril only if it can drag others along. Who, therefore, has less knowledge of the ways of Nature than the man who would ascribe to her best and most finished work this cruel and deadly vice ? Anger, as I have said, is bent on punishment, and that such a desire should find a harbour in man's most peaceful breast accords least of all with his nature. For human life is founded on kindness and concord, and is bound into an alliance for common help, not by terror, but by mutual love.

" What then ? " you say ; " is not correction some-times necessary ? " Of course it is ; but with

non enim nocet sed medetur specie nocendi. Quemadmodum quaedam hastilia detorta, ut corrigamus, adurimus et adactis cuneis, non ut frangamus sed ut explicemus, elidimus, sic ingenia vitio prava dolore 2 corporis animique corrigimus. Nempe medicus primo in levibus vitiis temptat non multum ex cotidiana consuetudine inflectere et cibis, potionibus, exercitationibus ordinem imponere ac valetudinem tantum mutata vitae dispositione firmare. Proximum est, ut modus proficiat; si modus et ordo non proficit, subducit aliqua et circumcidit; si ne adhoc quidem respondet, interdicit cibis et abstinentia corpus exonerat; si frustra molliora cesserunt, ferit venam membrisque, si adhaerentia nocent et morbum diffundunt, manus adfert; nec ulla dura videtur 3 curatio, cuius salutaris effectus est. Ita legum praesidem civitatisque rectorem decet, quam diu potest, verbis et his mollioribus ingenia curare, ut facienda suadeat cupiditatemque honesti et aequi conciliet animis faciatque vitiorum odium, pretium virtutium; transeat deinde ad tristiorem orationem, qua moneat adhuc et exprobret; novissime ad poenas et has adhuc leves, revocabiles decurrat; ultima supplicia sceleribus ultimis ponat, ut nemo pereat, nisi quem

---

ª *i.e.,* the poles or saplings from which spears were made.

discretion, not with anger. For it will not hurt, but will heal under the guise of hurting. As we apply the flame to certain spearshafts[a] when they are crooked in order to straighten them, and compress them by driving in wedges, not to crush them, but to take out their kinks, so through pain applied to body and mind we reform the natures of men that are distorted by vice. Manifestly, a physician, in the case of slight disorders, tries at first not to make much change in his patient's daily habits ; he lays down a regimen for food, drink, and exercise, and tries to improve his health only through a change in the ordering of his life. His next concern is to see that the amount is conducive to health. If the first amount and regimen fail to bring relief, he orders a reduction and lops off some things. If still there is no response, he prohibits food and disburdens the body by fasting. If these milder measures are unavailing he opens a vein, and then, if the limbs by continuing to be attached to the body are doing it harm and spreading the disease, he lays violent hands on them. No treatment seems harsh if its result is salutary. Similarly, it becomes a guardian of the law, the ruler of the state, to heal human nature by the use of words, and these of the milder sort, as long as he can, to the end that he may persuade a man to do what he ought to do, and win over his heart to a desire for the honourable and the just, and implant in his mind hatred of vice and esteem of virtue. Let him pass next to harsher language, in which he will still aim at admonition and reproof. Lastly, let him resort to punishment, yet still making it light and not irrevocable. Extreme punishment let him appoint only to extreme crime, so that no

4 perire etiam pereuntis intersit. Hoc uno medentibus erit dissimilis, quod illi quibus vitam non potuerunt largiri facilem exitum praestant, hic damnatos cum dedecore et traductione vita exigit, non quia delectetur ullius poena—procul est enim a sapiente tam inhumana feritas—sed ut documentum omnium sint, et quia vivi noluerunt prodesse, morte certe eorum res publica utatur. Non est ergo natura hominis poenae adpetens ; ideo ne ira quidem secundum
5 naturam hominis, quia poenae adpetens est. Et Platonis argumentum adferam—quid enim nocet alienis uti ex parte qua nostra sunt ?—: " Vir bonus," inquit, " non laedit." Poena laedit ; bono ergo poena non convenit, ob hoc nec ira, quia poena irae convenit. Si vir bonus poena non gaudet, non gaudebit ne eo quidem adfectu, cui poena voluptati est ; ergo non est naturalis ira.

1 7. Numquid, quamvis non sit naturalis ira, adsumenda est, quia utilis saepe fuit ? Extollit animos et incitat, nec quicquam sine illa magnificum in bello fortitudo gerit, nisi hinc flamma subdita est et hic stimulus peragitavit misitque in pericula audaces. Optimum itaque quidam putant temperare iram, non tollere, eoque detracto, quod exundat, ad salutarem

---

^a *Republic,* i. 335 D.

man will lose his life unless it is to the benefit even
of the loser to lose it. In only one particular will
he differ from the physician. For while the one
supplies to the patients to whom he has been unable
to give the boon of life an easy exit from it, the other
forcibly expels the condemned from life, covered
with disgrace and public ignominy, not because he
takes pleasure in the punishment of any one—for the
wise man is far from such inhuman ferocity—but that
they may prove a warning to all, and, since they were
unwilling to be useful while alive, that in death at
any rate they may be of service to the state. Man's
nature, then, does not crave vengeance; neither,
therefore, does anger accord with man's nature,
because anger craves vengeance. And I may adduce
here the argument of Plato—for what harm is there
in using the arguments of others, so far as they are
our own? "The good man," he says, "does no
injury." [a] Punishment injures; therefore punishment is not consistent with good, nor, for the same
reason, is anger, since punishment is consistent with
anger. If the good man rejoices not in punishment,
neither will he rejoice in that mood which takes
pleasure in punishment; therefore anger is contrary
to nature.

Although anger be contrary to nature, may it not
be right to adopt it, because it has often been useful?
It rouses and incites the spirit, and without it bravery
performs no splendid deed in war—unless it supplies
the flame, unless it acts as a goad to spur on brave
men and send them into danger. Therefore some
think that the best course is to control anger, not to
banish it, and by removing its excesses to confine it
within beneficial bounds, keeping, however, that

modum cogere, id vero retinere sine quo languebit
actio et vis ac vigor animi resolvetur.

2 Primum facilius est excludere perniciosa quam
regere et non admittere quam admissa moderari ;
nam cum se in possessione posuerunt, potentiora
3 rectore sunt nec recidi se minuive patiuntur. Deinde
ratio ipsa, cui freni traduntur, tam diu potens est
quam diu diducta est ab adfectibus ; si miscuit se
illis et inquinavit, non potest continere quos summovere potuisset. Commota enim semel et excussa
4 mens ei servit quo impellitur. Quarundam rerum
initia in nostra potestate sunt, ulteriora nos vi sua
rapiunt nec regressum relinquunt. Ut in praeceps
datis corporibus nullum sui arbitrium est nec resistere
morarive deiecta potuerunt, sed consilium omne et
paenitentiam irrevocabilis praecipitatio abscidit et
non licet eo non pervenire, quo non ire licuisset, ita
animus si in iram, amorem aliosque se proiecit adfectus, non permittitur reprimere impetum ; rapiat
illum oportet et ad imum agat pondus suum et
vitiorum natura proclivis.

1 8. Optimum est primum irritamentum irae protinus spernere ipsisque repugnare seminibus et dare
operam, ne incidamus in iram. Nam si coepit ferre
transversos, difficilis ad salutem recursus est, quoniam
nihil rationis est, ubi semel adfectus inductus est ius-

part without which action will be inert and the mind's force and energy broken.

In the first place, it is easier to exclude harmful passions than to rule them, and to deny them admittance than, after they have been admitted, to control them ; for when they have established themselves in possession, they are stronger than their ruler and do not permit themselves to be restrained or reduced. In the second place, Reason herself, to whom the reins of power have been entrusted, remains mistress only so long as she is kept apart from the passions : if once she mingles with them and is contaminated, she becomes unable to hold back those whom she might have cleared from her path. For when once the mind has been aroused and shaken, it becomes the slave of the disturbing agent. There are certain things which at the start are under our control, but later hurry us away by their violence and leave us no retreat. As a victim hurled from the precipice has no control of his body, and, once cast off, can neither stop nor stay, but, speeding on irrevocably, is cut off from all reconsideration and repentance and cannot now avoid arriving at the goal toward which he might once have avoided starting, so with the mind—if it plunges into anger, love, or the other passions, it has no power to check its impetus ; its very weight and the downward tendency of vice needs must hurry it on, and drive it to the bottom.

The best course is to reject at once the first incitement to anger, to resist even its small beginnings, and to take pains to avoid falling into anger. For if it begins to lead us astray, the return to the safe path is difficult, since, if once we admit the emotion and by our own free will grant it any authority, reason

que illi aliquod voluntate nostra datum est ; faciet de
2 cetero quantum volet, non quantum permiseris. In
primis, inquam, finibus hostis arcendus est ; nam cum
intravit et portis se intulit, modum a captivis non accipit. Neque enim sepositus est animus et extrinsecus
speculatur adfectus, ut illos non patiatur ultra quam
oportet procedere, sed in adfectum ipse mutatur ideoque non potest utilem illam vim et salutarem proditam
3 iam infirmatamque revocare. Non enim, ut dixi, se-
paratas ista sedes suas diductasque habent, sed
affectus et ratio in melius peiusque mutatio animi est.
Quomodo ergo ratio occupata et oppressa vitiis
resurget, quae irae cessit ? Aut quemadmodum
ex confusione se liberabit, in qua peiorum mixtura
4 praevaluit ? " Sed quidam," inquit, " in ira se continent." Utrum ergo ita ut nihil faciant eorum quae
ira dictat an ut aliquid ? Si nihil faciunt, apparet
non esse ad actiones rerum necessariam iram, quam
vos, quasi fortius aliquid ratione haberet, advocabatis.
5 Denique interrogo : valentior est quam ratio an
infirmior ? Si valentior, quomodo illi modum ratio
poterit imponere, cum parere nisi imbecilliora non
soleant ? Si infirmior est, sine hac per se ad rerum
effectus sufficit ratio nec desiderat inbecillioris auxi-
6 lium. " At irati quidam constant sibi et se continent."
126

becomes of no avail; after that it will do, not whatever you let it, but whatever it chooses. The enemy, I repeat, must be stopped at the very frontier; for if he has passed it, and advanced within the city-gates, he will not respect any bounds set by his captives. For the mind is not a member apart, nor does it view the passions merely objectively, thus forbidding them to advance farther than they ought, but it is itself transformed into the passion and is, therefore, unable to recover its former useful and saving power when this has once been betrayed and weakened. For, as I said before, these two do not dwell separate and distinct, but passion and reason are only the transformation of the mind toward the better or the worse. How, then, will the reason, after it has surrendered to anger, rise again, assailed and crushed as it is by vice? Or how shall it free itself from the motley combination in which a blending of all the worse qualities makes them supreme? "But," says some one, "there are those who control themselves even in anger." You mean, then, that they do none of the things that anger dictates, or only some of them? If they do none, it is evident that anger is not essential to the transactions of life, and yet you were advocating it on the ground that it is something stronger than reason. I ask, in fine, is anger more powerful or weaker than reason? If it is more powerful, how will reason be able to set limitations upon it, since, ordinarily, it is only the less powerful thing that submits? If it is weaker, then reason without it is sufficient in itself for the accomplishment of our tasks, and requires no help from a thing less powerful. Yet you say: "There are those who, even though angry, remain true to themselves

Quando? Cum iam ira evanescit et sua sponte decedit, non cum in ipso fervore est; tunc enim 7 potentior est. "Quid ergo? Non aliquando in ira quoque et dimittunt incolumes intactosque quos oderunt et a nocendo abstinent?" Faciunt. Quando? Cum adfectus repercussit adfectum et aut metus aut cupiditas aliquid impetravit. Non rationis tunc beneficio quievit, sed affectuum infida et mala pace.

1　9. Deinde nihil habet in se utile nec acuit animum ad res bellicas. Numquam enim virtus vitio adiuvanda est se contenta. Quotiens impetu opus est, non irascitur sed exsurgit et in quantum putavit opus esse concitatur remittiturque, non aliter quam quae tormentis exprimuntur tela in potestate mittentis sunt 2 in quantum torqueantur. "Ira," inquit Aristoteles, "necessaria est, nec quicquam sine illa expugnari potest, nisi illa implet animum et spiritum accendit; utendum autem illa est non ut duce sed ut milite." Quod est falsum. Nam si exaudit rationem sequiturque qua ducitur, iam non est ira, cuius proprium est contumacia; si vero repugnat et non ubi iussa est quiescit, sed libidine ferociaque provehitur, tam inutilis animi minister est quam miles, qui signum receptui 3 neglegit. Itaque si modum adhiberi sibi patitur, alio nomine appellanda est, desît ira esse, quam effrenatam

---

ª It is not known where.

and are self-controlled." But when are they so ? Only
when anger gradually vanishes and departs of its own
accord, not when it is at white heat ; then it is the
more powerful of the two. " What then ? " you say ;
" do not men sometimes even in the midst of anger
allow those whom they hate to get off safe and sound
and refrain from doing them injury ? " They do ;
but when ? When passion has beaten back passion,
and either fear or greed has obtained its end. Then
there is peace, not wrought through the good offices
of reason, but through a treacherous and evil agreement between the passions.

Again, anger embodies nothing useful, nor does
it kindle the mind to warlike deeds ; for virtue, being
self-sufficient, never needs the help of vice. Whenever there is need of violent effort, the mind does
not become angry, but it gathers itself together and
is aroused or relaxed according to its estimate of the
need ; just as when engines of war hurl forth their
arrows, it is the operator who controls the tension
with which they are hurled. "Anger," says
Aristotle,[a] " is necessary, and no battle can be won
without it—unless it fills the mind and fires the soul ;
it must serve, however, not as a leader, but as the
common soldier." But this is not true. For if it
listens to reason and follows where reason leads, it
is no longer anger, of which the chief characteristic is
wilfulness. If, however, it resists and is not submissive when ordered, but is carried away by its
own caprice and fury, it will be an instrument of
the mind as useless as is the soldier who disregards
the signal for retreat. If, therefore, anger suffers
any limitation to be imposed upon it, it must be
called by some other name—it has ceased to be anger ;

129

indomitamque intellego ; si non patitur, perniciosa
est nec inter auxilia numeranda ; ita aut ira non est
4 aut inutilis est. Nam si quis poenam exigit non
ipsius poenae avidus sed quia oportet, non est
adnumerandus iratis. Hic erit utilis miles qui scit
parere consilio ; adfectus quidem tam mali ministri
quam duces sunt.

1   10. Ideo numquam adsumet ratio in adiutorium
improvidos et violentos impetus, apud quos nihil ipsa
auctoritatis habeat, quos numquam comprimere possit,
nisi pares illis similisque opposuerit, ut irae metum,
2 inertiae iram, timori cupiditatem.[1] Absit hoc a
virtute malum, ut umquam ratio ad vitia confugiat !
Non potest hic animus fidele otium capere, quatiatur
necesse est fluctueturque, qui malis suis tutus est, qui
fortis esse nisi irascitur non potest, industrius nisi
cupit, quietus nisi timet : in tyrannide illi vivendum
est in alicuius adfectus venienti servitutem. Non
pudet virtutes in clientelam vitiorum demittere ?
3 Deinde desinit quicquam posse ratio, si nihil potest
sine adfectu, et incipit par illi similisque esse. Quid
enim interest, si aeque adfectus inconsulta res est
sine ratione quam ratio sine adfectu inefficax ? Par
utrumque est, ubi esse alterum sine altero non potest.
Quis autem sustineat adfectum exaequare rationi ?

----

[1] ut . . . cupiditatem *Gertz and Hermes omit.*

for I understand this to be unbridled and ungovernable. If it suffers no limitation, it is a baneful thing
and is not to be counted as a helpful agent. Thus
either anger is not anger or it is useless. For the
man who exacts punishment, not because he desires
punishment for its own sake, but because it is right
to inflict it, ought not to be counted as an angry man.
The useful soldier will be one who knows how to obey
orders ; the passions are as bad subordinates as
they are leaders.

Consequently, reason will never call to its help
blind and violent impulses over which it will itself
have no control, which it can never crush save by
setting against them equally powerful and similar
impulses, as fear against anger, anger against sloth,
greed against fear. May virtue be spared the
calamity of having reason ever flee for help to vice !
It is impossible for the mind to find here a sure
repose ; shattered and storm-tossed it must ever be
if it depends upon its worst qualities to save it, if it
cannot be brave without being angry, if it cannot
be industrious without being greedy, if it cannot be
quiet without being afraid—such is the tyranny
under which that man must live who surrenders to
the bondage of any passion. Is it not a shame to
degrade the virtues into dependence upon the vices ?
Again, reason ceases to have power if it has no power
apart from passion, and so gets to be on the same
level with passion and like unto it. For what difference is there, if passion without reason is a thing as
unguided as reason without passion is ineffective ?
Both are on the same level, if one cannot exist without the other. Yet who would maintain that passion
is on a level with reason ? " Passion," some one

4 " Ita," inquit, " utilis adfectus est, si modicus est."
Immo si natura utilis est. Sed si impatiens imperii
rationisque est, hoc dumtaxat moderatione con-
sequetur, ut quo minor fuerit, minus noceat : ergo
modicus affectus nihil aliud quam malum modicum est.
1   11. " Sed adversus hostes," inquit, " necessaria est
ira." Nusquam minus ; ubi non effusos esse oportet
impetus sed temperatos et oboedientes. Quid enim
est aliud quod barbaros tanto robustiores corporibus,
tanto patientiores laborum comminuat nisi ira in-
2 festissima sibi ? Gladiatores quoque ars tuetur, ira
denudat. Deinde quid opus est ira, cum idem proficiat ratio ? An tu putas venatorem irasci feris ?
Atqui et venientis excipit et fugientis persequitur,
et omnia illa sine ira facit ratio. Quid Cimbrorum
Teutonorumque tot milia superfusa Alpibus ita
sustulit, ut tantae cladis notitiam ad suos non nuntius
sed fama pertulerit, nisi quod erat illis ira pro virtute ?
Quae ut aliquando propulit stravitque obvia, ita
3 saepius sibi exitio est. Germanis quid est animosius ?
Quid ad incursum acrius ? Quid armorum cupidius,
quibus innascuntur innutriunturque, quorum unica
illis cura est in alia neglegentibus ? Quid induratius
ad omnem patientiam, ut quibus magna ex parte non
tegimenta corporum provisa sint, non suffugia adversus

ᵃ Leading nations of a vast horde of barbarians, who,
migrating from northern Germany (113-101 B.C.), alarmed
Italy by their repeated victories over Roman armies. Marius
defeated the Teutons at Aquae Sextiae in 102 B.C., and in the
following year, with Catulus, annihilated the Cimbrians on
the Raudine Plain.

says, " is useful, provided that it be moderate." No, only by its nature can it be useful. If, however, it will not submit to authority and reason, the only result of its moderation will be that the less there is of it, the less harm it will do. Consequently moderate passion is nothing else than a moderate evil.

" But against the enemy," it is said, " anger is necessary." Nowhere is it less so ; for there the attack ought not to be disorderly, but regulated and under control. What else is it, in fact, but their anger—its own worst foe—that reduces to impotency the barbarians, who are so much stronger of body than we, and so much better able to endure hardship ? So, too, in the case of gladiators skill is their protection, anger their undoing. Of what use, further, is anger, when the same end may be accomplished by reason ? Think you the hunter has anger toward wild beasts ? Yet when they come, he takes them, and when they flee, he follows, and reason does it all without anger. The Cimbrians and the Teutons [a] who poured over the Alps in countless thousands—what wiped them out so completely that even the news of the great disaster was carried to their homes, not by a messenger, but only by rumour, except that they substituted anger for valour ? Anger, although it will sometimes overthrow and lay low whatever gets in its way, yet more often brings destruction on itself. Who are more courageous than the Germans ? Who are bolder in a charge ? Who have more love of the arms to which they are born and bred, which to the exclusion of all else become their only care ? Who are more hardened to endurance of every kind, since they are, in large measure, provided with no protection for their bodies,

4 perpetuum caeli rigorem ? Hos tamen Hispani Galli-
que et Asiae Syriaeque molles bello viri, antequam
legio visatur, caedunt ob nullam aliam rem opportunos
quam iracundiam. Agedum illis corporibus, illis
animis delicias, luxum, opes ignorantibus da rationem,
da disciplinam : ut nil amplius dicam, necesse erit
5 certe nobis mores Romanos repetere. Quo alio
Fabius affectas imperii vires recreavit, quam quod
cunctari et trahere et morari sciit, quae omnia irati
nesciunt ? Perierat imperium, quod tunc in extremo
stabat, si Fabius tantum ausus esset quantum ira sua-
debat : habuit in consilio fortunam publicam et aestimatis viribus, ex quibus iam perire nihil sine universo
poterat, dolorem ultionemque seposuit in unam utili-
tatem et occasiones intentus ; iram ante vicit quam
6 Hannibalem. Quid Scipio ? Non relicto Hannibale et
Punico exercitu omnibusque, quibus irascendum erat,
bellum in Africam transtulit tam lentus, ut opinionem
7 luxuriae segnitiaeque malignis daret ? Quid alter
Scipio ? Non circa Numantiam multum diuque sedit
et hunc suum publicumque dolorem aequo animo
tulit, diutius Numantiam quam Carthaginem vinci ?
Dum circumvallat et includit hostem, eo compulit, ut

ᵃ A reference to the famous tactics of Quintus Fabius
Maximus, Cunctator, who, appointed dictator after the battle
of Lake Trasimenus (217 B.C.), harassed Hannibal by his
dilatory policy.

ᵇ During the winter of 205-204 B.C. Scipio lingered in
Sicily, perfecting plans for his expedition into Africa.

ᶜ P. Cornelius Scipio Aemilianus, conqueror of Carthage
(146 B.C.).

ᵈ Through the winter, spring, and summer of 134–133 B.C.

with no shelter against the continual rigour of the climate ? Yet these are they whom the Spaniards and the Gauls and men of Asia and Syria, uninured to war, cut down before they could even glimpse a Roman legion, the victims of nothing else than anger. But mark you, once give discipline to those bodies, give reason to those minds that are strangers still to pampered ways, excess, and wealth, and we Romans— to mention nothing further—shall assuredly be forced to return to the ancient Roman ways. How else did Fabius restore the broken forces of the state but by knowing how to loiter, to put off, and to wait [a] —things of which angry men know nothing ? The state, which was standing then in the utmost extremity, had surely perished if Fabius had ventured to do all that anger prompted. But he took into consideration the well-being of the state, and, estimating its strength, of which now nothing could be lost without the loss of all, he buried all thought of resentment and revenge and was concerned only with expediency and the fitting opportunity ; he conquered anger before he conquered Hannibal. And what of Scipio ? Did he not leave behind him Hannibal and the Carthaginian army and all those with whom he had reason to be angry, and dally so long [b] in transferring the war to Africa that he gave to evil-minded people the impression that he was a sensualist and a sluggard ? What, too, of the other Scipio ? [c] Did he not sit before Numantia, idling much and long, and bear unmoved the reproach to himself and to his country that it took longer to conquer Numantia than to conquer Carthage ? But by blockading and investing [d] the enemy he forced them to such straits that they perished by

8 ferro ipsi suo caderent. Non est itaque utilis ne in
proeliis quidem aut bellis ira ; in temeritatem enim
prona est et pericula, dum inferre vult, non cavet.
Illa certissima est virtus quae se diu multumque
circumspexit et rexit et ex lento ac destinato provexit.

1   12. " Quid ergo ? " inquit, " vir bonus non irascitur, si caedi patrem suum viderit, si rapi matrem ? "
Non irascetur, sed vindicabit, sed tuebitur. Quid
autem times, ne parum magnus illi stimulus etiam
sine ira pietas sit ? Aut dic eodem modo : " Quid
ergo ? Cum videat secari patrem suum filiumve,
vir bonus non flebit nec linquetur animo ? " Quae
accidere feminis videmus, quotiens illas levis periculi
2 suspicio perculit. Officia sua vir bonus exsequetur
inconfusus, intrepidus ; et sic bono viro digna faciet,
ut nihil faciat viro indignum. Pater caedetur, de-
fendam ; caesus est, exsequar, quia oportet, non quia
3 dolet. " Irascuntur boni viri pro suorum iniuriis." [1]
Cum hoc dicis, Theophraste, quaeris invidiam praeceptis fortioribus et relicto iudice ad coronam venis.
Quia unusquisque in eiusmodi suorum casu irascitur,
putas iudicaturos homines id fieri debere quod
faciunt ; fere enim iustum quisque affectum iudicat
4 quem adgnoscit. Sed idem faciunt, si calda non

---

[1] *The words* irascuntur . . . iniuriis *Gertz places here ; in*
AL they appear after adgnoscit *below.*

their own swords. Anger, therefore, is not expedient even in battle or in war ; for it is prone to rashness, and while it seeks to bring about danger, does not guard against it. The truest form of wisdom is to make a wide and long inspection, to put self in subjection, and then to move forward slowly and in a set direction.

"What then?" you ask; "will the good man not be angry if his father is murdered, his mother outraged before his eyes?" No, he will not be angry, but he will avenge them, will protect them. Why, moreover, are you afraid that filial affection, even without anger, may not prove a sufficiently strong incentive for him? Or you might as well say : "What then? if a good man should see his father or his son under the knife, will he not weep, will he not faint?" But this is the way we see women act whenever they are upset by the slightest suggestion of danger. The good man will perform his duties undisturbed and unafraid ; and he will in such a way do all that is worthy of a good man as to do nothing that is unworthy of a man. My father is being murdered—I will defend him ; he is slain—I will avenge him, not because I grieve, but because it is my duty. "Good men are made angry by the injuries to those they love." When you say this, Theophrastus, you seek to make more heroic doctrine unpopular—you turn from the judge to the bystanders. Because each individual grows angry when such a mishap comes to those he loves, you think that men will judge that what they do is the right thing to be done ; for as a rule every man decides that that is a justifiable passion which he acknowledges as his own. But they act in the same way if they

bene praebetur, si vitreum fractum est, si calceus luto
sparsus est. Non pietas illam iram sed infirmitas
movet, sicut pueris, qui tam parentibus amissis flebunt
5 quam nucibus. Irasci pro suis non est pii animi sed
infirmi ; illud pulchrum dignumque, pro parentibus,
liberis, amicis, civibus prodire defensorem ipso officio
ducente, volentem, iudicantem, providentem, non
impulsum et rabidum. Nullus enim affectus vindi-
candi cupidior est quam ira et ob id ipsum ad vindi-
candum inhabilis ; praerapida et amens, ut omnis
fere cupiditas, ipsa sibi in id in quod properat opponitur. Itaque nec in pace nec in bello umquam
bono fuit ; pacem enim similem belli efficit, in armis
vero obliviscitur Martem esse communem venitque
6 in alienam potestatem, dum in sua non est. Deinde
non ideo vitia in usum recipienda sunt, quia aliquando aliquid effecerunt ; nam et febres quaedam
genera valetudinis levant, nec ideo non ex toto illis
caruisse melius est. Abominandum remedi genus
est sanitatem debere morbo. Simili modo ira, etiam
si aliquando ut venenum et praecipitatio et nau-
fragium ex inopinato profuit, non ideo salutaris iudi-
canda est ; saepe enim saluti fuere pestifera.
1   13. Deinde quae habenda sunt, quo maiora eo
meliora et optabiliora sunt. Si iustitia bonum est,

---

* Cf. Shakespeare, *King Henry IV*, Pt. 2, Act 1, Sc. 1 :

    In poison there is physic ; and these news,
    Having been well, that would have made me sick,
    Being sick, have in some measure made me well.

are not well supplied with hot water, if a glass goblet is broken, if a shoe gets splashed with mud. Such anger comes, not from affection, but from a weakness—the kind we see in children, who will shed no more tears over lost parents than over lost toys. To feel anger on behalf of loved ones is the mark of a weak mind, not of a loyal one. For a man to stand forth as the defender of parents, children, friends, and fellow-citizens, led merely by his sense of duty, acting voluntarily, using judgement, using foresight, moved neither by impulse nor by fury—this is noble and becoming. Now no passion is more eager for revenge than anger, and for that very reason is unfit to take it; being unduly ardent and frenzied, as most lusts are, it blocks its own progress to the goal toward which it hastens. Therefore it has never been of advantage either in peace or in war ; for it makes peace seem like war, and amid the clash of arms it forgets that the War-god shows no favour and, failing to control itself, it passes into the control of another. Again, it does not follow that the vices are to be adopted for use from the fact that they have sometimes been to some extent profitable. For a fever may bring relief in certain kinds of sickness, and yet it does not follow from this that it is not better to be altogether free from fever. A method of cure that makes good health dependent upon disease must be regarded with detestation. In like manner anger, like poison, a fall, or a shipwreck, even if it has sometimes proved an unexpected good, ought not for that reason to be adjudged wholesome ; for ofttimes poisons have saved life.[a]

Again, if any quality is worth having, the more of it there is, the better and the more desirable it becomes.

nemo dicet meliorem futuram, si quid detractum ex
2 ea fuerit ; si fortitudo bonum est, nemo illam de-
siderabit ex aliqua parte deminui. Ergo et ira quo
maior hoc melior ; quis enim ullius boni accessionem
recusaverit ? Atqui augeri illam inutile est; ergo
et esse. Non est bonum quod incremento malum fit.
3 " Utilis," inquit, " ira est, quia pugnaciores facit."
Isto modo et ebrietas ; facit enim protervos et audaces
multique meliores ad ferrum fuere male sobrii ; isto
modo dic et phrenesin atque insaniam viribus neces-
4 sariam, quia saepe validiores furor reddit. Quid ?
Non aliquotiens metus ex contrario fecit audacem,
et mortis timor etiam inertissimos excitavit in proe-
lium ? Sed ira, ebrietas, metus aliaque eiusmodi
foeda et caduca irritamenta sunt nec virtutem in-
struunt, quae nihil vitiis eget, sed segnem alioqui
5 animum et ignavum paullum adlevant. Nemo irascendo fit fortior, nisi qui fortis sine ira non fuisset.
Ita non in adiutorium virtutis venit, sed in vicem.
Quid quod, si bonum esset ira, perfectissimum quemque sequeretur ? Atqui iracundissimi infantes
senesque et aegri sunt, et invalidum omne natura
querulum est.
1 14. " Non potest," inquit, " fieri " Theophrastus
" ut non vir bonus irascatur malis." Isto modo quo

If justice is a good, no one will say that it becomes a greater good after something has been withdrawn from it ; if bravery is a good, no one will desire it to be in any measure reduced. Consequently, also, the greater anger is, the better it is ; for who would oppose the augmentation of any good ? And yet, it is not profitable that anger should be increased ; therefore, that anger should exist either. That is not a good which by increase becomes an evil. " Anger is profitable," it is said, " because it makes men more warlike." By that reasoning, so is drunkenness too ; for it makes men forward and bold, and many have been better at the sword because they were the worse for drink. By the same reasoning you must also say that lunacy and madness are essential to strength, since frenzy often makes men more powerful. But tell me, does not fear, in the opposite way, sometimes make a man bold, and does not the terror of death arouse even arrant cowards to fight ? But anger, drunkenness, fear, and the like, are base and fleeting incitements and do not give arms to virtue, which never needs the help of vice ; they do, however, assist somewhat the mind that is otherwise slack and cowardly. No man is ever made braver through anger, except the one who would never have been brave without anger. It comes, then, not as a help to virtue, but as a substitute for it. And is it not true that if anger were a good, it would come naturally to those who are the most perfect ? But the fact is, children, old men, and the sick are most prone to anger, and weakness of any sort is by nature captious.

" It is impossible," says Theophrastus, " for a good man not to be angry with bad men." Accord-

melior quisque, hoc iracundior erit; vide ne contra
placidior solutusque affectibus et cui nemo odio sit.

2 Peccantis vero quid habet cur oderit, cum error illos
in eiusmodi delicta compellat? Non est autem pru-
dentis errantis odisse; alioqui ipse sibi odio erit.
Cogitet quam multa contra bonum morem faciat,
quam multa ex is, quae egit, veniam desiderent;
iam irascetur etiam sibi. Neque enim aequus iudex
aliam de sua, aliam de aliena causa sententiam fert.

3 Nemo, inquam, invenietur qui se possit absolvere, et
innocentem quisque se dicit respiciens testem, non
conscientiam. Quanto humanius mitem et patrium
animum praestare peccantibus et illos non persequi,
sed revocare! Errantem per agros ignorantia viae
melius est ad rectum iter admovere quam expellere.

1 15. Corrigendus est itaque, qui peccat, et admonitione et vi, et molliter et aspere, meliorque tam
sibi quam aliis faciendus non sine castigatione, sed
sine ira; quis enim cui medetur irascitur? At
corrigi nequeunt nihilque in illis lene aut spei bonae
capax est. Tollantur e coetu mortalium facturi
peiora quae contingunt, et quo uno modo possunt

2 desinant mali esse, sed hoc sine odio. Quid enim

ing to this, the better a man is, the more irascible he will be ; on the contrary, be sure that none is more peaceable, more free from passion, and less given to hate. Indeed, what reason has he for hating wrong-doers, since it is error that drives them to such mistakes ? But no man of sense will hate the erring ; otherwise he will hate himself. Let him reflect how many times he offends against morality, how many of his acts stand in need of pardon ; then he will be angry with himself also. For no just judge will pronounce one sort of judge-ment in his own case and a different one in the case of others. No one will be found, I say, who is able to acquit himself, and any man who calls himself innocent is thinking more of witnesses than con-science. How much more human to manifest toward wrong-doers a kind and fatherly spirit, not hunting them down but calling them back ! If a man has lost his way and is roaming across our fields, it is better to put him upon the right path than to drive him out.

And so the man who does wrong ought to be set right both by admonition and by force, by measures both gentle and harsh, and we should try to make him a better man for his own sake, as well as for the sake of others, stinting, not our reproof, but our anger. For what physician will show anger toward a patient ? " But," you say, " they are incapable of being reformed, there is nothing pliable in them, nothing that gives room for fair hope." Then let them be removed from human society if they are bound to make worse all that they touch, and let them, in the only way this is possible, cease to be evil—but let this be done without hatred. For what reason have I for

est, cur oderim eum, cui tum maxime prosum, cum
illum sibi eripio ? Num quis membra sua tunc odit,
cum abscidit ? Non est illa ira, sed misera curatio.
Rabidos effligimus canes et trucem atque immansue-
tum bovem occidimus et morbidis pecoribus, ne gre-
gem polluant, ferrum demittimus ; portentosos fetus
exstinguimus, liberos quoque, si debiles monstrosique
editi sunt, mergimus ; nec ira, sed ratio est a sanis
3 inutilia secernere. Nil minus quam irasci punientem
decet, cum eo magis ad emendationem poena proficiat, si iudicio lata est. Inde est, quod Socrates
servo ait : " Caederem te, nisi irascerer." Admoni-
tionem servi in tempus sanius distulit, illo tempore se admonuit. Cuius erit tandem temperatus
affectus, cum Socrates non sit ausus se irae com-
mittere ?

1 16. Ergo ad coercitionem errantium sceleratorum-
que irato castigatore non opus est ; nam cum ira
delictum animi sit, non oportet peccata corrigere
peccantem. " Quid ergo ? Non irascar latroni ?
Quid ergo ? Non irascar venefico ? " Non ; neque
enim mihi irascor, cum sanguinem mitto. Omne
2 poenae genus remedi loco admoveo. Tu adhuc in
prima parte versaris errorum nec graviter laberis sed
frequenter ; obiurgatio te primum secreta deinde
publicata emendare temptabit. Tu longius iam pro-
cessisti, quam ut possis verbis sanari ; ignominia

hating a man to whom I am offering the greatest service when I save him from himself? Does a man hate the members of his own body when he uses the knife upon them? There is no anger there, but the pitiful desire to heal. Mad dogs we knock on the head; the fierce and savage ox we slay; sickly sheep we put to the knife to keep them from infecting the flock; unnatural progeny we destroy; we drown even children who at birth are weakly and abnormal. Yet it is not anger, but reason that separates the harmful from the sound. For the one who administers punishment nothing is so unfitting as anger, since punishment is all the better able to work reform if it is bestowed with judgement. This is the reason Socrates says to his slave: " I would beat you if I were not angry." The slave's reproof he postponed to a more rational moment; at the time it was himself he reproved. Will there be any one, pray, who has passion under control, when even Socrates did not dare to trust himself to anger?

Consequently, there is no need that correction be given in anger in order to restrain the erring and the wicked. For since anger is a mental sin, it is not right to correct wrong-doing by doing wrong. " What then? " you exclaim; " shall I not be angry with a robber? Shall I not be angry with a poisoner? " No; for I am not angry with myself when I let my own blood. To every form of punishment will I resort, but only as a remedy. If you are lingering as yet in the first stage of error and are lapsing, not seriously, but often, I shall try to correct you by chiding, first in private, then in public. If you have already advanced so far that words can no longer bring you to your senses, then you shall be

contineberis.[1] Tibi fortius aliquid et quod sentias inurendum est; in exilium et loca ignota mitteris. In te duriora remedia iam solida nequitia desiderat; 3 et vincula publica et carcer adhibebitur. Tibi insanabilis animus et sceleribus scelera contexens, et iam non causis, quae numquam malo defuturae sunt, impelleris, sed satis tibi est magna ad peccandum causa peccare, perbibisti nequitiam et ita visceribus immiscuisti, ut nisi cum ipsis exire non possit; olim miser mori quaeris; bene de te merebimur, auferemus tibi istam qua vexas, vexaris insaniam et per tua alienaque volutato supplicia id quod unum tibi bonum superest repraesentabimus, mortem. Quare irascar cui cum maxime prosum? Interim optimum 4 misericordiae genus est occidere. Si intrassem valetudinarium exercitus ut sciens aut domus divitis, non idem imperassem omnibus per diversa aegrotantibus; varia in tot animis vitia video et civitati curandae adhibitus sum; pro cuiusque morbo medicina quaeratur, hunc sanet verecundia, hunc peregrinatio, 5 hunc dolor, hunc egestas, hunc ferrum. Itaque etsi perversa induenda magistratui vestis et convocanda classico contio est, procedam in tribunal non furens

[1] *Hermes, after Pincianus, inserts* non.

---

[a] The meaning of *perversa vestis* is not clear, but the phrase evidently implies some unusual manner of wearing the toga affected by the magistrate presiding at a trial on a capital charge.

[b] By an old custom, when a citizen was arraigned on a capital charge before the centuriate assembly, the trumpet was sounded in various public places and before the house of the accused.

held in check by public disgrace. Should it be necessary to brand you in more drastic fashion, with a punishment you can feel, you shall be sent into exile, banished to an unknown region. Should your wickedness have become deep-rooted, demanding harsher remedies to meet your case, to chains and the state-prison we shall have resort. If with mind incurable you link crime to crime and are actuated no longer by the excuses which will never fail the evil man, but wrong-doing itself becomes to you pretext enough for doing wrong; if you have drained the cup of wickedness and its poison has so mingled with your vitals that it cannot issue forth without them; if, poor wretch! you have long desired to die, then we shall do you good service—we shall take from you that madness by which, while you harass others, you yourself are harassed, and to you who have long wallowed in the suffering of yourself and others we shall gladly give the only boon still left for you, death! Why should I be angry with a man to whom I am giving the greatest help? Sometimes the truest form of pity is to kill. If with the training of an expert physician I had entered a hospital or a rich man's household, I should not have prescribed the same treatment to all, when their diseases differed. Diverse, too, are the ills I see in countless minds, and I am called to cure the body politic; for each man's malady the proper treatment should be sought; let this one be restored by his own self-respect, this one by a sojourn abroad, this one by pain, this one by poverty, this one by the sword! Accordingly, even if as a magistrate I must put on my robe awry[a] and summon the assembly by the trumpet,[b] I shall

nec infestus sed vultu legis et illa sollemnia verba
leni magis gravique quam rabida voce concipiam et
agi lege[1] iubebo non iratus sed severus ; et cum
cervicem noxio imperabo praecidi et cum parricidas
insuam culleo et cum mittam in supplicium militare
et cum Tarpeio proditorem hostemve publicum im-
ponam, sine ira eo vultu animoque ero, quo serpentes
6 et animalia venenata percutio. " Iracundia opus est
ad puniendum." Quid ? Tibi lex videtur irasci iis
quos non novit, quos non vidit, quos non futuros
sperat ? Illius itaque sumendus est animus, quae
non irascitur, sed constituit. Nam si bono viro ob
mala facinora irasci convenit, et ob secundas res
malorum hominum invidere conveniet. Quid enim
est indignius quam florere improbos[2] quosdam et eos
indulgentia fortunae abuti, quibus nulla potest satis
mala inveniri fortuna ? Sed tam commoda illorum
sine invidia videbit quam scelera sine ira ; bonus
7 iudex damnat improbanda, non odit. " Quid ergo ?
Non, cum eiusmodi aliquid sapiens habebit in manibus,
tangetur animus eius eritque solito commotior ? "
Fateor ; sentiet levem quendam tenuemque motum ;
nam, ut dicit Zenon, in sapientis quoque animo, etiam
cum vulnus sanatum est, cicatrix manet. Sentiet

---

[1] lege *added by Gertz, after Pincianus.*
[2] improbos *added by Gemoll.*

advance to the high tribunal, not in rage nor in enmity, but with the visage of the law, and as I pronounce those solemn words my voice will not be fierce, but rather grave and gentle, and not with anger, but with sternness, I shall order the law to be enforced. And when I command a criminal to be beheaded, or sew up a parricide in the sack,[a] or send a soldier to his doom, or stand a traitor or a public enemy upon the Tarpeian Rock, I shall have no trace of anger, but shall look and feel as I might if I were killing a snake or any poisonous creature. "We have to be angry," you say, "in order to punish." What! Think you the law is angry with men it does not know, whom it has never seen, who it hopes will never be? The spirit of the law, therefore, we should make our own—the law which shows not anger but determination. For if it is right for a good man to be angry at the crimes of wicked men, it will also be right for him to be envious of their prosperity. And what, indeed, seems more unjust than that certain reprobates should prosper and become the pets of fortune—men for whom there could be found no fortune bad enough? But the good man will no more view their blessings with envy than he views their crimes with anger. A good judge condemns wrongful deeds, but he does not hate them. "What then?" you say; "when the wise man shall have something of this sort to deal with, will not his mind be affected by it, will it not be moved from its usual calm?" I admit that it will; it will experience some slight and superficial emotion. For as Zeno says: "Even the wise man's mind will keep its scar long after the wound has healed." He will

[a] *i.e.*, to be drowned.

149

itaque suspiciones quasdam et umbras affectuum, ipsis quidem carebit.

1   17. Aristoteles ait affectus quosdam, si quis illis bene utatur, pro armis esse. Quod verum foret, si velut bellica instrumenta sumi deponique possent induentis arbitrio. Haec arma, quae Aristoteles virtuti dat, ipsa per se pugnant, non expectant manum, 2 et habent, non habentur.   Nil aliis instrumentis opus est, satis nos instruxit ratione natura. Hoc dedit telum firmum, perpetuum, obsequens, nec anceps nec quod in dominum remitti posset. Non ad providendum tantum, sed ad res gerendas satis est per se ipsa ratio ; etenim quid est stultius quam hanc ab iracundia petere praesidium, rem stabilem ab incerta, fidelem 3 ab infida, sanam ab aegra ? Quid, quod ad actiones quoque, in quibus solis opera iracundiae videtur necessaria, multo per se ratio fortior est ? Nam cum iudicavit aliquid faciendum, in eo perseverat ; nihil enim melius inventura est se ipsa, quo mutetur ; ideo 4 stat semel constitutis.   Iram saepe misericordia retro egit ; habet enim non solidum robur sed vanum tumorem violentisque principiis utitur, non aliter quam qui a terra venti surgunt et fluminibus paludibusque concepti sine pertinacia vehementes sunt. 5 Incipit magno impetu, deinde deficit ante tempus fatigata, et, quae nihil aliud quam crudelitatem ac

---

a *Cf.* the citation in chap. ix.

experience, therefore, certain suggestions and shadows of passion, but from passion itself he will be free.

Aristotle says [a] that certain passions, if one makes a proper use of them, serve as arms. And this would be true if, like the implements of war, they could be put on and laid aside at the pleasure of the user. But these " arms " which Aristotle would grant to virtue fight under their own orders ; they await no man's gesture and are not possessed, but possess. Nature has given to us an adequate equipment in reason ; we need no other implements. This is the weapon she has bestowed ; it is strong, enduring, obedient, not double-edged or capable of being turned against its owner. Reason is all-sufficient in itself, serving not merely for counsel, but for action as well. What, really, is more foolish than that reason should seek protection from anger—that which is steadfast from that which is wavering, that which is trustworthy from that which is untrustworthy, that which is well from that which is sick ? Even in matters of action, in which alone the help of anger seems necessary, is it not true that reason, if left to itself, has far more power ? For reason, having decided upon the necessity of some action, persists in her purpose, since she herself can discover no better thing to put in her place ; therefore her determinations, once made, stand. But anger is often forced back by pity ; for it has no enduring strength, but is a delusive inflation, violent at the outset. It is like the winds that rise from off the earth ; generated from streams and marshes they have vehemence, but do not last. So anger begins with a mighty rush, then breaks down from untimely exhaustion, and though all its thoughts had been concerned with

nova genera poenarum versaverat, cum animadver-
tendum est, iam fracta lenisque est. Affectus cito
6 cadit, aequalis est ratio. Ceterum etiam ubi perse-
veravit ira, nonnumquam, si plures sunt qui perire
meruerunt, post duorum triumve sanguinem occidere
desinit. Primi eius ictus acres sunt ; sic serpentium
venena a cubili erepentium nocent, innoxii dentes
7 sunt, cum illos frequens morsus exhausit. Ergo non
paria patiuntur qui paria commiserant, et saepe qui
minus commisit plus patitur, quia recentiori obiectus
est. Et in totum inaequalis est ; modo ultra quam
oportet excurrit, modo citerius debito resistit ; sibi
enim indulget et ex libidine iudicat et audire non
vult et patrocinio non relinquit locum et ea tenet
quae invasit et eripi sibi iudicium suum, etiam si
pravum est, non sinit.

1   18. Ratio utrique parti tempus dat, deinde advoca-
tionem et sibi petit, ut excutiendae veritati spatium
habeat ; ira festinat. Ratio id iudicare vult quod
aequum est ; ira id aequum videri vult quod iudicavit.
2 Ratio nil praeter ipsum de quo agitur spectat ;
ira vanis et extra causam obversantibus commovetur.
Vultus illam securior, vox clarior, sermo liberior, cultus
delicatior, advocatio ambitiosior, favor popularis ex-
asperant ; saepe infesta patrono reum damnat ; etiam

cruelty and unheard-of forms of torture, yet when the time is ripe for punishment it has already become crippled and weak. Passion quickly falls, reason is balanced. But even if anger persists, it will often happen that having taken the blood of two or three victims it will cease to slay, although there are more who deserve to die. Its first blows are fierce ; so serpents when they first crawl from their lair are charged with venom, but their fangs are harmless after they have been drained by repeated biting. Consequently, not all who have sinned alike are punished alike, and often he who has committed the smaller sin receives the greater punishment, because he was subjected to anger when it was fresh. And anger is altogether unbalanced ; it now rushes farther than it should, now halts sooner than it ought. For it indulges its own impulses, is capricious in judgement, refuses to listen to evidence, grants no opportunity for defence, maintains whatever position it has seized, and is never willing to surrender its judgement even if it is wrong.

Reason grants a hearing to both sides, then seeks to postpone action, even its own, in order that it may gain time to sift out the truth ; but anger is precipitate. Reason wishes the decision that it gives to be just ; anger wishes to have the decision which it has given seem the just decision. Reason considers nothing except the question at issue ; anger is moved by trifling things that lie outside the case. An over-confident demeanour, a voice too loud, boldness of speech, foppishness in dress, a pretentious show of patronage, popularity with the public—these inflame anger. Many times it will condemn the accused because it hates his lawyer ; even if the truth is

si ingeritur oculis veritas, amat et tuetur errorem ;
coargui non vult et in male coeptis honestior illi
pertinacia videtur quam paenitentia.

3   Cn. Piso fuit memoria nostra vir a multis vitiis in-
teger, sed pravus et cui placebat pro constantia rigor.
Is cum iratus duci iussisset eum, qui ex commeatu sine
commilitone redierat, quasi interfecisset quem non
exhibebat, roganti tempus aliquod ad conquirendum
non dedit.   Damnatus extra vallum productus est et
iam cervicem porrigebat, cum subito apparuit ille
4 commilito qui occisus videbatur.   Tunc centurio
supplicio praepositus condere gladium speculatorem
iubet, damnatum ad Pisonem reducit redditurus
Pisoni innocentiam ; nam militi fortuna reddiderat.
Ingenti concursu deducuntur complexi alter alterum
cum magno gaudio castrorum commilitones.   Con-
scendit tribunal furens Piso ac iubet duci utrumque,
et eum militem qui non occiderat et eum qui non
5 perierat.   Quid hoc indignius ?   Quia unus innocens
apparuerat, duo peribant.   Piso adiecit et tertium.
Nam ipsum centurionem, qui damnatum reduxerat,
duci iussit.   Constituti sunt in eodem illo loco perituri
6 tres ob unius innocentiam.   O quam sollers est
iracundia ad fingendas causas furoris !   " Te," inquit,
" duci iubeo, quia damnatus es ; te, quia causa dam-

---

a That grave *inflexibility* of soul
   Which Reason can't convince, nor fear control.
                              Churchill, *Gotham*, iii. 335 f.

piled up before its very eyes, it loves error and clings to it ; it refuses to be convinced, and having entered upon wrong it counts persistence to be more honourable than penitence.

There was Gnaeus Piso, whom I can remember ; a man free from many vices, but misguided, in that he mistook inflexibility *a* for firmness. Once when he was angry he ordered the execution of a soldier who had returned from leave of absence without his comrade, on the ground that if the man did not produce his companion, he had killed him ; and when the soldier asked for a little time to institute a search, the request was refused. The condemned man was led outside the rampart, and as he was in the act of presenting his neck, there suddenly appeared the very comrade who was supposed to have been murdered. Hereupon the centurion in charge of the execution bade the guardsman sheathe his sword, and led the condemned man back to Piso in order to free Piso from blame ; for Fortune had freed the soldier. A huge crowd amid great rejoicing in the camp escorted the two comrades locked in each other's arms. Piso mounted the tribunal in a rage, and ordered both soldiers to be led to execution, the one who had done no murder and the one who had escaped it ! Could anything have been more unjust than this ? Two were dying because one had been proved innocent. But Piso added also a third ; for he ordered the centurion who had brought back the condemned man to be executed as well. On account of the innocence of one man three were appointed to die in the selfsame place. O how clever is anger in devising excuses for its madness ! " You," it says, " I order to be executed because you were condemned ; you,

nationis commilitoni fuisti ; te, quia iussus occidere
imperatori non paruisti." Excogitavit quemadmodum
tria crimina faceret, quia nullum invenerat.

1   19. Habet, inquam, iracundia hoc mali ; non
vult regi. Irascitur veritati ipsi, si contra voluntatem
suam apparuit ; cum clamore et tumultu et totius
corporis iactatione quos destinavit insequitur adiectis
2 conviciis maledictisque. Hoc non facit ratio ; sed si
ita opus est, silens quietaque totas domus funditus
tollit et familias rei publicae pestilentes cum coniugi-
bus ac liberis perdit, tecta ipsa diruit et solo exaequat
et inimica libertati nomina exstirpat. Hoc non
frendens nec caput quassans nec quicquam indecorum
iudici faciens, cuius tum maxime placidus esse debet
3 et in statu vultus, cum magna pronuntiat. " Quid
opus est," inquit Hieronymus, " cum velis caedere
aliquem, tua prius labra mordere ? " Quid, si ille
vidisset desilientem de tribunali proconsulem et fasces
lictori auferentem et suamet vestimenta scindentem,
4 quia tardius scindebantur aliena ? Quid opus est
mensam evertere ? Quid pocula adfligere ? Quid se
in columnas impingere ? Quid capillos avellere, femur
pectusque percutere ? Quantam iram putas, quae,
quia in alium non tam cito quam vult erumpit, in se

156

because you were the cause of your comrade's condemnation; you, because you did not obey your commander when you were ordered to kill." It thought out three charges because it had grounds for none.

Anger, I say, has this great fault—it refuses to be ruled. It is enraged against truth itself if this is shown to be contrary to its desire. With outcry and uproar and gestures that shake the whole body it pursues those whom it has marked out, heaping upon them abuse and curses. Not thus does reason act. But if need should so require, it silently and quietly wipes out whole families root and branch, and households that are baneful to the state it destroys together with wives and children; it tears down their very houses, levelling them to the ground, and exterminates the very names of the foes of liberty. All this it will do, but with no gnashing of the teeth, no wild tossing of the head, doing nothing that would be unseemly for a judge, whose countenance should at no time be more calm and unmoved than when he is delivering a weighty sentence. "What is the need," asks Hieronymus,[a] "of biting your own lips before you start to give a man a thrashing?" What if he had seen a proconsul leap down from the tribunal, snatch the fasces from the lictor, and tear his own clothes because some victim's clothes were still untorn! What is to be gained by overturning the table, by hurling cups upon the floor, by dashing oneself against pillars, tearing the hair, and smiting the thigh and the breast? How mighty is the anger, think you, which turns back upon itself because it cannot be vented upon another as speedily as it

[a] See Index.

revertitur ? Tenentur itaque a proximis et rogantur, ut sibi ipsi placentur.

5 Quorum nil facit quisquis vacuus ira meritam cuique poenam iniungit. Dimittit saepe eum, cuius peccatum deprendit. Si paenitentia facti spem bonam pollicetur, si intellegit non ex alto venire nequitiam, sed summo, quod aiunt, animo inhaerere, dabit impunitatem nec accipientibus nocituram nec dantibus ;

6 nonnumquam magna scelera levius quam minora compescet, si illa lapsu, non crudelitate commissa sunt, his inest latens et operta et inveterata calliditas ; idem delictum in duobus non eodem malo afficiet, si alter per neglegentiam admisit, alter curavit ut

7 nocens esset. Hoc semper in omni animadversione servabit, ut sciat alteram adhiberi, ut emendet malos, alteram, ut tollat ; in utroque non praeterita, sed futura intuebitur—nam, ut Plato ait, nemo prudens punit, quia peccatum est, sed ne peccetur ; revocari enim praeterita non possunt, futura prohibentur—, et quos volet nequitiae male cedentis exempla fieri, palam occidet, non tantum ut pereant ipsi, sed ut

8 alios pereundo deterreant. Haec cui expendenda aestimandaque sunt, vides quam debeat omni perturbatione liber accedere ad rem summa diligentia

---

^a *Laws* xi. 934 A.

desires ! And so such men are seized by the by-standers and begged to become at peace with themselves.

None of these things will he do, who, being free from anger, imposes upon each one the punishment that he merits. He will often let a man go free even after detecting his guilt. If regret for the act warrants fair hope, if he discerns that the sin does not issue from the inmost soul of the man, but, so to speak, is only skin-deep, he will grant him impunity, seeing that it will injure neither the recipient nor the giver. Sometimes he will ban great crimes less ruthlessly than small ones, if these, in the one case, were committed not in cruelty but in a moment of weakness, and, in the other, were instinct with secret, hidden, and long-practised cunning. To two men guilty of the same offence he will mete out different punishment, if one sinned through careless-ness, while the other intended to be wicked. Always in every case of punishment he will keep before him the knowledge that one form is designed to make the wicked better, the other to remove them ; in either case he will look to the future, not to the past. For as Plato says [a] : " A sensible person does not punish a man because he has sinned, but in order to keep him from sin ; for while the past cannot be recalled, the future may be forestalled." And he will openly kill those whom he wishes to have serve as examples of the wickedness that is slow to yield, not so much that they themselves may be destroyed as that they may deter others from destruction. These are the things a man must weigh and consider, and you see how free he ought to be from all emotion when he proceeds to deal with a matter that requires the

tractandam, potestatem vitae necisque ; male irato
ferrum committitur.

1 20. Ne illud quidem iudicandum est, aliquid iram
ad magnitudinem animi conferre. Non est enim illa
magnitudo ; tumor est. Nec corporibus copia vitiosi
umoris intentis morbus incrementum est sed pestilens
2 abundantia. Omnes, quos vecors animus supra cogitationes extollit humanas, altum quiddam et sublime
spirare se credunt ; ceterum nil solidi subest, sed in
ruinam prona sunt quae sine fundamentis crevere.
Non habet ira cui insistat. Non ex firmo mansuroque
oritur, sed ventosa et inanis est tantumque abest a
magnitudine animi, quantum a fortitudine audacia,
a fiducia insolentia, ab austeritate tristitia, a severi-
3 tate crudelitas. Multum, inquam, interest inter sub-
limem animum et superbum. Iracundia nihil amplum
decorumque molitur ; contra mihi videtur veternosi
et infelicis animi, imbecillitatis sibi conscii, saepe
indolescere, ut exulcerata et aegra corpora, quae ad
tactus levissimos gemunt. Ita ira muliebre maxime
ac puerile vitium est. " At incidit et in viros." Nam
viris quoque puerilia ac muliebria ingenia sunt.
4 " Quid ergo ? Non aliquae voces ab iratis emittuntur
quae magno emissae videantur animo ? " Immo[1]
veram ignorantibus magnitudinem, qualis illa dira
et abominanda : " Oderint, dum metuant." Sullano
scias saeculo scriptam. Nescio utrum sibi peius

[1] immo *added by Madvig.*

---

[a] Accius, *Atreus* (*Trag. Rom. Frag.* v., Ribbeck).

utmost caution—the use of power over life and death.
'Tis ill trusting an angry man with a sword.

And you must not suppose this, either—that anger
contributes anything to greatness of soul. That is
not greatness, it is a swelling ; nor when disease dis-
tends the body with a mass of watery corruption is
the result growth, but a pestilent excess. All whom
frenzy of soul exalts to powers that are more than
human believe that they breathe forth something
lofty and sublime ; but it rests on nothing solid, and
whatever rises without a firm foundation is liable
to fall. Anger has nothing on which to stand ; it
springs from nothing that is stable and lasting, but
is a puffed-up, empty thing, as far removed from
greatness of soul as foolhardiness is from bravery,
arrogance from confidence, sullenness from austerity,
or cruelty from sternness. The difference between
a lofty and a haughty soul, I say, is great. Anger
aims at nothing splendid or beautiful. On the other
hand, it seems to me to show a feeble and harassed
spirit, one conscious of its own weakness and over-
sensitive, just as the body is when it is sick and
covered with sores and makes moan at the slightest
touch. Thus anger is a most womanish and childish
weakness. " But," you will say, " it is found in
men also." True, for even men may have childish
and womanish natures. " What then ? " you cry ;
" do not the utterances of angry men sometimes
seem to be the utterances of a great soul ? " Yes,
to those who do not know what true greatness is.
Take the famous words : " Let them hate if only
they fear," [a] which are so dread and shocking that
you might know that they were written in the times
of Sulla. I am not sure which wish was worse—that

optaverit, ut odio esset, an ut timori. "Oderint."
Occurrit illi futurum, ut exsecrentur, insidientur,
opprimant. Quid adiecit ? Di illi male faciant, adeo
repperit dignum odio remedium. "Oderint "—quid
tum ? Dum pareant ? Non ; dum probent ? Non ;
quid ergo ? "Dum timeant." Sic ne amari quidem
5 vellem. Magno hoc dictum spiritu putas ? Falleris ;
nec enim magnitudo ista est sed immanitas.

Non est quod credas irascentium verbis, quorum
strepitus magni, minaces sunt, intra mens pavidissima.
6 Nec est quod existimes verum esse, quod apud
disertissimum virum T. Livium dicitur : "Vir ingenii
magni magis quam boni." Non potest istud separari :
aut et bonum erit aut nec magnum, quia magnitudinem animi inconcussam intellego et introrsus
solidam et ab imo parem firmamque, qualis inesse
7 malis ingeniis non potest. Terribilia enim esse et
tumultuosa et exitiosa possunt ; magnitudinem quidem, cuius firmamentum roburque bonitas est, non
habebunt. Ceterum sermone, conatu et omni extra
8 paratu facient magnitudinis fidem ; eloquentur aliquid, quod tu magni animi[1] putes, sicut C. Caesar,
qui iratus caelo, quod obstreperetur pantomimis,
quos imitabatur studiosius quam spectabat, quodque comessatio sua fulminibus terreretur—prorsus
parum certis—ad pugnam vocavit Iovem et

[1] animi *added by Gertz.*

---

[a] *Frag.* 54 Hertz.
[b] *i.e.*, Caligula, of whose impiety Suetonius (xxii.) records
many instances.

he should be hated, or that he should be feared. "Let them hate," quoth he; then he bethinks him that there will come a time when men will curse him, plot against him, overpower him—so what did he add? O may the gods curse him for devising so hateful a cure for hate! "Let them hate"—and then what? If only they obey? No! If only they approve? No! What then? "If only they fear!" On such terms I should not have wished even to be loved. You think this the utterance of a great soul? You deceive yourself; for there is nothing great in it—it is monstrous.

You need put no trust in the words of the angry, for their noise is loud and threatening, but within, their heart is very cowardly. Nor need you count as true the saying found in that most eloquent writer, Titus Livius[a]: "A man whose character was great rather than good." In character there can be no such separation; it will either be good or else not great, because greatness of soul, as I conceive it, is a thing unshakable, sound to the core, uniform and strong from top to bottom—something that cannot exist in evil natures. Evil men may be terrible, turbulent, and destructive, but greatness they will never have, for its support and stay is goodness. Yet by speech, by endeavour, and by all outward display they will give the impression of greatness; they will make utterances which you may think bespeak the great soul, as in the case of Gaius Caesar.[b] He grew angry at heaven because its thunder interrupted some pantomimists, whom he was more anxious to imitate than to watch, and when its thunderbolts—surely they missed their mark —affrighted his own revels, he challenged Jove to

quidem sine missione, Homericum illum exclamans versum:

Ἤ μ' ἀνάειρ' ἢ ἐγὼ σέ.

9 Quanta dementia fuit! Putavit aut sibi noceri ne ab Iove quidem posse aut se nocere etiam Iovi posse. Non puto parum momenti hanc eius vocem ad incitandas coniuratorum mentes addidisse; ultimae enim patientiae visum est eum ferre, qui Iovem non ferret!

1 21. Nihil ergo in ira, ne cum videtur quidem vehemens et deos hominesque despiciens, magnum, nihil nobile est. Aut si videtur alicui magnum animum ira producere, videatur et luxuria—ebore sustineri vult, purpura vestiri, auro tegi, terras transferre, maria concludere, flumina praecipitare, nemora
2 suspendere; videatur et avaritia magni animi—acervis auri argentique incubat et provinciarum nominibus agros colit et sub singulis vilicis latiores
3 habet fines quam quos consules sortiebantur; videatur et libido magni animi—transnat freta, puerorum greges castrat, sub gladium mariti venit morte contempta; videatur et ambitio magni animi—non est contenta honoribus annuis; si fieri potest, uno nomine occupare fastus vult, per omnem orbem titulos
4 disponere. Omnia ista, non refert in quantum procedant extendantque se, angusta sunt, misera, depressa; sola sublimis et excelsa virtus est, nec quicquam magnum est nisi quod simul placidum.

---

[a] *Iliad*, xxiii. 724. After a protracted wrestling-bout, Ajax thus challenges Odysseus to some decisive manœuvre.

[b] The reference is to artificial lakes and cascades.

fight, even to the death, shouting in the words of Homer :

Or uplift me, or I will thee.[a]

What madness ! He thought that not even Jove could harm him, or that he could harm even Jove. I suppose that these words of his had no little weight in arousing the minds of conspirators ; for to put up with a man who could not put up with Jove seemed the limit of endurance !

There is in anger, consequently, nothing great, nothing noble, even when it seems impassioned, contemptuous alike of gods and men. Else let him who thinks that anger reveals the great soul, think that luxury does the same ; it desires to rest on ivory, to be arrayed in purple, to be roofed with gold, to remove lands, to confine the waters of the sea, to hurl rivers headlong,[b] to hang gardens in the air. Let him think that avarice also betokens the great soul ; it broods over heaps of gold and silver, it tills fields that are provinces in all but name, and holds under a single steward broader acres than were allotted once to consuls. Let him also think that lust betokens the great soul ; it swims across straits, it unsexes lads by the score, and despising death braves the husband's sword. And let him think that ambition also betokens the great soul ; it is not content with annual office ; it would fill the calendar with only one name if that might be, and set up its memorials throughout all the world. Such qualities, it matters not to what height or length they reach, are all narrow, pitiable, grovelling. Virtue alone is lofty and sublime, and nothing is great that is not at the same time tranquil.

LIBER IV

AD NOVATVM

DE IRA

LIBER II

1 **1.** Primus liber, Novate, benigniorem habuit materiam ; facilis enim in proclivia vitiorum decursus est. Nunc ad exiliora veniendum est ; quaerimus enim ira utrum iudicio an impetu incipiat, id est utrum sua sponte moveatur an quemadmodum pleraque, quae intra nos non[1] insciis nobis oriuntur.
2 Debet autem in haec se demittere disputatio, ut ad illa quoque altiora possit exsurgere. Nam et in corpore nostro ossa nervique et articuli, firmamenta totius et vitalia, minime speciosa visu, prius ordinantur, deinde haec, ex quibus omnis in faciem adspectumque decor est ; post haec omnia, qui maxime oculos rapit, color ultimus perfecto iam corpore adfunditur.
3 Iram quin species oblata iniuriae moveat non est dubium ; sed utrum speciem ipsa statim sequatur et non accedente animo excurrat, an illo adsentiente

---

[1] non *added by Hermes.*

BOOK IV

TO NOVATUS

ON ANGER

BOOK II

My first book, Novatus, had a more bountiful theme; for easy is the descent into the downward course of vice.[a] Now we must come to narrower matters; for the question is whether anger originates from choice or from impulse, that is, whether it is aroused of its own accord, or whether, like much else that goes on within us, it does not arise without our knowledge. But the discussion must be lowered to the consideration of these things in order that it may afterwards rise to the other, loftier, themes. For in our bodies, too, there comes first the system of bones, sinews, and joints, which form the framework of the whole and are vital parts, yet are by no means fair to look upon; next the parts on which all the comeliness of face and appearance depend, and after all these, when the body is now complete, there is added last that which above all else captivates the eye, the colour.

There can be no doubt that anger is aroused by the direct impression of an injury; but the question is whether it follows immediately upon the impression and springs up without assistance from the mind, or whether it is aroused only with the assent of the mind.

167

4 moveatur quaerimus. Nobis placet nihil illam per
se audere sed animo adprobante ; nam speciem
capere acceptae iniuriae et ultionem eius concupiscere
et utrumque coniungere, nec laedi se debuisse et
vindicari debere, non est eius impetus, qui sine
5 voluntate nostra concitatur. Ille simplex est, hic compositus et plura continens ; intellexit aliquid, in-
dignatus est, damnavit, ulciscitur : haec non possunt
fieri, nisi animus eis quibus tangebatur adsensus est.

1   2. " Quorsus," inquis, " haec quaestio pertinet ? "
Ut sciamus quid sit ira.   Nam si invitis nobis nascitur,
numquam rationi succumbet.   Omnes enim motus,
qui non voluntate nostra fiunt, invicti et inevitabiles
sunt, ut horror frigida aspersis, ad quosdam tactus
aspernatio ; ad peiores nuntios subriguntur pili et
rubor ad improba verba suffunditur sequiturque
vertigo praerupta cernentis. Quorum quia nihil in
nostra potestate est, nulla quo minus fiant ratio
2 persuadet.   Ira praeceptis fugatur ; est enim volun-
tarium animi vitium, non ex his, quae condicione
quadam humanae sortis eveniunt ideoque etiam sa-
pientissimis accidunt, inter quae et primus ille ictus
animi ponendus est, qui nos post opinionem iniuriae
3 movet.   Hic subit etiam inter ludicra scaenae spec-

Our opinion is that it ventures nothing by itself, but acts only with the approval of the mind. For to form the impression of having received an injury and to long to avenge it, and then to couple together the two propositions that one ought not to have been wronged and that one ought to be avenged—this is not a mere impulse of the mind acting without our volition. The one is a single mental process, the other a complex one composed of several elements ; the mind has grasped something, has become indignant, has condemned the act, and now tries to avenge it. These processes are impossible unless the mind has given assent to the impressions that moved it.

"But," you ask, "what is the purpose of such an inquiry ?" I answer, in order that we may know what anger is ; for if it arises against our will, it will never succumb to reason. For all sensations that do not result from our own volition are uncontrolled and unavoidable, as, for example, shivering when we are dashed with cold water and recoilment from certain contacts ; bad news makes the hair stand on end, vile language causes a blush to spread, and when one looks down from a precipice, dizziness follows. Because none of these things lies within our control, no reasoning can keep them from happening. But anger may be routed by precepts ; for it is a weakness of the mind that is subject to the will, not one of those things that result from some condition of the general lot of man and therefore befall even the wisest, among which must be placed foremost that mental shock which affects us after we have formed the impression of a wrong committed. This steals upon us even from the sight of plays upon the stage

tacula et lectiones rerum vetustarum. Saepe Clodio
Ciceronem expellenti et Antonio occidenti videmur
irasci ; quis non contra Mari arma, contra Sullae
proscriptionem concitatur ? Quis non Theodoto et
Achillae et ipsi puero non puerile auso facinus in-
4 festus est ? Cantus nos nonnumquam et citata
modulatio instigat Martiusque ille tubarum sonus ;
movet mentes et atrox pictura et iustissimorum
5 suppliciorum tristis adspectus ; inde est quod ad-
ridemus ridentibus et contristat nos turba maerentium
et effervescimus ad aliena certamina. Quae non sunt
irae, non magis quam tristitia est, quae ad conspectum
mimici naufragii contrahit frontem, non magis quam
timor, qui Hannibale post Cannas moenia circum-
sidente lectorum percurrit animos, sed omnia ista
motus sunt animorum moveri nolentium nec adfectus
6 sed principia proludentia adfectibus. Sic enim militaris
viri in media pace iam togati aures tuba suscitat
equosque castrenses erigit crepitus armorum. Alexandrum aiunt Xenophanto canente manum ad arma
misisse.
1 3. Nihil ex his, quae animum fortuito impellunt,
adfectus vocari debet ; ista, ut ita dicam, patitur
magis animus quam facit. Ergo adfectus est non ad
oblatas rerum species moveri, sed permittere se illis

ᵃ The youthful king Ptolemy XII., who compassed the
murder of Pompey when he sought refuge in Egypt after
the battle of Pharsalus (48 B.C.). Achillas, commander of
the army, and Theodotus, the king's adviser, shared the
responsibility of the crime.
ᵇ Timotheus is the name of the flutist in other versions of
the story ; cf. Dion Chrys. Or. i. 1 ; Suidas, s.v.

and from reading of happenings of long ago. How often we seem to grow angry with Clodius for banishing Cicero, with Antony for killing him! Who is not aroused against the arms which Marius took up, against the proscription which Sulla used? Who is not incensed against Theodotus and Achillas, and the child himself [a] who dared an unchildish crime? Singing sometimes stirs us, and quickened rhythm, and the well-known blare of the War-god's trumpets; our minds are perturbed by a shocking picture and by the melancholy sight of punishment even when it is entirely just; in the same way we smile when others smile, we are saddened by a throng of mourners, and are thrown into a ferment by the struggles of others. Such sensations, however, are no more anger than that is sorrow which furrows the brow at sight of a mimic shipwreck, no more anger than that is fear which thrills our minds when we read how Hannibal after Cannae beset the walls of Rome, but they are all emotions of a mind that would prefer not to be so affected; they are not passions, but the beginnings that are preliminary to passions. So, too, the warrior in the midst of peace, wearing now his civilian dress, will prick up his ears at the blast of a trumpet, and army horses are made restive by the clatter of arms. It is said that Alexander, when Xenophantus [b] played the flute, reached for his weapons.

None of these things which move the mind through the agency of chance should be called passions; the mind suffers them, so to speak, rather than causes them. Passion, consequently, does not consist in being moved by the impressions that are presented to the mind, but in surrendering to these and follow-

2 et hunc fortuitum motum prosequi. Nam si quis
pallorem et lacrimas procidentis et irritationem umoris
obsceni altumve suspirium et oculos subito acriores
aut quid his simile indicium adfectus animique signum
putat, fallitur nec intellegit corporis hos esse pulsus.
3 Itaque et fortissimus plerumque vir dum armatur
expalluit et signo pugnae dato ferocissimo militi
paulum genua tremuerunt et magno imperatori antequam inter se acies arietarent cor exsiluit et oratori
eloquentissimo dum ad dicendum componitur summa
4 riguerunt. Ira non moveri tantum debet sed ex-
currere ; est enim impetus ; numquam autem impetus
sine adsensu mentis est, neque enim fieri potest ut de
ultione et poena agatur animo nesciente. Putavit se
aliquis laesum, voluit ulcisci, dissuadente aliqua causa
statim resedit. Hanc iram non voco, motum animi
rationi parentem ; illa est ira, quae rationem trans-
5 silit, quae secum rapit. Ergo prima illa agitatio
animi, quam species iniuriae incussit, non magis ira
est quam ipsa iniuriae species ; ille sequens impetus,
qui speciem iniuriae non tantum accepit sed adpro-
bavit, ira est, concitatio animi ad ultionem voluntate
et iudicio pergentis. Numquam dubium est quin
timor fugam habeat, ira impetum ; vide ergo an putes
aliquid sine adsensu mentis aut peti posse aut caveri.

ing up such a chance prompting. For if any one supposes that pallor, falling tears, prurient itching or deep-drawn sigh, a sudden brightening of the eyes, and the like, are an evidence of passion and a manifestation of the mind, he is mistaken and fails to understand that these are disturbances of the body. And so very often even the bravest man turns pale while he fits on his arms, the knees of the boldest soldier often tremble a little when the battle-signal is given, the mighty commander has his heart in his throat before the battle-lines clash, and while the most eloquent orator is getting ready to speak, his extremities become rigid. Anger must not only be aroused but it must rush forth, for it is an active impulse ; but an active impulse never comes without the consent of the will, for it is impossible for a man to aim at revenge and punishment without the cognizance of his mind. A man thinks himself injured, wishes to take vengeance, but dissuaded by some consideration immediately calms down. This I do not call anger, this prompting of the mind which is submissive to reason ; anger is that which over-leaps reason and sweeps it away. Therefore that primary disturbance of the mind which is excited by the impression of injury is no more anger than the impression of injury is itself anger ; the active impulse consequent upon it, which has not only admitted the impression of injury but also approved it, is really anger—the tumult of a mind proceeding to revenge by choice and determination. There can never be any doubt that as fear involves flight, anger involves assault ; consider, therefore, whether you believe that anything can either be assailed or avoided without the mind's assent.

173

1   4. Et ut scias quemadmodum incipiant adfectus
aut crescant aut efferantur, est primus motus non
voluntarius, quasi praeparatio adfectus et quaedam
comminatio ; alter cum voluntate non contumaci,
tamquam oporteat me vindicari, cum laesus sim, aut
oporteat hunc poenas dare, cum scelus fecerit ; tertius
motus est iam impotens, qui non si oportet ulcisci vult,
2 sed utique, qui rationem evicit.   Primum illum animi
ictum effugere ratione non possumus, sicut ne illa
quidem quae diximus accidere corporibus, ne nos
oscitatio aliena sollicitet, ne oculi ad intentationem
subitam digitorum conprimantur.   Ista non potest
ratio vincere, consuetudo fortasse et adsidua ob-
servatio extenuat.   Alter ille motus, qui iudicio
nascitur, iudicio tollitur.

1   5. Illud etiamnunc quaerendum est, ii qui vulgo
saeviunt et sanguine humano gaudent an irascantur,
cum eos occidunt, a quibus nec acceperunt iniuriam
nec accepisse ipsi se existimant ; qualis fuit Apollo-
2 dorus aut Phalaris.   Haec non est ira, feritas est ;
non enim quia accepit iniuriam nocet, sed parata est,
dum noceat, vel accipere, nec illi verbera lacerationes-
3 que in ultionem petuntur sed in voluptatem.   Quid
ergo est[1] ?   Origo huius mali ab ira est, quae ubi

---

[1] est *Hermes after Gertz.*

a See Index.

That you may know, further, how the passions begin, grow, and run riot, I may say that the first prompting is involuntary, a preparation for passion, as it were, and a sort of menace ; the next is combined with an act of volition, although not an unruly one, which assumes that it is right for me to avenge myself because I have been injured, or that it is right for the other person to be punished because he has committed a crime ; the third prompting is now beyond control, in that it wishes to take vengeance, not if it is right to do so, but whether or no, and has utterly vanquished reason. We can no more avoid by the use of reason that first shock which the mind experiences than we can avoid those effects mentioned before which the body experiences—the temptation to yawn when another yawns, and winking when fingers are suddenly pointed toward the eyes. Such impulses cannot be overcome by reason, although perchance practice and constant watchfulness will weaken them. Different is that prompting which is born of the judgement, is banished by the judgement.

This point also must now be considered, whether those who are habitually cruel and rejoice in human blood are angry when they kill people from whom they have neither received injury nor think even themselves that they have received one ; of such sort were Apollodorus [a] and Phalaris.[a] But this is not anger, it is brutality ; for it does not harm because it has received an injury, but it is even ready to receive one provided that it can harm, and its purpose in desiring to beat and to mangle is not vengeance but pleasure. And why does it happen ? The source of this evil is anger, and when anger from

175

frequenti exercitatione et satietate in oblivionem
clementiae venit et omne foedus humanum eiecit
animo, novissime in crudelitatem transit. Rident
itaque gaudentque et voluptate multa perfruuntur
plurimumque ab iratorum vultu absunt, per otium
saevi.

4   Hannibalem aiunt dixisse, cum fossam sanguine
humano plenam vidisset : " O formonsum spectaculum ! " Quanto pulchrius illi visum esset, si flumen
aliquod lacumque complesset ! Quid mirum, si hoc
maxime spectaculo caperis innatus sanguini et ab
infante caedibus admotus ? Sequetur te fortuna
crudelitati tuae per viginti annos secunda dabitque
oculis tuis gratum ubique spectaculum ; videbis istud
et circa Trasumennum et circa Cannas et novissime
5 circa Carthaginem tuam. Volesus nuper sub divo
Augusto proconsul Asiae, cum trecentos uno die
securi percussisset, incedens inter cadavera vultu
superbo, quasi magnificum quiddam conspiciendum-
que fecisset, graece proclamavit : " O rem regiam ! "
Quid hic rex fecisset ? Non fuit haec ira sed maius
malum et insanabile.

1   6. " Virtus," inquit, " ut honestis rebus propitia
est, ita turpibus irata esse debet." Quid, si dicat virtutem et humilem et magnam esse debere ? Atqui
hoc dicit, illam[1] extolli vult et deprimi, quoniam
laetitia ob recte factum clara magnificaque est, ira
ob alienum peccatum sordida et angusti pectoris est.

---

[1] illam *Hermes, after Müller* : qui illam *MSS.*

oft-repeated indulgence and surfeit has arrived at a disregard for mercy and has expelled from the mind every conception of the human bond, it passes at last into cruelty. And so these men laugh and rejoice and experience great pleasure, and wear a countenance utterly unlike that of anger, making a pastime of ferocity.

When Hannibal saw a trench flowing with human blood, he is said to have exclaimed, " O beauteous sight ! " How much more beautiful would it have seemed to him if the blood had filled some river or lake ! What wonder, O Hannibal, if you, born to bloodshed and from childhood familiar with slaughter, find especial delight in this spectacle ? A fortune will attend you that for twenty years will gratify your cruelty, and will everywhere supply to your eyes the welcome sight ; you will see it at Trasumennus and at Cannae, and last of all at your own Carthage ! Only recently Volesus, governor of Asia under the deified Augustus, beheaded three hundred persons in one day, and as he strutted among the corpses with the proud air of one who had done some glorious deed worth beholding, he cried out in Greek, " What a kingly act ! " But what would he have done if he had been a king ? No, this was not anger, but an evil still greater and incurable.

" If," some one argues, " virtue is well disposed toward what is honourable, it is her duty to feel anger toward what is base." What if he should say that virtue must be both low and great ? And yet this is what he does say—he would have her be both exalted and debased, since joy on account of a right action is splendid and glorious, while anger on account of another's sin is mean and narrow-minded.

2 Nec umquam committet virtus, ut vitia, dum com-
pescit, imitetur ; iram ipsam castigandam habet, quae
nihilo melior est, saepe etiam peior is delictis quibus
irascitur. Gaudere laetarique proprium et naturale
virtutis est ; irasci non est ex dignitate eius, non
magis quam maerere. Atqui iracundiae tristitia
comes est et in hanc omnis ira vel post paenitentiam
3 vel post repulsam revolvitur. Et si sapientis est
peccatis irasci, magis irascetur maioribus et saepe
irascetur ; sequitur, ut non tantum iratus sit sapiens,
sed iracundus. Atqui si nec magnam iram nec
frequentem in animo sapientis locum habere credimus, quid est, quare non ex toto illum hoc adfectu
4 liberemus ? Modus enim esse non potest, si pro facto
cuiusque irascendum est ; nam aut iniquus erit, si
aequaliter irascetur delictis inaequalibus, aut ira-
cundissimus, si totiens excanduerit quotiens iram
scelera meruerint.

1 7. Et quid indignius quam sapientis adfectum ex
aliena pendere nequitia ? Desinet ille Socrates posse
eundem vultum domum referre, quem domo extulerat ? Atqui si irasci sapiens turpiter factis debet
et concitari contristarique ob scelera, nihil est
aerumnosius sapiente ; omnis illi per iracundiam
2 maeroremque vita transibit. Quod enim momentum
erit, quo non improbanda videat ? Quotiens pro-
cesserit domo, per sceleratos illi avarosque et prodigos

And virtue will never be guilty of simulating vice in the act of repressing it ; anger in itself she considers reprehensible, for it is in no way better, often even worse, than those shortcomings which provoke anger. The distinctive and natural property of virtue is to rejoice and be glad ; it no more comports with her dignity to be angry than to be sad. But sorrow is the companion of anger, and all anger comes round to this as the result either of remorse or of defeat. Besides, if it is the part of a wise man to be angry at sin, the greater this is the more angry will he be, and he will be angry often ; it follows that the wise man will not only become angry, but will be prone to anger. But if we believe that neither great anger nor frequent anger has a place in the mind of a wise man, is there any reason why we should not free him from this passion altogether ? No limit, surely, can be set if the degree of his anger is to be determined by each man's deed. For either he will be unjust if he has equal anger toward unequal delinquencies, or he will be habitually angry if he blazes up every time crimes give him warrant.

And what is more unworthy of the wise man than that his passion should depend upon the wickedness of others ? Shall great Socrates lose the power to carry back home the same look he had brought from home ? But if the wise man is to be angered by base deeds, if he is to be perturbed and saddened by crimes, surely nothing is more woeful than the wise man's lot ; his whole life will be passed in anger and in grief. For what moment will there be when he will not see something to disapprove of ? Every time he leaves his house, he will have to walk among criminals and misers and spendthrifts and

179

et impudentis et ob ista felices incedendum erit; nusquam oculi eius flectentur, ut non quod indignentur inveniant. Deficiet, si totiens a se iram 3 quotiens causa poscet exegerit. Haec tot milia ad forum prima luce properantia quam turpes lites, quanto turpiores advocatos habent! Alius iudicia patris accusat, quae vereri satius fuit, alius cum matre consistit, alius delator venit eius criminis, cuius manifestior reus est; et iudex damnaturus quae fecit eligitur et corona pro mala causa stat[1] bona patroni voce corrupta.

1 8. Quid singula persequor? Cum videris forum multitudine refertum et saepta concursu omnis frequentiae plena et illum circum, in quo maximam sui partem populus ostendit, hoc scito, istic tantundem 2 esse vitiorum quantum hominum. Inter istos quos togatos vides nulla pax est; alter in alterius exitium levi compendio ducitur; nulli nisi ex alterius iniuria quaestus est; felicem oderunt, infelicem contemnunt; maiorem gravantur, minori graves sunt; diversis stimulantur cupiditatibus; omnia perdita ob levem voluptatem praedamque cupiunt. Non alia quam in ludo gladiatorio vita est cum isdem bibentium 3 pugnantiumque. Ferarum iste conventus est, nisi quod illae inter se placidae sunt morsuque similium abs-

---

[1] stat *Gertz, omitted by Hermes.*

profligates — men who are happy in being such.
Nowhere will he turn his eyes without finding something to move them to indignation. He will give out
if he forces himself to be angry every time occasion
requires. All these thousands hurrying to the forum
at break of day—how base their cases, and how
much baser are their advocates ! One assails his
father's will, which it were more fitting that he
respect ; another arraigns his mother at the bar ;
another comes as an informer of the very crime in
which he is more openly the culprit ; the judge,
too, is chosen who will condemn the same deeds
that he himself has committed, and the crowd, misled by the fine voice of a pleader, shows favour to
a wicked cause.

But why recount all the different types ? Whenever you see the forum with its thronging multitude,
and the polling-places filled with all the gathered
concourse, and the great Circus where the largest
part of the populace displays itself, you may be sure
that just as many vices are gathered there as men.
Among those whom you see in civilian garb there is
no peace ; for a slight reward any one of them can
be led to compass the destruction of another ; no
one makes gain save by another's loss ; the prosperous they hate, the unprosperous they despise ;
superiors they loathe, and to inferiors are loathsome ;
they are goaded on by opposite desires ; they desire
for the sake of some little pleasure or plunder to
see the whole world lost. They live as though they
were in a gladiatorial school—those with whom they
eat, they likewise fight. It is a community of wild
beasts, only that beasts are gentle toward each other
and refrain from tearing their own kind, while men

tinent, hi mutua laceratione satiantur. Hoc omnino[1]
ab animalibus mutis differunt, quod illa mansuescunt
alentibus, horum rabies ipsos a quibus est nutrita
depascitur.

1   9. Numquam irasci desinet sapiens, si semel
coeperit. Omnia sceleribus ac vitiis plena sunt ; plus
committitur quam quod possit coercitione sanari.
Certatur ingenti quidem nequitiae certamine. Maior
cottidie peccandi cupiditas, minor verecundia est ;
expulso melioris aequiorisque respectu quocumque
visum est libido se impingit, nec furtiva iam scelera
sunt. Praeter oculos eunt, adeoque in publicum
missa nequitia est et in omnium pectoribus evaluit, ut
2 innocentia non rara sed nulla sit. Numquid enim
singuli aut pauci rupere legem ? Undique velut signo
dato ad fas nefasque miscendum coorti sunt :

> Non hospes ab hospite tutus,
> non socer a genero ; fratrum quoque gratia rara est.
> Imminet exitio vir coniugis, illa mariti ;
> lurida terribiles miscent aconita novercae ;
> filius ante diem patrios inquirit in annos.

3 Et quota ista pars scelerum est ! Non descripsit
castra ex uno partu contraria et parentium liberorumque sacramenta diversa, subiectam patriae civis
manu flammam et agmina infestorum equitum ad in-
quirendas proscriptorum latebras circumvolitantia et
violatos fontes venenis et pestilentiam manu factam et
praeductam obsessis parentibus fossam, plenos carce-

---

[1] hoc omnino *Vahlen* : hoc in uno *A.*

---

[a] Ovid, *Met.* i. 144 *sqq.*

glut themselves with rending one another. They differ from the dumb animals in this alone—that animals grow gentle toward those who feed them, while men in their madness prey upon the very persons by whom they are nurtured.

Never will the wise man cease to be angry if once he begins. Every place is full of crime and vice; too many crimes are committed to be cured by any possible restraint. Men struggle in a mighty rivalry of wickedness. Every day the desire for wrong-doing is greater, the dread of it less; all regard for what is better and more just is banished, lust hurls itself wherever it likes, and crimes are now no longer covert. They stalk before our very eyes, and wickedness has come to such a public state, has gained such power over the hearts of all, that innocence is not rare—it is non-existent. For is it only the particular man or the few who break the law? On every hand, as if at a given signal, men rise to level all the barriers of right and wrong :

> No guest from host is safe, nor daughter's sire
> From daughter's spouse; e'en brothers' love is rare.
> The husband doth his wife, she him, ensnare ;
> Ferocious stepdames brew their ghastly banes ;
> The son too soon his father's years arraigns.[a]

And yet how few of all the crimes are these ! The poet makes no mention of the battling camps that claim a common blood, of the parents and the children sundered by a soldier's oath, of the flames a Roman hand applied to Rome, of the hostile bands of horsemen that scour the land to find the hiding-places of citizens proscribed, of springs defiled by poison, of plague the hand of man has made, of the trench flung around beleaguered parents, of crowded prisons, of

183

res et incendia totas urbes concremantia dominationes-
que funestas et regnorum publicorumque exitiorum
clandestina consilia, et pro gloria habita, quae quam
diu opprimi possunt, scelera sunt, raptus ac stupra et
4 ne os quidem libidini exceptum. Adde nunc publica
periuria gentium et rupta foedera et in praedam[1]
validioris quidquid non resistebat abductum, circum-
scriptiones, furta, fraudes, infitiationes, quibus trina
non sufficiunt fora. Si tantum irasci vis sapientem,
quantum scelerum indignitas exigit, non irascendum
illi sed insaniendum est.

1   10. Illud potius cogitabis, non esse irascendum
erroribus. Quid enim, si quis irascatur in tenebris
parum vestigia certa ponentibus? Quid, si quis
surdis imperia non exaudientibus? Quid, si pueris,
quod neglecto dispectu officiorum ad lusus et ineptos
aequalium iocos spectent? Quid, si illis irasci velis,
qui,[2] quod aegrotant senescunt, fatigantur? Inter
cetera mortalitatis incommoda et hoc est, caligo
mentium nec tantum necessitas errandi sed errorum
2 amor. Ne singulis irascaris, universis ignoscendum
est, generi humano venia tribuenda est. Si irasceris
iuvenibus senibusque, quod peccant, irascere et[3] infantibus : peccaturi sunt. Numquis irascitur pueris,
quorum aetas nondum novit rerum discrimina? Maior

---

[1] *so editors* : praedam *A* : pro praeda *Gertz.*
[2] qui *added by Hermes.*
[3] et *added by Gertz.*

---

a i.e., the Roman Forum, the Forum of Julius Caesar,
and the Forum of Augustus.

fires that burn whole cities to the ground, of baleful tyrannies and secret plots for regal power and for subversion of the state, of acts that now are glorified, but still are crimes so long as power endures to crush them, rape and lechery and the lust that spares not even human mouths. Add now to these, public acts of perjury between nations, broken treaties, and all the booty seized when resistance could not save it from the stronger, the double-dealings, the thefts and frauds and debts disowned—for such crimes all three forums *a* supply not courts enough! If you expect the wise man to be as angry as the shamefulness of crimes compels, he must not be angry merely, but go mad.

This rather is what you should think—that no one should be angry at the mistakes of men. For tell me, should one be angry with those who move with stumbling footsteps in the dark? with those who do not heed commands because they are deaf? with children because forgetting the observance of their duties they watch the games and foolish sports of their playmates? Would you want to be angry with those who become weary because they are sick or growing old? Among the various ills to which humanity is prone there is this besides—the darkness that fills the mind, and not so much the necessity of going astray, as the love of straying. That you may not be angry with individuals, you must forgive mankind at large, you must grant indulgence to the human race. If you are angry with the young and the old because they sin, be angry with babes as well; they are destined to sin. But who is angry with children who are still too young to have the power of discrimination? Yet to be a human being is an even

est excusatio et iustior hominem esse quam puerum.
3 Hac condicione nati sumus, animalia obnoxia non
paucioribus animi quam corporis morbis, non quidem
obtusa nec tarda, sed acumine nostro male utentia,
alter alteri vitiorum exempla. Quisquis sequitur prio-
res male iter ingressos, quidni habeat excusationem,
4 cum publica via erraverit? In singulos severitas
imperatoris destringitur, at necessaria venia est, ubi
totus deseruit exercitus. Quid tollit iram sapientis?
Turba peccantium. Intellegit quam et iniquum sit et
periculosum irasci publico vitio.

5 Heraclitus quotiens prodierat et tantum circa se
male viventium, immo male pereuntium viderat,
flebat, miserebatur omnium, qui sibi laeti felicesque
occurrebant, miti animo, sed nimis imbecillo, et ipse
inter deplorandos erat. Democritum contra aiunt
numquam sine risu in publico fuisse; adeo nihil illi
videbatur serium eorum quae serio gerebantur. Ubi
istic irae locus est? Aut ridenda omnia aut flenda
sunt.

6 Non irascetur sapiens peccantibus. Quare? Quia
scit neminem nasci sapientem sed fieri, scit paucis-
simos omni aevo sapientis evadere, quia condicionem
humanae vitae perspectam habet, nemo autem
naturae sanus irascitur. Quid enim, si mirari velit
186

greater and truer excuse for error than to be a child.
This is the lot to which we are born—we are creatures
subject to as many ills of the mind as of the body,
and though our power of discernment is neither
blunted nor dull, yet we make poor use of it and
become examples of vice to each other. If any one
follows in the footsteps of others who have taken
the wrong road, should he not be excused because
it was the public highway that led him astray?
Upon the individual soldier the commander may
unsheathe all his sternness, but he needs must for-
bear when the whole army deserts. What, then,
keeps the wise man from anger? The great mass
of sinners. He understands both how unjust and
how dangerous it is to grow angry at universal sin.

Whenever Heraclitus went forth from his house
and saw all around him so many men who were
living a wretched life—no, rather, were dying a
wretched death—he would weep, and all the joyous
and happy people he met stirred his pity; he was
gentle-hearted, but too weak, and was himself one of
those who had need of pity. Democritus, on the
other hand, it is said, never appeared in public
without laughing; so little did the serious pursuits
of men seem serious to him. Where in all this is
there room for anger? Everything gives cause for
either laughter or tears.

The wise man will have no anger toward sinners.
Do you ask why? Because he knows that no one is
born wise but becomes so, knows that only the fewest
in every age turn out wise, because he has fully
grasped the conditions of human life, and no sensible
man becomes angry with nature. Think you a sane
man would marvel because apples do not hang from

non in silvestribus dumis poma pendere ? Quid, si miretur spineta sentesque non utili aliqua fruge compleri ? Nemo irascitur, ubi vitium natura defendit. 7 Placidus itaque sapiens et aequus erroribus, non hostis sed corrector peccantium, hoc cottidie procedit animo : " Multi mihi occurrent vino dediti, multi libidinosi, multi ingrati, multi avari, multi furiis ambitionis agitati." Omnia ista tam propitius aspiciet 8 quam aegros suos medicus. Numquid ille, cuius navigium multam undique laxatis compagibus aquam trahit, nautis ipsique navigio irascitur ? Occurrit potius et aliam excludit undam, aliam egerit, manifesta foramina praecludit, latentibus et ex occulto sentinam ducentibus labore continuo resistit, nec ideo intermittit, quia quantum exhaustum est subnascitur. Lento adiutorio opus est contra mala continua et fecunda, non ut desinant, sed ne vincant.

1   11. " Utilis est," inquit, " ira, quia contemptum effugit, quia malos terret." Primum ira, si quantum minatur valet, ob hoc ipsum quod terribilis est et invisa est ; periculosius est autem timeri quam despici. Si vero sine viribus est, magis exposita contemptui est et derisum non effugit ; quid enim est iracundia in supervacuum tumultuante frigidius ? 2 Deinde non ideo quaedam, quia sunt terribiliora,

the brambles of the woodland ? Would he marvel because thorns and briars are not covered with some useful fruit ? No one becomes angry with a fault for which nature stands sponsor. And so the wise man is kindly and just toward errors, he is not the foe, but the reformer of sinners, and as he issues forth each day his thought will be : " I shall meet many who are in bondage to wine, many who are lustful, many ungrateful, many grasping, many who are lashed by the frenzy of ambition." He will view all these things in as kindly a way as a physician views the sick. When the skipper finds that his ship has sprung her seams and in every part is letting in a copious flow of water, does he then become angry with the seamen and with the ship herself ? No, he rushes rather to the rescue and shuts out a part of the flood, a part he bales out, and he closes up the visible openings, the hidden leaks that secretly let water into the hold he tries to overcome by ceaseless labour, and he does not relax his effort simply because as much water springs up as is pumped out. The succour against continuous and prolific evils must be tenacious, aimed not at their cessation but against their victory.

" Anger," it is said, " is expedient because it escapes contempt, because it terrifies the wicked." In the first place, if the power of anger is commensurate with its threats, for the very reason that it is terrible it is likewise hated ; besides, it is more dangerous to be feared than to be scorned. If, however, anger is powerless, it is even more exposed to contempt and does not escape ridicule. For what is more silly than the futile blustering of anger ? In the second place, because certain things are more

potiora sunt, nec hoc sapienti dici velim : " Quod ferae,
sapientis quoque telum est, timeri." Quid ? Non
timetur febris, podagra, ulcus malum ? Numquid
ideo quicquam in istis boni est ? An contra omnia
despecta foedaque et turpia, ipsoque eo timentur ?
Sic ira per se deformis est et minime metuenda, at
timetur a pluribus sicut deformis persona ab in-
3 fantibus. Quid, quod semper in auctores redundat
timor nec quisquam metuitur ipse securus ? Occurrat
hoc loco tibi Laberianus ille versus, qui medio civili
bello in theatro dictus totum in se populum non aliter
convertit, quam si missa esset vox publici adfectus :

Necesse est multos timeat quem multi timent.

4 Ita natura constituit, ut quidquid alieno metu magnum est, a suo non vacet. Leonum quam pavida
sunt ad levissimos sonos pectora ! Acerrimas feras
umbra et vox et odor insolitus exagitat. Quidquid
terret et trepidat. Non est ergo quare concupiscat
quisquam sapiens timeri, nec ideo iram magnum
quiddam putet, quia formidini est, quoniam quidem
etiam contemptissima timentur ut venena et ossa
5 pestifera et morsus.[1] Nec mirum est, cum maximos
ferarum greges linea pinnis distincta contineat et in

---

[1] venena . . . morsus *so A* : mortifera *for* pestifera *L* :
venenato bestiae pestiferae morsu *Haupt* : venenato aspis
viperave morsu *Gertz* : venenato serpens pestifera morsu
Hermes.

---

[a] Laberius 126 (*Com. Rom. Frag.* Ribbeck).
[b] By Laberius himself, impersonating a Syrian slave, in
the presence of Julius Caesar, at whom it was aimed ; *cf.*
Macrobius, *Sat.* ii. 7. 4.
[c] If " contemptible," probably the trumpery of magic !
[d] For their use in magic see Hor. *Sat.* i. 8. 22 ; Tac.
Ann. ii. 69. 5.

terrible, they are not for that reason preferable, and
I would not have it said to the wise man : " The
wild beast and the wise man have the same weapon ;
they are feared." What ? Is not a fever feared,
the gout, a malignant sore ? And do they for that
reason have any good in them ? Or are they, on
the contrary, all despised and loathsome and ugly,
and for this and no other reason are feared ? So
anger is in itself only repulsive and is by no means
to be dreaded, yet most people fear it just as children
fear a repulsive mask. And what of the fact that
fear always recoils upon those who inspire it and
that no one who is feared is himself unafraid ? You
may recall in this connexion the famous line of
Laberius :

Full many he must fear whom many fear,[a]

which when delivered in the theatre [b] in the height
of civil war caught the ear of the whole people as if
utterance had been given to the people's voice.
Nature has so ordained it that whatever is mighty
through the fear that others feel is not without its
own. How even the lion's heart quakes at the
slightest sound ! The boldest of wild beasts is
startled by a shadow or a voice or an unfamiliar
smell. Whatever terrifies must also tremble. There
is no reason, then, why any wise man should desire
to be feared, nor should he think that anger is a
mighty thing simply because it arouses dread, since
even the most contemptible things, such as poisonous
brews [c] and noxious bones [d] and bites are likewise
feared. Since a cord hung with feathers will stop
the mightiest droves of wild beasts and guide them
into traps, it is not strange that this from the very

insidias agat, ab ipso effectu dicta formido ; vanis
enim vana terrori sunt. Curriculi motus rotarumque
versata facies leones redegit in caveam, elephantos
6 porcina vox terret. Sic itaque ira metuitur, quomodo
umbra ab infantibus, a feris rubens pinna.[a] Non ipsa
in se quicquam habet firmum aut forte, sed leves
animos movet.
1   12. " Nequitia," inquit, " de rerum natura tollenda
est, si velis iram tollere ; neutrum autem potest
fieri." Primum potest aliquis non algere, quamvis
ex rerum natura hiemps sit, et non aestuare, quamvis
menses aestivi sint. Aut loci beneficio adversus in-
temperiem anni tutus est aut patientia corporis
2 sensum utriusque pervicit. Deinde verte istud :
necesse est prius virtutem ex animo tollas quam
iracundiam recipias, quoniam cum virtutibus vitia
non coeunt, nec magis quisquam eodem tempore et
iratus potest esse et vir bonus quam aeger et sanus.[b]
3 " Non potest," inquit, " omnis ex animo ira tolli,
nec hoc hominis natura patitur." Atqui nihil est
tam difficile et arduum quod non humana mens vincat
et in familiaritatem perducat adsidua meditatio,
nullique sunt tam feri et sui iuris adfectus, ut non
4 disciplina perdomentur. Quodcumque sibi imperavit
animus, obtinuit. Quidam ne umquam riderent consecuti sunt ; vino quidam, alii venere, quidam omni
umore interdixere corporibus ; alius contentus brevi

---

[a] *Cf.* Virgil, *Aen.* xii. 750 *sq.*:

> cervum aut puniceae saeptum formidine pennae
> venator cursu canis et latratibus instat.

[b] The implication would then be that if a man cannot
banish anger, no man can be virtuous.

result should be called a " scare " [a]; for to the foolish foolish things are terrible. The speeding of the race-chariot and the sight of its revolving wheels will drive back lions to their cage, and elephants are terrified by the squealing of a pig. And so we fear anger just as children fear the dark and wild beasts fear a gaudy feather. Anger in itself has nothing of the strong or the heroic, but shallow minds are affected by it.

" Wickedness," it is said, " must be eliminated from the scheme of nature, if you would eliminate anger ; neither, however, is possible." In the first place, one *can* avoid being cold although in the scheme of nature it is winter, and one *can* avoid being hot although the hot months are here. A man may either be protected against the inclemency of the season by a favourable place of residence, or he may by physical endurance subdue the sensation of both heat and cold. In the second place, reverse [b] this statement : A man must banish virtue from his heart before he can admit wrath, since vices do not consort with virtues, and a man can no more be both angry and good at the same time than he can be sick and well. " But it is not possible," you say, " to banish anger altogether from the heart, nor does the nature of man permit it." Yet nothing is so hard and difficult that it cannot be conquered by the human intellect and be brought through persistent study into intimate acquaintance, and there are no passions so fierce and self-willed that they cannot be subjugated by discipline. Whatever command the mind gives to itself holds its ground. Some have reached the point of never smiling, some have cut themselves off from wine, others from sexual pleasure, others from every kind of drink ; another, satisfied by short

somno vigiliam indefatigabilem extendit; didicerunt
tenuissimis et adversis funibus currere et ingentia
vixque humanis toleranda viribus onera portare et in
immensam altitudinem mergi ac sine ulla respirandi
5 vice perpeti maria. Mille sunt alia, in quibus pertinacia impedimentum omne transcendit ostenditque
nihil esse difficile cuius sibi ipsa mens patientiam in-
diceret. Istis quos paulo ante rettuli aut nulla tam perti-
nacis studii aut non digna merces fuit—quid enim magnificum consequitur ille qui meditatus est per intentos
funes ire? qui sarcinae ingenti cervices supponere?
qui somno non summittere oculos? qui penetrare in
imum mare?—et tamen ad finem operis non magno
6 auctoramento labor pervenit. Nos non advocabimus
patientiam, quos tantum praemium expectat, felicis
animi immota tranquillitas? Quantum est effugere
maximum malum, iram, et cum illa rabiem, saevitiam,
crudelitatem, furorem, alios comites eius adfectus!

1   13. Non est quod patrocinium nobis quaeramus
et excusatam licentiam, dicentes aut utile id esse aut
inevitabile; cui enim tandem vitio advocatus defuit?
Non est quod dicas excidi non posse; sanabilibus
aegrotamus malis ipsaque nos in rectum genitos natura, si emendari velimus, iuvat. Nec, ut quibusdam
visum est, arduum in virtutes et asperum iter est;

---

^a The thought is a commonplace and is found as early as
Hesiod, *Works and Days*, 289 *sqq.*:

> Τῆς δ' ἀρετῆς ἱδρῶτα θεοὶ προπάροιθεν ἔθηκαν
> ἀθάνατοι· μακρὸς δὲ καὶ ὄρθιος οἶμος ἐς αὐτὴν
> καὶ τρηχὺς τὸ πρῶτον.

Cf. the beginning of Aristotle's *Hymn to Virtue* (Bergk,
Poet. Lyr. Graec. ii. p. 360):

> Ἀρετά, πολύμοχθε γένει βροτείῳ,
> θήραμα κάλλιστον βίῳ.

sleep, prolongs his waking hours unwearied ; some have learned to run on very small and slanting ropes, to carry huge burdens that are scarcely within the compass of human strength, to dive to unmeasured depths and to endure the sea without any drawing of breath. There are a thousand other instances to show that persistence surmounts every obstacle and that nothing is really difficult which the mind enjoins itself to endure. The men I mentioned a little while ago had either no reward for their unflagging zeal or none worthy of it—for what glory does he attain who has trained himself to walk a tight rope, to carry a huge load upon his shoulders, to withhold his eyes from sleep, to penetrate to the bottom of the sea ?—and yet by effort they attained the end for which they worked although the remuneration was not great. Shall we, then, not summon ourselves to endurance when so great a reward awaits us—the unbroken calm of the happy soul ? How great a blessing to escape anger, the greatest of all ills, and along with it madness, ferocity, cruelty, rage, and the other passions that attend anger !

It is not for us to seek a defence for ourselves and an excuse for such indulgence by saying that it is either expedient or unavoidable ; for what vice, pray, has ever lacked its defender ? It is not for you to say that anger cannot be eradicated ; the ills from which we suffer are curable, and since we are born to do right, nature herself helps us if we desire to be improved. Nor, as some think, is the path to the virtues steep and rough [a] ; they are reached by a

2 plano adeuntur. Non vanae vobis auctor rei venio. Facilis est ad beatam vitam via ; inite modo bonis auspiciis ipsisque dis bene iuvantibus. Multo difficilius est facere ista quae facitis. Quid est animi quiete otiosius, quid ira laboriosius ? Quid clementia remissius, quid crudelitate negotiosius ? Vacat pudicitia, libido occupatissima est. Omnium denique virtutum tutela facilis est, vitia magno coluntur.

3 Debet ira removeri—hoc ex parte fatentur etiam qui dicunt esse minuendam ; tota dimittatur, nihil profutura est. Sine illa facilius rectiusque scelera tollentur, mali punientur et transducentur in melius. Omnia quae debet sapiens sine ullius malae rei ministerio efficiet nihilque admiscebit, cuius modum sollicitius observet.

1 14. Numquam itaque iracundia admittenda est ; aliquando simulanda, si segnes audientium animi concitandi sunt, sicut tarde consurgentis ad cursum equos stimulis facibusque subditis excitamus. Aliquando incutiendus est iis metus apud quos ratio non proficit ; irasci quidem non magis utile est quam maerere, quam

2 metuere. " Quid ergo ? Non incidunt causae quae iram lacessant ? " Sed tunc maxime illi opponendae manus sunt. Nec est difficile vincere animum, cum athletae quoque in vilissima sui parte occupati tamen ictus doloresque patiantur, ut vires caedentis exhauriant, nec cum ira suadet, feriant, sed cum occasio.

level road. It is no idle tale that I come to tell you. The road to the happy life is an easy one; do but enter on it—with good auspices and the good help of the gods themselves! It is far harder to do what you are now doing. What is more reposeful than peace of mind, what more toilsome than anger? What is more disengaged than mercy, what more busy than cruelty? Chastity keeps holiday, while lust is always occupied. In short, the maintenance of all the virtues is easy, but it is costly to cultivate the vices. Anger must be dislodged—even those who say that it ought to be reduced admit this in part; let us be rid of it altogether, it can do us no good. Without it we shall more easily and more justly abolish crimes, punish the wicked, and set them upon the better path. The wise man will accomplish his whole duty without the assistance of anything evil, and he will associate with himself nothing which needs to be controlled with anxious care.

Wrath is therefore never admissible; sometimes we must feign it if we have to arouse the sluggish minds of our hearers, just as we apply goads and brands to arouse horses that are slow in starting upon their course. Sometimes we must strike fear into the hearts of those with whom reason is of no avail; yet it is no more expedient to be angry than to be sad or to be afraid. "What then?" you say; "do not incidents occur which provoke anger?" Yes, but it is then most of all that we must grapple with it hand to hand. Nor is it difficult to subdue the spirit, since even athletes, concerned as they are with man's basest part, nevertheless endure blows and pain in order that they may drain the strength of their assailant and strike, not when anger, but

3 Pyrrhum maximum praeceptorem certaminis gymnici
solitum aiunt iis quos exercebat praecipere, ne
irascerentur ; ira enim perturbat artem et qua noceat
tantum aspicit. Saepe itaque ratio patientiam suadet,
ira vindictam, et qui primis defungi malis potuimus, in
4 maiora devolvimur. Quosdam unius verbi contumelia
non aequo animo lata in exilium proiecit, et qui levem
iniuriam silentio ferre noluerant, gravissimis malis
obruti sunt, indignatique aliquid ex plenissima
libertate deminui servile in sese adtraxerunt iugum.

1 15. " Ut scias," inquit, " iram habere in se generosi
aliquid, liberas videbis gentes, quae iracundissimae
sunt, ut Germanos et Scythas." Quod evenit, quia
fortia solidaque natura ingenia, antequam disciplina
molliantur, prona in iram sunt. Quaedam enim non
nisi melioribus innascuntur ingeniis, sicut valida
arbusta laeta quamvis neclecta tellus creat, et alta
2 fecundi soli silva est. Itaque et ingenia natura fortia
iracundiam ferunt nihilque tenue et exile capiunt
ignea et fervida, sed imperfectus illis vigor est ut
omnibus, quae sine arte ipsius tantum naturae bono
exsurgunt, sed nisi cito domita sunt, quae fortitudini
3 apta erant, audaciae temeritatique consuescunt. Quid?
Non mitioribus animis vitia leniora coniuncta sunt, ut

when advantage, prompts. Pyrrhus, the most famous trainer for gymnastic contests, made it a rule, it is said, to warn those whom he was training against getting angry; for anger confounds art and looks only for a chance to injure. Often, therefore, reason counsels patience, but anger revenge, and when we have been able to escape our first misfortunes, we are plunged into greater ones. Some have been cast into exile because they could not bear calmly one insulting word, and those who had refused to bear in silence a slight wrong have been crushed with the severest misfortunes, and, indignant at any diminution of the fullest liberty, have brought upon themselves the yoke of slavery.

" That you may be convinced," says our opponent, " that anger does have in it something noble, you will see that such nations as are free—for example, the Germans and Scythians—are those which are most prone to anger." The reason of this is that natures which are inherently brave and sturdy are prone to anger before they become softened by discipline. For certain qualities are innate only in better natures, just as rich ground, although it is neglected, produces a strong growth and a tall forest is the mark of fertile soil. And so natures that have innate vigour likewise produce wrath, and being hot and fiery they have no room for anything weak and feeble, but their energy is defective, as is the case with everything that springs up without cultivation through the bounty merely of nature herself; yes, and, unless such natures are quickly tamed, what was a disposition to bravery tends to become recklessness and temerity. And tell me, is it not with the more gentle tempers that the milder faults, such as pity

199

misericordia et amor et verecundia ? Itaque saepe
tibi bonam indolem malis quoque suis ostendam ; sed
non ideo vitia non sunt, si naturae melioris indicia sunt.
4 Deinde omnes istae feritate liberae gentes leonum
luporumque ritu ut servire non possunt, ita nec
imperare ; non enim humani vim ingenii, sed feri
et intractabilis habent ; nemo autem regere potest
5 nisi qui et regi. Fere itaque imperia penes eos
fuere populos, qui mitiore caelo utuntur. In frigora
septemtrionemque vergentibus immansueta ingenia
sunt, ut ait poeta :

Suoque simillima caelo.

1 16. "Animalia," inquit, "generosissima habentur,
quibus multum inest irae." Errat qui ea in exemplum
hominis adducit, quibus pro ratione est impetus ; homini pro impetu ratio est. Sed ne illis quidem omnibus idem prodest ; iracundia leones adiuvat, pavor
2 cervos, accipitrem impetus, columbam fuga. Quid,
quod ne illud quidem verum est, optima animalia esse
iracundissima ? Feras putem, quibus ex raptu alimenta
sunt, meliores quo iratiores ; patientiam laudaverim
boum et equorum frenos sequentium. Quid est autem
cur hominem ad tam infelicia exempla revoces, cum
habeas mundum deumque, quem ex omnibus animali-

ᵃ *Frag. Poet. Rom.* p. 359. 25 Baehrens.

and love and bashfulness, are found combined? Accordingly, I can often prove to you even by a man's own evils that his natural bent is good; but these evils are none the less vices even though they are indicative of a superior nature. Then, again, all those peoples which are, like lions and wolves, free by reason of their very wildness, even as they cannot submit to servitude, neither can they exercise dominion; for the ability they possess is not that of a human being but of something wild and ungovernable; and no man is able to rule unless he can also submit to be ruled. Consequently, the peoples who have held empire are commonly those who live in a rather mild climate. Those who lie toward the frozen north have savage tempers—tempers which, as the poet says, are

Most like their native skies.[a]

" Those animals," you say, " which are much given to anger are held to be the noblest." But it is wrong for one to hold up the creatures in whom impulse takes the place of reason as a pattern for a human being; in man reason takes the place of impulse. But not even in the case of such animals is the same impulse equally profitable for all; anger serves the lion, fear the stag, aggressiveness the hawk, cowardice the dove. But what if it is not even true that it is the best animals that are most prone to anger? Wild beasts which gain their food by rapine, I can believe, do so the better the angrier they are; but it is the endurance of the ox and the horse, obedient to the rein, that I would commend. For what reason, however, do you direct man to such miserable standards when you have the universe and God, whom man of all creatures alone com-

3 bus, ut solus imitetur, solus intellegit? "Simplicissimi," inquit, "omnium habentur iracundi." Fraudulentis enim et versutis comparantur et simplices videntur, quia expositi sunt. Quos quidem non simplices dixerim sed incautos; stultis, luxuriosis nepotibusque hoc nomen imponimus et omnibus vitiis parum callidis.

1 17. "Orator," inquit, "iratus aliquando melior est." Immo imitatus iratum; nam et histriones in pronuntiando non irati populum movent, sed iratum bene agentes; et apud iudices itaque et in contione et ubicumque alieni animi ad nostrum arbitrium agendi sunt, modo iram, modo metum, modo misericordiam, ut aliis incutiamus, ipsi simulabimus, et saepe id, quod veri adfectus non effecissent, effecit imitatio adfectuum. "Languidus," inquit, "animus est qui 2 ira caret." Verum est, si nihil habet ira valentius. Nec latronem oportet esse nec praedam, nec misericordem nec crudelem; illius nimis mollis animus, huius nimis durus est. Temperatus sit sapiens et ad res fortius agendas non iram sed vim adhibeat.

1 18. Quoniam quae de ira quaeruntur tractavimus, accedamus ad remedia eius. Duo autem, ut opinor, sunt: ne incidamus in iram et ne in ira peccemus. Ut in corporum cura alia de tuenda valetudine, alia de restituenda praecepta sunt, ita aliter iram debemus

prehends in order that he alone may imitate him? "Those who are prone to anger," you say, "are of all men considered the most ingenuous." Yes, in contrast with the tricky and the crafty they do seem ingenuous because they are undisguised. I, however, should call them, not ingenuous, but reckless; that is the term we apply to fools, to voluptuaries and spendthrifts, and to all who ill disguise their vices.

"The orator," you say, "at times does better when he is angry." Not so, but when he pretends to be angry. For the actor likewise stirs an audience by his declamation not when he is angry, but when he plays well the rôle of the angry man; consequently before a jury, in the popular assembly, and wherever we have to force our will upon the minds of other people, we must pretend now anger, now fear, now pity, in order that we may inspire others with the same, and often the feigning of an emotion produces an effect which would not be produced by genuine emotion. "The mind that is devoid of anger," you say, "is inert." Very true, unless it is actuated by something more powerful than anger. A man should be neither a highwayman nor his victim, neither soft-hearted nor cruel; the one is too mild in spirit, the other too harsh. Let the wise man show moderation, and to situations that require strong measures let him apply, not anger, but force.

Having dealt with the questions that arise concerning anger, let us now pass to the consideration of its remedies. In my opinion, however, there are but two rules—not to fall into anger, and in anger to do no wrong. Just as in caring for the body certain rules are to be observed for guarding the health, others for restoring it, so we must use one means

repellere, aliter compescere. Ut vitemus, quaedam
ad universam vitam pertinentia praecipientur ; ea in
educationem et in sequentia tempora dividentur.

2 Educatio maximam diligentiam plurimumque pro-
futuram desiderat ; facile est enim teneros adhuc
animos componere, difficulter reciduntur vitia quae
nobiscum creverunt.

1 19. Opportunissima ad iracundiam fervidi animi
natura est. Nam cum elementa sint quattuor, ignis,
aquae, aëris, terrae, potestates pares his sunt, fervida,
frigida, arida atque umida. Et locorum itaque et animalium et corporum et morum varietates mixtura
elementorum facit, et proinde aliquo magis incumbunt
ingenia, prout alicuius elementi maior vis abundavit.
Inde quasdam umidas vocamus aridasque regiones et
calidas et frigidas. Eadem animalium hominumque

2 discrimina sunt ; refert quantum quisque umidi in
se calidique contineat ; cuius in illo elementi portio
praevalebit, inde mores erunt. Iracundos fervida
animi natura faciet, est enim actuosus et pertinax
ignis ; frigidi mixtura timidos facit, pigrum est enim

3 contractumque frigus. Volunt itaque quidam ex
nostris iram in pectore moveri effervescente circa cor
sanguine ; causa cur hic potissimum adsignetur irae
locus non alia est, quam quod in toto corpore calidis-

4 simum pectus est. Quibus umidi plus inest, eorum

---

^a In the order of the corresponding elements these are:
hot, moist, cold, dry. According to the Stoic view, in the
processes of nature the four elements were changed from one
into the other in fixed order. *Cf.* Cicero, *De Nat. Deor.* ii.
33. 84 : "nam ex terra aqua, ex aqua oritur aër, ex aëre
aether (*i.e.* ignis); deinde retrorsum vicissim ex aethere aër,
inde aqua, ex aqua terra infima."

to repel anger, another to restrain it. In order that we may avoid anger, certain rules will be laid down which apply to the whole period of life; these will fall under two heads—the period of education and the later periods of life.

The period of education calls for the greatest, and what will also prove to be the most profitable, attention; for it is easy to train the mind while it is still tender, but it is a difficult matter to curb the vices that have grown up with us.

The fiery mind is by its nature most liable to wrath. For as there are the four elements of fire, water, air, and earth, so there are the corresponding properties, the hot, the cold, the dry, and the moist.[a] Accordingly, the various differences of regions, of animals, of substances, and of characters are caused by the mingling of the elements; consequently, also, dispositions show a greater bent in some one direction, according as they abound in a larger supply of some one element. Hence it is that we call some regions moist, some dry, some hot, some cold. The same distinctions apply to animals and to men; it makes a great difference how much of the moist and the hot each man has in him; his character will be determined by that element in him of which he will have a dominant proportion. A fiery constitution of mind will produce wrathful men, for fire is active and stubborn; a mixture of cold makes cowards, for cold is sluggish and shrunken. Consequently, some of our school hold that anger is aroused in the breast by the boiling of the blood about the heart; the reason why this particular spot is assigned to anger is none other than the fact that the warmest part of the whole body is the breast. In the case of those who have more of

205

paulatim crescit ira, quia non est paratus illis calor
sed motu adquiritur ; itaque puerorum feminarumque
irae acres magis quam graves sunt levioresque dum
incipiunt. Siccis aetatibus vehemens robustaque est
ira, sed sine incremento, non multum sibi adiciens,
quia inclinaturum calorem frigus insequitur. Senes
difficiles et queruli sunt, ut aegri et convalescentes et
quorum aut lassitudine aut detractione sanguinis ex-
5 haustus est calor ; in eadem causa sunt siti fameque
tabidi et quibus exsangue corpus est maligneque
alitur et deficit. Vinum incendit iras, quia calorem
auget ; pro cuiusque natura quidam ebrii efferves-
cunt, quidam saucii. Neque ulla alia causa est, cur
iracundissimi sint flavi rubentesque, quibus talis
natura color est, qualis fieri ceteris inter iram solet ;
mobilis enim illis agitatusque sanguis est.

1 20. Sed quemadmodum natura quosdam proclives
in iram facit, ita multae incidunt causae, quae idem
possint quod natura. Alios morbus aut iniuria corporum in hoc perduxit, alios labor aut continua pervigilia noctesque sollicitae et desideria amoresque ;
quidquid aliud aut corpori nocuit aut animo, aegram
2 mentem in querellas parat. Sed omnia ista initia
causaeque sunt ; plurimum potest consuetudo, quae
si gravis est, alit vitium. Naturam quidem mutare
difficile est, nec licet semel mixta nascentium
elementa convertere ; sed in hoc nosse profuit, ut

---

[a] Apparently the dominating element, and consequently
the natural tendency, varies according to age and condition.

[b] Designating conditions where in the combination of the
dry, the hot, and the cold, cold becomes dominant. "Cold"
was the property of air, and this element was associated with
calmness and poise (Lucretius, iii. 292 sq.). We may think
here, probably, of the middle periods of life.

[c] i.e., of the body.

the moist in them, anger grows up gradually because
they have no heat ready at hand but obtain it by
movement; and so the anger of children *a* and women
is more vehement than serious, and it is lighter at the
start. In the dry periods of life *b* anger is powerful
and strong, but is without increase, showing little
gain because cold succeeds heat,*c* which is now on the
decline. Old men are simply testy and querulous,
as also are invalids and convalescents and all whose
heat has been drained either by exhaustion or by
loss of blood; the same is the condition of those who
are gaunt from thirst and hunger and of those whose
bodies are anaemic and ill-nourished and weak. Wine
kindles anger because it increases the heat; some
boil over when they are drunk, others when they are
simply tipsy, each according to his nature. And the
only reason why red-haired and ruddy people are
extremely hot-tempered is that they have by nature
the colour which others are wont to assume in anger;
for their blood is active and restless.

But while nature makes certain persons prone to
anger, there are likewise many accidental causes
which are just as effective as nature. Some are
brought into this condition by sickness or injury of
the body, others by toil or unceasing vigils, by
nights of anxiety, by yearnings and the affairs of
love; whatever else impairs either body or mind,
produces a diseased mental state prone to complaint.
But these are all only beginnings and causes; habit
counts for most, and if this is deep-seated, it fosters
the fault. As for nature, it is difficult to alter it, and
we may not change the elements that were combined
once for all at our birth; but it is profitable to know
this to the end that fiery temperaments may be

calentibus ingeniis subtrahas vinum, quod pueris
Plato negandum putat et ignem vetat igne incitari.
Ne cibis quidem implendi sint ; distendentur enim
3 corpora et animi cum corpore tumescent. Labor illos
citra lassitudinem exerceat, ut minuatur, non ut
consumatur calor nimiusque ille fervor despumet.
Lusus quoque proderunt ; modica enim voluptas laxat
4 animos et temperat. Umidioribus siccioribusque et
frigidis non est ab ira periculum, sed ignaviora vitia
metuenda sunt, pavor et difficultas et desperatio et
suspiciones. Extollenda itaque fovendaque talia
ingenia et in laetitiam evocanda sunt. Et quia aliis
contra iram, aliis contra tristitiam remediis utendum
est nec dissimillimis tantum ista sed contrariis
curanda sunt, semper ei occurremus quod in-
creverit.

1   21. Plurimum, inquam, proderit pueros statim
salubriter institui ; difficile autem regimen est, quia
dare debemus operam, ne aut iram in illis nutriamus
2 aut indolem retundamus. Diligenti observatione res
indiget ; utrumque enim, et quod extollendum et
quod deprimendum est, similibus alitur, facile autem
3 etiam adtendentem similia decipiunt. Crescit licentia
spiritus, servitute comminuitur ; adsurgit, si lau-
datur et in spem sui bonam adducitur, sed eadem
ista insolentiam et iracundiam generant ; itaque

---

a Laws, ii. 666 **A**.

kept away from wine, which Plato [a] thinks ought to be forbidden to children, protesting against adding fire to fire. Neither should such men gorge themselves with food ; for their bodies will be distended and their spirits will become swollen along with the body. They should get exercise in toil, stopping short of exhaustion, to the end that their heat may be reduced, but not used up, and that their excessive fever may subside. Games also will be beneficial ; for pleasure in moderation relaxes the mind and gives it balance. The more moist and the drier natures, and also the cold, are in no danger from anger, but they must beware of faults that are more base—fear, moroseness, discouragement, and suspicion. And so such natures have need of encouragement and indulgence and the summons to cheerfulness. And since certain remedies are to be employed against anger, others against sullenness, and the two faults are to be cured, not merely by different, but even by contrary, methods, we shall always attack the fault that has become the stronger.

It will be of the utmost profit, I say, to give children sound training from the very beginning ; guidance, however, is difficult, because we ought to take pains neither to develop in them anger nor to blunt their native spirit. The matter requires careful watching ; for both qualities—that which should be encouraged and that which should be checked—are fed by like things, and like things easily deceive even a close observer. By freedom the spirit grows, by servitude it is crushed ; if it is commended and is led to expect good things of itself, it mounts up, but these same measures breed insolence and temper ; therefore we must guide the

sic inter utrumque regendus est, ut modo frenis
4 utamur modo stimulis. Nihil humile, nihil servile
patiatur ; numquam illi necesse sit rogare sup-
pliciter nec prosit rogasse, potius causae suae et
prioribus factis et bonis in futurum promissis donetur.
5 In certaminibus aequalium nec vinci illum patiamur
nec irasci ; demus operam, ut familiaris sit iis cum
quibus contendere solet, ut in certamine adsuescat
non nocere velle sed vincere ; quotiens superaverit
et dignum aliquid laude fecerit, attolli non gestire
patiamur, gaudium enim exultatio, exultationem
6 tumor et nimia aestimatio sui sequitur Dabimus
aliquod laxamentum, in desidiam vero otiumque
non resolvemus et procul a contactu deliciarum re-
tinebimus ; nihil enim magis facit iracundos quam
educatio mollis et blanda. Ideo unicis quo plus
indulgetur, pupillisque quo plus licet, corruptior
animus est. Non resistet offensis cui nihil umquam
negatum est, cuius lacrimas sollicita semper mater
7 abstersit, cui de paedagogo satisfactum est. Non
vides, ut maiorem quamque fortunam maior ira
comitetur ? In divitibus et nobilibus et magistratibus
praecipue apparet, cum quidquid leve et inane in
animo erat secunda se aura sustulit. Felicitas

---

^a *i.e.*, the slave who was the child's special guardian, not
his teacher.

child between the two extremes, using now the curb, now the spur. He should be subjected to nothing that is humiliating, nothing that is servile ; it should never be necessary for him to beg submissively, nor should begging ever prove profitable—rather let his own desert and his past conduct and good promise of it in the future be rewarded. In struggles with his playmates we should not permit him either to be beaten or to get angry ; we should take pains to see that he is friendly toward those with whom it is his practice to engage in order that in the struggle he may form the habit of wishing not to hurt his opponent but merely to win. Whenever he gets the upper hand and does something praiseworthy, we should allow him to be encouraged but not elated, for joy leads to exultation, exultation to over-conceit and a too high opinion of oneself. We shall grant him some relaxation, though we shall not let him lapse into sloth and ease, and we shall keep him far from all taint of pampering ; for there is nothing that makes the child hot-tempered so much as a soft and coddling bringing up. Therefore the more an only child is indulged, and the more liberty a ward is allowed, the more will his disposition be spoiled. He will not withstand rebuffs who has never been denied anything, whose tears have always been wiped away by an anxious mother, who has been allowed to have his own way with his tutor.[a] Do you not observe that with each advancing grade of fortune there goes the greater tendency to anger ? It is especially apparent in the rich, in nobles, and in officials when all that was light and trivial in their mind soars aloft upon the breeze of good fortune. Prosperity fosters wrath when the crowd

iracundiam nutrit, ubi aures superbas adsentatorum turba circumstetit : " Tibi enim ille respondeat ? non pro fastigio te tuo metiris ; ipse te proicis " et alia quibus vix sanae et ab initio bene fundatae
8 mentes restiterunt. Longe itaque ab adsentatione pueritia removenda est ; audiat verum. Et timeat interim, vereatur semper, maioribus adsurgat. Nihil per iracundiam exoret ; quod flenti negatum fuerit, quieto offeratur. Et divitias parentium in conspectu
9 habeat, non in usu. Exprobrentur illi perperam facta. Pertinebit ad rem praeceptores paedagogosque pueris placidos dari. Proximis adplicatur omne quod tenerum est et in eorum similitudinem crescit ; nutricum et paedagogorum rettulere mox
10 adulescentium mores. Apud Platonem educatus puer cum ad parentes relatus vociferantem videret patrem : " Numquam," inquit, " hoc apud Platonem vidi." Non dubito quin citius patrem imitatus sit
11 quam Platonem. Tenuis ante omnia victus sit[1] et non pretiosa vestis et similis cultus cum aequalibus. Non irascetur aliquem sibi comparari quem ab initio multis parem feceris.
1 22. Sed haec ad liberos nostros pertinent ; in nobis quidem sors nascendi et educatio nec vitii locum nec iam praecepti habet ; sequentia ordinanda

[1] sit *added by Ruhkopf.*

[a] *i.e.*, of older people. The discussion here passes to the second topic formulated in ch. 18. 2.

[b] In the earlier discussion the reverse was true—anger was associated with the fortune of birth (ch. 19), and precept with the corrective value of education (ch. 21).

of flatterers, gathered around, whispers to the proud ear : " What, should that man answer *you* back ? Your estimate of yourself does not correspond with your importance ; you demean yourself "—these and other adulations, which even the sensible and originally well-poised mind resists with difficulty. Childhood, therefore, should be kept far from all contact with flattery ; let a child hear the truth, sometimes even let him fear, let him be respectful always, let him rise before his elders. Let him gain no request by anger ; when he is quiet let him be offered what was refused when he wept. Let him, moreover, have the sight but not the use of his parents' wealth. When he has done wrong, let him be reproved. It will work to the advantage of children to give them teachers and tutors of a quiet disposition. Every young thing attaches itself to what is nearest and grows to be like it ; the character of their nurses and tutors is presently reproduced in that of the young men. There was a boy who had been brought up in the house of Plato, and when he had returned to his parents and saw his father in a blustering rage, his comment was : " I never saw this sort of thing at Plato's." I doubt not that he was quicker to copy his father than he was to copy Plato ! Above all, let his food be simple, his clothing inexpensive, and his style of living like that of his companions. The boy will never be angry at some one being counted equal to himself, whom you have from the first treated as the equal of many.

But these rules apply to our children. In our case,[a] however, our lot at birth and our education give no excuse—the one for the vice, or the other, any longer, for instruction[b] ; it is their

2 sunt. Contra primas itaque causas pugnare debemus. Causa autem iracundiae opinio iniuriae est,
cui non facile credendum est. Ne apertis quidem
manifestisque statim accedendum ; quaedam enim
3 falsa veri speciem ferunt. Dandum semper est
tempus ; veritatem dies aperit. Ne sint aures
criminantibus faciles ; hoc humanae naturae vitium
suspectum notumque nobis sit, quod, quae inviti
audimus, libenter credimus et, antequam iudicemus,
4 irascimur. Quid, quod non criminationibus tantum,
sed suspicionibus impellimur et ex vultu risuque
alieno peiora interpretati innocentibus irascimur ?
Itaque agenda est contra se causa absentis et in
suspenso ira retinenda ; potest enim poena dilata
exigi, non potest exacta revocari.

1   23. Notus est ille tyrannicida, qui imperfecto opere
comprehensus et ab Hippia tortus, ut conscios
indicaret, circumstantes amicos tyranni nominavit
quibusque maxime caram salutem eius sciebat ; et
cum ille singulos, ut nominati erant, occidi iussisset,
interroganti, ecquis superesset, " Tu," inquit, " solus ;
neminem enim alium cui carus esses reliqui." Effecit
ira, ut tyrannus tyrannicidae manus accommodaret
2 et praesidia sua gladio suo caederet. Quanto ani-

ᵃ *i.e.*, of birth and education.
ᵇ See Index.

consequences[a] that we must regulate. We ought, therefore, to make our fight against the primary causes. Now the cause of anger is an impression of injury, and to this we should not easily give credence. We ought not to be led to it quickly even by open and evident acts ; for some things are false that have the appearance of truth. We should always allow some time ; a day discloses the truth. Let us not give ready ear to traducers ; this weakness of human nature let us recognize and mistrust—we are glad to believe what we are loth to hear, and we become angry before we can form a judgement about it. And what is to be said when we are actuated, not merely by charges, but by bare suspicions, and having put the worse interpretation on another's look or smile, become angry at innocent men ? Therefore we should plead the cause of the absent person against ourselves, and anger should be held in abeyance ; for punishment postponed can still be exacted, but once exacted it cannot be recalled.

Every one knows the story of the tyrannicide who having been arrested before he had finished his task was put to torture by Hippias[b] in order that he might be forced to reveal his accomplices ; whereupon he named the friends of the tyrant who were gathered around him, the very ones to whom, as he knew, the safety of the tyrant was especially dear. After Hippias had ordered them to be slain one by one, as they were named, he asked whether there was still any other. " No," said the man, " you alone remain ; for I have left no one else who cares anything about you." The result of his anger was that the tyrant lent his might to the tyrant-slayer and slew his own protectors with his own sword.

mosius Alexander! Qui cum legisset epistulam
matris, qua admonebatur, ut a veneno Philippi
medici caveret, acceptam potionem non deterritus
3 bibit. Plus sibi de amico suo credidit. Dignus fuit
qui innocentem haberet, dignus qui faceret! Hoc
eo magis in Alexandro laudo, quia nemo tam obnoxius
irae fuit; quo rarior autem moderatio in regibus,
4 hoc laudanda magis est. Fecit hoc et C. Caesar
ille qui victoria civili clementissime usus est; cum
scrinia deprendisset epistularum ad Cn. Pompeium
missarum ab iis, qui videbantur aut in diversis aut
in neutris fuisse partibus, combussit. Quamvis
moderate soleret irasci, maluit tamen non posse;
gratissimum putavit genus veniae nescire quid
quisque peccasset.

1 24. Plurimum mali credulitas facit. Saepe ne
audiendum quidem est, quoniam in quibusdam rebus
satius est decipi quam diffidere. Tollenda ex animo
suspicio et coniectura, fallacissima irritamenta.
" Ille me parum humane salutavit; ille osculo meo
non adhaesit; ille inchoatum sermonem cito abrupit;
ille ad cenam non vocavit; illius vultus aversior
2 visus est." Non deerit suspicioni argumentatio.
Simplicitate opus est et benigna rerum aestimatione.
Nihil nisi quod in oculos incurret manifestumque
erit credamus, et quotiens suspicio nostra vana

---

^a *i.e.*, his own judgement.

How much more courageous was Alexander ! After
reading a letter from his mother warning him to
beware of poison from his physician Philip, he took
the draught and drank it without alarm. In the
case of his own friend he trusted himself [a] more. He
deserved to find him innocent, deserved to prove
him so ! I applaud this all the more in Alexander
because no man was so prone to anger ; but the
rarer self-control is among kings, the more praiseworthy it becomes. The great Gaius Caesar also
showed this, he who, victorious in civil war, used his
victory most mercifully ; having apprehended some
packets of letters written to Gnaeus Pompeius by those
who were believed to belong either to the opposing
side or to the neutral party, he burned them. Although he was in the habit, within bounds, of indulging in anger, yet he preferred being unable to do so ;
he thought that the most gracious form of pardon
was not to know what the offence of each person had
been.

Credulity is a source of very great mischief.
Often one should not even listen to report, since
under some circumstances it is better to be deceived
than to be suspicious. Suspicion and surmise—
provocations that are most deceptive—ought to be
banished from the mind. " That man did not give
me a civil greeting ; that one did not return my
kiss ; that one broke off the conversation abruptly ;
that one did not invite me to dinner ; that one
seemed to avoid seeing me." Pretext for suspicion
will not be lacking. But there is need of frankness
and generosity in interpreting things. We should
believe only what is thrust under our eyes and
becomes unmistakable, and every time our suspicion

apparuerit, obiurgemus credulitatem ; haec enim
castigatio consuetudinem efficiet non facile credendi.

1 25. Inde et illud sequitur, ut minimis sordi-
dissimisque rebus non exacerbemur. Parum agilis
est puer aut tepidior aqua poturo aut turbatus torus
aut mensa neglegentius posita—ad ista concitari
insania est. Aeger et infelicis valetudinis est quem
levis aura contraxit, adfecti oculi quos candida vestis
obturbat, dissolutus deliciis cuius latus alieno labore
2 condoluit. Mindyriden aiunt fuisse ex Sybaritarum
civitate, qui cum vidisset fodientem et altius rastrum
adlevantem, lassum se fieri questus vetuit illum opus
in conspectu suo facere ; idem habere se peius
questus est, quod foliis rosae duplicatis incubuisset.
3 Ubi animum simul et corpus voluptates corrupere,
nihil tolerabile videtur, non quia dura, sed quia
mollis patitur. Quid est enim, cur tussis alicuius
aut sternutamentum aut musca parum curiose fugata
in rabiem agat aut obversatus canis aut clavis ne-
4 glegentis servi manibus elapsa ? Feret iste aequo
animo civile convicium et ingesta in contione curiave
maledicta, cuius aures tracti subsellii stridor offendit ? Perpetietur hic famem et aestivae expeditio-
nis sitim, qui puero male diluenti nivem irascitur ?

---

^a Wine was often drunk mixed with hot water ; *cf.* Mart.
i. 11. 3.

proves to be groundless we should chide our credulity; for this self-reproof will develop the habit of being slow to believe.

Next, too, comes this—that we should not be exasperated by trifling and paltry incidents. A slave is too slow, or the water for the wine[a] is lukewarm, or the couch-cushion disarranged, or the table too carelessly set—it is madness to be incensed by such things. The man is ill or in a poor state of health who shrinks from a slight draught; something is wrong with a man's eyes if they are offended by white clothing; the man is enfeebled by soft living who gets a pain in his side from seeing somebody else at work! The story is that there was once a citizen of Sybaris, a certain Mindyrides, who, seeing a man digging and swinging his mattock on high, complained that it made him weary and ordered the man not to do such work in his sight; the same man complained that he felt worse because the rose-leaves upon which he had lain were crumpled! When pleasures have corrupted both mind and body, nothing seems to be tolerable, not because the suffering is hard, but because the sufferer is soft. For why is it that we are thrown into a rage by somebody's cough or sneeze, by negligence in chasing a fly away, by a dog's hanging around, or by the dropping of a key that has slipped from the hands of a careless servant? The poor wretch whose ears are hurt by the grating of a bench dragged across the floor—will he be able to bear with equanimity the strife of public life and the abuse rained down upon him in the assembly or in the senate-house? Will he be able to endure the hunger and the thirst of a summer campaign who gets angry at his slave for being careless in mixing

Nulla itaque res magis iracundiam alit quam luxuria intemperans et impatiens ; dure tractandus animus est, ut ictum non sentiat nisi gravem.

1   26. Irascimur aut iis, a quibus ne accipere quidem potuimus iniuriam, aut iis, a quibus accipere in-
2 iuriam potuimus.   Ex prioribus quaedam sine sensu sunt, ut liber, quem minutioribus litteris scriptum saepe proiecimus et mendosum laceravimus, ut vestimenta, quae, quia displicebant, scidimus.   His irasci quam stultum est, quae iram nostram nec meruerunt
3 nec sentiunt !   " Sed offendunt nos videlicet qui illa fecerunt."   Primum saepe antequam hos apud nos distinguamus irascimur.   Deinde fortasse ipsi quoque artifices excusationes iustas afferent.   Alius non potuit melius facere quam fecit, nec ad tuam contumeliam parum didicit ; alius non in hoc ut te offenderet fecit.   Ad ultimum quid est dementius quam bilem in homines collectam in res effundere ?
4 Atqui ut his irasci dementis est, quae anima carent, sic mutis animalibus, quae nullam iniuriam nobis faciunt, quia velle non possunt ; non est enim iniuria nisi a consilio profecta.   Nocere itaque nobis possunt ut ferrum aut lapis, iniuriam quidem facere non
5 possunt. Atqui contemni se quidam putant, ubi idem equi obsequentes alteri equiti, alteri contumaces sunt, tamquam iudicio, non consuetudine

---

ᵃ *i.e.*, with the wine.

the snow [a] ? Nothing, therefore, is more conducive to anger than the intemperance and intolerance that comes from soft living ; the mind ought to be schooled by hardship to feel none but a crushing blow.

Our anger is stirred either by those from whom we could not have received any injury at all, or by those from whom we might have received one. To the former class belong certain inanimate things, such as the manuscript which we often hurl from us because it is written in too small a script or tear up because it is full of mistakes, or the articles of clothing which we pull to pieces because we do not like them. But how foolish it is to get angry at these things which neither deserve our wrath nor feel it ! " But of course," you say, " it is those who made them who have given us the affront." But, in the first place, we often get angry before we make this distinction clear to our minds ; in the second place, perhaps also the makers themselves will have reasonable excuses to offer : this one could not do better work than he did, and it was not out of disrespect for you that he was poor at his trade ; another did not aim to affront you by what he did. In the end what can be madder than to accumulate spleen against men and then vent it upon things ? But as it is the act of a madman to become angry at things without life, it is not less mad to be angry at dumb animals, which do us no injury because they cannot will to do so ; for there can be no injury unless it arises from design. Therefore they can harm us just as the sword or a stone may do, but they cannot injure us. But some people think that a man is insulted when the same horses which are submissive to one rider are rebellious toward another, just as if it were due to the animal's

et arte tractandi quaedam quibusdam subiectiora
6 sint. Atqui ut his irasci stultum est, ita pueris et
non multum a puerorum prudentia distantibus;
omnia enim ista peccata apud aequum iudicem pro
innocentia habent imprudentiam.

1 27. Quaedam sunt quae nocere non possunt
nullamque vim nisi beneficam et salutarem habent,
ut di immortales, qui nec volunt obesse nec possunt;
natura enim illis mitis et placida est, tam longe re-
2 mota ab aliena iniuria quam a sua. Dementes itaque
et ignari veritatis illis imputant saevitiam maris,
immodicos imbres, pertinaciam hiemis, cum interim
nihil horum quae nobis nocent prosuntque ad nos
proprie derigatur. Non enim nos causa mundo
sumus hiemem aestatemque referendi; suas ista
leges habent, quibus divina exercentur. Nimis nos
suspicimus, si digni nobis videmur propter quos tanta
moveantur. Nihil ergo horum in nostram iniuriam
3 fit, immo contra nihil non ad salutem. Quaedam
esse diximus quae nocere non possint, quaedam quae
nolint. In iis erunt boni magistratus parentesque
et praeceptores et iudices, quorum castigatio sic
accipienda est quomodo scalpellum et abstinentia
4 et alia quae profutura torquent. Affecti sumus

choice and not rather to the rider's practised skill in management that certain animals prove more tractable to certain men. But it is as foolish to be angry with these as it is to be angry with children and all who are not much different from children in point of wisdom ; for in the eyes of a just judge all such mistakes can plead ignorance as the equivalent of innocence.

But there are certain agents that are unable to harm us and have no power that is not beneficent and salutary, as, for example, the immortal gods, who neither wish nor are able to hurt ; for they are by nature mild and gentle, as incapable of injuring others as of injuring themselves. Those, therefore, are mad and ignorant of truth who lay to the gods' charge the cruelty of the sea, excessive rains, and the stubbornness of winter, whereas all the while none of the phenomena which harm or help us are planned personally for us. For it is not because of us that the universe brings back winter and summer ; these have their own laws, by which the divine plan operates. We have too high a regard for ourselves if we deem ourselves worthy to be the cause of such mighty movements. Therefore none of these phenomena takes place for the purpose of injuring us, nay, on the contrary, they all tend toward our benefit. I have said that there are certain agents that cannot, certain ones that would not, harm us. To the latter class will belong good magistrates and parents, teachers and judges, and we ought to submit to the chastening they give in the same spirit in which we submit to the surgeon's knife, a regimen of diet, and other things which cause suffering that they may bring profit. We have been visited with

poena ; succurrat non tantum quid patiamur, sed
quid fecerimus, in consilium de vita nostra mittamur ;
si modo verum ipsi nobis dicere voluerimus, pluris
litem nostram aestimabimus.

1   28. Si volumus aequi rerum omnium iudices esse,
hoc primum nobis persuadeamus, neminem nostrum
esse sine culpa ; hinc enim maxima indignatio
oritur : " Nihil peccavi " et " nihil feci." Immo
nihil fateris ! Indignamur aliqua admonitione aut
coercitione nos castigatos, cum illo ipso tempore
peccemus, quod adicimus malefactis adrogantiam
2 et contumaciam. Quis est iste qui se profitetur
omnibus legibus innocentem ? Ut hoc ita sit, quam
angusta innocentia est ad legem bonum esse !
Quanto latius officiorum patet quam iuris regula !
Quam multa pietas, humanitas, liberalitas, iustitia,
fides exigunt, quae omnia extra publicas tabulas
3 sunt ! Sed ne ad illam quidem artissimam innocentiae formulam praestare nos possumus. Alia
fecimus, alia cogitavimus, alia optavimus, aliis
favimus ; in quibusdam innocentes sumus, quia non
4 successit. Hoc cogitantes aequiores simus delin-
quentibus, credamus obiurgantibus ; utique bonis
ne irascamur (cui enim non, si bonis quoque ?),
minime diis ; non enim illorum vi,[1] sed lege mor-

----

[1] vi *added by Hermes.*

punishment; then let it bring up the thought, not so much of what we suffer, as of what we have done; let us summon ourselves to give a verdict upon our past life; if only we are willing to be frank with ourselves, we shall assess our fines at a still higher figure.

If we are willing in all matters to play the just judge, let us convince ourselves first of this—that no one of us is free from fault. For most of our indignation arises from our saying, "I am not to blame," "I have done nothing wrong." Say, rather, you admit nothing wrong! We chafe against the censure of some reprimand or chastisement although at the very time we are at fault because we are adding to wrong-doing arrogance and obstinacy. What man is there who can claim that in the eyes of every law he is innocent? But assuming that this may be, how limited is the innocence whose standard of virtue is the law! How much more comprehensive is the principle of duty than that of law! How many are the demands laid upon us by the sense of duty, humanity, generosity, justice, integrity—all of which lie outside the statute books! But even under that other exceedingly narrow definition of innocence we cannot vouch for our claim. Some sins we have committed, some we have contemplated, some we have desired, some we have encouraged; in the case of some we are innocent only because we did not succeed. Bearing this in mind, let us be more just to transgressors, more heedful to those who rebuke us; especially let us not be angry with the good (for who will escape if we are to be angry even with the good?), and least of all with the gods. For it is not by their power,

talitatis patimur quidquid incommodi accidit. " At morbi doloresque incurrunt." Utique aliquo defungendum est domicilium putre sortitis.

Dicetur aliquis male de te locutus; cogita an 5 prior feceris, cogita de quam multis loquaris. Cogitemus, inquam, alios non facere iniuriam sed reponere, alios pro nobis facere, alios coactos facere, alios ignorantes, etiam eos, qui volentes scientesque faciunt, ex iniuria nostra non ipsam iniuriam petere; aut dulcedine urbanitatis prolapsus est, aut fecit aliquid, non ut nobis obesset, sed quia consequi ipse non poterat, nisi nos repulisset; saepe adulatio, 6 dum blanditur, offendit. Quisquis ad se rettulerit, quotiens ipse in suspicionem falsam inciderit, quam multis officiis suis fortuna speciem iniuriae induerit, quam multos post odium amare coeperit, poterit non statim irasci, utique si sibi tacitus ad singula quibus offenditur dixerit: " Hoc et ipse commisi." 7 Sed ubi tam aequum iudicem invenies? Is qui nullius non uxorem concupiscit et satis iustas causas putat amandi, quod aliena est, idem uxorem suam aspici non vult; et fidei acerrimus exactor est perfidus, et mendacia persequitur ipse periurus, et litem sibi inferri aegerrime calumniator patitur; pudicitiam servulorum suorum adtemptari non vult

but by the terms of our mortality, that we are forced to suffer whatever ill befalls. " But," you say, " sickness and pain assail us." At any rate there must be an ending some time, seeing that we have been given a crumbling tenement !

It will be said that some one spoke ill of you ; consider whether you spoke ill of him first, consider how many there are of whom you speak ill. Let us consider, I say, that some are not doing us an injury but repaying one, that others are acting for our good, that some are acting under compulsion, others in ignorance, that even those who are acting intention- ally and wittingly do not, while injuring us, aim only at the injury ; one slipped into it allured by his wit, another did something, not to obstruct us, but because he could not reach his own goal without pushing us back; often adulation, while it flatters, offends. If any one will recall how often he himself has fallen under undeserved suspicion, how many of his good services chance has clothed with the appear- ance of injury, how many persons whom once he hated he learned to love, he will be able to avoid all hasty anger, particularly if as each offence occurs he will first say to himself in silence : " I myself have also been guilty of this." But where will you find a judge so just ? The man who covets everybody's wife and considers the mere fact that she belongs to another an ample and just excuse for loving her— this same man will not have his own wife looked at ; the strictest enforcer of loyalty is the traitor, the punisher of falsehood is himself a perjurer, and the trickster lawyer deeply resents an indictment being brought against himself ; the man who has no regard for his own chastity will permit no tampering with

8 qui non pepercit suae. Aliena vitia in oculis habemus, a tergo nostra sunt ; inde est quod tempestiva
filii convivia pater deterior filio castigat, et nihil
alienae luxuriae ignoscit qui nihil suae negavit, et
homicidae tyrannus irascitur, et punit furta sacrilegus.
Magna pars hominum est quae non peccatis irascitur
sed peccantibus. Faciet nos moderatiores respectus
nostri, si consuluerimus nos : " Numquid et ipsi
aliquid tale commisimus ? Numquid sic erravimus ?
Expeditne nobis ista damnare ? "[a]

1   29. Maximum remedium irae mora est. Hoc ab
illa pete initio, non ut ignoscat, sed ut iudicet : graves
habet impetus primos ; desinet, si expectat. Nec
universam illam temptaveris tollere ; tota vincetur,
2 dum partibus carpitur. Ex is, quae nos offendunt,
alia renuntiantur nobis, alia ipsi audimus aut videmus.
De iis, quae narrata sunt, non debemus cito credere ;
multi mentiuntur, ut decipiant, multi, quia decepti
sunt. Alius criminatione gratiam captat et fingit
iniuriam, ut videatur doluisse factam ; est aliquis
malignus et qui amicitias cohaerentis diducere velit ;
est subdicax[1] et qui spectare ludos cupiat et ex
3 longinquo tutoque speculetur quos conlisit. De
parvola summa iudicaturo tibi res sine teste non
probaretur, testis sine iureiurando non valeret,

---

[1] subdicax *Badstübner* : subprocax *Lipsius* : suspicax *AL*.

[a] *Cf.* Catullus, xxii. 20 *sq.* :
        suus cuique attributus est error :
    sed non videmus manticae quod in tergo est.

that of his slaves. The vices of others we keep before our eyes, our own behind our back[a]; hence it happens that a father who is even worse than his son rebukes his son's untimely revels, that a man does not pardon another's excesses who sets no bound to his own, that the murderer stirs a tyrant's wrath, and the temple-robber punishes theft. It is not with the sins but with the sinners that most men are angry. We shall become more tolerant from self-inspection if we cause ourselves to consider : " Have we ourselves never been guilty of such an act ? Have we never made the same mistake ? Is it expedient for us to condemn such conduct ? "

The best corrective of anger lies in delay. Beg this concession from anger at the first, not in order that it may pardon, but in order that it may judge. Its first assaults are heavy ; it will leave off if it waits. And do not try to destroy it all at once ; attacked piecemeal, it will be completely conquered. Of the things which offend us some are reported to us, others we ourselves hear or see. As to what is told us, we should not be quick to believe ; many falsify in order that they may deceive ; many others, because they themselves are deceived. One courts our favour by making an accusation and invents an injury in order to show that he regrets the occurrence ; then there is the man who is spiteful and wishes to break up binding friendships, and the one who is sharp-tongued and, eager to see the sport, watches from a safe distance the friends whom he has brought to blows. If the question of even a small payment should come before you to be judged, you would require a witness to prove the claim, the witness would have no weight except on oath, you

utrique parti dares actionem, dares tempus, non semel audires ; magis enim veritas elucet quo saepius ad manum venit. Amicum condemnas de praesentibus ? Antequam audias, antequam interroges, antequam illi aut accusatorem suum nosse liceat aut crimen, irasceris ? Iam enim, iam 4 utrimque quid diceretur audisti ? Hic ipse, qui ad te detulit, desinet dicere, si probare debuerit. " Non est," inquit, " quod me protrahas ; ego productus negabo ; alioqui nihil umquam tibi dicam." Eodem tempore et instigat et ipse se certamini pugnaeque subtrahit. Qui dicere tibi nisi clam non vult, paene non dicit. Quid est iniquius quam secreto credere, palam irasci ?

1 30. Quorundam ipsi testes sumus ; in his naturam excutiemus voluntatemque facientium. Puer est ; aetati donetur, nescit an peccet. Pater est ; aut tantum profuit, ut illi etiam iniuriae ius sit, aut fortasse ipsum hoc meritum eius est quo offendimur. Mulier est ; errat. Iussus est ; necessitati quis nisi iniquus suscenset ? Laesus est ; non est iniuria pati quod prior feceris. Iudex est ; plus credas illius sententiae quam tuae. Rex est ; si nocentem punit,

would grant to both parties the right of process,
you would allow them time, you would give more
than one hearing ; for the oftener you come to
close quarters with truth, the more it becomes
manifest. Do you condemn a friend on the spot ?
Will you be angry with him before you hear his side,
before you question him, before he has a chance to
know either his accuser or the charge ? What, have
you already heard what is to be said on both sides ?
The man who gave you the information will of his
own accord stop talking if he is forced to prove what
he says. " No need to drag me forward," he says ; " if
I am brought forward I shall make denial ; otherwise, I shall never tell you anything." At one and
the same time he both goads you on and withdraws
himself from the strife and the battle. The man
who is unwilling to tell you anything except in
secret has, we may almost say, nothing to tell. What
is more unfair than to give credence secretly but to
be angry openly ?

To some offences we can bear witness ourselves ;
in such cases we shall search into the character and
the purpose of the offender. Does a child offend ?
Excuse should be made for his age—he does not
know what is wrong. A father ? Either ·he has
been so good to us that he has the right even to
injure us, or mayhap the very act which offends us
is really a service. A woman ? It was a blunder.
Some one under orders ? What fair-minded person
chafes against the inevitable ? Some one who has been
wronged ? There is no injustice in your having to
submit to that which you were the first to inflict.
Is it a judge ? You should trust his opinion more
than your own. Is it a king ? If he punishes you

2 cede iustitiae, si innocentem, cede fortunae. Mutum
animal est aut simile muto; imitaris illud, si irasceris.
Morbus est aut calamitas; levius transiliet sus-
tinentem. Deus est; tam perdis operam cum illi
irasceris, quam cum illum alteri precaris iratum.
Bonus vir est qui iniuriam fecit; noli credere.
Malus; noli mirari; dabit poenas alteri quas debet
tibi, et iam sibi dedit qui peccavit.

1 31. Duo sunt, ut dixi, quae iracundiam concitent:
primum, si iniuriam videmur accepisse—de hoc satis
dictum est; deinde, si inique accepisse—de hoc
dicendum est. Iniqua quaedam iudicant homines,
quia pati non debuerint, quaedam, quia non spera-
verint. Indigna putamus quae inopinata sunt;
2 itaque maxime commovent, quae contra spem ex-
pectationemque evenerunt, nec aliud est quare in
domesticis minima offendant, in amicis iniuriam
3 vocemus neglegentiam. "Quomodo ergo," inquit,
"inimicorum nos iniuriae movent?" Quia non ex-
pectavimus illas aut certe non tantas. Hoc efficit
amor nostri nimius. Inviolatos nos etiam inimicis
iudicamus esse debere; regis quisque intra se animum
4 habet, ut licentiam sibi dari velit, in se nolit. Itaque
nos aut insolentia iracundos facit aut ignorantia
rerum; quid enim mirum est malos mala facinora

when you are guilty, submit to justice, if when you
are innocent, submit to fortune. A dumb animal
perhaps, or something just as dumb? You become
like it if you get angry. Is it a sickness or a misfortune? It will pass by more lightly if you bear
up under it. Is it God? You waste your pains
when you become angry with him as much as when
you pray him to be angry with another. Is it a good
man who has done you injury? Do not believe it.
A bad man? Do not be surprised; he will suffer
from another the punishment which is due from you,
and he who has sinned has already punished himself.

There are, as I have said, two conditions under
which anger is aroused: first, if we think that we
have received an injury—about this enough has been
said; second, if we think that we have received it
unjustly—about this something must now be said.
Men judge some happenings to be unjust because
they did not deserve them, some merely because
they did not expect them. What is unexpected we
count undeserved. And so we are mightily stirred
by all that happens contrary to hope and expectation,
and this is the only reason why in domestic affairs we
are vexed by trifles, why in the case of friends we call
neglect a wrong. "Why, then," you query, "do
the wrongs done by our enemies stir us?" Because
we did not expect them, or at any rate not wrongs
so serious. This, in turn, is due to excessive self-
love. We decide that we ought not to be harmed
even by our enemies; each one in his heart has
the king's point of view, and is willing to use licence,
but unwilling to suffer from it. And so it is either
arrogance or ignorance that makes us prone to
anger; for what is there surprising in wicked men's

233

edere ? Quid novi est, si inimicus nocet, amicus
offendit, filius labitur, servus peccat ? Turpissimam
aiebat Fabius imperatori excusationem esse : " Non
putavi," ego turpissimam homini puto. Omnia puta,
expecta ; etiam in bonis moribus aliquid exsistet
5 asperius. Fert humana natura insidiosos animos,
fert ingratos, fert cupidos, fert impios. Cum de
unius moribus iudicabis, de publicis cogita.

Ubi maxime gaudebis, maxime metues. Ubi
tranquilla tibi omnia videntur, ibi nocitura non
desunt sed quiescunt. Semper futurum aliquid
quod te offendat existima. Gubernator numquam
ita totos sinus securus explicuit, ut non expedite
6 ad contrahendum armamenta disponeret. Illud
ante omnia cogita, foedam esse et exsecrabilem vim
nocendi et alienissimam homini, cuius beneficio etiam
saeva mansuescunt. Aspice elephantorum iugo
colla summissa et taurorum pueris pariter ac feminis
persultantibus terga impune calcata et repentis inter
pocula sinusque innoxio lapsu dracones et intra
domum ursorum leonumque ora placida tractantibus
adulantisque dominum feras; pudebit cum anima-
7 libus permutasse mores. Nefas est nocere patriae ;
ergo civi quoque, nam hic pars patriae est—sanctae
partes sunt, si universum venerabile est,—ergo et
homini, nam hic in maiore tibi urbe civis est. Quid

---

^a Cf. Pliny, Nat. Hist. viii. 2. 4 : " Romae iuncti primum
subiere currum Pompei Magni Africano triumpho."

^b Cf. Martial v. 31. 1-4 :

> aspice quam placidis insultet turba iuvencis
> et sua quam facilis pondera taurus amet ;
> cornibus hic pendet summis, vagus ille per armos
> currit et in toto ventilat arma bove.

^c i.e., by letting anger turn us into brutes, which are
naturally fierce.

practising wicked deeds ? Why is it strange if an enemy injures us, a friend offends us, a son errs, or a servant blunders ? Fabius used to say that the excuse, " I did not think," was the one most shameful for a commander ; I think it most shameful for any man. Think of everything, expect everything ; even in good characters some unevenness will appear. Human nature begets hearts that are deceitful, that are ungrateful, that are covetous, that are undutiful. When you are about to pass judgement on one single man's character, reflect upon the general mass.

When you are about to rejoice most, you will have most to fear. When everything seems to you to be peaceful, the forces that will harm are not non-existent, but inactive. Always believe that there will come some blow to strike you. No skipper is ever so reckless as to unfurl all his canvas without having his tackle in order for quickly shortening sail. Above all, bear this in mind, that the power of injury is vile and detestable and most unnatural for man, by whose kindness even fierce beasts are tamed. Look how elephants ^a submit their necks to the yoke, how boys and women alike leap upon bulls ^b and tread their backs unhurt, how serpents crawl in harmless course among our cups and over our laps, how gentle are the faces of bears and lions when their trainers are inside their cages, and how wild beasts fawn upon their keeper—we shall blush to have ex-changed characters with the beasts ^c! To injure one's country is a crime ; consequently, also, to injure a fellow-citizen—for he is a part of the country, and if we reverence the whole, the parts are sacred—con-sequently to injure any man is a crime, for he is your fellow-citizen in the greater commonwealth. What

235

si nocere velint manus pedibus, manibus oculi?
Ut omnia inter se membra consentiunt, quia singula
servari totius interest, ita homines singulis parcent,
quia ad coetum geniti sunt, salva autem esse societas
8 nisi custodia et amore partium non potest. Ne
viperas quidem et natrices, et si qua morsu aut ictu
nocent, effligeremus, si in reliquum mansuefacere
possemus aut efficere, ne nobis aliisve periculo essent.
Ergo ne homini quidem nocebimus, quia peccavit,
sed ne peccet, nec umquam ad praeteritum, sed ad
futurum poena referetur; non enim irascitur, sed
cavet. Nam si puniendus est cuicumque pravum
maleficumque ingenium est, poena neminem excipiet.
1 32. "At enim ira habet aliquam voluptatem et
dulce est dolorem reddere." Minime; non enim ut
in beneficiis honestum est merita meritis repensare,
ita iniurias iniuriis. Illic vinci turpe est, hic vincere.
Inhumanum verbum est et quidem pro iusto receptum ultio, et talio non multum differt[1] nisi ordine;
qui dolorem regerit tantum excusatius peccat.
2 M. Catonem ignorans[2] in balineo quidam percussit
imprudens; quis enim illi sciens faceret iniuriam?
Postea satis facienti Cato: "Non memini," inquit,

---

[1] et quidem . . . differt *AL*: ultio et *deleted by most
editors*: et vitiose quidem pro iusto receptum, talio. *proposed by Gertz*: et quidem pro iusta receptum ultione
"talio." Non multum differt nisi ordine, qui dolorem
regerit: *P. Thomas*.
[2] ignorans *most editors consider a gloss on* imprudens.

---

[a] In the code of the XII. Tables *talio* is the Mosaic "an
eye for an eye," and *ultio* (*dolorem reg. rere*), says Seneca,
is merely a more excusable form of this savage law,

if the hands should desire to harm the feet, or the eyes the hands? As all the members of the body are in harmony one with another because it is to the advantage of the whole that the individual members be unharmed, so mankind should spare the individual man, because all are born for a life of fellowship, and society can be kept unharmed only by the mutual protection and love of its parts. We would not crush even a viper or a water-snake or any other creature that harms by bite or sting if we could make them kindly in future, or keep them from being a source of danger to ourselves and others. Neither, therefore, shall we injure a man because he has done wrong, but in order to keep him from doing wrong, and his punishment shall never look to the past, but always to the future; for that course is not anger, but precaution. For if every one whose nature is evil and depraved must be punished, punishment will exempt no one.

"But of course there is some pleasure in anger," you say, "and it is sweet to return a smart." Not at all; for it is not honourable, as in acts of kindness to requite benefits with benefits, so to requite injuries with injuries. In the one case it is shameful to be outdone, in the other not to be outdone. "Revenge" is an inhuman word and yet one accepted as legitimate, and "retaliation" is not much different except in rank; the man who returns a smart commits merely the more pardonable sin.[a] Once when Marcus Cato was in the public bath, a certain man, not knowing him, struck him unwittingly; for who would knowingly have done injury to that great man? Later, when the man was making apology, Cato said, "I do not recall that I received

"me percussum." Melius putavit non agnoscere
3 quam vindicare. "Nihil," inquis, "illi post tantam
petulantiam mali factum est?" Immo multum
boni; coepit Catonem nosse. Magni animi est
iniurias despicere; ultionis contumeliosissimum genus
est non esse visum dignum, ex quo peteretur ultio.
Multi leves iniurias altius sibi demisere, dum vindicant. Ille magnus et nobilis, qui more magnae
ferae latratus minutorum canum securus exaudit.

1   33. "Minus," inquit, "contemnemur, si vindi-
caverimus iniuriam." Si tamquam ad remedium
venimus, sine ira veniamus, non quasi dulce sit
vindicari, sed quasi utile; saepe autem satius fuit
dissimulare quam ulcisci. Potentiorum iniuriae
hilari vultu, non patienter tantum ferendae sunt;
facient iterum, si se fecisse crediderint. Hoc habent
pessimum animi magna fortuna insolentes: quos
2 laeserunt et oderunt. Notissima vox est eius qui
in cultu regum consenuerat. Cum illum quidam
interrogaret, quomodo rarissimam rem in aula con-
secutus esset, senectutem: "Iniurias," inquit, "ac-
cipiendo et gratias agendo." Saepe adeo iniuriam
vindicare non expedit, ut ne fateri quidem expediat.
3 C. Caesar Pastoris splendidi equitis Romani filium
cum in custodia habuisset munditiis eius et cul-

a blow." It was better, he thought, to ignore the incident than to resent it. "Then the fellow," you ask, "got no punishment for such an act of rudeness?" No, but much good—he began to know Cato. Only a great soul can be superior to injury; the most humiliating kind of revenge is to have it appear that the man was not worth taking revenge upon. Many have taken slight injuries too deeply to heart in the act of revenging them. He is a great and noble man who acts as does the lordly wild beast that listens unconcernedly to the baying of tiny dogs.

"If we avenge an injury," you say, "we shall be less subject to contempt." If we must resort to a remedy, as it were, for contempt, let us do so without anger—not with the plea that revenge is sweet, but that it is expedient; it is often, however, better to feign ignorance of an act than to take vengeance for it. Injuries from the more powerful must be borne, not merely with submission, but even with a cheerful countenance; they will repeat the offence if they are convinced that they have succeeded once. Men whose spirit has grown arrogant from the great favour of fortune have this most serious fault—those whom they have injured they also hate. The words of the man who had grown old in doing homage to kings are familiar to all. When some one asked him how he had attained what was so rarely achieved at court, namely old age, he replied, "By accepting injuries and returning thanks for them." So far from its being expedient to avenge injuries, it is often inexpedient even to acknowledge them. Gaius Caesar, offended with the son of Pastor, a distinguished Roman knight, because of his foppishness and his too elaborately dressed hair, sent him to

tioribus capillis offensus, rogante patre ut salutem
sibi filii concederet, quasi de supplicio admonitus
duci protinus iussit; ne tamen omnia inhumane
faceret adversum patrem, ad cenam illum eo die
4 invitavit. Venit Pastor vultu nihil exprobrante.
Propinavit illi Caesar heminam et posuit illi custodem;
perduravit miser, non aliter quam si fili sanguinem
biberet. Unguentum et coronas misit et observare
iussit an sumeret; sumpsit. Eo die, quo filium
extulerat, immo quo non extulerat, iacebat conviva
centesimus et potiones vix honestas natalibus liberorum podagricus senex hauriebat, cum interim non
lacrimam emisit, non dolorem aliquo signo erumpere
passus est; cenavit tamquam pro filio exorasset.
5 Quaeris, quare? Habebat alterum. Quid ille
Priamus? Non dissimulavit iram et regis genua
complexus est, funestam perfusamque cruore fili
manum ad os suum retulit, cenavit? Sed tamen
sine unguento, sine coronis, et illum hostis saevis-
simus multis solaciis, ut cibum caperet, hortatus est,
non ut pocula ingentia super caput posito custode
6 siccaret. Contempsisses[1] Romanum patrem, si sibi
timuisset; nunc iram compescuit pietas. Dignus
fuit cui permitteretur a convivio ad ossa fili legenda

---

[1] contempsisses *Hermes, after Gertz* : contempsisset *AL.*

---

[a] *Cf. Iliad*, xxiv. 477-479, for the incident. Achilles had
slain Hector, and Priam, a suppliant in the lodge of the
victor, now seeks to ransom the body of his son.

prison ; when the father begged that his son's life might be spared, Caesar, just as if he had been reminded to punish him, ordered him to be executed forthwith ; yet in order not to be wholly brutal to the father, he invited him to dine with him that day. Pastor actually came and showed no reproach in his countenance. Caesar, taking a cup, proposed his health and set some one to watch him ; the poor wretch went through with it, although he seemed to be drinking the blood of his son. Caesar then sent him perfume and garlands of flowers and gave orders to watch whether he used them : he used them. On the very day on which he had buried—no, before he had yet buried—his son, he took his place among a hundred dinner-guests, and, old and gouty as he was, drained a draught of wine that would scarce have been a seemly potion even on the birthday of one of his children, all the while shedding not a single tear nor by any sign suffering his grief to be revealed ; at the dinner he acted as if he had obtained the pardon he had sought for his son. Do you ask why ? He had a second son. And what did great Priam do ? Did he not disguise his anger and embrace the knees of the king ? Did he not carry to his lips the murderous hand all stained with the blood of his son ?[a] Did he not dine ? True, but there was no perfume for him, no garlands, and his bloodthirsty enemy with many soft words pressed him to take food, and did not force him to drain huge beakers while some one stood over him to watch. The Roman father you would have despised if his fears had been for himself ; as it was, affection curbed his anger. He deserved to be permitted to leave the banquet in order that he might gather up the bones of his son, but that

discedere ; ne hoc quidem permisit benignus interim
et comis adulescens ; propinationibus senem crebris,
ut cura leniretur admonens, lacessebat ; contra ille
se laetum et oblitum, quid eo actum esset die,
praestitit. Perierat alter filius, si carnifici conviva
non placuisset.

1   34. Ergo ira abstinendum est, sive par est qui
lacessendus est sive superior sive inferior. Cum
pare contendere anceps est, cum superiore furiosum,
cum inferiore sordidum. Pusilli hominis et miseri
est repetere mordentem. Mures formicaeque, si
manum admoveris, ora convertunt; imbecillia se
2 laedi putant, si tanguntur. Faciet nos mitiores, si
cogitaverimus, quid aliquando nobis profuerit ille
cui irascimur, et meritis offensa redimetur. Illud
quoque occurrat, quantum nobis commendationis
allatura sit clementiae fama, quam multos venia
3 amicos utiles fecerit. Ne irascamur inimicorum et
hostium liberis, inter Sullanae crudelitatis exempla
est, quod ab re publica liberos proscriptorum sub-
movit. Nihil est iniquius quam aliquem heredem
4 paterni odii fieri. Cogitemus, quotiens ad ignoscendum difficiles erimus, an expediat nobis omnes
inexorabiles esse. Quam saepe veniam qui negavit
petît ! Quam saepe eius pedibus advolutus est,
quem a suis reppulit ! Quid est gloriosius quam

stripling prince, all the while so kindly and polite, did not permit even this ; pledging the old man's health again and again, he tortured him by urging him to lighten his sorrow, while on the other hand the father made a show of being happy and oblivious of all that had been done that day. The other son was doomed, had the guest displeased the executioner.

We must, therefore, refrain from anger, whether he be an equal or a superior or an inferior who provokes its power. A contest with one's equal is hazardous, with a superior mad, with an inferior degrading. It is a petty and sorry person who will bite back when he is bitten. Mice and ants, if you bring your hand near them, do turn at you ; feeble creatures think they are hurt if they are only touched. It will make us more kindly if we remember the benefit we once received from him who now provokes our anger, and let his kindnesses atone for his offence. Let us also bear in mind how much approval we shall gain from a reputation for forbearance, how many have been made useful friends through forgiveness. From the examples of Sulla's cruelty comes the lesson that we should feel no anger toward the children of personal and political enemies, since he removed from the state even the children of the proscribed. There is no greater injustice than to make a man the inheritor of hatred borne toward his father. Whenever we are loth to pardon, let us consider whether we ourselves should benefit if all men were inexorable. How often has he who refused forgiveness sought it ! How often has he grovelled at the feet of the man whom he had repulsed from his own ! What is more splendid than to exchange

iram amicitia mutare? Quos populus Romanus
fideliores habet socios quam quos habuit pertina-
cissimos hostes? Quod hodie esset imperium, nisi
salubris providentia victos permiscuisset victoribus?
5 Irascetur aliquis; tu contra beneficiis provoca.
Cadit statim simultas ab altera parte deserta; nisi
paria non pugnant. Sed utrimque certabit ira,
concurritur, ille est melior qui prior pedem rettulit;
victus est qui vicit. Percussit te, recede; referiendo
enim et occasionem saepius feriendi dabis et excusationem; non poteris revelli, cum voles.

1 35. Numquid velit quisquam tam graviter hostem
ferire, ut relinquat manum in vulnere et se ab ictu
revocare non possit? Atqui tale ira telum est;
vix retrahitur. Arma nobis expedita prospicimus,
gladium commodum et habilem; non vitabimus
impetus animi istos[1] graves et onerosos et irre-
2 vocabiles? Ea demum velocitas placet, quae ubi
iussa est vestigium sistit nec ultra destinata pro-
currit flectique et a cursu ad gradum reduci potest;
aegros scimus nervos esse, ubi invitis nobis moventur;
senex aut infirmi corporis est, qui cum ambulare
vult currit. Animi motus eos putemus sanissimos
validissimosque, qui nostro arbitrio ibunt, non suo
ferentur.

3 Nihil tamen aeque profuerit quam primum intueri
deformitatem rei, deinde periculum. Non est ullius

---

[1] istos *Gertz*: . . . hos $A^1 A^5$.

anger for friendship? What more faithful allies does the Roman people possess than those who were once its most stubborn foes? Where would the empire be to-day had not a sound foresight united the victors and the vanquished into one? Does a man get angry? Do you on the contrary challenge him with kindness. Animosity, if abandoned by one side, forthwith dies; it takes two to make a fight. But if anger shall be rife on both sides, if the conflict comes, he is the better man who first withdraws; the vanquished is the one who wins. If some one strikes you, step back; for by striking back you will give him both the opportunity and the excuse to repeat his blow; when you later wish to extricate yourself, it will be impossible.

Would any one want to stab an enemy with such force as to leave his own hand in the wound and be unable to recover himself from the blow? But such a weapon is anger; it is hard to draw back. We take care to have light arms, a handy and nimble sword; shall we not avoid those mental outbursts that are clumsy, unwieldy, and beyond control? The only desirable speed is that which will check its pace when ordered, which will not rush past the appointed goal, and can be altered and reduced from running to a walk; when our muscles twitch against our will, we know that they are diseased; he who runs when he tries to walk is either old or broken in body. In the operations of the mind we should deem those to be the sanest and the soundest which will start at our pleasure, not rush on at their own.

Nothing, however, will prove as profitable as to consider first the hideousness of the thing, and then its danger. No other emotion has an outward aspect

adfectus facies turbatior ; pulcherrima ora foedavit,
torvos vultus ex tranquillissimis reddit ; linquit
decor omnis iratos, et sive amictus illis compositus
est ad legem, trahent vestem omnemque curam sui
effundent, sive capillorum natura vel arte iacentium
non informis habitus, cum animo inhorrescunt ;
tumescunt venae ; concutietur crebro spiritu pectus,
rabida vocis eruptio colla distendet ; tum artus
trepidi, inquietae manus, totius corporis fluctuatio.
4 Qualem intus putas esse animum, cuius extra imago
tam foeda est ? Quanto illi intra pectus terribilior
vultus est, acrior spiritus, intentior impetus, rupturus
5 se nisi eruperit ! Quales sunt hostium vel ferarum
caede madentium aut ad caedem euntium aspectus,
qualia poetae inferna monstra finxerunt succincta
serpentibus et igneo flatu, quales ad bella excitanda
discordiamque in populos dividendam pacemque
lacerandam teterrimae inferum exeunt : talem
nobis iram figuremus, flamma lumina ardentia,
sibilo mugituque et gemitu et stridore et si qua his
invisior vox est perstrepentem, tela manu utraque
quatientem (neque enim illi se tegere curae est),
torvam cruentamque et cicatricosam et verberibus
suis lividam, incessus vaesani, offusam multa caligine,
incursitantem, vastantem fugantemque et omnium
odio laborantem, sui maxime, si aliter nocere non
possit, terras, maria, caelum ruere cupientem,

so disordered : it makes ugly the most beautiful
faces ; through it the most peaceful countenance
becomes transformed and fierce ; from the angry all
grace departs ; if they were well-kempt and modish
in their dress, they will let their clothing trail and
cast off all regard for their person ; if their hair was
disposed by nature or by art in smooth and becoming
style, it bristles up in sympathy with their state of
mind ; the veins swell, the breast will be racked
by incessant panting, the neck will be distended
by the frantic outrush of the voice ; then the limbs
tremble, the hands are restless, the whole body is
agitated.   What state of mind, think you, lies within
when its outward manifestation is so horrible ?
Within the man's breast how much more terrible
must be the expression, how much fiercer the breathing, how much more violent the strain of his fury,
that would itself burst unless it found an outburst !
As is the aspect of an enemy or wild beasts wet with
the blood of slaughter or bent upon slaughter ; as are
the hellish monsters of the poet's brain, all girt about
with snakes and breathing fire ; as are those most
hideous shapes that issue forth from hell to stir up
wars and scatter discord among the peoples and
tear peace all to shreds ; as such let us picture anger—
its eyes aflame with fire, blustering with hiss and
roar and moan and shriek and every other noise
more hateful still if such there be, brandishing
weapons in both hands (for it cares naught for self-
protection !), fierce and bloody, scarred, and black
and blue from its own blows, wild in gait, enveloped
in deep darkness, madly charging, ravaging and routing, in travail with hatred of all men, especially of
itself, and ready to overturn earth and sea and sky

6 infestam pariter invisamque. Vel, si videtur, sit qualis apud vates nostros est :

> Sanguineum quatiens dextra Bellona flagellum,
> aut scissa gaudens vadit Discordia palla,

aut si qua magis dira facies excogitari diri adfectus potest.

1 36. Quibusdam, ut ait Sextius, iratis profuit aspexisse speculum ; perturbavit illos tanta mutatio sui ; velut in rem praesentem adducti non agnoverunt se. Et quantulum ex vera deformitate imago illa 2 speculo repercussa reddebat ? Animus si ostendi et si in ulla materia perlucere posset, intuentis nos confunderet ater maculosusque et aestuans et distortus et tumidus. Nunc quoque tanta deformitas eius est per ossa carnesque et tot impedimenta effluentis ; quid si nudus ostenderetur ? 3 Speculo quidem neminem deterritum ab ira credideris : quid ergo est[1] ? Qui ad speculum venerat, ut se mutaret, iam mutaverat ; iratis quidem nulla est formonsior effigies quam atrox et horrida, qualesque esse etiam videri volunt.

4 Magis illud videndum est, quam multis ira per se nocuerit. Alii nimio fervore rupere venas et sanguinem supra vires elatus clamor egessit et

---

[1] est *added by Gertz.*

---

a An adaptation of Virgil, *Aeneid*, viii. 702 *sq.* :
> Et scissa gaudens vadit Discordia palla,
> quam cum sanguineo sequitur Bellona flagello.

if it can find no other way to harm, equally hating and hated.   Or, if you will, let us take the picture from our poets :

> Flaunting her bloody scourge the War-dame strides,
> Or Discord glorying in her tattered robe.[a]

Or make you any other picture of this dread passion that can be devised still more dread.

As Sextius remarks, it has been good for some people to see themselves in a mirror while they are angry ;   the great change in themselves alarmed them ;   brought, as it were, face to face with the reality they did not recognize themselves.   And how little of the real ugliness did that image reflected in the mirror disclose !   If the soul could be shown, if it were in some substance through which it might shine, its black and mottled, inflamed, distorted and swollen appearance would confound us as we gazed upon it.   Even as it is, though it can only come to the surface through flesh, bones, and so many obstacles, its hideousness is thus great—what if it could be shown stark naked ?   You may perhaps think that no one has really been frightened out of anger by a mirror.   Well, what then ?   The man who had gone to the mirror in order to effect a change in himself was already a changed man ;   while men remain angry no image is more beautiful than one which is fierce and savage, and they wish also to look the sort they wish to be.

This, rather, is what we ought to realize—how many men anger in and of itself has injured.   Some through too much passion have burst their veins, a shout that strains our strength has carried with it blood, and too powerful a rush of tears to the eyes

luminum suffudit aciem in oculos vehementius umor
egestus et in morbos aegri reccidere.   Nulla celerior
5 ad insaniam via est.   Multi itaque continuaverunt
irae furorem nec quam expulerant mentem umquam
receperunt.   Aiacem in mortem egit furor, in
furorem ira.   Mortem liberis, egestatem sibi, ruinam
domui imprecantur et irasci se negant non minus
quam insanire furiosi.   Amicissimis hostes vitandique
carissimis, legum nisi qua nocent immemores, ad
minima mobiles, non sermone, non officio adiri faciles,
per vim omnia gerunt, gladiis et pugnare parati et
6 incumbere.   Maximum enim illos malum cepit et
omnia exsuperans vitia.   Alia paulatim intrant,
repentina et universa vis huius est.   Omnis denique
alios affectus sibi subicit.   Amorem ardentissimum
vincit, transfoderunt itaque amata corpora et in
eorum quos occiderant iacuere complexibus ; avaritiam, durissimum malum minimeque flexibile, ira
calcavit adactam[1] opes suas spargere et domui
rebusque in unum conlatis inicere ignem.   Quid ?
Non ambitiosus magno aestimata proiecit insignia
honoremque delatum reppulit ?   Nullus affectus est,
in quem non ira dominetur.

[1] adactam *Michaelis and Gertz* : adacta *A.*

---

[a] A reference to Ajax's act of self-destruction.

has blurred the sharpness of their vision, and sickly people have fallen back into illnesses. There is no quicker road to madness. Many, therefore, have continued in the frenzy of anger, and have never recovered the reason that had been unseated. It was frenzy that drove Ajax to his death and anger drove him into frenzy. These all call down death upon their children, poverty upon themselves, destruction upon their house, and they deny that they are angry just as the frenzied deny that they are mad. They become enemies to their closest friends and have to be shunned by those most dear; regardless of all law except as a means to injure, swayed by trifles, difficult to approach by either word or kindly act, they conduct themselves always with violence and are ready either to fight with the sword or to fall upon it.[a] For the fact is that the greatest of all evils, the vice that surpasses all others, has laid hold upon them. Other ills come gradually, but the power of this is sudden and complete. In short, it brings into subjection all other passions. It conquers the most ardent love, and so in anger men have stabbed the bodies that they loved and have lain in the arms of those whom they had slain ; avarice, the most stubborn and unbending evil, has been trodden under foot by anger after being forced to scatter her wealth and to set fire to her home and all her collected treasure. Tell me, has not also the ambitious man torn off the highly prized insignia of his office and rejected the honour that had been conferred ? There is no passion of any kind over which anger does not hold mastery.

LIBER V

AD NOVATVM

DE IRA

LIBER III

1 1. Quod maxime desiderasti, Novate, nunc facere temptabimus, iram excidere animis aut certe refrenare et impetus eius inhibere. Id aliquando palam aperteque faciendum est, ubi minor vis mali patitur, aliquando ex occulto, ubi nimium ardet omnique impedimento exasperatur et crescit; refert quantas vires quamque integras habeat, utrum reverberanda et agenda retro sit an cedere ei debeamus, dum tempestas prima desaevit, ne remedia ipsa secum ferat.

2 Consilium pro moribus cuiusque capiendum erit; quosdam enim preces vincunt; quidam insultant instantque summissis, quos terrendo placabimus; alios obiurgatio, alios confessio, alios pudor coepto deiecit, alios mora, lentum praecipitis mali remedium,

3 ad quod novissime descendendum est. Ceteri enim adfectus dilationem recipiunt et curari tardius

252

BOOK V

TO NOVATUS

ON ANGER

BOOK III

WE shall now, Novatus, attempt to do what you have especially desired—we shall try to banish anger from the mind, or at least to bridle and restrain its fury. This must be done sometimes plainly and openly, whenever a slighter attack of the malady makes this possible, sometimes secretly, when its flame burns hot and every obstacle but intensifies and increases its power; it depends upon how much strength and vigour it has whether we ought to beat back its attack and force a retreat, or should yield before it until the first storm of its fury has passed, in order to keep it from sweeping along with it the very means of relief.

Each man's character will have to determine his plan of action: some men yield to entreaty; some trample and stamp upon those who give way, and we shall quiet these by making them fear; some are turned from their course by reproof, others by a confession of guilt, others by shame, others by procrastination—a slow remedy, this last, for a swift disorder, to be used only as a last resort. For while the other passions admit of postponement and may

253

possunt, huius incitata et se ipsa rapiens violentia
non paulatim procedit sed, dum incipit, tota est;
nec aliorum more vitiorum sollicitat animos, sed
abducit et impotentes sui cupidosque vel communis
mali exagitat, nec in ea tantum in quae destinavit,
4 sed in occurrentia obiter[1] furit.   Cetera vitia impellunt animos, ira praecipitat. Etiam si resistere
contra affectus suos non licet, at certe affectibus
ipsis licet stare; haec non secus quam fulmina
procellaeque et si qua alia irrevocabilia sunt, quia
non eunt, sed cadunt, vim suam magis ac magis
5 intendit. Alia vitia a ratione, hoc a sanitate de-
sciscit; alia accessus lenes habent et incrementa
fallentia; in iram deiectus animorum est. Nulla
itaque res urget magis attonita et in vires suas prona
et, sive successit, superba, sive frustratur, insana;
ne repulsa quidem in taedium acta, ubi adversarium
fortuna subduxit, in se ipsa morsus suos vertit. Nec
refert quantum sit ex quo surrexerit; ex levissimis
enim in maxima evadit.

1   2. Nullam transit aetatem, nullum hominum genus
excipit. Quaedam gentes beneficio egestatis non
novere luxuriam; quaedam, quia exercitae et vagae
sunt, effugere pigritiam; quibus incultus mos
agrestisque vita est, circumscriptio ignota est et
fraus et quodcumque in foro malum nascitur. Nulla
gens est, quam non ira instiget, tam inter Graios

---

[1] obiter *A*[1] : ob iter *C. F. W. Müller.*

be cured more leisurely, this one in hurried and self-driven violence does not advance by slow degrees, but becomes full-grown the moment it begins; and, unlike the other vices, it does not seduce but abducts the mind, and it goads on those that, lacking all self-control, desire, if need be, the destruction of all, and its fury falls not merely upon the objects at which it aims, but upon all that meet it by the way. The other vices incite the mind, anger overthrows it. Even if a man may not resist his passions, yet at least the passions themselves may halt; anger intensifies its vehemence more and more, like the lightning's stroke, the hurricane, and the other things that are incapable of control for the reason that they not merely move, but fall. Other vices are a revolt against intelligence, this against sanity; the others approach gently and grow up unnoticed, but the mind plunges headlong into anger. Therefore no more frenzied state besets the mind, none more reliant upon its own power, none more arrogant if it is successful, none more insane if it is baffled; since it is not reduced to weariness even by defeat, if chance removes its foe it turns its teeth upon itself. And the source from which it springs need not be great; for rising from most trivial things it mounts to monstrous size.

It passes by no time of life, makes exception of no class of men. Some races by the blessing of poverty know nothing of luxury; some because they are restless and wandering have escaped sloth; the uncivilized state of some and their rustic mode of life keep them strangers to trickery and deception and all the evil that the forum breeds. But there lives no race that does not feel the goad of anger,

quam inter barbaros potens, non minus perniciosa
leges metuentibus quam quibus iura distinguit
2 modus virium. Denique cetera singulos corripiunt,
hic unus adfectus est, qui interdum publice con-
cipitur. Numquam populus universus feminae amore
flagravit, nec in pecuniam aut lucrum tota civitas
spem suam misit; ambitio viritim singulos occupat;
3 impotentia una est malum publicum. Saepe in iram
uno agmine itum est; viri feminae, senes pueri,
principes vulgusque consensere, et tota multitudo
paucissimis verbis concitata ipsum concitatorem
antecessit; ad arma protinus ignesque discursum
est et indicta finitimis bella aut gesta cum civibus;
4 totae cum stirpe omni crematae domus et modo
eloquio favorabili habitus in multo honore iram
suae contionis excepit; in imperatorem suum
legiones pila torserunt; dissedit plebs tota cum
patribus; publicum consilium senatus non expectatis
dilectibus nec nominato imperatore subitos irae suae
duces legit ac per tecta urbis nobiles consectatus
5 viros supplicium manu sumpsit; violatae legationes
rupto iure gentium rabiesque infanda civitatem tulit,
nec datum tempus, quo resideret tumor publicus,
sed deductae protinus classes et oneratae tumul-
tuario milite; sine more, sine auspiciis populus ductu
irae suae egressus fortuita raptaque pro armis gessit,

which masters alike both Greeks and barbarians, and
is no less ruinous to those who respect the law than
to those who make might the only measure of their
right. Lastly, though the other vices lay hold of
individual men, this is the only passion that can at
times possess a whole state. No entire people has
ever burned with love for a woman, no whole state
has set its hope upon money or gain; ambition is
personal and seizes upon the individual; only fury
is an affliction of a whole people. Often in a single
mass they rush into anger; men and women, old men
and boys, the gentry and the rabble, are all in full
accord, and the united body, inflamed by a very
few incendiary words, outdoes the incendiary himself;
they fly forthwith to fire and sword, and proclaim
war against their neighbours or wage it against their
countrymen; whole houses are consumed, root and
branch, and the man who but lately was held in high
esteem and applauded for his eloquence receives now
the anger of his following; legions hurl their javelins
upon their own commanders; all the commoners are
at discord with the nobles; the senate, the high
council of the state, without waiting to levy troops,
without appointing a commander, chooses impromptu
agents of its wrath, and hunting down its high-born
victims throughout the houses of the city, takes
punishment in its own hand; embassies are outraged,
the law of nations is broken, and unheard of madness
sweeps the state, and no time is given for the public
ferment to subside, but fleets are launched forthwith
and loaded with hastily gathered troops; without
training, without auspices, under the leadership of its
own anger, the populace goes forth, snatching up for
arms whatever chance has offered, and then atones

deinde magna clade temeritatem audacis irae luit.
6 Hic barbaris forte ruentibus in bella exitus est ;
cum mobiles animos species iniuriae perculit, aguntur
statim et qua dolor traxit ruinae modo legionibus
incidunt incompositi, interriti, incauti, pericula adpetentes sua ; gaudent feriri et instare ferro et tela
corpore urgere et per suum vulnus exire.

1   3. " Non est," inquis, " dubium, quin magna ista
et pestifera sit vis ; ideo quemadmodum sanari
debeat monstra." Atqui, ut in prioribus libris dixi,
stat Aristoteles defensor irae et vetat illam nobis
exsecari ; calcar ait esse virtutis, hac erepta inermem
animum et ad conatus magnos pigrum inertemque
2 fieri. Necessarium est itaque foeditatem eius ac
feritatem coarguere et ante oculos ponere quantum
monstri sit homo in hominem furens quantoque
impetu ruat non sine pernicie sua perniciosus et ea
deprimens, quae mergi nisi cum mergente non
3 possunt. Quid ergo ? Sanum hunc aliquis vocat,
qui velut tempestate correptus non it sed agitur et
furenti malo servit, nec mandat ultionem suam, sed
ipse eius exactor animo simul ac manu saevit caris-
simorum eorumque quae mox amissa fleturus est
4 carnifex ? Hunc aliquis affectum virtuti adiutorem

---

for the rash daring of its anger by a great disaster. Such is the outcome, when barbarians rush haphazard into war; the moment their excitable minds are roused by the semblance of injury, they are forthwith in action, and where their resentment draws them, like an avalanche they fall upon our legions—all unorganized, unfearful, and unguarded, seeking their own destruction; with joy they are struck down, or press forward upon the sword, or thrust their bodies upon the spear, or perish from a self-made wound.

"There can be no doubt," you say, "that such a force is powerful and pernicious; show, therefore, how it is to be cured." And yet, as I said in my earlier books,[a] Aristotle stands forth as the defender of anger, and forbids us to cut it out; it is, he claims, a spur to virtue, and if the mind is robbed of it, it becomes defenceless and grows sluggish and indifferent to high endeavour. Therefore our first necessity is to prove its foulness and fierceness, and to set before the eyes what an utter monster a man is when he is enraged against a fellow-man, with what fury he rushes on working destruction—destructive of himself as well and wrecking what cannot be sunk unless he sinks with it. Tell me, then, will any one call the man sane who, just as if seized by a hurricane, does not walk but is driven along, and is at the mercy of a raging demon, who entrusts not his revenge to another, but himself exacts it, and thus, bloodthirsty alike in purpose and in deed, becomes the murderer of those persons who are dearest and the destroyer of those things for which, when lost, he is destined ere long to weep? Can any one assign this passion to virtue as its supporter and consort

comitemque dat consilia, sine quibus virtus nihil
gerit, obturbantem ? Caducae sinistraeque sunt
vires et in malum suum validae, in quas aegrum
5 morbus et accessio erexit. Non est ergo quod me
putes tempus in supervacuis consumere, quod iram,
quasi dubiae apud homines opinionis sit, infamem,
cum sit aliquis et quidem de illustribus philosophis,
qui illi indicat operas et tamquam utilem ac spiritus
subministrantem in proelia, in actus rerum, ad
omne, quodcumque calore aliquo gerendum est,
6 vocet. Ne quem fallat tamquam aliquo tempore,
aliquo loco profutura, ostendenda est rabies eius
effrenata et attonita apparatusque illi reddendus
est suus, eculei et fidiculae et ergastula et cruces
et circumdati defossis corporibus ignes et cadavera
quoque trahens uncus, varia vinculorum genera,
varia poenarum, lacerationes membrorum, inscrip-
tiones frontis et bestiarum immanium caveae—inter
haec instrumenta collocetur ira dirum quiddam
atque horridum stridens, omnibus per quae furit
taetrior.

1   4. Ut de ceteris dubium sit, nulli certe adfectui
peior est vultus, quem in prioribus libris descrip-
simus : asperum et acrem et nunc subducto re-
trorsus sanguine fugatoque pallentem, nunc in os

---

a The course of the thought is : The question whether
anger is a good or an evil is not, as might be thought, so
clearly settled that further discussion of it is unnecessary ;
for so great a philosopher as Aristotle found anger commend-
able for certain purposes.
    b *Cf.* i. 1. 3-7.

when it confounds the resolves without which virtue accomplishes nothing ? Transient and baneful, and potent only for its own harm, is the strength which a sick man acquires from the rising of his fever. Therefore when I decry anger on the assumption that men are not agreed [a] in their estimate of it, you are not to think that I am wasting time on a superfluous matter ; for there is one, and he, too, a distinguished philosopher, who ascribes to it a function, and on the ground that it is useful and conducive to energy would evoke it for the needs of battle, for the business of state—for any undertaking, in fact, that requires some fervour for its accomplishment. To the end that no one may be deceived into supposing that at any time, in any place, it will be profitable, the unbridled and frenzied madness of anger must be exposed, and there must be restored to it the trappings that are its very own—the torture-horse, the cord, the jail, the cross, and fires encircling living bodies implanted in the ground, the drag-hook that seizes even corpses, and all the different kinds of chains and the different kinds of punishment, the rending of limbs, the branding of foreheads, the dens of frightful beasts—in the midst of these her implements let anger be placed, while she hisses forth her dread and hideous sounds, a creature more loathsome even than all the instruments through which she vents her rage.

Whatever doubt there may be concerning anger in other respects, there is surely no other passion whose countenance is worse—that countenance which we have pictured in the earlier books [b]—now harsh and fierce, now pale by reason of the backward flow and dispersing of the blood, now flushed

omni calore ac spiritu verso subrubicundum et
similem cruento, venis tumentibus, oculis nunc
trepidis et exsilientibus, nunc in uno obtutu defixis
2 et haerentibus ; adice dentium inter se arietatorum
ut aliquem esse cupientium non alium sonum quam
est apris tela sua adtritu acuentium ; adice articulorum crepitum, cum se ipsae manus frangunt, et
pulsatum saepius pectus, anhelitus crebros tractosque
altius gemitus, instabile corpus, incerta verba subitis
exclamationibus, trementia labra interdumque com-
3 pressa et dirum quiddam exsibilantia. Ferarum,
me hercules, sive illas fames agitat sive infixum
visceribus ferrum, minus taetra facies est, etiam
cum venatorem suum semianimes morsu ultimo
petunt, quam hominis ira flagrantis. Age, si exaudire
voces ac minas vacet, qualia excarnificati animi
4 verba sunt ! Nonne revocare se quisque ab ira volet,
cum intellexerit illam a suo primum malo incipere ?
Non vis ergo admoneam eos, qui iram summa potentia
exercent et argumentum virium existimant et in
magnis magnae fortunae bonis ponunt paratam
ultionem, quam non sit potens, immo ne liber quidem
5 dici possit irae suae captivus ? Non vis admoneam,
quo diligentior quisque sit et ipse se circumspiciat,
alia animi mala ad pessimos quosque pertinere,
iracundiam etiam eruditis hominibus et in alia sanis
inrepere ? Adeo ut quidam simplicitatis indicium

and seemingly steeped in blood when all the heat
and fire of the body has been turned toward the face,
with swollen veins, with eyes now restless and
darting, now fastened and motionless in one fixed
gaze ; mark, too, the sound of clashing teeth, as if
their owners were bent on devouring somebody, like
the noise the wild boar makes when he sharpens his
tusks by rubbing ; mark the crunching of the joints
as the hands are violently crushed together, the
constant beating of the breast, the quick breathing
and deep-drawn sighs, the unsteady body, the
broken speech and sudden outcries, the lips now
trembling, now tight and hissing out a curse. Wild
beasts, I swear, whether tormented by hunger or by
the steel that has pierced their vitals—even when,
half dead, they rush upon their hunter for one last
bite—are less hideous in appearance than a man
inflamed by anger. If you are free to listen to his
cries and threats, hear what language issues from
his tortured soul ! Will not every one be glad to
check any impulse to anger when he realizes that it
begins by working harm, first of all, to himself ? If
there are those who grant full sway to anger and
deem it a proof of power, who count the opportunity
of revenge among the great blessings of great estate,
would you not, then, have me remind them that a
man is not powerful—no, cannot even be called free—
if he is the captive of his anger ? To the end that
each one may be more careful and may set a guard
upon himself, would you not have me remind him
that while other base passions affect only the worst
type of men, wrath steals upon those also who are
enlightened and otherwise sane ? So true is this,
that there are some who call wrath a sign of in-

iracundiam dicant et vulgo credatur facillimus quisque huic obnoxius.

1   5. " Quorsus," inquis, " hoc pertinet ? " Ut nemo se iudicet tutum ab illa, cum lenes quoque natura et placidos in saevitiam ac violentiam evocet. Quemadmodum adversus pestilentiam nihil prodest firmitas corporis et diligens valetudinis cura—promiscue enim imbecilla robustaque invadit—, ita ab ira tam inquietis moribus periculum est quam compositis et remissis, quibus eo turpior ac periculosior est, quo
2 plus in illis mutat. Sed cum primum sit non irasci, secundum desinere, tertium alienae quoque irae mederi, dicam primum quemadmodum in iram non incidamus, deinde quemadmodum nos ab illa liberemus, novissime quemadmodum irascentem retineamus placemusque et ad sanitatem reducamus.

3   Ne irascamur praestabimus, si omnia vitia irae nobis subinde proposuerimus et illam bene aestimaverimus. Accusanda est apud nos, damnanda ; perscrutanda eius mala et in medium protrahenda sunt ; ut qualis sit appareat, comparanda cum
4 pessimis est. Avaritia adquirit et contrahit, quo aliquis melior utatur ; ira impendit, paucis gratuita est. Iracundus dominus quot in fugam servos egit, quot in mortem ! Quanto plus irascendo quam id erat, propter quod irascebatur, amisit ! Ira patri luctum, marito divortium attulit, magistratui odium,
5 candidato repulsam. Peior est quam luxuria, quoniam

---

[a] *Cf.* ii. 16. 3.

genuousness,[a] and that it is commonly believed that the best-natured people are most liable to it !

"What," you say, "is the purpose of this ?" That no man may consider himself safe from anger, since it summons even those who are naturally kind and gentle into acts of cruelty and violence. As soundness of body and a careful regard for health avail nothing against the plague—for it attacks indiscriminately the weak and the strong—so calm and languid natures are in no less danger from anger than the more excitable sort, and the greater the change it works in these, the greater is their disgrace and danger. But since the first requirement is not to become angry, the second, to cease from anger, the third, to cure also the anger of others, I shall speak first of how we may avoid falling into anger, next of how we may free ourselves from it, and lastly of how we may curb an angry man—how we may calm him and restore him to sanity.

We shall forestall the possibility of anger if we repeatedly set before ourselves its many faults and shall rightly appraise it. Before our own hearts we must arraign it and convict it ; we must search out its evils and drag them into the open ; in order that it may be shown as it really is, it should be compared with all that is worst. Man's avarice assembles and gathers wealth for some one who is better to use ; but anger is a spender—few indulge in it without cost. How many slaves a master's anger has driven to flight, how many to death ! How much more serious was his loss from indulging in anger than was the incident which caused it ! Anger brings to a father grief, to a husband divorce, to a magistrate hatred, to a candidate defeat. It is worse

illa sua voluptate fruitur, haec alieno dolore. Vincit
malignitatem et invidiam ; illae enim infelicem fieri
volunt, haec facere ; illae fortuitis malis delectantur,
haec non potest expectare fortunam—nocere ei
6 quem odit, non noceri vult. Nihil est simultatibus
gravius, has ira conciliat ; nihil est bello funestius,
in hoc potentium ira prorumpit ; ceterum etiam illa
plebeia ira et privata inerme et sine viribus bellum
est. Praeterea ira, ut seponamus, quae mox secutura
sunt, damna, insidias, perpetuam ex certaminibus
mutuis sollicitudinem, dat poenas dum exigit ;
naturam hominis eiurat : illa in amorem hortatur,
haec in odium ; illa prodesse iubet, haec nocere.
7 Adice quod, cum indignatio eius a nimio sui suspectu
veniat et animosa videatur, pusilla est et angusta ;
nemo enim non eo, a quo se contemptum iudicat,
minor est. At ille ingens animus et verus aestimator
8 sui non vindicat iniuriam, quia non sentit. Ut tela
a duro resiliunt et cum dolore caedentis solida feriuntur, ita nulla magnum animum iniuria ad sensum
sui adducit, fragilior eo quod petit. Quanto pulchrius velut nulli penetrabilem telo omnis iniurias
contumeliasque respuere ! Ultio doloris confessio
est ; non est magnus animus, quem incurvat iniuria.

than wantonness, since that finds satisfaction in its own enjoyment, this in another's pain. It exceeds spite and envy; for they desire a man to be unhappy, while anger tries to make him so; they delight in the ills that chance may bring, while it cannot wait for chance—to the man it hates it not merely wishes harm to come, but brings it. There is nothing more baleful than enmity, yet it is anger that breeds it; nothing is more deadly than war, yet in that the anger of the powerful finds its vent; none the less anger in the common folk or private persons is also war—war without arms and without resources. Moreover, leaving out of account the immediate consequences that will come from anger, such as losses of money, plots, and the never-ending anxiety of mutual strife, anger pays for the penalty it exacts—it renounces human nature, which incites to love, whereas it incites to hate; which bids us help, whereas it bids us injure. And besides, though its chafing originates in an excess of self-esteem and seems to be a show of spirit, it is petty and narrow-minded; for no man can fail to be inferior to the one by whom he regards himself despised. But the really great mind, the mind that has taken the true measure of itself, fails to revenge injury only because it fails to perceive it. As missiles rebound from a hard surface, and the man who strikes solid objects is hurt by the impact, so no injury whatever can cause a truly great mind to be aware of it, since the injury is more fragile than that at which it is aimed. How much more glorious it is for the mind, impervious, as it were, to any missile, to repel all insults and injuries! Revenge is the confession of a hurt; no mind is truly great that

Aut potentior te aut imbecillior laesit ; si imbecillior, parce illi, si potentior, tibi.

1   6. Nullum est argumentum magnitudinis certius quam nihil posse quo instigeris accidere. Pars superior mundi et ordinatior ac propinqua sideribus nec in nubem cogitur nec in tempestatem impellitur nec versatur in turbinem ; omni tumultu caret, inferiora fulminantur.   Eodem modo sublimis animus, quietus semper et in statione tranquilla conlocatus, omnia infra[1] se premens, quibus ira contrahitur, modestus et venerabilis est et dispositus ; quorum
2 nihil invenies in irato.   Quis enim traditus dolori et furens non primam reiecit verecundiam ?   Quis impetu turbidus et in aliquem ruens non quidquid in se venerandi habuit abiecit ?   Cui officiorum numerus aut ordo constitit incitato ?   Quis linguae temperavit ?   Quis ullam partem corporis tenuit ?
3 Quis se regere potuit immissum ?   Proderit nobis illud Democriti salutare praeceptum, quo monstratur tranquillitas, si neque privatim neque publice multa aut maiora viribus nostris egerimus.   Numquam tam feliciter in multa discurrenti negotia dies transit, ut non aut ex homine aut ex re offensa
4 nascatur, quae animum in iras paret. Quemadmodum per frequentia urbis loca properanti in multos incursitandum est et aliubi labi necesse est, aliubi

---

[1] infra *inferior* MSS. : intra *AL.*

---

[a] The Stoic doctrine of apathy (ἀπάθεια)—the exemption from emotion, which was the negative aspect of virtue; Horace's *nil admirari* (*Epistles*, i. 6).
[b] *Cf.* Diels, *Die Fragmente der Vorsokratiker, Demokritos,* 3.

bends before injury. The man who has offended you is either stronger or weaker than you : if he is weaker, spare him ; if he is stronger, spare yourself.

There is no surer proof of greatness than to be in a state where nothing can possibly happen to disturb you. The higher region of the universe, being better ordered and near to the stars, is condensed into no cloud, is lashed into no tempest, is churned into no whirlwind ; it is free from all turmoil ; it is in the lower regions that the lightnings flash. In the same way the lofty mind is always calm, at rest in a quiet haven [a] ; crushing down all that engenders anger, it is restrained, commands respect, and is properly ordered. In an angry man you will find none of these things. For who that surrenders to anger and rage does not straightway cast behind him all sense of shame ? Who that storms in wild fury and assails another does not cast aside whatever he had in him that commands respect ? Who that is enraged maintains the full number or the order of his duties ? Who restrains his tongue ? Who controls any part of his body ? Who is able to rule the self that he has set loose ? We shall do well to heed that sound doctrine of Democritus [b] in which he shows that tranquillity is possible only if we avoid most of the activities of both private and public life, or at least those that are too great for our strength. The man who engages in many affairs is never so fortunate as to pass a day that does not beget from some person or some circumstance a vexation that fits the mind for anger. Just as a man hurrying through the crowded sections of the city cannot help colliding with many people, and in one place is sure to slip, in another to be held back,

retineri, aliubi respergi, ita in hoc vitae actu dis-
sipato et vago multa impedimenta, multae querellae
incidunt. Alius spem nostram fefellit, alius distulit, alius intercepit; non ex destinato proposita
5 fluxerunt. Nulli fortuna tam dedita est, ut multa
temptanti ubique respondeat. Sequitur ergo, ut
is, cui contra quam proposuerat aliqua cesserunt,
impatiens hominum rerumque sit, ex levissimis
causis irascatur nunc personae, nunc negotio, nunc
6 loco, nunc fortunae, nunc sibi. Itaque ut quietus
possit esse animus, non est iactandus nec multarum,
ut dixi, rerum actu fatigandus nec magnarum
supraque vires adpetitarum. Facile est levia aptare
cervicibus et in hanc aut illam partem transferre
sine lapsu; at quae alienis in nos manibus imposita
aegre sustinemus, victi in proximo effundimus.
Etiam dum stamus sub sarcina, impares oneri vac-
cillamus.

1 7. Idem accidere in rebus civilibus ac domesticis
scias. Negotia expedita et habilia sequuntur ac-
torem; ingentia et supra mensuram gerentis nec
dant se facile et, si occupata sunt, premunt atque
abducunt administrantem tenerique iam visa cum
ipso cadunt. Ita fit, ut frequenter irrita sit eius
voluntas, qui non quae facilia sunt adgreditur, sed
2 vult facilia esse quae adgressus est. Quotiens

in another to be splashed, so in this diverse and restless activity of life many hindrances befall us and
many occasions for complaint. Our hopes one man
deceives, another defers, another destroys ; our pro-
jects do not proceed as they were planned. To no
man is Fortune so wholly submissive that she will
always respond if often tried. The result is, consequently, that when a man finds that some of his
plans have turned out contrary to his expectations,
he becomes impatient with men and things, and on
the slightest provocation becomes angry now with
a person, now with his calling, now with his place
of abode, now with his luck, now with himself. In
order, therefore, that the mind may have peace, it
must not be tossed about, it must not, as I have
said, be wearied by activity in many or great affairs,
or by attempting such as are beyond its powers. It
is easy to fit the shoulders to light burdens, and to
shift the load from this side to that without slipping ;
but it is hard to support what others' hands have
laid upon us, and exhausted we cast the load upon a
neighbour. Even while we stand beneath the burden,
we stagger if we are too weak to bear its weight.

In public and in private affairs, be sure, the same
condition holds. Light and easy tasks accept the
control of the doer ; those that are heavy and beyond
the capacity of the performer are not easily mastered ;
and if they are undertaken, they outweigh his efforts
and run away with him, and just when he thinks he
has them in his grasp, down they crash and bring him
down with them. So it happens that the man who
is unwilling to approach easy tasks, yet wishes to
find easy the tasks he approaches, is often disappointed in his desire. Whenever you would

aliquid conaberis, te simul et ea, quae paras quibusque
pararis ipse, metire ; faciet enim te asperum paenitentia operis infecti. Hoc interest utrum quis
fervidi sit ingenii an frigidi atque humilis ; generoso
repulsa iram exprimet, languido inertique tristitiam.
Ergo actiones nostrae nec parvae sint nec audaces et
improbae, in vicinum spes exeat, nihil conemur,
quod mox adepti quoque successisse miremur.

1   8. Demus operam, ne accipiamus iniuriam, quia
ferre nescimus. Cum placidissimo et facillimo et
minime anxio morosoque vivendum est ; sumuntur a
conversantibus mores et ut quaedam in contactos corporis vitia transiliunt, ita animus mala sua proximis
2 tradit. Ebriosus convictores in amorem meri traxit,
impudicorum coetus fortem quoque et, si liceat,[1]
virum emolliit, avaritia in proximos virus suum transtulit. Eadem ex diverso ratio virtutum est, ut omne
quod secum habent mitigent ; nec tam valetudini
profuit utilis regio et salubrius caelum quam animis
3 parum firmis in turba meliore versari. Quae res
quantum possit intelleges, si videris feras quoque
convictu nostro mansuescere nullique etiam immani
bestiae vim suam permanere, si hominis contubernium
diu passa est ; retunditur omnis asperitas paulatim-

---

[1] si liceat *mss.* : *ingenious is* siliceum *Pincianus, but in
usage the transferred meaning is* " *hard-hearted* " : solidum
Cornelissen : si placet *Gertz* : si lis erat *Petschenig*.

attempt anything, measure yourself and at the same time the undertaking—both the thing you intend and the thing for which you are intended ; for the regret that springs from an unaccomplished task will make you bitter. It makes some difference whether a man is of a fiery or of a cold and submissive nature; the man of spirit will be driven by defeat to anger, a dull and sluggish nature to sorrow. Let our activities, consequently, be neither petty, nor yet bold and presumptuous ; let us restrict the range of hope ; let us attempt nothing which later, even after we have achieved it, will make us surprised that we have succeeded.

Since we do not know how to bear injury, let us endeavour not to receive one. We should live with a very calm and good-natured person—one that is never worried or captious ; we adopt our habits from those with whom we associate, and as certain diseases of the body spread to others from contact, so the mind transmits its faults to those near-by. The drunkard lures his boon companions into love of wine ; shameless company corrupts even the strong man and, perchance, the hero ; avarice transfers its poison to its neighbours. The same principle holds good of the virtues, but with the opposite result—that they ameliorate whatever comes in contact with them ; an invalid does not benefit so much from a suitable location or a more healthful climate as does the mind which lacks strength from association with a better company. You will understand what a powerful factor this is if you observe that even wild animals grow tame from intercourse with us, and that all beasts, no matter how savage, after enduring long companionship with man cease to be violent ; all

que inter placida dediscitur. Accedit huc, quod non tantum exemplo melior fit qui cum quietis hominibus vivit, sed quod causas irascendi non invenit nec vitium suum exercet. Fugere itaque debebit omnis quos irritaturos iracundiam sciet. 4 " Qui sunt," inquis, " isti ? " Multi ex variis causis idem facturi : offendet te superbus contemptu, dicax contumelia, petulans iniuria, lividus malignitate, pugnax contentione, ventosus et mendax vanitate ; non feres a suspicioso timeri, a pertinace vinci, a 5 delicato fastidiri. Elige simplices, faciles, moderatos, qui iram tuam nec evocent et ferant. Magis adhuc proderunt summissi et humani et dulces, non tamen usque in adulationem, nam iracundos nimia assentatio 6 offendit. Erat certe amicus noster vir bonus, sed irae paratioris, cui non magis tutum erat blandiri quam male dicere.

Caelium oratorem fuisse iracundissimum constat. Cum quo, ut aiunt, cenabat in cubiculo lectae patientiae cliens, sed difficile erat illi in copulam coniecto rixam eius cum quo cohaerebat effugere ; optimum iudicavit quidquid dixisset sequi et secundas agere. Non tulit Caelius adsentientem et exclamavit : " Dic aliquid contra, ut duo simus ! " Sed ille quoque, quod non irasceretur, iratus cito sine adver-

their fierceness is blunted and gradually amid peaceful conditions is forgotten. Moreover, the man who lives with tranquil people not only becomes better from their example, but finding no occasions for anger he does not indulge in his weakness. It will, therefore, be a man's duty to avoid all those who he knows will provoke his anger. " Just whom do you mean ? " you ask. There are many who from various causes will produce the same result. The proud man will offend you by his scorn, the caustic man by an insult, the forward man by an affront, the spiteful man by his malice, the contentious by his wrangling, the windy liar by his hollowness ; you will not endure to be feared by a suspicious man, to be outdone by a stubborn one, or to be despised by a coxcomb. Choose frank, good-natured, temperate people, who will not call forth your anger and yet will bear with it. Still more helpful will be those who are yielding and kindly and suave—not, however, to the point of fawning, for too much cringing incenses hot-tempered people. I, at any rate, had a friend, a good man, but too prone to anger, whom it was not less dangerous to wheedle than to curse.

It is well known that Caelius, the orator, was very hot-tempered. A client of rare forbearance was, as the story goes, once dining with Caelius in his chamber, but it was difficult for him, having got into such close quarters, to avoid a quarrel with the companion at his side ; so he decided that it was best to agree with whatever Caelius said and to play up to him. Caelius, however, could not endure his compliant attitude, and cried out, " Contradict me, that there may be two of us ! " But even he, angry because he was not angered, quickly subsided when

7 sario desît. Eligamus ergo vel hos potius, si conscii
nobis iracundiae sumus, qui vultum nostrum ac
sermonem sequantur. Facient quidem nos delicatos
et in malam consuetudinem inducent nihil contra
voluntatem audiendi, sed proderit vitio suo inter-
vallum et quietem dare. Difficiles quoque et
indomiti natura blandientem ferent. Nihil asperum
8 territumque palpanti est. Quotiens disputatio lon-
gior et pugnacior erit, in prima resistamus, antequam
robur accipiat. Alit se ipsa contentio et demissos
altius tenet. Facilius est se a certamine abstinere
quam abducere.

1 9. Studia quoque graviora iracundis omittenda
sunt aut certe citra lassitudinem exercenda, et
animus non inter plura[1] versandus, sed artibus
amoenis tradendus. Lectio illum carminum obleniat
et historia fabulis detineat; mollius delicatiusque
2 tractetur. Pythagoras perturbationes animi lyra
componebat; quis autem ignorat lituos et tubas
concitamenta esse, sicut quosdam cantus blandi-
menta, quibus mens resolvatur? Confusis oculis
prosunt virentia et quibusdam coloribus infirma
acies adquiescit, quorundam splendore praestringitur;
3 sic mentes aegras studia laeta permulcent. Forum,
advocationes, iudicia fugere debemus et omnia quae
exulcerant vitium, aeque cavere lassitudinem corpo-

---

[1] inter plura *A* : inter dura *Gertz.*

he had no antagonist. Consequently, if we are conscious of being hot-tempered, let us rather pick out those who will be guided by our looks and by our words. Such men, it is true, will pamper us and lead us into the harmful habit of hearing nothing that we do not like, but there will be the advantage of giving our weakness a period of respite. Even those who are churlish and intractable by nature will endure caressing ; no creature is savage and frightened if you stroke it. Whenever a discussion tends to be too long or too quarrelsome, let us check it at the start before it gains strength. Controversy grows of itself and holds fast those that have plunged in too deeply. It is easier to refrain than to retreat from a struggle.

Hot-tempered people should also abstain from the more burdensome pursuits, or at least should not ply these to the point of exhaustion, and the mind should not be engaged by too many interests, but should surrender itself to such arts as are pleasurable. Let it be soothed by the reading of poetry and gripped by the tales of history ; it should be much coddled and pampered. Pythagoras used to calm his troubled spirit with the lyre ; and who does not know that the clarion and the trumpet act as incitements to the mind, and that, similarly, certain songs are a soothing balm that brings it relaxation ? Green things are good for disordered eyes, and certain colours are restful to weak vision, while by the brightness of others it is blinded. So pleasant pursuits soothe the troubled mind. We should shun the courts, court-appearances, and trials, and everything that aggravates our weakness, and we should equally guard against physical exhaustion ; for this destroys what-

ris; consumit enim quidquid in nobis mite placidum-
4 que est et acria concitat. Ideo quibus stomachus
suspectus est, processuri ad res agendas maioris
negotii bilem cibo temperant, quam maxime movet
fatigatio, sive quia calorem in media compellit et
nocet sanguini cursumque eius venis laborantibus
sistit, sive quia corpus attenuatum et infirmum
incumbit animo; certe ob eandem causam ira-
cundiores sunt valetudine aut aetate fessi. Fames
quoque et sitis ex isdem causis vitanda est; exasperat
5 et incendit animos. Vetus dictum est a lasso rixam
quaeri; aeque autem et ab esuriente et a sitiente
et ab omni homine quem aliqua res urit. Nam ut
ulcera ad levem tactum, deinde etiam ad suspicionem
tactus condolescunt, ita animus adfectus minimis
offenditur, adeo ut quosdam salutatio et epistula
et oratio et interrogatio in litem evocent. Numquam
sine querella aegra tanguntur.

1   10. Optimum est itaque ad primum mali sensum
mederi sibi, tum verbis quoque suis minimum liber-
2 tatis dare et inhibere impetum. Facile est autem
adfectus suos, cum primum oriuntur, deprehendere;
morborum signa praecurrunt. Quemadmodum tem-
pestatis ac pluviae ante ipsas notae veniunt, ita irae,
amoris omniumque istarum procellarum animos
3 vexantium sunt quaedam praenuntia. Qui comitiali
vitio solent corripi, iam adventare valetudinem
intellegunt, si calor summa deseruit et incertum

ever gentleness and mildness we have and engenders sharpness. Those, therefore, who distrust their digestion, before they proceed to the performance of tasks of unusual difficulty, allay their bile with food ; for fatigue especially arouses the bile, possibly because it drives the body's heat toward the centre, vitiates the blood, and stops its circulation by clogging the veins, or because the body when it is worn and feeble weighs down the mind. For the same reason, undoubtedly, those who are broken by ill-health and age are more irascible than others. Hunger and thirst also, for the same reasons, must be avoided ; they exasperate and irritate the mind. There is an old proverb that " the tired man seeks a quarrel," but it applies just as well to the hungry and thirsty man, and to any man who chafes under something. For just as a bodily sore hurts under the slightest touch, afterwards even at the suggestion of a touch, so the disordered mind takes offence at the merest trifles, so that even, in the case of some people, a greeting, a letter, a speech, or a question provokes a dispute. There will always be a protest if you touch a sore spot.

It is best, therefore, to treat the malady as soon as it is discovered ; then, too, to allow oneself the least possible liberty of speech, and to check impulsiveness. It is easy, moreover, to detect one's passion as soon as it is born ; sickness is preceded by symptoms. Just as the signs of storm and rain appear before the storms themselves, so there are certain forerunners of anger, of love, and of all those tempests that shake the soul. Those who are subject to fits of epilepsy know that the attack is coming on if heat leaves their extremities, if their sight wavers,

lumen nervorumque trepidatio est, si memoria
sublabitur caputque versatur ; solitis itaque remediis
incipientem causam occupant, et odore gustuque
quidquid est quod alienat animos repellitur, aut
fomentis contra frigus rigoremque pugnatur ; aut
si[1] parum medicina profecit, vitaverunt turbam et
4 sine teste ceciderunt.   Prodest morbum suum nosse
et vires eius antequam spatientur opprimere. Videamus quid sit, quod nos maxime concitet. Alium
verborum, alium rerum contumeliae movent ; hic
vult nobilitati, hic formae suae parci ; hic elegantis-
simus haberi cupit, ille doctissimus ; hic superbiae
impatiens est, hic contumaciae ; ille servos non putat
dignos quibus irascatur, hic intra domum saevus est,
foris mitis ; ille rogari invidiam iudicat, hic non rogari
contumeliam.   Non omnes ab eadem parte feriuntur ; scire itaque oportet, quid in te imbecillum sit,
ut id maxime protegas.

1   11. Non expedit omnia videre, omnia audire.
Multae nos iniuriae transeant, ex quibus plerasque
non accipit qui nescit.   Non vis esse iracundus ?
Ne fueris curiosus.   Qui inquirit quid in se dictum
sit, qui malignos sermones, etiam si secreto habiti
sunt, eruit, se ipse inquietat. Quaedam inter-
pretatio eo perducit, ut videantur iniuriae ; itaque
alia differenda sunt, alia deridenda, alia donanda.

---

[1] aut si *A* : [aut] si *Hermes.*

if there is a twitching of the muscles, or if memory forsakes them and the head swims; therefore by customary remedies they try to forestall the disease in its incipiency, and they ward off whatever it is that causes unconsciousness by smelling or tasting something, or they battle against cold and stiffness with hot applications; or if the remedy is of no avail, they escape from the crowd and fall where no one may see. It is well to understand one's malady and to break its power before it spreads. Let us discern what it is that especially irritates us. One man is stirred by insulting words, another by insulting actions; this man craves respect for his rank, this one for his person; this one wishes to be considered a fine gentleman, that one a fine scholar; this one cannot brook arrogance, this one obstinacy; that one does not think his slaves worthy of his wrath, this one is violent inside his house and mild outside; that man considers it a disgrace to be put up for office, this one an insult not to be put up. We are not all wounded at the same spot; therefore you ought to know what your weak spot is in order that you may especially protect it.

It is well not to see everything, not to hear everything. Many affronts may pass by us; in most cases the man who is unconscious of them escapes them. Would you avoid being provoked? Then do not be inquisitive. He who tries to discover what has been said against him, who unearths malicious gossip even if it was privately indulged in, is responsible for his own disquietude. There are words which the construction put upon them can make appear an insult; some, therefore, ought to be put aside, others derided, others condoned. In various

2 Circumscribenda multis modis ira est; pleraque
in lusum iocumque vertantur. Socraten aiunt
colapho percussum nihil amplius dixisse quam
molestum esse, quod nescirent homines, quando
3 cum galea prodire deberent. Non quemadmodum
facta sit iniuria refert, sed quemadmodum lata;
nec video quare difficilis sit moderatio, cum sciam
tyrannorum quoque tumida et fortuna et licentia
4 ingenia familiarem sibi saevitiam repressisse. Pisi-
stratum certe, Atheniensium tyrannum, memoriae
proditur, cum multa in crudelitatem eius ebrius
conviva dixisset nec deessent qui vellent manus ei
commodare, et alius hinc alius illinc faces subderent,
placido animo tulisse et hoc irritantibus respondisse,
non magis illi se suscensere quam si quis obligatis
oculis in se incurrisset.

1   12. Magna pars querellas manu fecit aut falsa
suspicando aut levia adgravando. Saepe ad nos ira
venit, saepius nos ad illam. Quae numquam arces-
2 senda est; etiam cum incidit, reiciatur. Nemo dicit
sibi: " Hoc propter quod irascor aut feci aut fecisse
potui "; nemo animum facientis, sed ipsum aestimat
factum. Atqui ille intuendus est, voluerit an inciderit, coactus sit an deceptus, odium secutus sit

282

ways anger must be circumvented; most offences
may be turned into farce and jest. Socrates, it is
said, when once he received a box on the ear, merely
declared that it was too bad that a man could not
tell when he ought to wear a helmet while taking
a walk. Not how an affront is offered, but how it is
borne is our concern; and I do not see why it is
difficult to practise restraint, since I know that even
despots, though their hearts were puffed up with
success and privilege, have nevertheless repressed
the cruelty that was habitual to them. At any rate,
there is the story handed down about Pisistratus, the
Athenian despot—that once when a tipsy table-
guest had declaimed at length about his cruelty,
and there was no lack of those who would gladly
place their swords at the service of their master, and
one from this side and another from that supplied
fuel to the flame, the tyrant, none the less, bore the
incident calmly, and replied to those who were goad-
ing him on that he was no more angry at the man
than he would be if some one ran against him blind-
fold.

A great many manufacture grievances either by
suspecting the untrue or by exaggerating the trivial.
Anger often comes to us, but more often we go to it.
It should never be invited; even when it falls upon
us, it should be repulsed. No man ever says to
himself, " I myself have done, or at least might have
done, this very thing that now makes me angry ";
no one considers the intention of the doer, but
merely the deed. Yet it is to the doer that we
should give thought—whether he did it intentionally
or by accident, whether under compulsion or by
mistake, whether he was led on by hatred or by the

an praemium, sibi morem gesserit an manum alteri
commodaverit. Aliquid aetas peccantis facit, aliquid
fortuna, ut ferre aut pati[1] aut humanum sit aut
3 humile.[2] Eo nos loco constituamus, quo ille est cui
irascimur ; nunc facit nos iracundos iniqua nostri
aestimatio et quae facere vellemus pati nolumus.
4 Nemo se differt ; atqui maximum remedium irae
dilatio est, ut primus eius fervor relanguescat et
caligo quae premit mentem aut residat aut minus
densa sit. Quaedam ex his, quae te praecipitem
ferebant, hora, non tantum dies molliet, quaedam
ex toto evanescent ; si nihil egerit petita advocatio,
apparebit iam iudicium esse, non iram. Quidquid
voles quale sit scire, tempori trade ; nihil diligenter
5 in fluctu cernitur. Non potuit impetrare a se Plato
tempus, cum servo suo irasceretur, sed ponere illum
statim tunicam et praebere scapulas verberibus
iussit sua manu ipse caesurus ; postquam intellexit
irasci se, sicut sustulerat manum suspensam detinebat
et stabat percussuro similis ; interrogatus deinde
ab amico, qui forte intervenerat, quid ageret :
" Exigo," inquit, " poenas ab homine iracundo."
6 Velut stupens gestum illum saevituri deformem
sapienti viro servabat, oblitus iam servi, quia alium
quem potius castigaret invenerat. Itaque abstulit

---

[1] aut pati *A* : ac pati *Hermes, after Lipsius.*
[2] humile *A* : non humile *Hermes, after Madvig.*

hope of reward, whether he was pleasing himself or lending aid to another. The age of the offender counts for something, his station for something, so that to tolerate or to submit becomes merely indulgence or deference. Let us put ourselves in the place of the man with whom we are angry ; as it is, an unwarranted opinion of self makes us prone to anger, and we are unwilling to bear what we ourselves would have been willing to inflict. No one makes himself wait ; yet the best cure for anger is waiting, to allow the first ardour to abate and to let the darkness that clouds the reason either subside or be less dense. Of the offences which were driving you headlong, some an hour will abate, to say nothing of a day, some will vanish altogether ; though the postponement sought shall accomplish nothing else, yet it will be evident that judgement now rules instead of anger. If ever you want to find out what a thing really is, entrust it to time ; you can see nothing clearly in the midst of the billows. Plato once, when he was angry with his slave, was unable to impose delay upon himself, and, bent upon flogging him with his own hand, ordered him forthwith to take off his shirt and bare his shoulders for the blows ; but afterwards realizing that he was angry he stayed his uplifted hand, and just as he was stood with his hand in the air like one in the act of striking. Later, when a friend who happened to come in asked him what he was doing, he said, " I am exacting punishment from an angry man." As if stunned he maintained that attitude, unbecoming to a philosopher, of one on the point of venting his passion, forgetful now of the slave since he had found another whom he was more anxious to punish. He therefore denied

sibi in suos potestatem et ob peccatum quoddam commotior : " Tu," inquit, " Speusippe, servulum 7 istum verberibus obiurga ; nam ego irascor." Ob hoc non cecidit, propter quod alius cecidisset. " Irascor," inquit ; " plus faciam quam oportet, libentius faciam ; non sit iste servus in eius potestate qui in sua non est." Aliquis vult irato committi ultionem, cum Plato sibi ipse imperium abrogaverit ? Nihil tibi liceat, dum irasceris. Quare ? Quia vis omnia licere.

1   13. Pugna tecum ipse ! Si vis[1] vincere iram, non potest te illa. Incipis vincere, si absconditur, si illi exitus non datur. Signa eius obruamus et illam quantum fieri potest occultam secretamque teneamus. 2 Cum magna id nostra molestia fiet, cupit enim exilire et incendere oculos et mutare faciem ; sed si eminere illi extra nos licuit, supra nos est. In imo pectoris secessu recondatur feraturque, non ferat ; immo in contrarium omnia eius indicia flectamus. Vultus remittatur, vox lenior sit, gradus lentior ; paulatim 3 cum exterioribus interiora formantur. In Socrate irae signum erat vocem summittere, loqui parcius. Apparebat tunc illum sibi obstare. Deprendebatur itaque a familiaribus et coarguebatur, nec erat illi exprobratio latitantis irae ingrata. Quidni gauderet,

---

[1] vis *added by Hermes, after Madvig.*

himself all power over his own household, and once, when he was deeply provoked at some fault, he said, "Do you, Speusippus, punish this dog of a slave with a whip, for I am angry." His reason for not striking was the very reason that would have caused another to strike. "I am angry," said he; "I should do more than I ought, and with too much satisfaction; this slave should not be in the power of a master who is not master of himself." Can any one wish to entrust punishment to an angry man when even Plato denied himself this authority? Let nothing be lawful to you while you are angry. Do you ask why? Because then you wish everything to be lawful.

Fight against yourself! If you will to conquer anger, it cannot conquer you. If it is kept out of sight, if it is given no outlet, you begin to conquer. Let us conceal its signs, and so far as it is possible let us keep it hidden and secret. We shall have great trouble in doing this, for it is eager to leap forth and fire the eyes and transform the countenance; but if we allow it to show itself outside of us, at once it is on top of us. It should be kept hidden in the deepest depths of the heart and it should not drive, but be driven; and more, all symptoms of it let us change into just the opposite. Let the countenance be unruffled, let the voice be very gentle, the step very slow; gradually the inner man conforms itself to the outer. In the case of Socrates, it was a sign of anger if he lowered his voice and became sparing of speech. It was evident then that he was struggling against himself. And so his intimate friends would find him out and accuse him, yet he was not displeased by the charge of concealing his anger. Why

287

quod iram suam multi intellegerent, nemo sentiret?
Sensissent autem, nisi ius amicis obiurgandi se
4 dedisset, sicut ipse sibi in amicos sumpserat. Quanto
magis hoc nobis faciendum est! Rogemus amicissimum quemque, ut tunc maxime libertate adversus
nos utatur, cum minime illam pati poterimus, nec
adsentiatur irae nostrae; contra potens malum et
apud nos gratiosum, dum consipimus, dum nostri
5 sumus, advocemus. Qui vinum male ferunt et
ebrietatis suae temeritatem ac petulantiam metuunt,
mandant suis, ut e convivio auferantur; intemperantiam in morbo suam experti parere ipsis in
6 adversa valetudine vetant. Optimum est notis
vitiis impedimenta prospicere et ante omnia ita
componere animum, ut etiam gravissimis rebus
subitisque concussus iram aut non sentiat aut magnitudine inopinatae iniuriae exortam in altum retrahat
7 nec dolorem suum profiteatur. Id fieri posse
apparebit, si pauca ex turba ingenti exempla pro-
tulero, ex quibus utrumque discere licet, quantum
mali habeat ira, ubi hominum praepotentium potestate tota utitur, quantum sibi imperare possit,
ubi metu maiore compressa est.

1   14. Cambysen regem nimis deditum vino Praexaspes unus ex carissimis monebat, ut parcius
biberet, turpem esse dicens ebrietatem in rege,
quem omnium oculi auresque sequerentur.   Ad haec

should he not have been happy that many perceived his anger, yet no man felt it ? But they would have felt it, had his friends not been granted the same right to criticize him which he himself claimed over them. How much more ought we to do this ! Let us beg all our best friends to use to the utmost such liberty toward us, especially when we are least able to bear it, and let there be no approval of our anger. While we are sane, while we are ourselves, let us ask help against an evil that is powerful and oft indulged by us. Those who cannot carry their wine discreetly and fear that they will be rash and insolent in their cups, instruct their friends to remove them from the feast ; those who have learned that they are unreasonable when they are sick, give orders that in times of illness they are not to be obeyed. It is best to provide obstacles for recognized weaknesses, and above all so to order the mind that even when shaken by most serious and sudden happenings it either shall not feel anger, or shall bury deep any anger that may arise from the magnitude of the unexpected affront and shall not acknowledge its hurt. That this can be done will become clear if from a great array of instances I shall cite a few examples ; from these you may learn two things— how great evil there is in anger when it wields the complete power of supremely powerful men, and how great control it can impose upon itself when restrained by the stronger influence of fear.

Since Cambyses was too much addicted to wine, Praexaspes, one of his dearest friends, urged him to drink more sparingly, declaring that drunkenness is disgraceful for a king, towards whom all eyes and ears are turned. To this Cambyses replied : " To

ille: "Ut scias," inquit, "quemadmodum numquam excidam mihi, adprobabo iam et oculos post vinum 2 in officio esse et manus." Bibit deinde liberalius quam alias capacioribus scyphis et iam gravis ac vinolentus obiurgatoris sui filium procedere ultra limen iubet adlevataque super caput sinistra manu stare. Tunc intendit arcum et ipsum cor adulescentis, id enim petere se dixerat, figit rescissoque pectore haerens in ipso corde spiculum ostendit ac respiciens patrem interrogavit, satisne certam haberet manum. At ille negavit Apollinem potuisse certius 3 mittere. Dii illum male perdant animo magis quam condicione mancipium! Eius rei laudator fuit, cuius nimis erat spectatorem fuisse. Occasionem blanditiarum putavit pectus filii in duas partes diductum et cor sub vulnere palpitans. Controversiam illi facere de gloria debuit et revocare iactum, ut regi liberet in ipso patre certiorem manum 4 ostendere! O regem cruentum! O dignum in quem omnium suorum arcus verterentur! Cum exsecrati fuerimus illum convivia suppliciis funeribusque solventem, tamen sceleratius telum illud laudatum est quam missum. Videbimus quomodo se pater gerere debuerit stans super cadaver fili sui caedemque illam, cuius et testis fuerat et causa. Id de quo nunc agitur apparet, iram supprimi posse.

convince you that I never lose command of myself, I shall proceed to prove to you that my eyes and my hands perform their duty in spite of wine." Thereupon taking larger cups he drank more recklessly than ever, and when at length he was heavy and besotted with wine, he ordered the son of his critic to proceed beyond the threshold and stand there with his left hand lifted above his head. Then he drew his bow and shot the youth through the very heart—he had mentioned this as his mark—and cutting open the breast of the victim he showed the arrow-head sticking in the heart itself, and then turning toward the father he inquired whether he had a sufficiently steady hand. But he replied that Apollo himself could not have made a more unerring shot. Heaven curse such a man, a bondslave in spirit even more than in station! He praised a deed, which it were too much even to have witnessed. The breast of his son that had been torn asunder, his heart quivering from its wound, he counted a fitting pretext for flattery. He ought to have provoked a dispute with him about his boast and called for another shot, that the king might have the pleasure of displaying upon the person of the father himself an even steadier hand! What a bloodthirsty king! What a worthy mark for the bows of all his followers! Though we may execrate him for terminating a banquet with punishment and death, yet it was more accursed to praise that shot than to make it. We shall see later how the father should have borne himself as he stood over the corpse of his son, viewing that murder of which he was both the witness and the cause. The point now under discussion is clear, namely, that it is possible to suppress anger. He

5 Non male dixit regi, nullum emisit ne calamitosi quidem verbum, cum aeque cor suum quam fili transfixum videret. Potest dici merito devorasse verba; nam si quid tamquam iratus dixisset, nihil tamquam 6 pater facere potuisset. Potest, inquam, videri sapientius se in illo casu gessisse, quam cum de potandi modo praeciperet ei, quem satius erat vinum quam sanguinem bibere, cuius manus poculis occupari pax erat. Accessit itaque ad numerum eorum, qui magnis cladibus ostenderunt, quanti constarent regum amicis bona consilia.

1   15. Non dubito quin Harpagus quoque tale aliquid regi suo Persarumque suaserit, quo offensus liberos illi epulandos adposuit et subinde quaesiit, an placeret conditura; deinde ut satis illum plenum malis suis vidit, adferri capita illorum iussit et quomodo esset acceptus interrogavit. Non defuerunt misero verba, non os concurrit: "Apud regem," 2 inquit, "omnis cena iucunda est." Quid hac adulatione profecit? Ne ad reliquias invitaretur. Non veto patrem damnare regis sui factum, non veto quaerere dignam tam truci portento poenam, sed hoc interim colligo, posse etiam ex ingentibus malis nascentem iram abscondi et ad verba contraria sibi 3 cogi. Necessaria ista est doloris refrenatio, utique

did not curse the king, he let slip no word even of anguish, though he saw his own heart pierced as well as his son's. It may be said that he was right to choke back words ; for even if he had spoken as an angry man, he could have accomplished nothing as a father. He may, I say, be thought to have acted more wisely in that misfortune than he had done in recommending moderation in drinking to a man who would have much better drunk wine than blood, with whom peace meant that his hands were busy with the wine-cup. He, therefore, added one more to the number of those who have shown by bitter misfortune the price a king's friends pay for giving good advice.

I doubt not that Harpagus also gave some such advice to his king, the king of the Persians, who, taking offence thereat, caused the flesh of Harpagus's own children to be set before him as a course in the banquet, and kept inquiring whether he liked the cooking ; then when he saw him sated with his own ills, he ordered the heads of the children to be brought in, and inquired what he thought of his entertainment. The poor wretch did not lack words, his lips were not sealed. "At the king's board," he said, "any kind of food is delightful." And what did he gain by this flattery ? He escaped an invitation to eat what was left. I do not say that a father must not condemn an act of his king, I do not say that he should not seek to give so atrocious a monster the punishment he deserves, but for the moment I am drawing this conclusion—that it is possible for a man to conceal the anger that arises even from a monstrous outrage and to force himself to words that belie it. Such restraint of distress is necessary, particularly for

hoc sortitis vitae genus et ad regiam adhibitis mensam.
Sic estur apud illos, sic bibitur, sic respondetur,
funeribus suis adridendum est. An tanti sit vita
videbimus ; alia ista quaestio est. Non consolabimur
tam triste ergastulum, non adhortabimur ferre
imperia carnificum ; ostendemus in omni servitute
apertam libertati viam. Si aeger animus et suo vitio
4 miser est, huic miserias finire secum licet. Dicam
et illi, qui in regem incidit sagittis pectora amicorum
petentem, et illi, cuius dominus liberorum visceribus patres saturat : "Quid gemis, demens? Quid
expectas, ut te aut hostis aliquis per exitium gentis
tuae vindicet aut rex a longinquo potens advolet ?
Quocumque respexeris, ibi malorum finis est. Vides
illum praecipitem locum ? Illac ad libertatem
descenditur. Vides illud mare, illud flumen, illum
puteum ? Libertas illic in imo sedet. Vides illam
arborem brevem, retorridam, infelicem ? Pendet
inde libertas. Vides iugulum tuum, guttur tuum,
cor tuum ? Effugia servitutis sunt. Nimis tibi
operosos exitus monstro et multum animi ac roboris
exigentes ? Quaeris quod sit ad libertatem iter ?
Quaelibet in corpore tuo vena ! "

1 16. Quam diu quidem nihil tam intolerabile nobis
videtur, ut nos expellat e vita, iram, in quocumque

those whose lot is cast in this sort of life and who are invited to the board of kings. So must they eat in that company, so must they drink, so must they answer, so must they mock at the death of their dear ones. Whether the life is worth the price we shall see ; that is another question. We shall not condole with such a chain-gang of prisoners so wretched, we shall not urge them to submit to the commands of their butchers ; we shall show that in any kind of servitude the way lies open to liberty. If the soul is sick and because of its own imperfection unhappy, a man may end its sorrows and at the same time himself. To him to whom chance has given a king that aims his shafts at the breasts of his friends, to him who has a master that gorges fathers with the flesh of their children, I would say : " Madman, why do you moan ? Why do you wait for some enemy to avenge you by the destruction of your nation, or for a mighty king from afar to fly to your rescue ? In whatever direction you may turn your eyes, there lies the means to end your woes. See you that precipice ? Down that is the way to liberty. See you that sea, that river, that well ? There sits liberty—at the bottom. See you that tree, stunted, blighted, and barren ? Yet from its branches hangs liberty. See you that throat of yours, your gullet, your heart ? They are ways of escape from servitude. Are the ways of egress I show you too toilsome, do they require too much courage and strength ? Do you ask what is the highway to liberty ? Any vein in your body ! "

So long indeed as there shall be no hardship so intolerable in our opinion as to force us to abandon life, let us, no matter what our station in life may

erimus statu, removeamus. Perniciosa est servientibus. Omnis enim indignatio in tormentum
suum proficit et imperia graviora sentit quo con-
tumacius patitur. Sic laqueos fera, dum iactat,
adstringit ; sic aves viscum, dum trepidantes ex-
cutiunt, plumis omnibus inlinunt. Nullum tam
artum est iugum, quod non minus laedat ducentem
quam repugnantem. Unum est levamentum malorum ingentium, pati et necessitatibus suis obsequi.
2 Sed cum utilis sit servientibus adfectuum suorum
et huius praecipue rabidi atque effreni continentia,
utilior est regibus. Perierunt omnia, ubi quantum
ira suadet fortuna permittit, nec diu potest quae
multorum malo exercetur potentia stare ; peri-
clitatur enim, ubi eos, qui separatim gemunt, communis metus iunxit. Plerosque itaque modo singuli
mactaverunt, modo universi, cum illos conferre in
3 unum iras publicus dolor coegisset. Atqui plerique
sic iram quasi insigne regium exercuerunt, sicut
Dareus, qui primus post ablatum Mago imperium
Persas et magnam partem orientis obtinuit. Nam
cum bellum Scythis indixisset orientem cingentibus,
rogatus ab Oeobazo nobili sene, ut ex tribus liberis
unum in solacium patri relinqueret, duorum opera
uteretur, plus quam rogabatur pollicitus omnis se
illi dixit remissurum et occisos in conspectu parentis
4 abiecit, crudelis futurus, si omnis abduxisset. At

---

[a] The false Smerdis, dethroned 521 B.C. Cf. Herodotus,
iii. 70 ff.
[b] The true founder of the Persian empire, Darius extended
his supremacy as far as the Indus.

be, keep ourselves from anger. It is harmful for all who serve. For any sort of chafing grows to self-torture, and the more rebellious we are under authority, the more oppressive we feel it to be. So a wild beast by struggling but tightens its noose ; so birds by trying in their alarm to get free from bird-lime, smear all their plumage with it. No yoke is so tight but that it hurts less to carry it than to struggle against it. The only relief for great misfortunes is to bear them and submit to their coercion. But though it is expedient for subjects to control their passions, especially this mad and unbridled one, it is even more expedient for kings. When his position permits a man to do all that anger prompts, general destruction is let loose, nor can any power long endure which is wielded for the injury of many ; for it becomes imperilled when those who separately moan in anguish are united by a common fear. Consequently, many kings have been the victims now of individual, now of concerted, violence, at times when a general animosity had forced men to gather together their separate angers into one. Yet many kings have employed anger as if it were the badge of regal power ; for example Darius, who after the dethronement of the Magian *a* became the first ruler of the Persians and of a great part of the East.*b* For after he had declared war on the Scythians who were on his eastern border, Oeobazus, an aged noble, besought him to use the services of two of his sons, but to leave one out of the three as a comfort to his father. Promising more than was asked, and saying that he would exempt all three, Darius flung their dead bodies before their father's eyes—for it would have been cruelty if he had taken them all with him !

quanto Xerses facilior ! Qui Pythio quinque filiorum
patri unius vacationem petenti, quem vellet eligere
permisit, deinde quem elegerat in partes duas
distractum ab utroque viae latere posuit et hac
victima lustravit exercitum. Habuit itaque quem
debuit exitum; victus et late longeque fusus ac
stratam ubique ruinam suam cernens medius inter
suorum cadavera incessit.

1 17. Haec barbaris regibus feritas in ira fuit, quos
nulla eruditio, nullus litterarum cultus imbuerat.
Dabo tibi ex Aristotelis sinu regem Alexandrum, qui
Clitum carissimum sibi et una educatum inter epulas
transfodit manu quidem sua, parum adulantem et
pigre ex Macedone ac libero in Persicam servitutem
2 transeuntem. Nam Lysimachum aeque familiarem
sibi leoni obiecit. Numquid ergo hic Lysimachus
felicitate quadam dentibus leonis elapsus ob hoc,
3 cum ipse regnaret, mitior fuit ? Nam Telesphorum
Rhodium amicum suum undique decurtatum, cum
aures illi nasumque abscidisset, in cavea velut novum
aliquod animal et invisitatum diu pavit, cum oris
detruncati mutilatique deformitas humanam faciem
perdidisset ; accedebat fames et squalor et inluvies
4 corporis in stercore suo destituti ; callosis super

But how much kinder was Xerxes! For he, when Pythius, the father of five sons, begged for the exemption of one, permitted him to choose the one he wished; then he tore into halves the son who had been chosen, and placing a half on each side of the road offered the body as an expiatory sacrifice for the success of the army. And so the army met the fate it deserved. Defeated, routed far and wide, and seeing its own destruction spread on every side, between two lines of the dead bodies of its comrades it trudged along.

Such was the ferocity of barbarian kings when in anger—men who had had no contact with learning or the culture of letters. But I shall now show you a king from the very bosom of Aristotle, even Alexander, who in the midst of a feast with his own hand stabbed Clitus, his dearest friend, with whom he had grown up, because he withheld his flattery and was reluctant to transform himself from a Macedonian and a free man into a Persian slave. Lysimachus, likewise a familiar friend, he threw to a lion. Though Lysimachus escaped by some good luck from the lion's teeth, was he therefore, in view of this experience, a whit more kind when he himself became king? Not so, for Telesphorus the Rhodian, his own friend, he completely mutilated, and when he had cut off his ears and nose, he shut him up in a cage as if he were some strange and unknown animal and for a long time lived in terror of him, since the hideousness of his hacked and mutilated face had destroyed every appearance of a human being; to this were added starvation and squalor and the filth of a body left to wallow in its own dung; further more, his hands and knees becoming all calloused—

haec genibus manibusque, quas in usum pedum angustiae loci cogebant, lateribus vero adtritu exulceratis non minus foeda quam terribilis erat forma eius visentibus, factusque poena sua monstrum misericordiam quoque amiserat. Tamen, cum dissimillimus esset homini qui illa patiebatur, dissimilior erat qui faciebat.

1   18. Utinam ista saevitia intra peregrina exempla mansisset nec in Romanos mores cum aliis adventiciis vitiis etiam suppliciorum irarumque barbaria transisset ! M. Mario, cui vicatim populus statuas posuerat, cui ture ac vino supplicabat, L. Sulla praefringi crura, erui oculos, amputari linguam, manus iussit et, quasi totiens occideret quotiens vulnerabat, 2 paulatim et per singulos artus laceravit. Quis erat huius imperii minister ? Quis nisi Catilina iam in omne facinus manus exercens ? Is illum ante bustum Quinti Catuli carpebat gravissimus mitissimi viri cineribus, supra quos vir mali exempli, popularis tamen et non tam immerito quam nimis amatus per stillicidia sanguinem dabat. Dignus erat Marius qui illa pateretur, Sulla qui iuberet, Catilina qui faceret, sed indigna res publica quae in corpus suum pariter et hostium et vindicum gladios reciperet. 3 Quid antiqua perscrutor ? Modo C. Caesar Sex.

for by the narrowness of his quarters he was forced
to use these instead of feet—his sides, too, a mass of
sores from rubbing, to those who beheld him his
appearance was no less disgusting than terrible, and
having been turned by his punishment into a monster
he had forfeited even pity. Yet, while he who
suffered these things was utterly unlike a human
being, he who inflicted them was still less like one.

Would to heaven that the examples of such cruelty
had been confined to foreigners, and that along with
other vices from abroad the barbarity of torture and
such venting of anger had not been imported into the
practices of Romans! Marcus Marius, to whom the
people erected statues in every street, whom they
worshipped with offerings of frankincense and wine—
this man by the command of Lucius Sulla had his
ankles broken, his eyes gouged out, his tongue and
his hands cut off, and little by little and limb by limb
Sulla tore him to pieces, just as if he could make
him die as many times as he could maim him. And
who was it who executed this command? Who but
Catiline, already training his hands to every sort of
crime? He hacked him to pieces before the tomb
of Quintus Catulus, doing violence to the ashes of
that gentlest of men, above which a hero—of evil
influence, no doubt, yet popular and loved not so
much undeservedly as to excess—shed his blood
drop by drop. It was meet that a Marius should
suffer these things, that a Sulla should give the
orders, and that a Catiline should execute them, but
it was not meet that the state should receive in her
breast the swords of her enemies and her protectors
alike. But why do I search out ancient crimes?
Only recently Gaius Caesar slashed with the scourge

Papinium, cui pater erat consularis, Betilienum
Bassum quaestorem suum, procuratoris sui filium,
aliosque et senatores et equites Romanos uno die
flagellis cecidit, torsit, non quaestionis sed animi
4 causa ; deinde adeo impatiens fuit differendae
voluptatis, quam ingentem crudelitas eius sine
dilatione poscebat, ut in xysto maternorum hortorum,
qui porticum a ripa separat, inambulans quosdam
ex illis cum matronis atque aliis senatoribus ad
lucernam decollaret. Quid instabat ? Quod periculum aut privatum aut publicum una nox minabatur ?
Quantulum fuit lucem expectare denique, ne
senatores populi Romani soleatus occideret !

1   19. Quam superba fuerit crudelitas eius ad rem
pertinet scire, quamquam aberrare alicui possimus
videri et in devium exire ; sed hoc ipsum pars
erit irae super solita saevientis. Ceciderat flagellis
senatores ; ipse effecit, ut dici posset "solet fieri."
Torserat per omnia, quae in rerum natura tristissima
sunt, fidiculis, talaribus, eculeo, igne, vultu suo.
2 Et hoc loco respondebitur : " Magnam rem ! si tres
senatores quasi nequam mancipia inter verbera et
flammas divisit homo, qui de toto senatu trucidando
cogitabat, qui optabat, ut populus Romanus unam
cervicem haberet, ut scelera sua tot locis ac tem-
poribus diducta in unum ictum et unum diem
cogeret." Quid tam inauditum quam nocturnum

---

^a Literally "sandals," a conventional detail of Roman
dinner-dress.

and tortured Sextus Papinius, whose father had been consul, and Betilienus Bassus, his own quaestor and the son of his procurator, and others, both Roman senators and knights, all in one day—and not to extract information but for amusement. Then so impatient was he of postponing his pleasure—a pleasure so great that his cruelty demanded it without delay—that he decapitated some of his victims by lamplight, as he was strolling with some ladies and senators on the terrace of his mother's gardens, which runs between the colonnade and the bank of the river. But what was the pressing need ? What public or private danger was threatened by a single night's delay ? How small a matter it would have been if he had waited just till dawn, so as not to kill the senators of the Roman people in his pumps *a* !

It is relevant, too, to note the insolence of his cruelty, though some one may consider that we are straying from the subject and embarking upon a digression ; but such insolence will be an element in cruelty when it is extravagant in its fury. He had scourged senators, but he himself made it possible to say, " An ordinary event." He had tortured them by every unhappy device in existence—by the cord, by knotted bones, by the rack, by fire, by his own countenance. But here also will come the answer : " A great matter, truly ! Because three senators, as if no better than worthless slaves, were mangled by whip and flame at the behest of a man who contemplated murdering the whole senate, a man who used to wish that the Roman people had only one neck in order that he might concentrate into one day and one stroke all his crimes, now spread over so many places and times." What was ever so unheard of as an

supplicium ? Cum latrocinia tenebris abscondi
soleant, animadversiones, quo notiores sunt, plus
3 in exemplum emendationemque proficiant. Et hoc
loco respondebitur mihi : "Quod tanto opere ad-
miraris, isti beluae cotidianum est ; ad hoc vivit,
ad hoc vigilat, ad hoc lucubrat." Nemo certe
invenietur alius, qui imperaverit omnibus iis, in quos
animadverti iubebat, os inserta spongea includi, ne
vocis emittendae haberent facultatem. Cui umquam
morituro non est relictum qua gemeret ? Timuit,
ne quam liberiorem vocem extremus dolor mitteret,
ne quid quod nollet audiret ; sciebat autem in-
numerabilia esse, quae obicere illi nemo nisi periturus
4 auderet. Cum spongeae non invenirentur, scindi
vestimenta miserorum et in os farciri pannos imperavit. Quae ista saevitia est ? Liceat ultimum
spiritum trahere, da exiturae animae locum, liceat
5 illam non per vulnus emittere ! Adicere his longum
est, quod patres quoque occisorum eadem nocte
dimissis per domos centurionibus confecit, id est,
homo misericors luctu liberavit ! Non enim Gai
saevitiam, sed irae, propositum est describere, quae
non tantum viritim furit sed gentes totas lancinat,
sed urbes et flumina et tuta ab omni sensu doloris
converberat.

1   20. Sic rex Persarum totius populi nares recidit

---

^a See the story of Cyrus and the river Gyndes, *De Ira*, iii.
21 ; of Xerxes' rage against the Hellespont, Herodotus, vii.
35.

execution by night ? Though robberies are generally curtained by darkness, the more publicity punishments have, the more may they avail as an admonition and warning. But here also I shall hear the answer : "That which surprises you so much is the daily habit of that beast ; for this he lives, for this he loses sleep, for this he burns the midnight oil." But surely you will find no other man who has bidden that the mouths of all those who were to be executed by his orders should be gagged by inserting a sponge, in order that they might not even have the power to utter a cry. What doomed man was ever before deprived of the breath with which to moan ? Caesar feared lest the man's last agony should give utterance to some speech too frank, lest he might hear something that he would rather not. He was well aware, too, that there were countless crimes, with which none but a dying man would dare reproach him. If no sponges were to be found, he ordered the garments of the poor wretches to be torn up, and their mouths to be stuffed with the strips. What savagery is this ? Let a man draw his last breath, leave a passage for his departing soul, let it have some other course of exit than a wound ! It would be tedious to add more—how he sent officers to the homes of his victims, and on that same night made away with their fathers too—that is, out of human pity he freed the fathers from their sorrow ! And, indeed, my purpose is not to picture the cruelty of Gaius, but the cruelty of anger, which not only vents its fury on a man here and there, but rends in pieces whole nations, which lashes cities and rivers ^a and lifeless things that are immune to all feeling of pain.

Thus, the king of the Persians cut off the noses of

in Syria, unde Rhinocolura loco nomen est. Peper-
cisse illum iudicas, quod non tota capita praecidit ?
2 Novo genere poenae delectatus est. Tale aliquid
passi forent et Aethiopes, qui ob longissimum vitae
spatium Macrobioe appellantur ; in hos enim, quia
non supinis manibus exceperant servitutem missisque
legatis libera responsa dederant, quae contumeliosa
reges vocant, Cambyses fremebat et non provisis
commeatibus, non exploratis itineribus, per invia,
per arentia trahebat omnem bello utilem turbam.
Cui intra primum iter deerant necessaria, nec quicquam subministrabat sterilis et inculta humanoque
3 ignota vestigio regio. Sustinebant famem primo
tenerrima frondium et cacumina arborum, tum coria
igne mollita et quidquid necessitas cibum fecerat ;
postquam inter harenas radices quoque et herbae
defecerant apparuitque inops etiam animalium
solitudo, decimum quemque sortiti alimentum ha-
4 buerunt fame saevius. Agebat adhuc regem ira
praecipitem, cum partem exercitus amisisset, partem
comedisset, donec timuit, ne et ipse vocaretur ad
sortem. Tum demum signum receptui dedit. Serva-
bantur interim generosae illi aves et instrumenta
epularum camelis vehebantur, cum sortirentur
milites eius, quis male periret, quis peius viveret.

a whole population in Syria, whence it gets its name of " Land-of-the-stump-nosed." Think you he was merciful because he did not cut off their entire heads ? No, he got some pleasure from a new kind of punishment. And the Ethiopians, who on account of the prodigiously long time they live are known as the " Longevals," might also have suffered some such fate. For Cambyses became enraged against them because, instead of embracing servitude with outstretched arms, they sent envoys and made reply in the independent words which kings call insults ; wherefore, without providing supplies, without investigating the roads, through a trackless and desert region he hurried against them his whole host of fighting men. During the first day's march his food supplies began to fail, and the country itself, barren and uncultivated and untrodden by the foot of man, furnished them nothing. At first the tenderest parts of leaves and shoots of trees satisfied their hunger, then skins softened by fire and whatever necessity forced them to use as food. After, amid the desert sands, even roots and herbage failed them, and they viewed a wilderness destitute also of animal life, choosing every tenth man by lot, they secured the nutriment that was more cruel than hunger. And still the king was driven headlong onwards by his anger, until having lost one part of his army and having devoured another part, he began to fear that he too might be summoned to the choice by lot. Only then did he give the signal for retreat. And all the while fowls of choice breed were being kept for him, and camels carried supplies for his feasts, while his soldiers drew lots to discover who should miserably perish, who should more miserably live.

1 21. Hic iratus fuit genti et ignotae et immeritae, sensurae tamen ; Cyrus flumini. Nam cum Babylona oppugnaturus festinaret ad bellum, cuius maxima momenta in occasionibus sunt, Gynden late fusum amnem vado transire temptavit, quod vix tutum est, etiam cum sensit aestatem et ad minimum 2 deductus est. Ibi unus ex iis equis, qui trahere regium currum albi solebant, abreptus vehementer commovit regem ; iuravit itaque se amnem illum regis comitatus auferentem eo redacturum, ut 3 transiri calcarique etiam a feminis posset. Hoc deinde omnem transtulit belli apparatum et tam diu adsedit operi, donec centum et octoginta cuniculis divisum alveum in trecentos et sexaginta rivos dispergeret, siccum relinqueret in diversum fluentibus 4 aquis. Periit itaque et tempus, magna in magnis rebus iactura, et militum ardor, quem inutilis labor fregit, et occasio adgrediendi imparatos, dum ille 5 bellum indictum hosti cum flumine gerit. Hic furor —quid enim aliud voces ?—Romanos quoque contigit. C. enim Caesar villam in Herculanensi pulcherrimam, quia mater sua aliquando in illa custodita erat, diruit fecitque eius per hoc notabilem fortunam ; stantem enim praenavigabamus, nunc causa dirutae quaeritur.

308

This man raged against a people unknown and inoffensive, yet able to feel his anger ; Cyrus, however, raged against a river. For when, with the purpose of taking Babylon, he was hastening to war —in which the favourable opportunity is of the utmost importance—he attempted to ford the river Gyndes, then in full flood, though such an undertaking is scarcely safe even after the river has felt the heat of summer and is reduced to its smallest volume. There, when one of the white horses which regularly drew the royal chariot was swept away, the king became mightily stirred. And so he swore that he would reduce that river, which was carrying away the retinue of the king, to such proportions that even women could cross it and trample it under foot. To this task, then, he transferred all his preparations for war, and having lingered thereat long enough to cut one hundred and eighty runways across the channel of the river, he distributed its water into three hundred and sixty runnels, which flowing in different directions left the channel dry. And so he sacrificed time, a serious loss in important operations, the enthusiasm of his soldiers, which was crushed by the useless toil, and the opportunity of attacking the enemy unprepared, while he waged against a river the war he had declared against a foe. Such madness—for what else can you call it ?—has befallen Romans also. For Gaius Caesar destroyed a very beautiful villa near Herculaneum because his mother had once been imprisoned in it, and by his very act gave publicity to her misfortune ; for while the villa stood, we used to sail by unconcerned, but now people ask why it was destroyed.

1   22. Et haec cogitanda sunt exempla, quae vites,
et illa ex contrario, quae sequaris, moderata, lenia,
quibus nec ad irascendum causa defuit nec ad ulci-
2 scendum potestas.   Quid enim facilius fuit Antigono
quam duos manipulares duci iubere, qui incumbentes
regis tabernaculo faciebant, quod homines et pericu-
losissime et libentissime faciunt, de rege suo male
existimabant ? Audierat omnia Antigonus, utpote
cum inter dicentes et audientem palla interesset ;
quam ille leviter commovit et : " Longius," inquit,
3 " discedite, ne vos rex audiat." Idem quadam nocte,
cum quosdam ex militibus suis exaudisset omnia
mala imprecantis regi, qui ipsos in illud iter et in-
extricabile lutum deduxisset, accessit ad eos, qui
maxime laborabant, et cum ignorantis a quo adiu-
varentur explicuisset : " Nunc," inquit, " male dicite
Antigono, cuius vitio in has miserias incidistis ; ei
autem bene optate, qui vos ex hac voragine eduxit."
4 Idem tam miti animo hostium suorum male dicta
quam civium tulit. Itaque cum in parvulo quodam
castello Graeci obsiderentur et fiducia loci contemnentes hostem multa in deformitatem Antigoni
iocarentur et nunc staturam humilem, nunc collisum
nasum deriderent : " Gaudeo," inquit, " et aliquid
5 boni spero, si in castris meis Silenum habeo." Cum
hos dicaces fame domuisset, captis sic usus est, ut
eos qui militiae utiles erant in cohortes discriberet,
ceteros praeconi subiceret, idque se negavit facturum

These should be regarded as examples to be avoided ; the following, on the other hand, are to be imitated, being instances of restrained and gentle men, who lacked neither the provocation to anger nor the power of requital. What indeed would have been easier than for Antigonus to order the execution of the two common soldiers, who, while they leaned against the royal tent, expressed—as men will do with equally great danger and delight—their ill opinion of their king ? Antigonus heard everything, only a canvas intervening between the speakers and the listener ; this he gently shook and said, " Move a little farther off, for the king might hear you." Again, one night, when he overheard some of his soldiers invoking all kinds of curses upon the king for having led them into such a road and inextricable mud, he went up to those who were struggling most, and when he had got them out, without revealing who their helper was, he said, " Now curse Antigonus, by whose fault you have fallen upon this mishap, but bless him who has led you out of this swamp." He also bore the abuse of his enemies as calmly as that of his countrymen. And so, when he was besieging some Greeks in a small fort, and they, confident in their position, showed open contempt for the enemy, and cracking many jokes upon the ugliness of Antigonus scoffed now at his diminutive stature, now at his flattened nose, he merely said, " If I have a Silenus in my camp, I am fortunate and hope for good luck." When he had subdued these wags by hunger, he disposed of his captives as follows : those who were fit for military service he assigned to regiments ; the rest he put up at auction, saying that he would not have done

fuisse, nisi expediret iis dominum habere, qui tam malam haberent linguam.

1   23. Huius nepos fuit Alexander, qui lanceam in convivas suos torquebat, qui ex duobus amicis, quos paulo ante rettuli, alterum ferae obiecit, alterum sibi. Ex his duobus tamen qui leoni obiectus est

2 vixit. Non habuit hoc avitum ille vitium, ne paternum quidem ; nam si qua alia in Philippo virtus, fuit et contumeliarum patientia, ingens instrumentum ad tutelam regni. Demochares ad illum Parrhesiastes ob nimiam et procacem linguam appellatus inter alios Atheniensium legatos venerat. Audita benigne legatione Philippus : " Dicite," inquit, " mihi, facere quid possim, quod sit Atheniensibus gratum." Excepit Demochares et : " Te," inquit,

3 " suspendere." Indignatio circumstantium ad tam inhumanum responsum exorta erat ; quos Philippus conticiscere iussit et Thersitam illum salvum incolumemque dimittere. " At vos," inquit, " ceteri legati, nuntiate Atheniensibus multo superbiores esse, qui ista dicunt, quam qui impune dicta audiunt."

4   Multa et divus Augustus digna memoria fecit dixitque, ex quibus appareat iram illi non imperasse. Timagenes historiarum scriptor quaedam in ipsum, quaedam in uxorem eius et in totam domum dixerat nec perdiderat dicta ; magis enim circumfertur et

5 in ore hominum est temeraria urbanitas. Saepe illum Caesar monuit, moderatius lingua uteretur ;

---

   [a] A mistake. Alexander was the grandson of Amyntas ; Antigonus (Μονόφθαλμος) was one of Alexander's generals.
   [b] *i.e.*, " the Outspoken " (Παρρησιαστής).
   [c] A Greek in the camp before Troy, noted for his bold and impudent tongue.

so had it not seemed good for men who had such an evil tongue to find a master.

The grandson of this man was Alexander,[a] who used to hurl his spear at his dinner-guests, who, of the two friends mentioned above, exposed one to the fury of a wild beast, the other to his own. Of these two, however, the one who was thrown to a lion lived. Alexander did not get this weakness from his grandfather, nor from his father either; for if Philip possessed any virtues at all, among them was the ability to endure insults—a great help in the maintenance of a throne. Demochares, surnamed Parrhesiastes[b] on account of his bold and impudent tongue, came to him once in company with other envoys from the Athenians. Having granted the delegation a friendly hearing, Philip said, " Tell me what I can do that will please the Athenians." Demochares took him at his word and replied, " Hang yourself." All the bystanders flared up in indignation at such brutal words, but Philip bade them keep quiet and let that Thersites[c] withdraw safe and unharmed. " But you," he said, " you other envoys, go tell the Athenians that those who speak such words show far more arrogance than those who listen to them without retaliation."

The deified Augustus also did and said many things that are memorable, which prove that he was not ruled by anger. Timagenes, a writer of history, made some unfriendly remarks about the emperor himself, his wife, and all his family, and they had not been lost; for reckless wit gets bandied about more freely and is on everybody's lips. Often did Caesar warn him that he must have a more prudent tongue; when he persisted, he forbade

perseveranti domo sua interdixit. Postea Timagenes
in contubernio Pollionis Asinii consenuit ac tota
civitate direptus est. Nullum illi limen praeclusa
6 Caesaris domus abstulit. Historias, quas postea
scripserat, recitavit et libros acta Caesaris Augusti
continentis in igne posuit et combussit; inimicitias
gessit cum Caesare; nemo amicitiam eius extimuit,
nemo quasi fulguritum refugit, fuit qui praeberet
tam alte cadenti sinum. Tulit hoc, ut dixi, Caesar
7 patienter, ne eo quidem motus, quod laudibus suis
rebusque gestis manus attulerat; numquam cum
8 hospite inimici sui questus est. Hoc dumtaxat
Pollioni Asinio dixit: θηριοτροφεῖς; paranti deinde
excusationem obstitit et "Fruere," inquit, "mi
Pollio, fruere!" et cum Pollio diceret: "Si iubes,
Caesar, statim illi domo mea interdicam," "Hoc
me," inquit, "putas facturum, cum ego vos in
gratiam reduxerim?" Fuerat enim aliquando Tima-
geni Pollio iratus nec ullam aliam habuerat causam
desinendi, quam quod Caesar coeperat.
1   24. Dicat itaque sibi quisque, quotiens lacessitur:
"Numquid potentior sum Philippo? Illi tamen
impune male dictum est. Numquid in domo mea
plus possum quam toto orbe terrarum divus Augustus
potuit? Ille tamen contentus fuit a conviciatore
2 suo secedere." Quid est quare ego servi mei clarius
responsum et contumaciorem voltum et non per-

ᵃ There is greater wit in the Greek, which permits also
the interpretation "You keep a menagerie"—a common
amusement of rich men.

him the palace. After this, Timagenes lived to old age in the house of Asinius Pollio, and was lionized by the whole city. Though Caesar had excluded him from the palace, he was debarred from no other door. He gave readings of the history which he had written after the incident, and the books which contained the doings of Augustus Caesar he put in the fire and burned. He maintained hostility against Caesar, yet no one feared to be his friend, no one shrank from him as a blasted man ; though he fell from such a height, he found some one ready to take him to his bosom. As I have said, Caesar bore all of this patiently, not even moved by the fact that his renown and his achievements had been assailed ; he made no complaint against the host of his enemy. To Asinius Pollio he merely said, " You're keeping a wild beast." *a* Then, when the other was trying to offer some excuse, he stopped him and said, " Enjoy yourself, my dear Pollio, enjoy yourself ! " and when Pollio declared, " If you bid me, Caesar, I shall forthwith deny him the house," he replied, " Do you think that I would do this, when it was I who restored the friendship between you ? " For the fact is, Pollio had once had a quarrel with Timagenes, and his only reason for ending it was that Caesar had now begun one.

Whenever a man is provoked, therefore, let him say to himself, " Am I more mighty than Philip ? Yet he was cursed and did not retaliate. Have I more authority over my house than the deified Augustus had over all the world ? Yet he was content merely to keep away from his maligner." What right have I to make my slave atone by stripes and manacles for too loud a reply, too rebellious a

315

venientem usque ad me murmurationem flagellis
et compedibus expiem? Quis sum, cuius aures
laedi nefas sit? Ignoverunt multi hostibus; ego
non ignoscam pigris, neglegentibus, garrulis?
3 Puerum aetas excuset, feminam sexus, extraneum
libertas, domesticum familiaritas. Nunc primum
offendit, cogitemus quam diu placuerit; saepe et
alias offendit, feramus quod diu tulimus. Amicus
est, fecit quod noluit; inimicus, fecit quod debuit.
4 Prudentiori credamus, stultiori remittamus. Pro
quocumque illud nobis respondeamus, sapientis-
simos quoque viros multa delinquere, neminem esse
tam circumspectum, cuius non diligentia aliquando
sibi ipsa excidat, neminem tam maturum, cuius non
gravitatem in aliquod fervidius factum casus impingat,
neminem tam timidum offensarum, qui non in illas,
dum vitat, incidat.
1 25. Quomodo homini pusillo solacium in malis
fuit etiam magnorum virorum titubare fortunam,
et aequiore animo filium in angulo flevit, qui vidit
acerba funera etiam ex regia duci, sic animo aequiore
fert ab aliquo laedi, ab aliquo contemni, cuicumque
venit in mentem nullam esse tantam potentiam,
2 in quam non occurrat iniuria. Quod si etiam pru-
dentissimi peccant, cuius non error bonam causam
habet? Respiciamus quotiens adulescentia nostra
in officio parum diligens fuerit, in sermone parum
modesta, in vino parum temperans. Si iratus est,
demus illi spatium, quo dispicere quid fecerit possit;

look, a muttering of something that I do not quite hear ? Who am I that it should be a crime to offend my ears ? Many have pardoned their enemies ; shall I not pardon the lazy, the careless, and the babbler ? Let a child be excused by his age, a woman by her sex, a stranger by his independence, a servant by the bond of intercourse. Does some one offend for the first time ? Let us reflect how long he has pleased us. At other times and often has he given offence ? Let us bear longer what we have long borne. Is he a friend ? He has done what he did not mean to do. Is he an enemy ? He did what he had a right to do. One that is sensible let us believe, one that is foolish let us forgive. Whoever it may be, let us say to ourselves on his behalf that even the wisest men have many faults, that no man is so guarded that he does not sometimes let his diligence lapse, none so seasoned that accident does not drive his composure into some hot-headed action, none so fearful of giving offence that he does not stumble into it while seeking to avoid it.

As to the humble man, it brings comfort in trouble that great men's fortune also totters, and as he who weeps for his son in a hovel is more content if he has seen the piteous procession move from the palace also, so a man is more content to be injured by one, to be scorned by another, if he takes thought that no power is so great as to be beyond the reach of harm. But if even the wisest do wrong, whose sin will not have good excuse ? Let us look back upon our youth and recall how often we were too careless about duty, too indiscreet in speech, too intemperate in wine. If a man gets angry, let us give him enough time to discover what he has done ;

ipse se castigabit. Denique debeat poenas ; non
3 est quod cum illo paria faciamus. Illud non veniet
in dubium, quin se exemerit turbae et altius steterit
quisquis despexit lacessentis. Proprium est magnitudinis verae non sentire percussum. Sic immanis
fera ad latratum canum lenta respexit, sic irritus
ingenti scopulo fluctus adsultat. Qui non irascitur,
inconcussus iniuria perstitit, qui irascitur, motus
4 est. At ille, quem modo altiorem omni incommodo
posui, tenet amplexu quodam summum bonum, nec
homini tantum, sed ipsi fortunae respondet : " Omnia
licet facias, minor es, quam ut serenitatem meam
obducas. Vetat hoc ratio, cui vitam regendam dedi.
Plus mihi nocitura est ira quam iniuria. Quidni
plus ? Illius modus certus est, ista quo usque me
latura sit dubium est."

1   26. " Non possum," inquis, " pati ; grave est iniuriam sustinere." Mentiris ; quis enim iniuriam
non potest ferre, qui potest iram ? Adice nunc quod
id agis, ut et iram feras et iniuriam. Quare fers aegri
rabiem et phrenetici verba, puerorum protervas
manus ? Nempe quia videntur nescire quid faciant.
Quid interest, quo quisque vitio fiat imprudens ?
2 Imprudentia par in omnibus patrocinium est. " Quid
ergo ? " inquis, " impune illi erit ? " Puta velle te,

he will chastise himself. Suppose in the end he deserves punishment ; then there is no reason why we should match his misdeeds. There will be no doubt about this—that whoever scorns his tormentors removes himself from the common herd and towers above them. The mark of true greatness is not to notice that you have received a blow. So does the huge wild beast calmly turn and gaze at barking dogs, so does the wave dash in vain against a mighty cliff. The man who does not get angry stands firm, unshaken by injury ; he who gets angry is over-thrown. But he whom I have just set above the reach of all harm holds, as it were, in his arms the highest good, and not only to a man, but to Fortune herself, he will say : " Do what you will, you are too puny to disturb my serenity. Reason, to whom I have committed the guidance of my life, forbids it. My anger is likely to do me more harm than your wrong. And why not more ? The limit of the injury is fixed, but how far the anger will sweep me no man knows."

" I cannot," you say, " be forbearing ; it is difficult to submit to a wrong." That is not true ; for who that can tolerate anger will yet be unable to tolerate wrong ? Besides, what you now propose is to tolerate both anger and wrong. Why do you tolerate the delirium of a sick man, the ravings of a lunatic, or the wanton blows of children ? Because, of course, they seem not to know what they are doing. What difference does it make what weakness it is that makes a person irresponsible ? The plea of irresponsibility holds equally good for all. " What then ? " you say ; " shall the man go unpunished ? " Grant that you wish it so, nevertheless it will not be

tamen non erit ; maxima est enim factae iniuriae
poena fecisse, nec quisquam gravius adficitur quam
3 qui ad supplicium paenitentiae traditur. Deinde
ad condicionem rerum humanarum respiciendum
est, ut omnium accidentium aequi iudices simus ;
iniquus autem est, qui commune vitium singulis
obiecit. Non est Aethiopis inter suos insignitus
color, nec rufus crinis et coactus in nodum apud
Germanos virum dedecet. Nihil in uno iudicabis
notabile aut foedum, quod genti suae publicum est ;
et ista, quae rettuli, unius regionis atque anguli
consuetudo defendit. Vide nunc, quanto in iis
iustior venia sit, quae per totum genus humanum
4 vulgata sunt. Omnes inconsulti et improvidi sumus,
omnes incerti, queruli, ambitiosi,—quid lenioribus
verbis ulcus publicum abscondo ?—omnes mali
sumus. Quidquid itaque in alio reprenditur, id
unusquisque in sinu suo inveniet. Quid illius
pallorem, illius maciem notas ? Pestilentia est.
Placidiores itaque invicem simus ; mali inter malos
vivimus. Una nos res facere quietos potest, mutuae
5 facilitatis conventio. " Ille iam mihi nocuit, ego
illi nondum." Sed iam aliquem fortasse laesisti,
sed laedes. Noli aestumare hanc horam aut hunc
diem, totum inspice mentis tuae habitum ; etiam si
nihil mali fecisti, potes facere.

1   27. Quanto satius est sanare iniuriam quam

so ; for the greatest punishment of wrong-doing is the having done it, and no man is more heavily punished than he who is consigned to the torture of remorse. Again, we must consider the limitations of our human lot if we are to be just judges of all that happens ; he, however, is unjust who blames the individual for a fault that is universal. Amongst his own people the colour of the Ethiopian is not notable, and amongst the Germans red hair gathered into a knot is not unseemly for a man. You are to count nothing odd or disgraceful for an individual which is a general characteristic of his nation ; even those examples that I have cited can plead in defence the practice of some one section and corner of the world. Consider now how much more justly excuse may be made for those qualities that are common to the whole human race. We are all inconsiderate and unthinking, we are all untrustworthy, discontented, ambitious—why should I hide the universal sore by softer words ?—we are all wicked. And so each man will find in his own breast the fault which he censures in another. Why do you notice the pallor of A, the gauntness of B ? These qualities are epidemic ! And so let us be more kindly toward one another ; we being wicked live among the wicked. Only one thing can bring us peace—the compact of mutual indulgence. You say, perhaps, " That man has already injured me, but I have not yet injured him." But perhaps you have already harmed, perhaps you will some day harm, some man. Do not count only this hour or this day ; consider the whole character of your mind—even if you have done no wrong, you are capable of doing it.

How much better it is to heal than to avenge an

ulcisci ! Multum temporis ultio absumit, multis
se iniuriis obicit, dum una dolet ; diutius irascimur
omnes quam laedimur. Quanto melius est abire
in diversum nec vitia vitiis opponere ! Numquis
satis constare sibi videatur, si mulam calcibus repetat
2 et canem morsu ? " Ista," inquis, " peccare se
nesciunt." Primum quam iniquus est, apud quem
hominem esse ad impetrandam veniam nocet !
Deinde, si cetera animalia hoc irae tuae subducit,
quod consilio carent, eodem loco tibi sit quisquis
consilio caret ; quid enim refert an alia mutis dis-
similia habeat, si hoc, quod in omni peccato muta
3 defendit, simile habet, caliginem mentis ? Peccavit ;
hoc enim primum ? Hoc enim extremum ? Non
est quod illi credas, etiam si dixerit : " Iterum non
faciam." Et iste peccabit et in istum alius et tota
vita inter errores volutabitur. Mansuete imman-
4 sueta tractanda sunt. Quod in luctu dici solet
efficacissime, et in ira dicetur : utrum aliquando
desines an numquam ? Si aliquando, quanto satius
est iram relinquere quam ab ira relinqui ! An
semper haec concitatio permanebit ? Vides quam
impacatam tibi denunties vitam ? Qualis enim erit
5 semper tumentis ? Adice nunc quod, cum bene te
ipse succenderis et subinde causas, quibus stimuleris

injury ! Vengeance consumes much time, and it exposes the doer to many injuries while he smarts from one ; our anger always lasts longer than the hurt. How much better it is to take the opposite course and not to match fault with fault. Would any one think that he was well balanced if he repaid a mule with kicks and a dog with biting ? But you say, " Those creatures do not know that they are doing wrong." In the first place, how unjust is he in whose eyes being a man is fatal to obtaining pardon ! In the second place, if other creatures escape your anger for the very reason that they are lacking in understanding, every man who lacks understanding should hold in your eyes a like position. For what difference does it make that his other qualities are unlike those of dumb animals if he resembles them in the one quality that excuses dumb animals for every misdeed—a mind that is all darkness ? " He did wrong," you say. Well, was this the first time ? Will it be the last time ? You need not believe him even if he should say, " I will never do it again." He will go on sinning and some one else will sin against him, and the whole of life will be a tossing about amid errors. Unkindness must be treated with kindness. The words so often addressed to one in grief will prove most effective also for a man in anger : " Will you ever desist—or never ? " If ever, how much better it is to forsake anger than to wait for anger to forsake you ! Or shall this turmoil continue for ever ? Do you see to what life-long unrest you are dooming yourself ? For what will be the life of one who is always swollen with rage ? Besides, when you have successfully inflamed yourself with passion, and have repeatedly

renovaveris, sua sponte ira discedet et vires illi dies
subtrahet. Quanto satius est a te illam vinci quam
a se !

1   28. Huic irasceris, deinde illi ; servis, deinde
libertis ; parentibus, deinde liberis ; notis, deinde
ignotis ; ubique enim causae supersunt, nisi de-
precator animus accessit. Hinc te illo furor rapiet,
illinc alio, et novis subinde irritamentis orientibus
continuabitur rabies. Age, infelix, ecquando ama-
bis ? O quam bonum tempus in re mala perdis !
2 Quanto nunc erat satius amicos parare, inimicos
mitigare, rem publicam administrare, transferre in
res domesticas operam, quam circumspicere, quid
alicui facere possis mali, quod aut dignitati eius aut
patrimonio aut corpori vulnus infligas, cum id tibi
contingere sine certamine ac periculo non possit,
3 etiam si cum inferiore concurses ! Vinctum licet
accipias et ad arbitrium tuum omni patientiae
expositum ; saepe nimia vis caedentis aut articulum
loco movit aut nervum in his quos fregerat dentibus
fixit. Multos iracundia mancos, multos debiles
fecit, etiam ubi patientem est[1] nancta materiam.
Adice nunc quod nihil tam imbecille natum est, ut
sine elidentis periculo pereat ; imbecillos valentis-
4 simis alias dolor, alias casus exaequat. Quid, quod
pleraque eorum, propter quae irascimur, offendunt
nos magis quam laedunt ? Multum autem interest,

---

[1] est *added by Petschenig.*

renewed the causes that spur you on, your anger
will leave you of its own accord, and lapse of time
will reduce its power. How much better it is that
it should be vanquished by you than by itself!

You will be angry first with this man, then with
that one; first with slaves, then with freedmen;
first with parents, then with children; first with
acquaintances, then with strangers; for there are
causes enough everywhere unless the mind enters
to intercede. Rage will sweep you hither and yon,
this way and that, and your madness will be prolonged by new provocations that constantly arise.
Tell me, unhappy man, will you ever find time to
love? What precious time you are wasting upon
an evil thing! How much better would it be at this
present moment to be gaining friends, reconciling
enemies, serving the state, devoting effort to private
affairs, than to be casting about to see what evil you
can do to some man, what wound you may deal to
his position, his estate, or his person, although you
cannot attain this without struggle and danger even
if your adversary be an inferior! You may take
him in chains and at your pleasure expose him to
every test of endurance; but too great violence in
the striker has often dislocated a joint, or left a sinew
fastened in the very teeth it had broken. Anger has
left many a man crippled, many disabled, even when
it has found its victim submissive. Besides, there
lives no creature so weak that it will die without
trying to harm its destroyer; sometimes pain, sometimes a mishap, makes the weak a match for the
strongest. And is it not true that most of the things
that make us angry offend us more than they harm
us? But it makes a great difference whether a man

utrum aliquis voluntati meae obstet an desit, eripiat
an non det. Atqui in aequo ponimus, utrum aliquis
auferat an neget, utrum spem nostram praecidat
an differat, utrum contra nos faciat an pro se, amore
5 alterius an odio nostri. Quidam vero non tantum
iustas causas standi contra nos, sed etiam honestas
habent. Alius patrem tuetur, alius fratrem, alius
patriam, alius amicum ; his tamen non ignoscimus
id facientibus, quod nisi facerent improbaremus,
immo, quod est incredibile, saepe de facto bene
6 existimamus, de faciente male. At me hercules
vir magnus ac iustus fortissimum quemque ex
hostibus suis et pro libertate ac salute patriae per-
tinacissimum suspicit et talem sibi civem, talem
militem contingere optat.

1   29. Turpe est odisse quem laudes ; quanto vero
turpius ob id aliquem odisse, propter quod misericordia dignus est. Si captivus in servitutem subito
depressus reliquias libertatis tenet nec ad sordida
ac laboriosa ministeria agilis occurrit, si ex otio piger
equum vehiculumque domini cursu non exaequat,
si inter cottidiana pervigilia fessum somnus op-
pressit, si rusticum laborem recusat aut non fortiter
obiit a servitute urbana et feriata translatus ad
2 durum opus, distinguamus, utrum aliquis non possit
an nolit. Multos absolvemus, si coeperimus ante
iudicare quam irasci. Nunc autem primum impetum

thwarts my wish or fails to further it, whether he robs me or merely fails to give. And yet we attach the same value to both—whether a man deprives us of something or merely withholds it, whether he shatters our hope or defers it, whether he acts against us or in his own interest, whether from love of another or from hatred of us. Some men, indeed, have not only just, but even honourable, reasons for opposing us. One is protecting his father, another his brother, another his country, another his friend. Nevertheless, we do not excuse these for doing the very thing which we should blame them for not doing; nay, more, though it is quite unbelievable, we often think well of an act, but ill of its doer. But, in very truth, a great and just man honours those of his foes who are bravest and are most stubborn in the defence of the liberty and the safety of their country, and prays that fortune may grant him such men as fellow-citizens, such as fellow-soldiers.

It is base to hate a man who commands your praise, but how much baser to hate any one for the very reason that he deserves your pity. If a captive, suddenly reduced to servitude, still retains some traces of his freedom and does not run nimbly to mean and toilsome tasks, if sluggish from inaction he does not keep pace with the speed of his master's horse and carriage, if worn out by his daily vigils he yields to sleep, if when transferred to hard labour from service in the city with its many holidays he either refuses the toil of the farm or does not enter into it with energy—in such cases let us discriminate, asking whether he cannot or will not serve. We shall acquit many if we begin with discernment instead of with anger. But as it is, we obey our first impulse; then,

327

sequimur, deinde, quamvis vana nos concitaverint, perseveramus, ne videamur coepisse sine causa, et, quod iniquissimum est, pertinaciores nos facit iniquitas irae ; retinemus enim illam et augemus, quasi argumentum sit iuste irascentis graviter irasci.

1 30. Quanto melius est initia ipsa perspicere quam levia sint, quam innoxia ! Quod accidere vides animalibus mutis, idem in homine deprendes ; frivolis turbamur et inanibus. Taurum color rubicundus excitat, ad umbram aspis exsurgit, ursos leonesque mappa proritat ; omnia, quae natura fera 2 ac rabida sunt, consternantur ad vana. Idem inquietis et stolidis ingeniis evenit. Rerum suspicione feriuntur, adeo quidem, ut interdum iniurias vocent modica beneficia, in quibus frequentissima, certe acerbissima iracundiae materia est. Carissimis enim irascimur, quod minora nobis praestiterint quam mente conceperimus quamque alii tulerint, cum 3 utriusque rei paratum remedium sit. Magis alteri indulsit ; nostra nos sine comparatione delectent. Numquam erit felix, quem torquebit felicior. Minus habeo quam speravi ; sed fortasse plus speravi quam debui. Haec pars maxime metuenda est, hinc perniciosissimae irae nascuntur et sanctissima quaeque invasurae.

4 Divum Iulium plures amici confecerunt quam inimici, quorum non expleverat spes inexplebiles.

although we have been aroused by mere trifles, we continue to be angry for fear that we may seem to have had no reason to be so from the first, and—what is most unjust—the very injustice of our anger makes us the more obstinate. For we hold on to it and nurse it, as if the violence of our anger were proof of its justice.

How much better it is to perceive its first beginnings—how slight, how harmless they are! You will find that the same thing happens with a man which you observe in dumb animals; we are ruffled by silly and petty things. The bull is aroused by a red colour, the asp strikes at a shadow, bears and lions are irritated by a handkerchief; all creatures by nature wild and savage are alarmed by trifles. The same is true of men, whether they are by nature restless or inert. They are smitten with suspicions, so powerfully, even, that they sometimes call moderate benefits injuries; these are the most common, certainly the most bitter, source of anger. For we become angry at our dearest friends because they have bestowed less than we anticipated, and less than they conferred upon another; and yet for both troubles there is a ready remedy. More favour has been shown another; then let us without making comparison be pleased with what we have. That man will never be happy whom the sight of a happier man tortures. I may have less than I hoped for; but perhaps I hoped for more than I ought. It is from this direction that we have most to fear; from this springs the anger that is most destructive, that will assail all that is most holy.

Among those who dispatched the divine Julius there were more friends than enemies—friends whose insatiate hopes he had failed to satisfy. He wished

Voluit quidem ille—neque enim quisquam liberalius
victoria usus est, ex qua nihil sibi vindicavit nisi
dispensandi potestatem, — sed quemadmodum suf-
ficere tam improbis desideriis posset, cum tantum
omnes concupiscerent, quantum unus poterat?
5 Vidit itaque strictis circa sellam suam gladiis commilitones suos, Cimbrum Tillium, acerrimum paulo
ante partium defensorem, aliosque post Pompeium
demum Pompeianos. Haec res sua in reges arma
convertit fidissimosque eo compulit, ut de morte
eorum cogitarent, pro quibus et ante quos mori
votum habuerant.
1 31. Nulli ad aliena respicienti sua placent. Inde
diis quoque irascimur, quod aliquis nos antecedat,
obliti quantum hominum retro sit, et paucis inviden-
tem quantum sequatur a tergo ingentis invidiae.
Tanta tamen importunitas hominum est, ut, quamvis
multum acceperint, iniuriae loco sit plus accipere
2 potuisse. " Dedit mihi praeturam, sed consulatum
speraveram ; dedit duodecim fasces, sed non fecit
ordinarium consulem ; a me numerari voluit annum,
sed deest mihi ad sacerdotium ; cooptatus in col-
legium sum, sed cur in unum? Consummavit
dignitatem meam, sed patrimonio nihil contulit ;
ea dedit mihi, quae debebat alicui dare, de suo nihil
3 protulit." Age potius gratias pro his, quae accepisti ;
reliqua expecta et nondum plenum esse te gaude ;

---

    ^a *i.e.*, ironically, open enemies of Caesar.
    ^b Under the empire the term of the consular office was
shortened, and several pairs of consuls were nominated for
one year ; those who entered upon office at the beginning of
the year gave their names to the year (*consules ordinarii*),
and thus gained more prestige than the others (*consules
suffecti*).

indeed to do so—for no man ever made a more generous
use of victory, from which he claimed nothing for
himself except the right to give away—but how could
he gratify such unconscionable desires, since every one
of them coveted as much as any *one* could possibly
covet ? And so he saw his fellow-soldiers around
his chair with their swords drawn—Tillius Cimber, a
little while before the boldest defender of his cause,
and others who, after Pompey was no more, had at
length become Pompeians.[a] It is this that turns
against kings their own weapons, and drives their
most trusted followers to the point of planning for
the death of those for whom and before whom they
had vowed to die.

No man when he views the lot of others is content
with his own. This is why we grow angry even at the
gods, because some person is ahead of us, forgetting
how many men there are behind us, and how huge a
mass of envy follows at the back of him who envies but
a few. Nevertheless such is the presumptuousness
of men that, although they may have received much,
they count it an injury that they might have received
more. " He gave me the praetorship, but I had
hoped for the consulship ; he gave me the twelve
fasces, but he did not make me a regular consul ;
he was willing that my name should be attached to
the year,[b] but he disappointed me with respect to
the priesthood ; I was elected a member of the
college, but why of one only ? he crowned me with
public honour, but he added nothing to my patrimony ;
what he gave me he had to give to somebody—he
took nothing out of his own pocket." Express thanks
rather for what you have received ; wait for the rest,
and be glad that you are not yet surfeited. There is a

inter voluptates est superesse quod speres. Omnes
vicisti, primum esse te in animo amici tui laetare ;
multi te vincunt, considera, quanto antecedas plures
quam sequaris. Quod sit in te vitium maximum
quaeris ? Falsas rationes conficis ; data magno
aestumas, accepta parvo.

1   32. Aliud in alio nos deterreat. Quibusdam
timeamus irasci, quibusdam vereamur, quibusdam
fastidiamus. Magnam rem sine dubio fecerimus,
si servulum infelicem in ergastulum miserimus !
Quid properamus verberare statim, crura protinus
2 frangere ? Non peribit potestas ista, si differetur.
Sine id tempus veniat, quo ipsi iubeamus ; nunc ex
imperio irae loquemur ; cum illa abierit, tunc videbimus, quanto ista lis aestumanda sit. In hoc enim
praecipue fallimur ; ad ferrum venimus, ad capitalia
supplicia, et vinculis, carcere, fame vindicamus rem
3 castigandam flagris levioribus. " Quomodo," inquis,
" nos iubes intueri, quam omnia, per quae laedi
videamur, exigua, misera, puerilia sint ? " Ego
vero nihil magis suaserim quam sumere ingentem
animum et haec, propter quae litigamus, discurrimus,
anhelamus, videre quam humilia et abiecta sint,
nulli qui altum quiddam aut magnificum cogitat
respicienda.

1   33. Circa pecuniam plurimum vociferationis est.
Haec fora defetigat, patres liberosque committit,
venena miscet, gladios tam percussoribus quam legio-

pleasure in having something left to hope for. Have
you outstripped all others ? Rejoice that you are first
in the regard of your friend. Are there many who outstrip you ? Consider how many more you are ahead
of than behind. Do you ask me what is your greatest
fault ? Your book-keeping is wrong ; what you have
paid out you rate high; what you have received, low.

Different considerations should in different cases
restrain us. From some let fear stay our anger, from
others respect, from others pride. A fine thing we
shall have done, no doubt, if we send a wretched slave
to prison ! Why are we in such a hurry to flog him at
once, to break his legs forthwith ? Such power, though
deferred, will not perish. Wait for the time when
the order will be our own; at the moment we
shall speak under the dictation of anger ; when that
has passed, then we shall be able to see at what
value we should appraise the damage. For it is in
this that we are most liable to be wrong. We resort
to the sword and to capital punishment, and an act
that deserves the censure of a very light flogging
we punish by chains, the prison, and starvation.
" In what way," you ask, " do you bid us discover
how paltry, how pitiful, how childish are all those
things by which we think we are injured ? " I,
assuredly, could suggest nothing better than that you
acquire a truly great spirit, and that you realize how
sordid and worthless are all these things for the sake
of which we wrangle, rush to and fro, and pant ; these
do not deserve a thought from the man who has any
high and noble purpose

Most of the outcry is about money. It is this which
wearies the courts, pits father against son, brews
poisons, and gives swords alike to the legions and to

nibus tradit ; haec est sanguine nostro delibuta ;
propter hanc uxorum maritorumque noctes strepunt
litibus et tribunalia magistratuum premit turba,
reges saeviunt rapiuntque et civitates longo saecu-
lorum labore constructas evertunt, ut aurum argen-
2 tumque in cinere urbium scrutentur. Libet intueri
fiscos in angulo iacentis. Hi sunt propter quos oculi
clamore exprimantur, fremitu iudiciorum basilicae
resonent, evocati ex longinquis regionibus iudices
3 sedeant iudicaturi, utrius iustior avaritia sit. Quid
si ne propter fiscum quidem, sed pugnum aeris aut
imputatum a servo denarium senex sine herede
moriturus stomacho dirumpitur ? Quid si propter
usuram vel milensimam valetudinarius faenerator
distortis pedibus et manibus ad computandum non
relictis clamat ac per vadimonia asses suos in ipsis
4 morbi accessionibus vindicat ? Si totam mihi ex
omnibus metallis, quae cum maxime deprimimus,
pecuniam proferas, si in medium proicias quidquid
thensauri tegunt, avaritia iterum sub terras referente,
quae male egesserat, omnem istam congeriem non
putem dignam quae frontem viri boni contrahat.
Quanto risu prosequenda sunt quae nobis lacrimas
educunt !

1   34. Cedo nunc, persequere cetera, cibos, potiones
horumque causa paratas in ambitionem munditias,
verba contumeliosa, motus corporum parum honori-
ficos, contumacia iumenta et pigra mancipia, et

ª Literally, "interest of one thousandth," reckoned as a
monthly payment.   This rate of one and one-fifth per cent
per annum was absurdly low ; the usual rate was twelve
per cent.

cut-throats ; it is daubed with our blood ; because of
it husbands and wives make night hideous with their
quarrels, crowds swarm to the tribunals of the magistrates, kings rage and plunder and overthrow states
that have been built by the long labour of centuries,
in order that they may search for gold and silver
in the very ashes of cities. It is a pleasure, you say,
to see money-bags lying in the corner. But these
are what men shout for until their eyeballs start ; for
the sake of these the law-courts resound with the
din of trials, and jurors summoned from distant parts
sit in judgement to decide which man's greed has the
juster claim. But what if it is not even a bag of
money, but only a handful of copper or a silver piece,
reckoned by a slave, which causes an heirless old
man on the verge of the grave to split with rage ?
And what if it is only a paltry one per cent of
interest *a* that causes the money-lender, sick though
he be, with crippled feet and with gnarled hands
that no longer serve for counting money, to shout
aloud, and in the very throes of his malady to
require securities for his pennies ? If you were to
offer me all the money from all the mines, which
we are now so busy in digging, if you were to cast
before my eyes all the money that buried treasures
hold—for greed restores to earth what it once in
wickedness drew forth—I should not count that
whole assembled hoard worth even a good man's
frown. With what laughter should we attend the
things that now draw tears from our eyes !

Come, now, run through the other causes of anger
—foods, drinks, and the elegances we have devised
for them to gratify pride, insulting words, disrespect-
ful gestures, stubborn beasts of burden and lazy

suspiciones et interpretationes malignas vocis alienae,
quibus efficitur, ut inter iniurias naturae numeretur
sermo homini datus. Crede mihi, levia sunt propter
quae non leviter excandescimus, qualia quae pueros
2 in rixam et iurgium concitant. Nihil ex is, quae
tam tristes agimus, serium est, nihil magnum.
Inde, inquam, vobis ira et insania est, quod exigua
magno aestimatis. Auferre hic mihi hereditatem
voluit ; hic me diu in spem supremam captatis
criminatus est ; hic scortum meum concupivit.
3 Quod vinculum amoris esse debebat, seditionis atque
odi causa est, idem velle. Iter angustum rixas
transeuntium concitat, diffusa et late patens via ne
populos quidem collidit. Ista quae appetitis, quia
exigua sunt nec possunt ad alterum nisi alteri erepta
transferri, eadem affectantibus pugnas et iurgia
excitant.

1 35. Respondisse tibi servum indignaris libertum-
que et uxorem et clientem ; deinde idem de re
publica libertatem sublatam quereris, quam domi
sustulisti. Rursus, si tacuit interrogatus, contu-
2 maciam vocas. Et loquatur et taceat et rideat !
" Coram domino ? " inquis. Immo coram patre
familiae. Quid clamas ? Quid vociferaris ? Quid
flagella media cena petis, quod servi loquuntur, quod
non eodem loco turba contionis est, silentium soli-

ᵃ *Cf.* Sallust, *Catiline*, 20. 4 : "nam idem velle atque
idem nolle, ea demum firma amicitia est."

slaves, suspicion and the malicious misconstruction of another's words, the result of which is that the very gift of human speech is counted among the injustices of nature. Believe me, these things which incense us not a little are little things, like the trifles that drive children to quarrels and blows. Not one of them, though we take them so tragically, is a serious matter, not one is important. From this, I say, from the fact that you attach great value to petty things, come your anger and your madness. This man wanted to rob me of my inheritance; this one slandered me to people whom I had long courted in the expectation of a legacy; this one coveted my mistress. The desire for the same thing, which ought to have been a bond of love,[a] becomes the source of discord and of hatred. A narrow path drives passers-by to blows; on a wide and open road even a multitude will not jostle. Because the things you strive for are trifles, and yet cannot be given to one without robbing another, they provoke those desiring the same things to struggle and strife.

You are indignant because your slave, your freed-man, your wife, or your client answered you back; and then you complain that the state has been deprived of that liberty of which you have deprived your own household. Again, you call it obstinacy if a man keeps silent when he is questioned. But let him speak and let him keep silent and let him laugh! " In the presence of his master? " you ask. Yes, even in the presence of the head of the family. Why do you shout? Why do you rant? Why do you call for the whip in the midst of dinner, all because the slaves are talking, because there is not the silence of the desert in a room that holds a crowd big as a

3 tudinis? In hoc habes aures, ut non modulata
tantum et mollia et ex dulci tracta compositaque
accipiant; et risum audias oportet et fletum, et
blanditias et lites, et prospera et tristia, et hominum
voces et fremitus animalium latratusque. Quid
miser expavescis ad clamorem servi, ad tinnitum
aeris aut ianuae impulsum? Cum tam delicatus
4 fueris, tonitrua audienda sunt. Hoc, quod de
auribus dictum est, transfer ad oculos, qui non minus
fastidio laborant, si male instituti sunt. Macula
offenduntur et sordibus et argento parum splendido
5 et stagno non ad solum perlucente. Hi nempe oculi,
qui non ferunt nisi varium ac recenti cura nitens
marmor, qui mensam nisi crebris distinctam venis,
qui nolunt domi nisi auro pretiosiora calcari, aequis-
simo animo foris et scabras lutosasque semitas
spectant et maiorem partem occurrentium squa-
lidam, parietes insularum exesos, rimosos, inaequales.
Quid ergo aliud est, quod illos in publico non offendat,
domi moveat, quam opinio illic aequa et patiens,
domi morosa et querula?

1   36. Omnes sensus perducendi sunt ad firmitatem; natura patientes sunt, si animus illos desît
corrumpere, qui cotidie ad rationem reddendam
vocandus est. Faciebat hoc Sextius, ut consum-
mato die, cum se ad nocturnam quietem recepisset,

mass-meeting ? You do not have ears only for the purpose of listening to melodious sounds, soft and sweetly drawn and all in harmony ; you should also lend ear to laughter and weeping, to soft words and bitter, to happiness and sorrow, to the voices of men and the roars and barking of animals. Poor fellow ! why do you shudder at the shouting of a slave, at the rattling of bronze, or the banging of a door ? Although you are so sensitive, you have to listen to thunder. And all this which I have said about the ears you may apply as well to the eyes, which if they are not well schooled suffer not less from squeamishness. They are offended by a spot, by dirt, by tarnished silver, and by a pool that is not transparent to the bottom. These same eyes, forsooth, that cannot tolerate marble unless it is mottled and polished with recent rubbing, that cannot tolerate a table unless it is marked by many a vein, that at home would see under foot only pavements more costly than gold—these eyes when outside will behold, all unmoved, rough and muddy paths and dirty people, as are most of those they meet, and tenement walls crumbled and cracked and out of line. Why is it, then, that we are not offended on the street, yet are annoyed at home, except that in the one case we are in an unruffled and tolerant state of mind, and in the other are peevish and fault-finding ?

All our senses ought to be trained to endurance. They are naturally long-suffering, if only the mind desists from weakening them. This should be summoned to give an account of itself every day Sextius had this habit, and when the day was over and he had retired to his nightly rest, he would put

interrogaret animum suum : " Quod hodie malum
tuum sanasti ? Cui vitio obstitisti ? Qua parte
2 melior es ? " Desinet ira et moderatior erit, quae
sciet sibi cotidie ad iudicem esse veniendum. Quicquam ergo pulchrius hac consuetudine excutiendi
totum diem ? Qualis ille somnus post recognitionem
sui sequitur, quam tranquillus, quam altus ac liber,
cum aut laudatus est animus aut admonitus et
speculator sui censorque secretus cognovit de mori-
3 bus suis ! Utor hac potestate et cotidie apud me
causam dico. Cum sublatum e conspectu lumen
est et conticuit uxor moris iam mei conscia, totum
diem meum scrutor factaque ac dicta mea remetior ;
nihil mihi ipse abscondo, nihil transeo. Quare enim
quicquam ex erroribus meis timeam, cum possim
dicere :

4   " Vide ne istud amplius facias, nunc tibi ignosco.
In illa disputatione pugnacius locutus es ; noli
postea congredi cum imperitis ; nolunt discere, qui
numquam didicerunt. Illum liberius admonuisti
quam debebas, itaque non emendasti, sed offendisti.
De cetero vide, non tantum an verum sit quod dicis,
sed an ille cui dicitur veri patiens sit. Admoneri
bonus gaudet, pessimus quisque rectorem asperrime
patitur."

1   37. In convivio quorundam te sales et in dolorem
tuum iacta verba tetigerunt. Vitare volgares con-

these questions to his soul : " What bad habit have
you cured to-day ?   What fault have you resisted ?
In what respect are you better ? "   Anger will
cease and become more controllable if it finds that
it must appear before a judge every day.   Can anything be more excellent than this practice of thoroughly sifting the whole day ?   And how delightful the
sleep that follows this self-examination—how tranquil
it is, how deep and untroubled, when the soul has
either praised or admonished itself, and when this
secret examiner and critic of self has given report of
its own character !   I avail myself of this privilege,
and every day I plead my cause before the bar of
self.   When the light has been removed from sight,
and my wife, long aware of my habit, has become
silent, I scan the whole of my day and retrace all
my deeds and words.   I conceal nothing from myself,
I omit nothing.   For why should I shrink from any of
my mistakes, when I may commune thus with myself ?

" See that you never do that again ; I will pardon
you this time.   In that dispute, you spoke too
offensively ; after this don't have encounters with
ignorant people ; those who have never learned do
not want to learn.   You reproved that man more
frankly than you ought, and consequently you have
not so much mended him as offended him.   In the
future, consider not only the truth of what you say,
but also whether the man to whom you are speaking
can endure the truth.   A good man accepts reproof
gladly ; the worse a man is the more bitterly he
resents it."

At a banquet the wit of certain people and some
words aimed to sting you reached their mark.   But
remember to avoid the entertainments of the vulgar ;

victus memento ; solutior est post vinum licentia,
2 quia ne sobris quidem pudor est. Iratum vidisti
amicum tuum ostiario causidici alicuius aut divitis,
quod intrantem summoverat, et ipse pro illo iratus
extremo mancipio fuisti. Irasceris ergo catenario
cani ? Et hic, cum multum latravit, obiecto cibo
3 mansuescit. Recede longius et ride ! Nunc iste
se aliquem putat, quod custodit litigatorum turba
limen obsessum ; nunc ille, qui intra iacet, felix
fortunatusque est et beati hominis iudicat ac potentis
indicium difficilem ianuam. Nescit durissimum esse
ostium carceris. Praesume animo multa tibi esse
patienda. Numquis se hieme algere miratur ?
Numquis in mari nausiare, in via concuti ? Fortis
4 est animus ad quae praeparatus venit. Minus
honorato loco positus irasci coepisti convivatori,
vocatori, ipsi qui tibi praeferebatur. Demens, quid
interest, quam lecti premas partem ? Honestiorem
5 te aut turpiorem potest facere pulvinus ? Non
aequis quendam oculis vidisti, quia de ingenio tuo
male locutus est. Recipis hanc legem ? Ergo te
Ennius, quo non delectaris, odisset, et Hortensius,
si orationes eius improbares,[1] simultates tibi in-
diceret, et Cicero, si derideres carmina eius,

<hr />

[1] si . . . improbares *added by Haupt.*

after drinking their licence becomes too lax, because they want any sense of propriety even when they are sober. You saw one of your friends in a rage because the porter had thrust him out when he was trying to enter the house of some pettifogger or rich man, and you yourself on your friend's account became angry with that lowest kind of a slave. Will you then become angry with a chained watchdog ? He, too, after all his barking, will become gentle if you toss him food. Retire a little way and laugh ! As it is, the fellow thinks himself a somebody because he guards a threshold beset by a throng of litigants ; as it is, the gentleman who reclines within is blissful and blest and considers it the mark of a successful and powerful man to make it difficult to darken his door. He forgets that the hardest door of all to open is the prison's. Make up your mind that there are many things which you must bear. Is any one surprised that he is cold in winter ? That he is sick at sea ? That he is jolted about on the highroad ? The mind will meet bravely everything for which it has been prepared. Because you were given a less honourable place at the table, you began to get angry at your host, at the writer of the invitation, at the man himself who was preferred above you. Madman ! what difference does it make on what part of the couch you recline ? Can a cushion add to either your honour or your disgrace ? You did not look with fair eyes upon a certain man because he spoke ill of your talent. Do you accept this as a principle ? Then Ennius, whose poetry you do not like, would hate you, and Hortensius, if you disapproved of his speeches, would proclaim animosity to you, and Cicero, if you made fun of his poetry, would be your

inimicus esset. Vis tu aequo animo pati candidatus suffragia !

1 38. Contumeliam tibi fecit aliquis. Numquid maiorem quam Diogeni philosopho Stoico, cui de ira cum maxime disserenti adulescens protervus inspuit ? Tulit hoc ille leniter et sapienter : " Non quidem," inquit, " irascor, sed dubito tamen an

2 oporteat irasci." Quanto Cato[1] noster melius ! Qui, cum agenti causam in frontem mediam quantum poterat attracta pingui saliva inspuisset Lentulus ille patrum nostrorum memoria factiosus et impotens, abstersit faciem et : " Adfirmabo," inquit, " omnibus, Lentule, falli eos qui te negant os habere."

1 39. Contigit iam nobis, Novate, bene componere animum ; aut non sentit iracundiam aut superior est. Videamus quomodo alienam leniamus ; nec enim sani esse tantum volumus, sed sanare.

2 Primam iram non audebimus oratione mulcere. Surda est et amens ; dabimus illi spatium. Remedia in remissionibus prosunt. Nec oculos tumentis temptamus vim rigentem movendo incitaturi, nec cetera vitia, dum fervent. Initia morborum quies

3 curat. " Quantulum," inquis, " prodest remedium tuum, si sua sponte desinentem iram placat ! " Primum, ut citius desinat, efficit ; deinde custodit,

---

[1] Cato *added by Fickert* : quanto noster *A*.

---

*To reproduce the pun in the Latin the word must suggest also its vulgar use in the sense of " effrontery."

enemy. But when you are a candidate, you are willing to put up calmly—with the votes!

Some one, perhaps, has offered you an insult; was it any greater than the one Diogenes, the Stoic philosopher, suffered, who at the very time he was discoursing upon anger was spat upon by a shameless youth? Yet he bore this calmly and wisely. "Really, I am not angry," he said, "but nevertheless I am not sure but that I ought to be angry." Yet how much better the course of our own Cato! For when he was pleading a case, Lentulus, that factious and unruly man who lingers in the memory of our fathers, gathering as much thick saliva as he could, spat it full upon the middle of Cato's forehead. But he wiped it off his face and said, "To all who affirm that you have no cheek,[a] Lentulus, I'll swear that they are mistaken."

We have now succeeded, Novatus, in bringing composure to the mind; it either does not feel anger, or is superior to it. Let us now see how we may allay the anger of others. For we wish not merely to be healed ourselves, but also to heal.

We shall not venture to soothe the first burst of anger with words. It is both deaf and mad; we must give it room. Remedies are effective when the malady subsides. We do not tamper with the eyes when they are swollen—for in their stiff condition we are likely to irritate them by moving them— nor with other affected parts while they are inflamed. Rest is the cure in the first stages of illness. "How little," you say, "is your remedy worth, if it quiets anger when it is subsiding of its own accord!" In the first place, it makes it subside all the more quickly; in the second, it prevents its recurrence;

ne recidat; ipsum quoque impetum, quem non
audet lenire, fallet; removebit omnia ultionis
instrumenta, simulabit iram, ut tamquam adiutor
et doloris comes plus auctoritatis in consiliis habeat,
moras nectet et, dum maiorem poenam quaerit,
4 praesentem differet. Omni arte requiem furori
dabit. Si vehementior erit, aut pudorem illi cui non
resistat incutiet aut metum; si infirmior, sermones
inferet vel gratos vel novos et cupiditate cognoscendi
avocabit. Medicum aiunt, cum regis filiam curare
deberet nec sine ferro posset, dum tumentem
mammam leniter fovet, scalpellum spongea tectum
induxisse. Repugnasset puella remedio palam ad-
moto, eadem, quia non expectavit, dolorem tulit.
Quaedam non nisi decepta sanantur.

1   40. Alteri dices: " Vide ne inimicis iracundia tua
voluptati sit," alteri : " Vide ne magnitudo animi
tui creditumque apud plerosque robur cadat. In-
dignor me hercules et non invenio dolendi modum,
sed tempus expectandum est; dabit poenas; serva
istud in animo tuo; cum potueris, et pro mora
reddes." Castigare vero irascentem et ultro obirasci
2 incitare est; varie adgredieris blandeque, nisi forte
tanta persona eris, ut possis iram comminuere,

it will baffle, also, even the first outburst which it makes no effort to soothe, for it will remove all the weapons of revenge ; it will feign anger in order that, posing thus as a helper and comrade of our resentment, it may have more influence in counsel ; it will contrive delays, and will postpone immediate punishment by looking about for a heavier one. It will employ every artifice to give respite to the madness. If the victim grows violent, it will enforce on him a sense of shame or fear that he cannot resist ; if calmer, it will introduce conversation that is either interesting or novel, and will divert him by stirring his desire for knowledge. There is a story that once a physician had to cure the daughter of a king, and yet could not without using the knife. And so, while he was gently dressing her swollen breast, he inserted a lance concealed in a sponge. The girl would have fought against the remedy openly applied, but because she did not expect it, she endured the pain. Some matters are cured only by deception.

To one man you will say, " See to it that you do not by your anger give pleasure to your foes " ; to another, " See to it that you do not lose your greatness of mind and the reputation you have in the eyes of many for strength. By heavens, I myself am indignant and I am sorry beyond measure, but we must await our time. He shall pay the penalty ; keep that well in mind. When you can, you will make him pay for the delay as well." To reprove a man when he is angry and in turn to become angry at him serve only to increase his anger. You will approach him with various appeals and persuasively, unless you happen to be an important enough person to be able to quell his anger by the same tactics the

quemadmodum fecit divus Augustus, cum cenaret
apud Vedium Pollionem. Fregerat unus ex servis
eius crustallinum ; rapi eum Vedius iussit ne vulgari
quidem more periturum ; murenis obici iubebatur,
quas ingentis in piscina continebat. Quis non hoc
illum putaret luxuriae causa facere ? Saevitia erat.
3 Evasit e manibus puer et confugit ad Caesaris pedes
nihil aliud petiturus, quam ut aliter periret, ne esca
fieret. Motus est novitate crudelitatis Caesar et
illum quidem mitti, crustallina autem omnia coram
4 se frangi iussit complerique piscinam. Fuit Caesari
sic castigandus amicus ; bene usus est viribus suis :
" E convivio rapi homines imperas et novi generis
poenis lancinari ? Si calix tuus fractus est, viscera
hominis distrahentur ? Tantum tibi placebis, ut
5 ibi aliquem duci iubeas, ubi Caesar est ? " Sic cui
tantum potentiae est, ut iram ex superiore loco
adgredi possit, male tractet, at talem dumtaxat,
qualem modo rettuli, feram, immanem, sanguinariam,
quae iam insanabilis est, nisi maius aliquid extimuit.
1   41. Pacem demus animo, quam dabit praecep-
torum salutarium adsidua meditatio actusque rerum
boni et intenta mens ad unius honesti cupiditatem.
Conscientiae satis fiat, nil in famam laboremus.
2 Sequatur vel mala, dum bene merentis. " At

---

^a *Cf. De Clementia,* i. 18. 2.

deified Augustus used when he was dining with
Vedius Pollio.[a] When one of his slaves had broken
a crystal cup, Vedius ordered him to be seized and
doomed him to die, but in an extraordinary way—
he ordered him to be thrown to the huge lampreys,
which he kept in a fish-pond. Who would not
suppose that he did this merely for display ? It
was really out of cruelty. The lad slipped from his
captors and fled to Caesar's feet, begging only that
he might die some other way—anything but being
eaten. Caesar, shocked by such an innovation in
cruelty, ordered that the boy be pardoned, and,
besides, that all the crystal cups be broken before
his eyes and that the fish-pond be filled up. It was
so that it befitted Caesar to rebuke a friend ; he
employed his power rightly : " Do you order men
to be hurried from a banquet to death, and to be torn
to pieces by tortures of an unheard-of kind ? If your
cup was broken, is a man to have his bowels torn
asunder ? Will you vaunt yourself so much as to
order a man to be led to death in the very presence
of Caesar ? " Thus if any man's power is so great
that he can assail anger from an eminent position, let
him deal with it harshly, but only such anger as that
I have illustrated—fierce, inhuman, and bloodthirsty,
and now quite incurable unless it is made to fear
something more powerful.

Let us give to the soul that peace which is afforded
by constant meditation on wholesome instruction,
by noble deeds, and a mind intent upon the desire
for only what is honourable. Let us satisfy our
conscience ; for reputation let us strive not at all.
Let even a bad name attend us, provided that we
are really well-deserving. " But the populace," you

volgus animosa miratur et audaces in honore sunt,
placidi pro inertibus habentur." Primo forsitan
aspectu ; sed simul aequalitas vitae fidem fecit non
segnitiem illam animi esse sed pacem, veneratur illos
3 populus idem colitque. Nihil ergo habet in se utile
taeter iste et hostilis adfectus, at omnia ex contrario
mala, ferrum et ignes. Pudore calcato caedibus
inquinavit manus, membra liberorum dispersit, nihil
vacuum reliquit a scelere, non gloriae memor, non
infamiae metuens, inemendabilis, cum ex ira in
odium obcalluit.

1 42. Careamus hoc malo purgemusque mentem et
exstirpemus radicitus, quae quamvis tenuia undecum-
que haeserint renascentur, et iram non temperemus,
sed ex toto removeamus—quod enim malae rei
temperamentum est ? Poterimus autem, adnitamur
2 modo. Nec ulla res magis proderit quam cogitatio
mortalitatis. Sibi quisque atque alteri dicat : " Quid
iuvat tamquam in aeternum genitos iras indicere et
brevissimam aetatem dissipare ? Quid iuvat dies,
quos in voluptatem honestam impendere licet, in
dolorem alicuius tormentumque transferre ? Non
capiunt res istae iacturam nec tempus vacat perdere.
3 Quid ruimus in pugnam ? Quid certamina nobis
arcessimus ? Quid imbecillitatis obliti ingentia odia
suscipimus et ad frangendum fragiles consurgimus ?
Iam istas inimicitias, quas implacabili gerimus animo,

say, " admires spirited action, and the bold are held in honour while quiet people are considered in-effective." Perhaps so, at first sight. But when these have proved by the even tenor of their lives that they show, not inaction, but peace of mind, that same public will reverence and respect them. Consequently this hideous and ruinous passion serves not a single useful end, but, on the contrary, evil of every sort, the sword, and flame. Trampling under foot every scruple, it stains the hands with murder, it scatters abroad the limbs of children, it suffers no place to be free from crime, with no thought of glory, with no fear of disgrace, it is incurable when once, from anger, it has hardened into hate.

Let us be freed from this evil, let us clear it from our minds and tear it up by the roots, for if there should linger the smallest traces, it will grow again ; and let us not try to regulate our anger, but be rid of it altogether—for what regulation can there be of any evil thing ? Moreover, we can do it, if only we shall make the effort. And nothing will help us so much as pondering our mortality. Let each man say to himself and to his fellow-mortal : " Why do we, as if born to live for ever, take delight in pro-claiming our wrath and in wasting the little span of life ? Why do we delight to employ for somebody's distress and torture the days that we might devote to virtuous pleasure ? Your fortunes admit no squander-ing, and you have no spare time to waste. Why do we rush into the fray ? Why do we invite trouble for ourselves ? Why do we, forgetting our weakness, take up the huge burden of hate, and, easily broken as we are, rise up to break ? Soon a fever or some other bodily ill will stay that war of hatred, which

febris aut aliquod aliud malum corporis vetabit
4 geri ; iam par acerrimum media mors dirimet.
Quid tumultuamur et vitam seditiosi conturbamus ?
Stat supra caput fatum et pereuntis dies imputat
propiusque ac propius accedit ; istud tempus,
quod alienae destinas morti, fortasse circa tuam
est."

1 43. Quin potius vitam brevem colligis placidamque
et tibi et ceteris praestas ? Quin potius amabilem
te, dum vivis, omnibus, desiderabilem, cum ex-
cesseris, reddis ? Quid illum nimis ex alto tecum
agentem detrahere cupis ? Quid illum oblatrantem
tibi, humilem quidem et contemptum, sed superiori-
bus acidum ac molestum exterere viribus tuis
temptas ? Quid servo, quid domino, quid regi, quid
clienti tuo irasceris ? Sustine paulum ; venit ecce
2 mors quae vos pares faciat. Videre solemus inter
matutina harenae spectacula tauri et ursi pugnam
inter se colligatorum, quos, cum alter alterum
vexarunt, suus confector expectat. Idem facimus,
aliquem nobiscum adligatum lacessimus, cum victo
victorique finis et quidem maturus immineat. Quieti
potius pacatique quantulumcumque superest exi-
gamus ! Nulli cadaver nostrum iaceat invisum !
3 Saepe rixam conclamatum in vicinia incendium solvit
et interventus ferae latronem viatoremque diducit.
Colluctari cum minoribus malis non vacat, ubi metus
maior apparuit. Quid nobis cum dimicatione et
insidiis ? Numquid amplius isti cui irasceris quam

we now wage with such unrelenting purpose. Soon death will step in and part the fiercest pair of fighters. Why do we run riot and perturb life with our uproar? Fate looms above our heads, and scores up to our account the days as they go by, and draws ever nearer and nearer. That hour which you appoint for the death of another is perchance near your own."

Why do you not rather gather up your brief life and render it a peaceful one to yourself and all others? Why do you not rather make yourself beloved by all while you live, and regretted by all when you die? Why do you long to drag down the man who deals with you from too lofty a height? Why do you try with all your might to crush the man who rails against you, a low and contemptible fellow, but sharp-tongued and troublesome to his betters? Why are you angry with your slave, you with your master, you with your patron, you with your client? Wait a little. Behold, death comes, who will make you equals. At the morning performances in the arena we often see a battle between a bull and a bear tied together, and when they have harried each other, an appointed slayer awaits them. Their fate is ours; we harass some one bound closely to us, and yet the end, all too soon, threatens the victor and the vanquished. Rather let us spend the little time that is left in repose and peace! Let no man loathe us when we lie a corpse! A cry of fire in the neighbourhood often ends a fight, and the arrival of a wild beast rescues a traveller from the brigand. We have no time to struggle with lesser ills when a more threatening fear appears. Why do we concern ourselves with combat and with snares? Can you wish for the victim of your wrath a greater ill than death? Even

mortem optas? Etiam te quiescente morietur.
Perdis operam, si facere vis quod futurum est.
4 "Nolo," inquis, "utique occidere, sed exilio, sed
ignominia, sed damno adficere." Magis ignosco ei,
qui vulnus inimici quam qui pusulam concupiscit;
hic enim non tantum mali animi est, sed pusilli.
Sive de ultimis suppliciis cogitas sive de levioribus,
quantulum est temporis, quo aut ille poena sua
torqueatur aut tu malum gaudium ex aliena per-
5 cipias! Iam istum spiritum exspuemus. Interim,
dum trahimus, dum inter homines sumus, colamus
humanitatem. Non timori cuiquam, non periculo
simus, detrimenta, iniurias, convicia, vellicationes
contemnamus et magno animo brevia feramus incommoda. Dum respicimus, quod aiunt, versamus-
que nos, iam mortalitas aderit.

though you do not move a finger, he will die. You waste your pains if you wish to do what needs must be. "I do not wish," you say, "to kill him at all, but to punish him with exile, with public disgrace, with material loss." But I am more indulgent to the man who would give his enemy a wound than to the one who would give him a blister; for the latter has not only an evil mind, but a petty mind as well. Whether your thoughts run on tortures severe or slight, how short is the time in which either your victim can writhe under your torments, or you derive a wicked joy from another's pain! Soon shall we spew forth this frail spirit. Meanwhile, so long as we draw breath, so long as we live among men, let us cherish humanity. Let us not cause fear to any man, nor danger; let us scorn losses, wrongs, abuse, and taunts, and let us endure with heroic mind our short-lived ills. While we are looking back, as they say, and turning around, straightway death will be upon us.

AD NERONEM CAESAREM

DE CLEMENTIA

1 1. Scribere de clementia, Nero Caesar, institui, ut
quodam modo speculi vice fungerer et te tibi osten-
derem perventurum ad voluptatem maximam omnium. Quamvis enim recte factorum verus fructus
sit fecisse nec ullum virtutum pretium dignum illis
extra ipsas sit, iuvat inspicere et circumire bonam
conscientiam, tum immittere oculos in hanc immensam multitudinem discordem, seditiosam, im-
potentem, in perniciem alienam suamque pariter
exultaturam si hoc iugum fregerit, et ita loqui
2 secum : " Egone ex omnibus mortalibus placui
electusque sum, qui in terris deorum vice fungerer ?
Ego vitae necisque gentibus arbiter ; qualem
quisque sortem statumque habeat, in mea manu
positum est ; quid cuique mortalium fortuna datum
velit, meo ore pronuntiat ; ex nostro responso
laetitiae causas populi urbesque concipiunt ; nulla
pars usquam nisi volente propitioque me floret ;
haec tot milia gladiorum, quae pax mea comprimit,

TO THE EMPEROR NERO

ON MERCY

BOOK I

I HAVE undertaken, Nero Caesar, to write on the subject of mercy, in order to serve in a way the purpose of a mirror, and thus reveal you to yourself as one destined to attain to the greatest of all pleasures. For, though the true profit of virtuous deeds lies in the doing, and there is no fitting reward for the virtues apart from the virtues themselves, still it is a pleasure to subject a good conscience to a round of inspection, then to cast one's eyes upon this vast throng—discordant, factious, and unruly, ready to run riot alike for the destruction of itself and others if it should break its yoke—and finally to commune with oneself thus : " Have I of all mortals found favour with Heaven and been chosen to serve on earth as vicar of the gods ? I am the arbiter of life and death for the nations ; it rests in my power what each man's lot and state shall be ; by my lips Fortune proclaims what gift she would bestow on each human being ; from my utterance peoples and cities gather reasons for rejoicing ; without my favour and grace no part of the wide world can prosper ; all those many thousands of swords

ad nutum meum stringentur ; quas nationes funditus
excidi, quas transportari, quibus libertatem dari,
quibus eripi, quos reges mancipia fieri quorumque
capiti regium circumdari decus oporteat, quae ruant
3 urbes, quae oriantur, mea iuris dictio est. In hac
tanta facultate rerum non ira me ad iniqua supplicia
compulit, non iuvenilis impetus, non temeritas hominum et contumacia, quae saepe tranquillissimis
quoque pectoribus patientiam extorsit, non ipsa
ostentandae per terrores potentiae dira, sed frequens
magnis imperiis gloria. Conditum, immo con-
strictum apud me ferrum est, summa parsimonia
etiam vilissimi sanguinis ; nemo non, cui alia desunt,
4 hominis nomine apud me gratiosus est. Severitatem
abditam, at clementiam in procinctu habeo ; sic me
custodio, tamquam legibus, quas ex situ ac tenebris
in lucem evocavi, rationem redditurus sim. Alterius
aetate prima motus sum, alterius ultima ; alium
dignitati donavi, alium humilitati ; quotiens nullam
inveneram misericordiae causam, mihi peperci.[a]
Hodie dis inmortalibus, si a me rationem repetant,
adnumerare genus humanum paratus sum."
5 Potes hoc, Caesar, audacter praedicare omnia,
quae in fidem tutelamque tuam venerunt, tuta
haberi,[1] nihil per te neque vi neque clam adimi rei
publicae. Rarissimam laudem et nulli adhuc princi-

---

[1] -que tuam . . . tuta ha- *supplied by Gertz.*

---

[a] Literally, "I have spared myself" *i.e.*, by sparing
another, according to the reasoning set forth in i. 5. 1.

which my peace restrains will be drawn at my nod; what nations shall be utterly destroyed, which banished, which shall receive the gift of liberty, which have it taken from them, what kings shall become slaves and whose heads shall be crowned with royal honour, what cities shall fall and which shall rise— this it is mine to decree. With all things thus at my disposal, I have been moved neither by anger nor youthful impulse to unjust punishment, nor by the foolhardiness and obstinacy of men which have often wrung patience from even the serenest souls, nor yet by that vainglory which employs terror for the display of might—a dread but all too common use of great and lordly power. With me the sword is hidden, nay, is sheathed; I am sparing to the utmost of even the meanest blood; no man fails to find favour at my hands though he lack all else but the name of man. Sternness I keep hidden, but mercy ever ready at hand. I so hold guard over myself as though I were about to render an account to those laws which I have summoned from decay and darkness into the light of day. I have been moved to pity by the fresh youth of one, by the extreme old age of another; one I have pardoned for his high position, another for his humble state; whenever I found no excuse for pity, for my own sake I have spared.[a] To-day, if the immortal gods should require a reckoning from me, I am ready to give full tale of the human race."

This pronouncement, Caesar, you may boldly make, that whatever has passed into your trust and guardianship is still kept safe, that through you the state suffers no loss, either from violence or from fraud. It is the rarest praise, hitherto denied to all

pum concessam concupisti innocentiam. Non perdit operam nec bonitas ista tua singularis ingratos aut malignos aestimatores nancta est. Refertur tibi gratia ; nemo unus homo uni homini tam carus umquam fuit, quam tu populo Romano, magnum 6 longumque eius bonum. Sed ingens tibi onus imposuisti ; nemo iam divum Augustum nec Ti. Caesaris prima tempora loquitur nec, quod te imitari velit, exemplar extra te quaerit ; principatus tuus ad gustum[1] exigitur. Difficile hoc fuisset, si non naturalis tibi ista bonitas esset, sed ad tempus sumpta. Nemo enim potest personam diu ferre, ficta cito in naturam suam recidunt ; quibus veritas subest quaeque, ut ita dicam, ex solido enascuntur, tempore ipso in maius meliusque procedunt.

7 Magnam adibat aleam populus Romanus, cum incertum esset, quo se ista tua nobilis indoles daret ; iam vota publica in tuto sunt ; nec enim periculum est, ne te subita tui capiat oblivio. Facit quidem avidos nimia felicitas, nec tam temperatae cupiditates sunt umquam, ut in eo, quod contigit, desinant ; gradus a magnis ad maiora fit, et spes improbissimas complectuntur insperata adsecuti ; omnibus tamen nunc civibus tuis et haec confessio exprimitur esse felices et illa nihil iam his accedere bonis posse, nisi 8 ut perpetua sint. Multa illos cogunt ad hanc con-

---

[1] *So N* : augustum *most MSS.* : obrussam *Haase.*

other princes, that you have coveted for yourself—
innocence of wrong. Nor has the effort been in
vain, and that unparalleled goodness of yours has not
found men ungrateful or grudging in their appraise-
ment. Thanks are rendered to you ; no human
being has ever been so dear to another as you are
to the people of Rome—its great and lasting blessing.
But it is a mighty burden that you have taken upon
yourself ; no one to-day talks of the deified Augustus
or the early years of Tiberius Caesar, or seeks for
any model he would have you copy other than yourself ; the standard for your principate is the foretaste
you have given. This would have indeed been difficult if that goodness of yours were not innate but
only assumed for the moment. For no one can
wear a mask long ; the false quickly lapses back into
its own nature ; but whatever has truth for its
foundation, and whatever springs, so to speak, from
out the solid earth, grows by the mere passing of
time into something larger and better.

Great was the hazard that the Roman people
faced so long as it was uncertain what course those
noble talents of yours would take ; to-day the
prayers of the state are assured, for there is no danger
that you will be seized by sudden forgetfulness of
yourself. Over-much prosperity, it is true, makes
men greedy, and desires are never so well controlled
as to cease at the point of attainment ; the ascent
is from great to greater, and men embrace the
wildest hopes when once they have gained what they
did not hope for ; and yet to-day your subjects one
and all are constrained to confess that they are
happy, and, too, that nothing further can be added
to their blessings, except that these may last. Many

fessionem, qua nulla in homine tardior est : securitas
alta, adfluens, ius supra omnem iniuriam positum ;
obversatur oculis laetissima forma rei publicae, cui
ad summam libertatem nihil deest nisi pereundi
9 licentia. Praecipue tamen aequalis ad maximos
imosque pervenit clementiae tuae admiratio ; cetera
enim bona pro portione fortunae suae quisque sentit
aut expectat maiora minoraque, ex clementia omnes
idem sperant ; nec est quisquam, cui tam valde
innocentia sua placeat, ut non stare in conspectu
clementiam paratam humanis erroribus gaudeat.

1 2. Esse autem aliquos scio, qui clementia pessimum
quemque putent sustineri, quoniam nisi post crimen
supervacua est et sola haec virtus inter innocentes
cessat. Sed primum omnium, sicut medicinae apud
aegros usus, etiam apud sanos honor est, ita clementiam, quamvis poena digni invocent, etiam innocentes
colunt. Deinde habet haec in persona quoque
innocentium locum, quia interim fortuna pro culpa
est ; nec innocentiae tantum clementia succurrit,
sed saepe virtuti, quoniam quidem condicione tem-
porum incidunt quaedam, quae possint laudata
puniri. Adice, quod magna pars hominum est, quae
reverti ad innocentiam possit, si <poenae remissio
2 fuerit>.[1] Non tamen vulgo ignoscere decet ; nam
ubi discrimen inter malos bonosque sublatum est,
confusio sequitur et vitiorum eruptio ; itaque ad-

---

[1] si *Hosius after best mss. with a lacuna* : sed *AT*.

---

[a] Stoicism produced many " conscientious objectors "
who were high-minded, yet futile, opponents of imperial rule.

facts force them to this confession, which more than any other a man is loath to make : a security deep and abounding, and justice enthroned above all injustice ; before their eyes hovers the fairest vision of a state which lacks no element of complete liberty except the licence of self-destruction. Above all, however, alike to the highest and the lowest, extends the same admiration for your quality of mercy ; for although of other blessings each one experiences or expects a larger or smaller measure in proportion to his lot, yet from mercy men all hope to have the same ; nor is there any man so wholly satisfied with his own innocence as not to rejoice that mercy stands in sight, waiting for human errors.

I know, however, that there are some who think that mercy upholds the worst class of men, since it is superfluous unless there has been some crime, and since it alone of all the virtues finds no exercise among the guiltless. But, first of all, just as medicine is used by the sick, yet is held in honour by the healthy, so with mercy—though it is those who deserve punishment that invoke it, yet even the guiltless cherish it. Again, this virtue has scope even in the person of the guiltless, because at times fortune takes the place of guilt ; and not only does mercy come to the rescue of innocence, but often of righteousness also, inasmuch as, from the state of the times,[a] there arise certain acts which, while praised, may yet be punished. Then, too, there are a great many people who might be turned back to the path of virtue if [they are released from punishment]. Nevertheless, pardoning ought not to be too common ; for when the distinction between the bad and the good is removed, the result is confusion and an epidemic of

hibenda moderatio est, quae sanabilia ingenia distinguere a deploratis sciat. Nec promiscuam habere ac vulgarem clementiam oportet nec abscisam; nam tam omnibus ignoscere crudelitas quam nulli. Modum tenere debemus; sed quia difficile est temperamentum, quidquid aequo plus futurum est, in partem humaniorem praeponderet.

1 3. Sed haec suo melius loco dicentur. Nunc in tres partes omnem hanc materiam dividam. Prima erit manumissionis; secunda, quae naturam clementiae habitumque demonstret: nam cum sint vitia quaedam virtutes imitantia, non possunt secerni, nisi signa, quibus dinoscantur, impresseris; tertio loco quaeremus, quomodo ad hanc virtutem perducatur animus, quomodo confirmet eam et usu suam faciat.

2 Nullam ex omnibus virtutibus homini magis convenire, cum sit nulla humanior, constet necesse est non solum inter nos, qui hominem sociale animal communi bono genitum videri volumus, sed etiam inter illos, qui hominem voluptati donant, quorum omnia dicta factaque ad utilitates suas spectant; nam si quietem petit et otium, hanc virtutem naturae suae nanctus est, quae pacem amat et manus retinet.

3 Nullum tamen clementia ex omnibus magis quam regem aut principem decet. Ita enim magnae vires decori gloriaeque sunt, si illis salutaris potentia est; nam pestifera vis est valere ad nocendum. Illius demum magnitudo stabilis fundataque est, quem

---

a A reference to the Stoic emphasis upon the responsibility of the individual to the community.

b *i.e.*, the Epicureans.

vice. Therefore a wise moderation should be exercised which will be capable of distinguishing between curable and hopeless characters. Neither should we have indiscriminate and general mercy, nor yet preclude it; for it is as much a cruelty to pardon all as to pardon none. We should maintain the mean; but since a perfect balance is difficult, if anything is to disturb the equipoise it should turn the scale toward the kindlier side.

But these matters will be more fitly discussed in their proper place. Here I shall divide this subject as a whole into three parts. The first will treat of the remission of punishment; the second will aim to show the nature and aspect of mercy; for since there are certain vices which counterfeit virtues, they cannot be separated unless you stamp them with marks by which they may be known apart. In the third place I shall inquire how the mind is led to adopt this virtue, and how it establishes it and by practice makes it its own.

That no one of all the virtues is more seemly for a man, since none is more human, is a necessary conviction not only for those of us who maintain that man is a social creature, begotten for the common good,[a] but also for those who give man over to pleasure,[b] whose words and deeds all look to their own advantage. For if a man seeks calm and quiet, he finds this virtue, which loves peace and stays the hand, forthwith suited to his bent. Yet of all men none is better graced by mercy than a king or a prince. For great power confers grace and glory only when it is potent for benefit; it is surely a baneful might that is strong only for harm. He alone has firm and well-grounded greatness whom

omnes tam supra se esse quam pro se sciunt, cuius
curam excubare pro salute singulorum atque univer-
sorum cottidie experiuntur, quo procedente non,
tamquam malum aliquod aut noxium animal e cubili
prosilierit, diffugiunt, sed tamquam ad clarum ac
beneficum sidus certatim advolant. Obicere se
pro illo mucronibus insidiantium paratissimi et sub-
sternere corpora sua, si per stragem illi humanam
iter ad salutem struendum sit, somnum eius nocturnis excubiis muniunt, latera obiecti circumfusisque
defendunt, incurrentibus periculis se opponunt.

4   Non est hic sine ratione populis urbibusque consensus sic protegendi amandique reges et se suaque
iactandi, quocumque desideravit imperantis salus ;
nec haec vilitas sui est aut dementia pro uno capite
tot milia excipere ferrum ac multis mortibus unam
animam redimere nonnumquam senis et invalidi.

5   Quemadmodum totum corpus animo deservit et,
cum hoc tanto maius tantoque speciosius sit, ille in
occulto maneat tenuis et in qua sede latitet incertus,
tamen manus, pedes, oculi negotium illi gerunt,
illum haec cutis munit, illius iussu iacemus aut in-
quieti discurrimus, cum ille imperavit, sive avarus
dominus est, mare lucri causa scrutamur, sive
ambitiosus, iam dudum dextram flammis obiecimus
aut voluntarii terram subsiluimus, sic haec immensa
multitudo unius animae circumdata illius spiritu

all men know to be as much their friend as he is their superior ; whose concern they daily find to be vigilant for the safety of each and all ; upon whose approach they do not flee as if some monster or deadly beast had leaped from his lair, but rush eagerly forward as toward a bright and beneficent star. In his defence they are ready on the instant to throw themselves before the swords of assassins, and to lay their bodies beneath his feet if his path to safety must be paved with slaughtered men ; his sleep they guard by nightly vigils, his person they defend with an encircling barrier, against assailing dangers they make themselves a rampart.

Not without reason do cities and peoples show this accord in giving such protection and love to their kings, and in flinging themselves and all they have into the breach whenever the safety of their ruler craves it. Nor is it self-depreciation or madness when many thousands meet the steel for the sake of one man, and with many deaths ransom the single life, it may be, of a feeble dotard.

The whole body is the servant of the mind, and though the former is so much larger and so much more showy, while the unsubstantial soul remains invisible not knowing where its secret habitation lies, yet the hands, the feet, and the eyes are in its employ ; the outer skin is its defence ; at its bidding we lie idle, or restlessly run to and fro ; when it commands, if it is a grasping tyrant, we search the sea for gain ; if covetous of fame, ere now we have thrust a right hand into the flame, or plunged willingly into a chasm. In the same way this vast throng, encircling the life of one man, is ruled by his spirit, guided by his

regitur, illius ratione flectitur pressura se ac fractura
viribus suis, nisi consilio sustineretur.

1 4. Suam itaque incolumitatem amant, cum pro uno
homine denas legiones in aciem deducunt, cum in
primam frontem procurrunt et adversa vulneribus
pectora ferunt, ne imperatoris sui signa vertantur.
Ille est enim vinculum, per quod res publica cohaeret,
ille spiritus vitalis, quem haec tot milia trahunt nihil
ipsa per se futura nisi onus et praeda, si mens illa
imperii subtrahatur.

> Rege incolumi mens omnibus una;
> amisso rupere fidem.

2 Hic casus Romanae pacis exitium erit, hic tanti
fortunam populi in ruinas aget; tam diu ab isto
periculo aberit hic populus, quam diu sciet ferre
frenos, quos si quando abruperit vel aliquo casu
discussos reponi sibi passus non erit, haec unitas
et hic maximi imperii contextus in partes multas
dissiliet, idemque huic urbi finis dominandi erit,
3 qui parendi fuerit. Ideo principes regesque et
quocumque alio nomine sunt tutores status publici
non est mirum amari ultra privatas etiam necessi-
tudines; nam si sanis hominibus publica privatis
potiora sunt, sequitur, ut is quoque carior sit, in quem
se res publica convertit. Olim enim ita se induit
rei publicae Caesar, ut seduci alterum non posset
sine utriusque pernicie; nam et illi viribus opus
est et huic capite.

---

^a Virgil, *Georgics*, iv. 212, where he is speaking of bees
and their devotion to their " king."

reason, and would crush and cripple itself with its own power if it were not upheld by wisdom.

It is, therefore, their own safety that men love, when for one man they lead ten legions at a time into battle, when they rush to the forefront and expose their breasts to wounds that they may save the standards of their emperor from defeat. For he is the bond by which the commonwealth is united, the breath of life which these many thousands draw, who in their own strength would be only a burden to themselves and the prey of others if the great mind of the empire should be withdrawn.

> If safe their king, one mind to all ;
> Bereft of him, they troth recall.[a]

Such a calamity would be the destruction of the Roman peace, such a calamity will force the fortune of a mighty people to its downfall. Just so long will this people be free from that danger as it shall know how to submit to the rein ; but if ever it shall tear away the rein, or shall not suffer it to be replaced if shaken loose by some mishap, then this unity and this fabric of mightiest empire will fly into many parts, and the end of this city's rule will be one with the end of her obedience. Therefore it is not strange that kings and princes and guardians of the public order, whatever different name they bear, are held more dear even than those bound to us by private ties ; for if men of sense put public interests above private, it follows that he too is dearer upon whom the whole state centres. At an earlier day, in fact, Caesar so clothed himself with the powers of state that neither one could be withdrawn without the destruction of both. For while a Caesar needs power, the state also needs a head.

1 **5.** Longius videtur recessisse a proposito oratio
mea, at mehercules rem ipsam premit. Nam si, quod
adhuc colligit, tu animus rei publicae tuae es, illa
corpus tuum, vides, ut puto, quam necessaria sit
clementia ; tibi enim parcis, cum videris alteri
parcere. Parcendum itaque est etiam improbandis
civibus non aliter quam membris languentibus, et,
si quando misso sanguine opus est, sustinenda est
2 manus,[1] ne ultra, quam necesse sit, incidat. Est
ergo, ut dicebam, clementia omnibus quidem hominibus secundum naturam, maxime tamen decora
imperatoribus, quanto plus habet apud illos, quod
servet, quantoque in maiore materia apparet. Quantulum enim nocet privata crudelitas ! Principum
3 saevitia bellum est. Cum autem virtutibus inter
se sit concordia nec ulla altera melior aut honestior
sit, quaedam tamen quibusdam personis aptior est.
Decet magnanimitas quemlibet mortalem, etiam
illum, infra quem nihil est ; quid enim maius aut
fortius quam malam fortunam retundere ? Haec
tamen magnanimitas in bona fortuna laxiorem locum
habet meliusque in tribunali quam in plano con-
spicitur.

4 Clementia, in quamcumque domum pervenerit,
eam felicem tranquillamque praestabit, sed in regia,
quo rarior, eo mirabilior. Quid enim est memora-
bilius quam eum, cuius irae nihil obstat, cuius
graviori sententiae ipsi, qui pereunt, adsentiuntur,
quem nemo interpellaturus est, immo, si vehementius

---

[1] manus *added by Haase.*

My discourse seems to have withdrawn somewhat far from its purpose, but, in very truth, it bears closely upon the real issue. For if—and this is what thus far it is establishing—you are the soul of the state and the state your body, you see, I think, how requisite is mercy ; for you are merciful to yourself when you are seemingly merciful to another. And so even reprobate citizens should have mercy as being the weak members of the body, and if there should ever be need to let blood, the hand must be held under control to keep it from cutting deeper than may be necessary. The quality of mercy, then, as I was saying, is indeed for all men in accordance with nature, but in rulers it has an especial comeliness inasmuch as with them it finds more to save, and exhibits itself amid ampler opportunities. For how small the harm the cruelty of a private citizen can do ! But when princes rage there is war. Though, moreover, the virtues are at harmony with each other, and no one of them is better or more noble than another, yet to certain people a certain virtue will be more suited. Greatness of soul is a virtue that is seemly for every human being, even for him who is the lowliest of the lowly. For what is greater or braver than to beat down misfortune ? Yet this greatness of soul has freer play under circumstances of good fortune, and is shown to better advantage upon the judge's bench than on the floor.

Every house that mercy enters she will render peaceful and happy, but in the palace she is more wonderful, in that she is rarer. For what is more remarkable than that he whose anger nothing can withstand, to whose sentence, too heavy though it be, even the victims bow the head, whom, if he is very

excanduit, ne deprecaturus est quidem, ipsum sibi
manum inicere et potestate sua in melius placidiusque
uti hoc ipsum cogitantem : " Occidere contra legem
nemo non potest, servare nemo praeter me " ?
5 Magnam fortunam magnus animus decet, qui, nisi
se ad illam extulit et altior stetit, illam quoque infra
ad[1] terram deducit ; magni autem animi proprium
est placidum esse tranquillumque et iniurias atque
offensiones superne despicere. Muliebre est furere
in ira, ferarum vero nec generosarum quidem prae-
mordere et urguere proiectos. Elephanti leonesque
transeunt, quae impulerunt ; ignobilis bestiae per-
6 tinacia est. Non decet regem saeva nec inexorabilis
ira, non multum enim supra eum eminet, cui se
irascendo exaequat ; at si dat vitam, si dat dignitatem periclitantibus et meritis amittere, facit,
quod nulli nisi rerum potenti licet ; vita enim etiam
superiori eripitur, numquam nisi inferiori datur.
7 Servare proprium est excellentis fortunae, quae
numquam magis suspici debet, quam cum illi contigit idem posse quod dis, quorum beneficio in lucem
edimur tam boni quam mali. Deorum itaque sibi
animum adserens princeps alios ex civibus suis, quia
utiles bonique sunt, libens videat, alios in numerum
relinquat ; quosdam esse gaudeat, quosdam patiatur.
1 6. Cogitato, in hac civitate, in qua turba per

---

[1] ad *added by Lipsius.*

greatly incensed, no one will venture to gainsay,
nay, even to entreat—that this man should lay a
restraining hand upon himself, and use his power to
better and more peaceful ends when he reflects,
" Any one can violate the law to kill, none but I,
to save " ? A lofty spirit befits a lofty station, and
if it does not rise to the level of its station and even
stand above it, the other, too, is dragged downward
to the ground. Moreover, the peculiar marks of a
lofty spirit are mildness and composure, and the lofty
disregard of injustice and wrongs. It is for woman to
rage in anger, for wild beasts doubtless—and yet not
even the noble sort of these—to bite and worry their
prostrate victims. Elephants and lions pass by what
they have stricken down ; it is the ignoble beast that
is relentless. Cruel and inexorable anger is not
seemly for a king, for thus he does not rise much
above the other man, toward whose own level he
descends by being angry at him. But if he grants life,
if he grants position to those who have imperilled
and deserve to lose them, he does what none but a
sovereign may ; for one may take the life even of a
superior, but not give it ever except to an inferior.
To save life is the peculiar privilege of exalted station,
which never has a right to greater admiration than
when it has the good fortune to have the same power
as the gods, by whose kindness we all, the evil as well
as the good, are brought forth into the light. Let a
prince, therefore, appropriating to himself the spirit
of the gods, look with pleasure upon one class of his
citizens because they are useful and good ; others
let him leave to make up the count ; let him be glad
that some of them live, some let him merely endure.
Consider this city, in which the throng that streams

latissima itinera sine intermissione defluens eliditur,
quotiens aliquid obstitit, quod cursum eius velut
torrentis rapidi moraretur, in qua tribus eodem
tempore theatris caveae[1] postulantur, in qua con-
sumitur, quidquid terris omnibus aratur, quanta
solitudo ac vastitas futura sit, si nihil relinquitur,
2 nisi quod iudex severus absolverit. Quotus quisque
ex quaesitoribus est, qui non ex ipsa ea lege teneatur,
qua quaerit ? quotus quisque accusator vacat culpa ?
Et nescio, an nemo ad dandam veniam difficilior sit,
3 quam qui illam petere saepius meruit. Peccavimus
omnes, alii gravia, alii leviora, alii ex destinato, alii
forte impulsi aut aliena nequitia ablati ; alii in bonis
consiliis parum fortiter stetimus et innocentiam
inviti ac retinentes perdidimus ; nec deliquimus
tantum, sed usque ad extremum aevi delinquemus.
4 Etiam si quis tam bene iam purgavit animum, ut
nihil obturbare eum amplius ac fallere, ad
innocentiam tamen peccando pervenit.
1   7. Quoniam deorum feci mentionem, optime hoc
exemplum principi constituam, ad quod formetur,
ut se talem esse civibus, quales sibi deos velit.
Expedit ergo habere inexorabilia peccatis atque
erroribus numina, expedit usque ad ultimam infesta

---

[1] caveae *Hosius* : viae MSS.

---

[a] Those of Pompey, Marcellus, and Balbus, each of
which, it must be remembered, seated many thousands.
[b] *i.e.*, of the ideal wise man of the Stoics, so rarely produced.
Their doctrine that virtue is not merely the greatest but the
only good allowed no gradation of goodness or badness, and
frankly recognized the almost universal depravity of mankind. Seneca with his humane tendencies gives passionate
emphasis to this belief, making it the basis of a plea for
mercy and kindness.

ceaselessly through its widest streets is crushed
to pieces whenever anything gets in the way to
check its course as it streams like a rushing torrent,—
this city in which the seating space of three theatres [a]
is required at one time, in which is consumed all the
produce of the plough from every land ; consider how
great would be the loneliness and the desolation of it
if none should be left but those whom a strict judge
would acquit. How few inquisitors there are who
would escape conviction under the very law which
they cite for the inquisition ; how few accusers are
free from blame. And, I am inclined to think, no
one is more reluctant to grant pardon than he who
again and again has had reason to seek it. We have
all sinned—some in serious, some in trivial things ;
some from deliberate intention, some by chance
impulse, or because we were led away by the wickedness of others ; some of us have not stood strongly
enough by good resolutions, and have lost our
innocence against our will and though still clinging
to it ; and not only have we done wrong, but we
shall go on doing wrong to the very end of life. Even
if there is any one who has so thoroughly cleansed his
mind that nothing can any more confound him and
betray him, yet it is by sinning that he has reached
the sinless state.[b]

Since I have made mention of the gods, I shall do
very well to establish this as the standard after which
a prince should model himself—that he should wish
so to be to his subjects, as he would wish the gods to be
to himself. Is it, then, desirable to have deities that
cannot be moved to show mercy to our sins and
mistakes ? Is it desirable to have them our enemies
even to the point of our complete destruction ? And

perniciem? Et quis regum erit tutus, cuius non
2 membra haruspices colligant? Quod si di placabiles
et aequi delicta potentium non statim fulminibus
persequuntur, quanto aequius est hominem hominibus
praepositum miti animo exercere imperium et cogitare,
uter mundi status gratior oculis pulchriorque sit,
sereno et puro die, an cum fragoribus crebris omnia
quatiuntur et ignes hinc atque illinc micant! Atqui
non alia facies est quieti moratique imperii quam
3 sereni caeli et nitentis. Crudele regnum turbidum
tenebrisque obscurum est, inter trementes et ad
repentinum sonitum expavescentes ne eo quidem,
qui omnia perturbat, inconcusso. Facilius privatis
ignoscitur pertinaciter se vindicantibus; possunt
enim laedi, dolorque eorum ab iniuria venit; timent
praeterea contemptum, et non rettulisse laedentibus
gratiam infirmitas videtur, non clementia; at cui
ultio in facili est, is omissa ea certam laudem man-
4 suetudinis consequitur. Humili loco positis exercere
manum, litigare, in rixam procurrere ac morem irae
suae gerere liberius est; leves inter paria ictus sunt;
regi vociferatio quoque verborumque intemperantia
non ex maiestate est.

1 8. Grave putas eripi loquendi arbitrium regibus,
quod humillimi habent. " Ista," inquis, " servitus
est, non imperium." Quid? tu non experiris istud
nobis esse, tibi servitutem? Alia condicio est

---

a To be struck by lightning was interpreted by the sooth-
sayers as a sign of the displeasure of the gods.

376

what king will escape the danger of having the sooth-
sayers gather up his riven limbs ? [a] But if the gods,
merciful and just, do not instantly avenge with the
thunderbolt the shortcomings of the mighty, how
much more just is it for a man, set over men, to
exercise his power in gentle spirit and to ask himself which condition of the world is more pleasing
to the eye and more lovely—when the day is calm
and clear, or when all nature quakes with crash
upon crash of thunder, and hither and yonder the
lightnings flash ? And yet the aspect of a quiet and
well-ordered empire is not different from that of a
calm and shining sky. A reign that is cruel is stormy
and overcast with gloom, and, while men tremble and
grow pale at the sudden uproar, even he who is the
cause of all the turmoil does not fail to shudder. One
in private life, if he stubbornly seeks revenge, is more
easily pardoned ; for it is possible for him to receive
an injury, and his resentment springs from a sense
of wrong ; besides, he is afraid of being scorned, and,
when one is injured, the failure to make requital
seems a show of weakness, not of mercy. But the
man for whom vengeance is easy, by disregarding it,
gains assured praise for clemency. Those placed in
lowly station are more free to use force, to quarrel,
to rush into a brawl, and to indulge their wrath ;
when the odds are matched, blows fall light ; but in
a king, even loud speech and unbridled words ill
accord with his majesty.

You think that it is a serious matter to deprive
kings of the right of free speech, which belongs to
the humblest man. " That," you say, " is servitude,
not sovereignty." What ? are you not aware that
the sovereignty is ours, the servitude yours ? Far

eorum, qui in turba, quam non excedunt, latent,
quorum et virtutes, ut appareant, diu luctantur et
vitia tenebras habent ; vestra facta dictaque rumor
excipit, et ideo nullis magis curandum est, qualem
famam habeant, quam qui, qualemcumque meruerint,
2 magnam habituri sunt. Quam multa tibi non licent,
quae nobis beneficio tuo licent ! Possum in qualibet
parte urbis solus incedere sine timore, quamvis
nullus sequatur comes, nullus sit domi, nullus ad
latus gladius ; tibi in tua pace armato vivendum est.
Aberrare a fortuna tua non potes ; obsidet te et,
quocumque descendis, magno apparatu sequitur.
3 Est haec summae magnitudinis servitus non posse
fieri minorem ; sed cum dis tibi communis ipsa
necessitas est. Nam illos quoque caelum alligatos
tenet, nec magis illis descendere datum est quam
4 tibi tutum ; fastigio tuo adfixus es. Nostros motus
pauci sentiunt, prodire nobis ac recedere et mutare
habitum sine sensu publico licet ; tibi non magis
quam soli latere contingit. Multa circa te lux est,
omnium in istam conversi oculi sunt. Prodire te
5 putas ? Oriris. Loqui non potes, nisi ut vocem
tuam, quae ubique sunt gentes, excipiant ; irasci
non potes, nisi ut omnia tremant, quia[1] neminem
adfligere, nisi ut, quidquid circa fuerit, quatiatur.
Ut fulmina paucorum periculo cadunt, omnium metu,
sic animadversiones magnarum potestatum terrent

[1] quin *Baehrens* : quia MSS.

---

[a] *Prodeo* is the ordinary word for "going out of doors,"
orior is used of the sun.

different is the position of those who escape notice in a crowd that they do not overtop, whose virtues must struggle long in order to be seen, whose vices keep under the cover of obscurity ; but the words and deeds of such as you are caught up by rumour, and, consequently, none should be more concerned about the character of their reputation than those who, no matter what reputation they may deserve, are sure to have a great one. How many things there are which you may not do, which we, thanks to you, may do ! It is possible for me to walk alone without fear in any part of the city I please, though no companion attends me, though I have no sword at my house, none at my side ; you, amid the peace you create, must live armed. You cannot escape from your lot ; it besets you, and, whenever you leave the heights, it pursues you with its magnificence. In this lies the servitude of supreme greatness—that it cannot become less great ; but you share with the gods that inevitable condition. For even they are held in bondage by heaven, and it is no more lawful for them to leave the heights than it is safe for you ; you are nailed to your pinnacle. Our movements are noticed by few ; we may come forth and retire and change our dress without the world being aware ; you can no more hide yourself than the sun. A flood of light surrounds you ; towards it every one turns his eyes. Think you to " come forth " ? Nay, you rise.[a] You cannot speak but that all the nations of the earth hear your voice ; you cannot be angry without causing everything to tremble, because you cannot strike any one down without shaking all that is around him. As the lightning's stroke is dangerous for the few, though feared by all, so the punishment born of

latius quam nocent, non sine causa ; non enim, quantum fecerit, sed quantum facturus sit, cogitatur in
6 eo, qui omnia potest. Adice nunc, quod privatos
homines ad accipiendas iniurias opportuniores accep-
tarum patientia facit, regibus certior est ex man-
suetudine securitas, quia frequens vindicta paucorum
7 odium opprimit, omnium irritat. Voluntas oportet
ante saeviendi quam causa deficiat ; alioqui, quemadmodum praecisae arbores plurimis ramis repullulant
et multa satorum genera, ut densiora surgant,
reciduntur, ita regia crudelitas auget inimicorum
numerum tollendo ; parentes enim liberique eorum,
qui interfecti sunt, et propinqui et amici in locum
singulorum succedunt.

1 9. Hoc quam verum sit, admonere te exemplo
domestico volo. Divus Augustus fuit mitis princeps,
si quis illum a principatu suo aestimare incipiat ; in
communi quidem rei publicae gladium movit. Cum
hoc aetatis esset, quod tu nunc es, duodevicensimum
egressus annum, iam pugiones in sinum amicorum
absconderat, iam insidiis M. Antonii consulis latus
2 petierat, iam fuerat collega proscriptionis. Sed
cum annum quadragensimum transisset et in Gallia
moraretur, delatum est ad eum indicium L. Cinnam,
stolidi ingenii virum, insidias ei struere ; dictum

---

a *i.e.*, while associated with Antony and Lepidus in the
triumvirate.

b This allusion determines approximately the date of the
composition of the essay ; Nero's eighteenth birthday was
Dec. 15, A.D. 55. Octavius was really over twenty at the
time of the proscriptions mentioned.

c Cassius Dio, lv. 14-22, places the incident in Rome.
The story supplied the theme of Corneille's *Cinna*.

d Dio gives correctly the praenomen Gnaeus ; Lucius

great power causes wider terror than harm, and not
without reason ; for when the doer is omnipotent, men
consider not how much he has done, but how much he
is likely to do.   Consider, too, that whereas private
citizens, by enduring the wrongs already received,
lie more open to receiving others, yet kings by
clemency gain a security more assured, because
repeated punishment, while it crushes the hatred of
a few, stirs the hatred of all.   The inclination to vent
one's rage should be less strong than the provocation
for it ;   otherwise, just as trees that have been
trimmed throw out again countless branches, and as
many kinds of plants are cut back to make them grow
thicker, so the cruelty of a king by removing his
enemies increases their number ; for the parents and
children of those who have been killed, their relatives
too and their friends, step into the place of each
single victim.

By an example from your own family I wish to
remind you how true this is.   The deified Augustus
was a mild prince if one should undertake to judge
him from the time of his principate ; but when he
shared the state with others,[a] he wielded the sword.
When he was at your present age, having just passed
his eighteenth year,[b] he had already buried his
dagger in the bosom of friends ; he had already in
stealth aimed a blow at the side of the consul, Mark
Antony ;   he had already been a partner in proscription.   But when he had passed his fortieth year
and was staying in Gaul,[c] the information was brought
to him that Lucius Cinna,[d] a dull-witted man, was
concocting a plot against him.   He was told where

Cornelius Cinna, son-in-law of Pompey, was the father of the
conspirator.

SENECA

est, et ubi et quando et quemadmodum adgredi
3 vellet ; unus ex consciis deferebat. Constituit se
ab eo vindicare et consilium amicorum advocari
iussit. Nox illi inquieta erat, cum cogitaret adule-
scentem nobilem, hoc detracto integrum, Cn. Pompei
nepotem, damnandum ; iam unum hominem occidere
non poterat, cui M. Antonius proscriptionis edictum
4 inter cenam dictarat. Gemens subinde voces varias
emittebat et inter se contrarias : " Quid ergo ?
Ego percussorem meum securum ambulare patiar
me sollicito ? Ergo non dabit poenas, qui tot
civilibus bellis frustra petitum caput, tot navalibus,
tot pedestribus proeliis incolume, postquam terra
marique pax parata est, non occidere constituat,
sed immolare ? " (nam sacrificantem placuerat adoriri).
5 Rursus silentio interposito maiore multo voce sibi
quam Cinnae irascebatur : " Quid vivis, si perire
te tam multorum interest ? Quis finis erit suppliciorum ? Quis sanguinis ? Ego sum nobilibus adu-
lescentulis expositum caput, in quod mucrones
acuant ; non est tanti vita, si, ut ego non peream,
6 tam multa perdenda sunt." Interpellavit tandem
illum Livia uxor et : " Admittis," inquit, " muliebre
consilium ? Fac, quod medici solent, qui, ubi usitata
remedia non procedunt, temptant contraria. Severitate nihil adhuc profecisti ; Salvidienum Lepidus
secutus est, Lepidum Murena, Murenam Caepio,
Caepionem Egnatius, ut alios taceam, quos tantum

---

[a] *Cf.* Cassius Dio, xlviii. 33 ; Suetonius, *Augustus*, 66.
[b] Suetonius, *Aug.* 19, mentions these, in the same order,
and others.

and when and how he meant to attack him ; one of
the accomplices gave the information. Augustus
resolved to revenge himself upon the fellow, and
ordered a council of his friends to be called. He
spent a restless night, reflecting that it was a young
man of noble birth, blameless but for this act, the
grandson of Gnaeus Pompeius, who was to be condemned. He could not now bear to kill one man,
he to whom Mark Antony had dictated the edict of
proscription while they dined. He moaned, and now
and then would burst forth into fitful and inconsistent
speech : " What then ? shall I let my murderer walk
about in unconcern while I am filled with fear ?
What ! Shall he not pay the penalty who, sought
in vain as my life has been in so many civil wars,
saved unhurt in so many battles of fleets and armies,
now that peace prevails on land and sea, is determining
not to murder but to immolate me ? " (for the plan
was to attack him while offering sacrifice). Again,
after an interval of silence, in louder tone he would
express much greater indignation at himself than
at Cinna : " Why do you live on if so many are
concerned to have you die ? What end will there be
of punishments, and of bloodshed ? I am the obvious
victim for whom young men of noble birth should
whet their swords. If so many must perish in order
that I may not, my life is not worth the price." At
length Livia, his wife, broke in and said : " Will you
take a woman's advice ? Follow the practice of
physicians, who when the usual remedies do not
work try just the opposite. So far you have accomplished nothing by severity. Salvidienus [a] was followed by Lepidus, Lepidus by Murena, Murena by
Caepio, Caepio by Egnatius,[b] to say nothing of the

ausos pudet. Nunc tempta, quomodo tibi cedat
clementia; ignosce L. Cinnae. Deprensus est;
iam nocere tibi non potest, prodesse famae tuae
7 potest." Gavisus, sibi quod advocatum invenerat,
uxori quidem gratias egit, renuntiari autem extemplo
amicis, quos in consilium rogaverat, imperavit et
Cinnam unum ad se accersit dimissisque omnibus
e cubiculo, cum alteram Cinnae poni cathedram
iussisset: "Hoc," inquit, "primum a te peto, ne
me loquentem interpelles, ne medio sermone meo
proclames; dabitur tibi loquendi liberum tempus.
8 Ego te, Cinna, cum in hostium castris invenissem,
non factum tantum mihi inimicum sed natum,
servavi, patrimonium tibi omne concessi. Hodie
tam felix et tam dives es, ut victo victores invideant.
Sacerdotium tibi petenti praeteritis compluribus,
quorum parentes mecum militaverant, dedi; cum
9 sic de te meruerim, occidere me constituisti." Cum
ad hanc vocem exclamasset procul hanc ab se abesse
dementiam: "Non praestas," inquit, "fidem,
Cinna; convenerat, ne interloquereris. Occidere,
inquam, me paras"; adiecit locum, socios, diem,
ordinem insidiarum, cui commissum esset ferrum.
10 Et cum defixum videret nec ex conventione iam,
sed ex conscientia tacentem: "Quo," inquit, "hoc
animo facis? Ut ipse sis princeps? Male mehercules cum populo Romano agitur, si tibi ad im-

others whose monstrous daring makes one ashamed. Try now how mercy will work : pardon Lucius Cinna. He has been arrested ; now he cannot do you harm, but he can help your reputation." Happy to have found a supporter, he thanked his wife, then ordered that the request to the friends who had been asked to the conference be at once countermanded, and summoned only Cinna to his presence. Having sent every one else from the room, he ordered a second chair to be placed for Cinna and said : " My first request of you is, that you will not interrupt me while I am talking, that you will not in the course of my words utter a protest ; you will be given free opportunity to speak. Cinna, though I found you in the camp of the enemy, not made, but born, my deadly foe, I saved you, I allowed you to keep the whole of your father's estate. To-day you are so prosperous, so rich, that your conquerors envy you, the conquered. When you sought holy office, I gave it to you, passing over many whose fathers had fought under me. Though such is the service that I have done you, you have determined to kill me." When at these words Cinna cried out that he was far from such madness, he said : " You are not keeping faith, Cinna ; it was agreed that you were not to interrupt. You are making ready, I say, to kill me." He mentioned, further, the place, his confederates, the plan of the plot, the one who had been entrusted with the dagger. And when he saw that Cinna had dropped his eyes, silent now, not because of his compact, but because of his conscience, he said : " What is your purpose in this ? Is it that you your-self may become the prince ? On my word, the Roman people are hard put to it if nothing stands in the

perandum nihil praeter me obstat. Domum tueri tuam non potes, nuper libertini hominis gratia in privato iudicio superatus es ; adeo nihil facilius potes quam contra Caesarem advocare. Cedo, si spes tuas solus impedio, Paulusne te et Fabius Maximus et Cossi et Servilii ferent tantumque agmen nobilium non inania nomina praeferentium, sed eorum, qui imaginibus suis decori sint ? "

11 Ne totam eius orationem repetendo magnam partem voluminis occupem (diutius enim quam duabus horis locutum esse constat, cum hanc poenam, qua sola erat contentus futurus, extenderet) : " Vitam," inquit, " tibi, Cinna, iterum do, prius hosti, nunc insidiatori ac parricidae. Ex hodierno die inter nos amicitia incipiat ; contendamus, utrum ego meliore fide tibi vitam dederim an tu debeas."

12 Post hoc detulit ultro consulatum questus, quod non auderet petere. Amicissimum fidelissimumque habuit, heres solus illi fuit. Nullis amplius insidiis ab ullo petitus est.

1 10. Ignovit abavus tuus victis ; nam si non ignovisset, quibus imperasset ? Sallustium et Cocceios et Deillios et totam cohortem primae admissionis ex adversariorum castris conscripsit ; iam Domitios, Messalas, Asinios, Cicerones, quidquid floris erat in civitate, clementiae suae debebat. Ipsum Lepidum quam diu mori passus est ! Per multos annos

way of your ruling except me. You cannot guard your own house ; just lately the influence of a mere freedman defeated you in a private suit; plainly, nothing can be easier for you than to take action against Caesar! Tell me, if I alone block your hopes, will Paulus and Fabius Maximus and the Cossi and the Servilii and the great line of nobles, who are not the representatives of empty names, but add distinction to their pedigree—will these put up with you ? "

Not to fill up a great part of my book in repeating all his words—for he is known to have talked more than two hours, lengthening out this ordeal with which alone he intended to be content—at last he said : " Cinna, a second time I grant you your life ; the first time you were an open enemy, now, a plotter and a parricide. From this day let there be a beginning of friendship between us ; let us put to the test which one of us acts in better faith—I in granting you your life, or you in owing it to me." Later he, unsolicited, bestowed upon him the consul-ship, chiding him because he did not boldly stand for the office. He found Cinna most friendly and loyal, and became his sole heir. No one plotted against him further.

Your great-great-grandfather spared the van-quished ; for if he had not spared them, whom would he have had to rule ? Sallustius and a Cocceius and a Deillius and the whole inner circle of his court he recruited from the camp of his opponents ; and now it was his own mercifulness that gave him a Domitius, a Messala, an Asinius, a Cicero, and all the flower of the state. What a long time was granted even Lepidus to die ! For many

tulit ornamenta principis retinentem et pontificatum maximum non nisi mortuo illo transferri in se passus est ; maluit enim illum honorem vocari quam 2 spolium. Haec eum clementia ad salutem securitatemque perduxit ; haec gratum ac favorabilem reddidit, quamvis nondum subactis populi Romani cervicibus manum imposuisset ; haec hodieque praestat illi famam, quae vix vivis principibus servit. 3 Deum esse non tamquam iussi credimus ; bonum fuisse principem Augustum, bene illi parentis nomen convenisse fatemur ob nullam aliam causam, quam quod contumelias quoque suas, quae acerbiores principibus solent esse quam iniuriae, nulla crudelitate exsequebatur, quod probrosis in se dictis adrisit, quod dare illum poenas apparebat, cum exigeret, quod, quoscumque ob adulterium filiae suae damnaverat, adeo non occidit, ut dimissis quo tutiores essent, 4 diplomata daret. Hoc est ignoscere, cum scias multos futuros, qui pro te irascantur et tibi sanguine alieno gratificentur, non dare tantum salutem, sed praestare.

1 11. Haec Augustus senex aut iam in senectutem annis vergentibus ; in adulescentia caluit, arsit ira, multa fecit, ad quae invitus oculos retorquebat. Comparare nemo mansuetudini tuae audebit divum Augustum, etiam si in certamen iuvenilium annorum

---

^a The notorious Julia, banished by Augustus on account of her infidelity to Tiberius.

years he suffered him to retain the insignia of a
ruler, and only after the other's death did he permit
the office of chief pontiff to be transferred to himself; for he preferred to have it called an honour
rather than a spoil. This mercifulness led him on
to safety and security, this made him popular and
beloved, although the necks of the Roman people
had not yet been humbled when he laid hand upon
them; and to-day this preserves for him a reputation
which is scarcely within the power of rulers even
while they live. A god we believe him to be, but
not because we are bidden; that Augustus was a
good prince, that he well deserved the name of
father, this we confess for no other reason than
because he did not avenge with cruelty even the
personal insults which usually sting a prince more than
wrongs, because when he was the victim of lampoons
he smiled, because he seemed to suffer punishment
when he was exacting it, because he was so far from
killing the various men whom he had convicted of
intriguing with his daughter *a* that he banished
them for their greater safety, and gave them their
credentials. Not merely to grant deliverance, but
to guarantee it, when you know that there will be
many to take up your quarrel and do you the favour
of shedding an enemy's blood—this is really to
forgive.

Such was Augustus when he was old, or just upon
the verge of old age. In youth he was hot-headed,
flared up with anger, and did many things which he
looked back upon with regret. To compare the
mildness of the deified Augustus with yours no
one will dare, even if the years of youth shall
be brought into competition with an old age

389

deduxerit senectutem plus quam maturam ; fuerit
moderatus et clemens, nempe post mare Actiacum
Romano cruore infectum, nempe post fractas in
Sicilia classes et suas et alienas, nempe post Peru-
2 sinas aras et proscriptiones. Ego vero clementiam
non voco lassam crudelitatem ; haec est, Caesar,
clementia vera, quam tu praestas, quae non saevitiae
paenitentia coepit, nullam habere maculam, numquam civilem sanguinem fudisse ; haec est in
maxima potestate verissima animi temperantia et
humani generis comprendens ut sui amor non cupiditate aliqua, non temeritate ingenii, non priorum
principum exemplis corruptum, quantum sibi in
cives suos liceat, experiendo temptare, sed hebetare
3 aciem imperii sui. Praestitisti, Caesar, civitatem
incruentam, et hoc, quod magno animo gloriatus es
nullam te toto orbe stillam cruoris humani misisse,
eo maius est mirabiliusque, quod nulli umquam
citius gladius commissus est.

4 Clementia ergo non tantum honestiores sed
tutiores praestat ornamentumque imperiorum est
simul et certissima salus. Quid enim est, cur reges
consenuerint liberisque ac nepotibus tradiderint
regna, tyrannorum exsecrabilis ac brevis potestas
sit ? Quid interest inter tyrannum ac regem (species
enim ipsa fortunae ac licentia par est), nisi quod
tyranni in voluptatem saeviunt, reges non nisi ex
causa ac necessitate ?

1 12. " Quid ergo ? Non reges quoque occidere

---

[a] In the battle with Antony and Cleopatra (31 B.C.).

[b] When Sextus Pompey was defeated in 36 B.C.

[c] A rumour was current that Octavius after the siege of
Perusia (41-40 B.C.) sacrificed many of the captives at an
altar erected to Julius Caesar ; cf. Suetonius, *Augustus*, 15 ;
Cassius Dio, xlviii. 14.

that was more than ripe. Granted that he was
restrained and merciful—yes, to be sure, but it
was after Actium's waters had been stained[a] with
Roman blood, after his own and an enemy's fleet
had been wrecked off Sicily,[b] after the holocaust
of Perusia[c] and the proscriptions. I, surely, do not
call weariness of cruelty mercy. True mercy, Caesar,
is this which you display, which arises from no regret
for violence, that bears no stain and never shed a
compatriot's blood. In a position of unlimited power
this is in the truest sense self-control and an all-
embracing love of the human race even as of oneself—not to be perverted by any low desire, or by
hastiness of nature, or by the precedent of earlier
princes into testing by experiment what licence one
may employ against fellow-citizens, but rather to
dull the edge of supreme power. Your gift, Caesar,
is a state unstained by blood, and your prideful boast
that in the whole world you have shed not a drop
of human blood is the more significant and wonderful because no one ever had the sword put into his
hands at an earlier age.

Mercy, then, makes rulers not only more honoured,
but safer, and is at the same time the glory of
sovereign power and its surest protection. For why
is it that kings have grown old and have handed on
their thrones to children and grandchildren, while
a tyrant's sway is accursed and short ? What difference is there between a tyrant and a king (for they
are alike in the mere outward show of fortune and
extent of power), except that tyrants are cruel to
serve their pleasure, kings only for a reason and by
necessity ?

"What then ? " you say ; " do not kings also often

solent ? " Sed quotiens id fieri publica utilitas persuadet ; tyrannis saevitia cordi est. Tyrannus autem a rege factis distat, non nomine ; nam et Dionysius maior iure meritoque praeferri multis regibus potest, et L. Sullam tyrannum appellari quid prohibet, cui occidendi finem fecit inopia hostium ?

2 Descenderit licet e dictatura sua et se togae reddiderit, quis tamen umquam tyrannus tam avide humanum sanguinem bibit quam ille, qui septem milia civium Romanorum contrucidari iussit et, cum in vicino ad aedem Bellonae sedens exaudisset conclamationem tot milium sub gladio gementium, exterrito senatu : " Hoc agamus," inquit, " patres conscripti ; seditiosi pauculi meo iussu occiduntur " ?

3 Hoc non est mentitus ; pauci Sullae videbantur. Sed mox de Sulla, cum quaeremus, quomodo hostibus irascendum sit, utique si in hostile nomen cives et ex eodem corpore abrupti transierint ; interim, hoc quod dicebam, clementia efficit, ut magnum inter regem tyrannumque discrimen sit, uterque licet non minus armis valletur ; sed alter arma habet, quibus in munimentum pacis utitur, alter, ut magno timore magna odia compescat, nec illas ipsas manus,

4 quibus se commisit, securus adspicit. Contrariis in contraria agitur ; nam cum invisus sit, quia timetur,

kill ? " Yes, but only when they are induced to do
so for the good of the state. Tyrants take delight
in cruelty. But the difference between a tyrant
and a king is one of deeds, not of name ; for while
the elder Dionysius *a* may justly and deservedly be
counted better than many kings, what keeps Lucius
Sulla from being styled a tyrant, whose killing was
stopped only by a dearth of foes ? Though he
abdicated the dictatorship and returned to private
life, yet what tyrant ever drank so greedily of human
blood as he, who ordered seven thousand Roman
citizens to be butchered at one time, and who, as he
sat nearby at the temple of Bellona and heard the
mingled cry of the many thousands moaning beneath
the sword, said to the terror-stricken senate, " Let
us attend to business, Gentlemen of the Senate ;
only a few seditious persons are being killed by my
order " ? This was no lie ; to Sulla they seemed a
few. But more about Sulla by and by, when we shall
take up the question of the sort of anger we should
have for enemies, particularly if fellow-countrymen
have broken away from the body politic and passed
over into the category of enemies. Meanwhile, as I
was saying, it is mercy that makes the distinction
between a king and a tyrant as great as it is, though
both are equally fenced about with arms ; but the
one uses the arms which he has to fortify good-will,
the other to curb great hatred by great fear, and
yet the very hands to which he has entrusted himself
he cannot view without concern. Conflicting causes
force him to conflicting courses ; for since he is
hated because he is feared, he wishes to be feared

a See Index.

timeri vult, quia invisus est, et illo exsecrabili versu,
qui multos praecipites dedit, utitur :

Oderint, dum metuant,

ignarus, quanta rabies oriatur, ubi supra modum
odia creverunt.

Temperatus enim timor cohibet animos, adsiduus
vero et acer et extrema admovens in audaciam
5 iacentes excitat et omnia experiri suadet. Sic feras
linea et pinnae clusas contineant ; easdem a tergo
eques telis incessat, temptabunt fugam per ipsa,
quae fugerant, proculcabuntque formidinem. Acer-
rima virtus est, quam ultima necessitas extundit.
Relinquat oportet securi aliquid metus multoque
plus spei quam periculorum ostentet ; alioqui, ubi
quiescenti paria metuuntur, incurrere in pericula
iuvat et[1] aliena anima abuti.

1   13. Placido tranquilloque regi fida sunt auxilia
sua, ut quibus ad communem salutem utatur,
gloriosusque miles (publicae enim securitati se dare
operam videt) omnem laborem libens patitur ut
parentis custos ; at illum acerbum et sanguinarium
2 necesse est graventur stipatores sui. Non potest
habere quisquam bonae ac fidae voluntatis ministros,
quibus in tormentis ut eculeo et ferramentis ad
mortem paratis utitur, quibus non aliter quam bestiis
homines obiectat, omnibus reis aerumnosior ac
sollicitior, ut qui homines deosque testes facinorum
ac vindices timeat, eo perductus, ut non liceat illi

---

[1] *Hosius, after Haase, inserts* ut *after* et.

[a] A favourite quotation ; cf. *De Ira*, i. 20. 4 ; *De Clem.*
ii. 2. 2.

because he is hated, and not knowing what frenzy is engendered when hatred grows too great, he takes as a motto that accursed verse which has driven many to their fall :

> Let them hate, if only they fear.[a]

Now fear in moderation restrains men's passions, but the fear that is constant and sharp and brings desperation arouses the sluggish to boldness, and urges them to stop at nothing.   In the same way, a string of feathers may keep wild beasts hemmed in, but let a horseman come upon them from behind with javelins, and they will try to escape through the very objects that had made them run, and will trample down their fear.   No courage is so bold as that forced by utter desperation.   Fear should leave some sense of security, and hold out much more of hope than of peril; otherwise, if an inoffensive man is made to fear the same peril as others, he takes pleasure in rushing into peril and making an end of a life that is forfeit.

A king that is peaceable and gentle finds his guards trusty, since he employs them for the common safety, and the soldier, seeing that he is giving his service for the security of the state, is proud and willing to undergo any hardship as a protector of the father of his country ; but he that is harsh and bloodthirsty inevitably gets the ill-will of his own henchmen.   It is impossible for any one to hold the good-will and loyalty of servitors whom he uses, like the rack and the axe, as instruments of torture and death, to whom he flings men as he would to wild beasts ; no prisoner at the bar is so troubled and anxious as he, seeing that he is in fear of men and gods, the witnesses and the avengers of crimes, yet has reached a point where

mutare mores. Hoc enim inter cetera vel pessimum
habet crudelitas, perseverandum est nec ad meliora
patet regressus ; scelera enim sceleribus tuenda
sunt. Quid autem eo infelicius, cui iam esse malo
3 necesse est ? O miserabilem illum, sibi certe !
Nam ceteris misereri eius nefas sit, qui caedibus ac
rapinis potentiam exercuit, qui suspecta sibi cuncta
reddidit tam externa quam domestica, cum arma
metuat, ad arma confugiens, non amicorum fidei
credens, non pietati liberorum ; qui, ubi circumspexit, quaeque fecit quaeque facturus est, et
conscientiam suam plenam sceleribus ac tormentis
adaperuit, saepe mortem timet, saepius optat,
4 invisior sibi quam servientibus. E contrario is, cui
curae sunt universa, qui alia magis, alia minus tuetur,
nullam non rei publicae partem tamquam sui nutrit,
inclinatus ad mitiora, etiam si ex usu est animad-
vertere, ostendens quam invitus aspero remedio
manus admoveat, in cuius animo nihil hostile, nihil
efferum est, qui potentiam suam placide ac salu-
tariter exercet approbare imperia sua civibus cupiens,
felix abunde sibi visus, si fortunam suam publicarit,
sermone adfabilis, aditu accessuque facilis, vultu,
qui maxime populos demeretur, amabilis, aequis
desideriis propensus, etiam iniquis non[1] acerbus, a
5 tota civitate amatur, defenditur, colitur. Eadem de

---

[1] non *added by Haase.*

he has not the power to change his conduct. For added to all the rest, this is still cruelty's greatest curse—that one must persist in it, and no return to better things is open ; for crime must be safeguarded by crime. But what creature is more unhappy than the man who now cannot help being wicked ? A wretch to be pitied, at least by himself ! for that others should pity him would be a crime—a man who has utilized his power for murder and pillage, who has caused mistrust of all his dealings whether at home or abroad, who resorts to the sword because he fears the sword, who trusts neither the loyalty of friends nor the affection of his children ; who, when he has surveyed what he has done and what he intends to do, and has laid bare his conscience burdened with crimes and torturings, often fears to die but more often prays for death, more hateful as he is to himself than to his servitors. On the other hand, he whose care embraces all, who, while guarding here with greater vigilance, there with less, yet fosters each and every part of the state as a portion of himself ; who is inclined to the milder course even if it would profit him to punish, showing thus how loath he is to turn his hand to harsh correction ; whose mind is free from all hostility, from all brutality ; who so covets the approbation of his countrymen upon his acts as ruler that he wields his power with mildness and for their good ; who thinks himself aboundingly happy if he can make the public sharers in his own good fortune ; who is affable in speech, easy of approach and access, lovable in countenance, which most of all wins the affection of the masses, well-disposed to just petitions and even to the unjust not harsh—such a one the whole state loves, defends,

illo homines secreto loquuntur quae palam. Tollere
filios cupiunt et publicis malis sterilitas indicta
recluditur ; bene se meriturum de liberis suis
quisque non dubitat, quibus tale saeculum ostenderit.
Hic princeps suo beneficio tutus nihil praesidiis eget,
arma ornamenti causa habet.

1 **14.** Quod ergo officium eius est ? Quod bonorum
parentium, qui obiurgare liberos non numquam
blande, non numquam minaciter solent, aliquando
admonere etiam verberibus. Numquid aliquis sanus
filium a prima offensa exheredat ? Nisi magnae
et multae iniuriae patientiam evicerunt, nisi plus
est, quod timet, quam quod damnat, non accedit ad
decretorium stilum ; multa ante temptat, quibus
dubiam indolem et peiore iam loco positam revocet ;
simul deploratum est, ultima experitur. Nemo ad
supplicia exigenda pervenit, nisi qui remedia con-
2 sumpsit. Hoc, quod parenti, etiam principi faciendum est, quem appellavimus Patrem Patriae non
adulatione vana adducti. Cetera enim cognomina
honori data sunt ; Magnos et Felices et Augustos
diximus et ambitiosae maiestati quidquid potuimus
titulorum congessimus illis hoc tribuentes ; Patrem
quidem Patriae appellavimus, ut sciret datam sibi
potestatem patriam, quae est temperantissima
3 liberis consulens suaque post illos reponens. Tarde
sibi pater membra sua abscidat, etiam, cum absci-

---

^a *i.e.,* to disinheritance in his will.

and reveres. What people say of such a man is the same in secret as in public. They are eager to rear up sons, and the childlessness once imposed by public ills is now relaxed ; no one doubts that his children will have cause to thank him for permitting them to see so happy an age. Such a prince, protected by his own good deeds, needs no bodyguard ; the arms he wears are for adornment only.

What, then, is his duty ? It is that of the good parent who is wont to reprove his children sometimes gently, sometimes with threats, who at times admonishes them even by stripes. Does any father in his senses disinherit a son for his first offence ? Only when great and repeated wrong-doing has overcome his patience, only when what he fears outweighs what he reprimands, does he resort to the decisive pen [a] ; but first he makes many an effort to reclaim a character that is still unformed, though inclined now to the more evil side ; when the case is hopeless, he tries extreme measures. No one resorts to the exaction of punishment until he has exhausted all the means of correction. This is the duty of a father, and it is also the duty of a prince, whom not in empty flattery we have been led to call " the Father of his Country." For other designations have been granted merely by way of honour ; some we have styled " the Great," " the Fortunate," and " the August," and we have heaped upon pretentious greatness all possible titles as a tribute to such men ; but to " the Father of his Country " we have given the name in order that he may know that he has been entrusted with a father's power, which is most forbearing in its care for the interests of his children and subordinates his own to theirs. Slow would a father be to sever his own flesh

derit, reponere cupiat, et in abscidendo gemat
cunctatus multum diuque ; prope est enim, ut
libenter damnet, qui cito ; prope est, ut inique
puniat, qui nimis.

1   15. Trichonem equitem Romanum memoria nostra,
quia filium suum flagellis occiderat, populus graphiis
in foro confodit ; vix illum Augusti Caesaris auctoritas
infestis tam patrum quam filiorum manibus eripuit.

2 Tarium, qui filium deprensum in parricidii consilio
damnavit causa cognita, nemo non suspexit, quod
contentus exilio et exilio delicato Massiliae parri-
cidam continuit et annua illi praestitit, quanta
praestare integro solebat ; haec liberalitas effecit,
ut, in qua civitate numquam deest patronus peioribus,
nemo dubitaret, quin reus merito damnatus esset,
quem is pater damnare potuisset, qui odisse non
poterat.

3   Hoc ipso exemplo dabo, quem compares bono patri,
bonum principem. Cogniturus de filio Tarius advo-
cavit in consilium Caesarem Augustum ; venit in
privatos penates, adsedit, pars alieni consilii fuit,
non dixit : " Immo in meam domum veniat " ; quod
si factum esset, Caesaris futura erat cognitio, non
4 patris. Audita causa excussisque omnibus, et his,
quae adulescens pro se dixerat, et his, quibus argue-

ᵃ Cf. the story of Milo's enjoying in exile the mullets
of Marseilles in Cassius Dio, xl. 54.
400

and blood; aye, after severing he would yearn to restore them, and while severing he would groan aloud, hesitating often and long; for he comes near to condemning gladly who condemns swiftly, and to punishing unjustly who punishes unduly.

Within my memory the people in the forum stabbed Tricho, a Roman knight, with their writing-styles because he had flogged his son to death; Augustus Caesar's authority barely rescued him from the indignant hands of fathers no less than of sons. Tarius, on the other hand, having detected his son in a plot against his life, when after investigating the case he found him guilty, won the admiration of every one because, satisfying himself with exile—and a luxurious exile—he detained the parricide at Marseilles,[a] furnishing him with the same liberal allowance that he had been in the habit of giving him before his guilt; the effect of this generosity was that, in a community where a villain never lacks a defender, no one doubted that the accused man had been justly condemned, since the father who could not hate him had found it possible to condemn him.

I will now use this very case to show you an example of a good prince with whom you may compare the good father. When Tarius was ready to open the inquiry on his son, he invited Augustus Caesar to attend the council; Augustus came to the hearth of a private citizen, sat beside him, and took part in the deliberation of another household. He did not say, "Rather, let the man come to my house"; for, if he had, the inquiry would have been conducted by Caesar and not by the father. When the case had been heard and all the evidence had been sifted —what the young fellow said in his defence, and

batur, petit, ut sententiam suam quisque scriberet,
ne ea omnium fieret, quae Caesaris fuisset ; deinde,
priusquam aperirentur codicilli, iuravit se Tarii,
5 hominis locupletis, hereditatem non aditurum. Dicet
aliquis : " Pusillo animo timuit, ne videretur locum
spei suae aperire velle filii damnatione." Ego contra
sentio ; quilibet nostrum debuisset adversus opiniones
malignas satis fiduciae habere in bona conscientia,
principes multa debent etiam famae dare. Iuravit
6 se non aditurum hereditatem. Tarius quidem eodem
die et alterum heredem perdidit, sed Caesar libertatem sententiae suae redemit ; et postquam ap-
probavit gratuitam esse severitatem suam, quod
principi semper curandum est, dixit relegandum, quo
7 patri videretur. Non culleum, non serpentes, non
carcerem decrevit memor, non de quo censeret, sed
cui in consilio esset ; mollissimo genere poenae
contentum esse debere patrem dixit in filio adules-
centulo impulso in id scelus, in quo se, quod proximum
erat ab innocentia, timide gessisset ; debere illum
1 ab urbe et a parentis oculis submoveri. 16. O dignum,
quem in consilium patres advocarent ! O dignum,
quem coheredem innocentibus liberis scriberent !
Haec clementia principem decet ; quocumque
venerit, mansuetiora omnia faciat.

---

^a *i.e.*, Caesar as well as his son.
^b In early times the parricide was sewn into a sack with
a dog, a cock, a snake, and a monkey, and drowned.

what was brought up in accusation against him—
Caesar requested each man to give his verdict in
writing, lest all should vote according to his lead.
Then, before the tablets were opened, he solemnly
declared that he would accept no bequest from
Tarius, who was a rich man. Some will say, "He
showed weakness in fearing that he might seem to
be trying to clear the field for his own prospects by
sentencing the son." I think differently; any one
of us might well have had enough faith in his own
good conscience to withstand hostile criticism, but
princes are bound to give much heed even to report.
He solemnly declared that he would not accept a
bequest. Tarius did indeed on one and the same day
lose a second heir [a] also, but Caesar saved the integrity
of his vote; and after he had proved that his severity
was disinterested—for a prince should always have
regard for this—he said that the son ought to be
banished to whatever place the father should decide.
His sentence was not the sack,[b] nor serpents, nor
prison, since his thought was not of the man on whom
he was passing sentence, but of him for whom he
was acting as counsellor. He said that the mildest
sort of punishment ought to satisfy a father in the
case of a son who was very youthful and had been
moved to commit this crime, but in committing it
had shown himself faint-hearted—which was next
door to being innocent; therefore the son should be
banished from the city and from his father's sight.
How worthy he was of being asked by parents to
share their counsels! how worthy of being recorded
a co-heir with the children who were innocent! This
is the spirit of mercy that graces the prince; wherever
he goes he should make everything more peaceable.

Nemo regi tam vilis sit, ut illum perire non
2 sentiat, qualiscumque pars imperii est. In magna
imperia ex minoribus petamus exemplum. Non
unum est imperandi genus ; imperat princeps civibus
suis, pater liberis, praeceptor discentibus, tribunus
3 vel centurio militibus. Nonne pessimus pater vide-
bitur, qui adsiduis plagis liberos etiam ex levissimis
causis compescet ? Uter autem praeceptor liberalibus studiis dignior, qui excarnificabit discipulos, si
memoria illis non constiterit aut si parum agilis in
legendo oculus haeserit, an qui monitionibus et
verecundia emendare ac docere malit ? Tribunum
centurionemque da saevum : desertores faciet,
4 quibus tamen ignoscitur.ᵃ Numquidnam aequum est
gravius homini et durius imperari, quam imperatur
animalibus mutis ? Atqui equum non crebris verberibus exterret domandi peritus magister ; fiet
enim formidolosus et contumax, nisi eum blandiente
5 tactu permulseris. Idem facit ille venator, quique
instituit catulos vestigia sequi quique iam exercitatis
utitur ad excitandas vel persequendas feras : nec
crebro illis minatur (contundet enim animos et, quidquid est indolis, comminuetur trepidatione degeneri)
nec licentiam vagandi errandique passim concedit.
Adicias his licet tardiora agentes iumenta, quae,
cum ad contumeliam et miserias nata sint, nimia
saevitia cogantur iugum detractare.

ᵃ *i.e.*, though guilty of desertion.

In the eyes of a ruler let no man count for so little that his destruction is not noted; be he what he may, he is part of the realm. From the forms of lesser power let us draw a parallel for great power. There is more than one kind of power: a prince has power over his subjects, a father over his children, a teacher over his pupils, a tribune or a centurion over his soldiers. Will he not seem the worst sort of father who controls his children by constant whippings for even the most trifling offences? And of teachers, which will reflect more credit upon the liberal studies—the one who will draw the blood of his pupils if their memory is weak, or if the eye is not quick and lags in reading, or the one who chooses rather by kind admonition and a sense of shame to correct, and so to teach, his pupils? Show me a tribune or centurion that is harsh; he will cause deserters, who all the same [a] are pardonable. Is it just, I ask, that man should be subjected to severer and harsher rule than dumb beasts? And yet the horse is not plied with the lash and terrified by the horse-breaker who is an expert; for it will grow fearful and obstinate unless it is soothed with caressing hand. The same is true of the hunter, whether he is teaching young dogs to follow the trail, or makes use of those already trained for routing out the game or running it down: he neither employs constant threats (for that will break their spirit, and all their native qualities will be gradually lost in a timidity unworthy of their breed), nor does he allow them to range and roam around without restraint. This applies again to drivers of the more sluggish beasts of burden, which, though they are born to abuse and misery, may be driven to refuse the yoke by too much cruelty.

1   17. Nullum animal morosius est, nullum maiore
arte tractandum quam homo, nulli magis parcendum.
Quid enim est stultius quam in iumentis quidem et
canibus erubescere iras exercere, pessima autem
condicione sub homine[1] hominem esse ?   Morbis
medemur nec irascimur ; atqui et hic morbus est
animi ;   mollem medicinam desiderat ipsumque
2 medentem minime infestum aegro. Mali medici
est desperare, ne curet : idem in iis, quorum animus
adfectus est, facere debebit is, cui tradita salus
omnium est, non cito spem proicere nec mortifera
signa pronuntiare ; luctetur cum vitiis, resistat,
aliis morbum suum exprobret, quosdam molli
curatione decipiat citius meliusque sanaturus remediis fallentibus ; agat princeps curam non tantum
3 salutis, sed etiam honestae cicatricis. Nulla regi
gloria est ex saeva animadversione (quis enim
dubitat posse ?), at contra maxima, si vim suam
continet, si multos irae alienae eripuit, neminem
suae impendit.

1   18. Servis imperare moderate laus est. Et in
mancipio cogitandum est, non quantum illud impune
possit pati, sed quantum tibi permittat aequi bonique
natura, quae parcere etiam captivis et pretio paratis

homine *added by Lipsius.*

No creature is more difficult of temper, none needs to be handled with greater skill, than man, and to none should more mercy be shown. For what is more senseless than to subject man to the foulest treatment at the hands of man, while one will blush to vent his anger on beasts of burden and dogs? Diseases do not make us angry—we try to cure them; yet here too is a disease, but of the mind; it requires gentle treatment, and one to treat it who is anything but hostile to his patient. It is a poor physician that lacks faith in his ability to cure; and he who has been entrusted with the life of all the people ought to act upon the same principle in dealing with those whose mind is diseased; he ought not to be too quick to give up hope or to pronounce the symptoms fatal; he should wrestle with their troubles and stay them; some he should reproach with their malady, some he should dupe by a sugared dose in order to make a quicker and a better cure by using deceptive remedies; the aim of the prince should be not merely to restore the health, but also to leave no shameful scar. No glory redounds to a ruler from cruel punishment—for who doubts his ability to give it?—but, on the other hand, the greatest glory is his if he holds his power in check, if he rescues many from the wrath of others, if he sacrifices none to his own.

It is praiseworthy to use authority over slaves with moderation. Even in the case of a human chattel you should consider not how much he can be made to suffer without retaliating, but how much you are permitted to inflict by the principles of equity and right, which require that mercy should be shown even to captives and purchased slaves.

iubet. Quanto iustius iubet hominibus liberis,
ingenuis, honestis non ut mancipiis abuti sed ut his,
quos gradu antecedas quorumque tibi non servitus
2 tradita sit, sed tutela. Servis ad statuam licet con-
fugere ; cum in servum omnia liceant, est aliquid,
quod in hominem licere commune ius animantium
vetet. Quis non Vedium Pollionem peius oderat
quam servi sui, quod muraenas sanguine humano
saginabat et eos, qui se aliquid offenderant, in
vivarium, quid aliud quam serpentium, abici iubebat ?
O hominem mille mortibus dignum, sive devorandos
servos obiciebat muraenis, quas esurus erat, sive in
hoc tantum illas alebat, ut sic aleret.

3 Quemadmodum domini crudeles tota civitate
commonstrantur invisique et detestabiles sunt, ita
regum et iniuria latius patet et infamia atque odium
saeculis traditur ; quanto autem non nasci melius
fuit, quam numerari inter publico malo natos !

1 19. Excogitare nemo quicquam poterit, quod
magis decorum regenti sit quam clementia, quocumque modo is et quocumque iure praepositus
ceteris erit. Eo scilicet formosius id esse magnifi-
centiusque fatebimur, quo in maiore praestabitur
potestate, quam non oportet noxiam esse, si ad
2 naturae legem componitur. Natura enim commenta

With how much more justice do they require that free, free-born, and reputable men should not be treated as mere chattels, but as those who, out-stripped by you in rank, have been committed to your charge to be, not your slaves, but your wards. Even slaves have the right of refuge at the statue of a god; and although the law allows anything in dealing with a slave, yet in dealing with a human being there is an extreme which the right common to all living creatures refuses to allow. Who did not hate Vedius Pollio even more than his own slaves did, because he would fatten his lampreys on human blood, and order those who had for some reason incurred his displeasure to be thrown into his fish-pond—or why not say his snake-preserve? The monster! He deserved to die a thousand deaths, whether he threw his slaves as food to lampreys he meant to eat, or whether he kept lampreys only to feed them on such food!

Even as cruel masters are pointed at with scorn throughout the whole city, and are hated and loathed, so with kings; while the wrong they do extends more widely, the infamy and hatred which they incur is handed down to the ages. But how much better not to have been born than to be counted among those born to the public harm!

It will be impossible for one to imagine anything more seemly for a ruler than the quality of mercy, no matter in what manner or with what justice he has been set over other men. We shall admit, of course, that this quality is the more beautiful and wonderful, the greater the power under which it is displayed; and this power need not be harmful if it is adjusted to Nature's law. For Nature herself

est regem, quod et ex aliis animalibus licet cognoscere
et ex apibus ; quarum regi amplissimum cubile est
medioque ac tutissimo loco ; praeterea opere vacat
exactor alienorum operum, et amisso rege totum
dilabitur, nec umquam plus unum patiuntur melioremque pugna quaerunt ; praeterea insignis regi forma
est dissimilisque ceteris cum magnitudine tum
3 nitore. Hoc tamen maxime distinguitur : iracundissimae ac pro corporis captu pugnacissimae
sunt apes et aculeos in volnere relinquunt, rex ipse
sine aculeo est ; noluit illum natura nec saevum esse
nec ultionem magno constaturam petere telumque
detraxit et iram eius inermem reliquit.

Exemplar hoc magnis regibus ingens ; est enim
illi mos exercere se in parvis et ingentium rerum
4 documenta minima largiri.[1] Pudeat ab exiguis
animalibus non trahere mores, cum tanto hominum
moderatior esse animus debeat, quanto vehementius
nocet. Utinam quidem eadem homini lex esset
et ira cum telo suo frangeretur nec saepius liceret
nocere quam semel nec alienis viribus exercere
odia ! Facile enim lassaretur furor, si per se sibi
satis faceret et si mortis periculo vim suam effunderet.
5 Sed ne nunc quidem illi cursus tutus est ; tantum
enim necesse est timeat, quantum timeri voluit, et
manus omnium observet et eo quoque tempore,

---

[1] minima argere (agere) *O*: urgere *Haupt*: spargere
Madvig: largiri *ego scripsi*: in minima (*sc.* re) parere
Hosius: arguere *Ball*.

---

[a] Really the queen-bee.
[b] *Cf.* Virgil's mock-heroic description of the battle of the
bees in *Georgics*, iv. 67-87.
[c] *i.e.*, from the tiniest things.

conceived the idea of king, as we may recognize from the case of bees and other creatures ; the king [a] of the bees has the roomiest cell, placed in the central and safest spot ; besides, he does no work, but super-intends the work of the others, and if they lose their king, they all scatter ; they never tolerate more than one at a time, and they discover the best one by means of a fight [b] ; moreover the appearance of the king is striking and different from that of the others both in size and beauty. His greatest mark of dis-tinction, however, lies in this : bees are most easily provoked, and, for the size of their bodies, excellent fighters, and where they wound they leave their stings ; but the king himself has no sting. Nature did not wish him to be cruel or to seek a revenge that would be so costly, and so she removed his weapon, and left his anger unarmed.

Great kings will find herein a mighty precedent ; for it is Nature's way to exercise herself in small matters, and to bestow the tiniest [c] proofs of great principles. Shameful were it not to draw a lesson from the ways of the tiny creatures, since, as the mind of man has so much more power to do harm, it ought to show the greater self-control. Would at least that a man were subject to the same law, and that his anger broke off along with his weapon, and that he could not injure more than once or use the strength of others to wreak his hatred ; for he would soon grow weary of his rage if he had no instrument to satisfy it but himself, and if by giving rein to his violence he ran the risk of death. But even as it is, such a man has no safe course ; for he must fear as much as he wishes to be feared, must watch the hands of every person, and count himself

quo non captatur, peti se iudicet nullumque momentum immune a metu habeat. Hanc aliquis agere
vitam sustinet, cum liceat innoxium aliis, ob hoc
securum, salutare potentiae ius laetis omnibus
tractare ? Errat enim, si quis existimat tutum esse
ibi regem, ubi nihil a rege tutum est ; securitas
6 securitate mutua paciscenda est. Non opus est
instruere in altum editas arces nec in adscensum
arduos colles emunire nec latera montium abscidere,
multiplicibus se muris turribusque saepire : salvum
regem clementia in aperto praestabit. Unum est
inexpugnabile munimentum amor civium.   •

7   Quid pulchrius est quam vivere optantibus cunctis
et vota non sub custode nuncupantibus ? si paulum
valetudo titubavit, non spem hominum excitari,
sed metum ? nihil esse cuiquam tam pretiosum,
quod non pro salute praesidis sui commutatum velit ?
8 O ne ille, cui contingit, ut sibi quoque vivere debeat ; in hoc adsiduis bonitatis argumentis probavit
non rem publicam suam esse, sed se rei publicae. Quis
huic audeat struere aliquod periculum ? Quis ab hoc
non, si possit, fortunam quoque avertere velit, sub
quo iustitia, pax, pudicitia, securitas, dignitas florent,
sub quo opulenta civitas copia bonorum omnium
abundat ? Nec alio animo rectorem suum intuetur,
quam, si di immortales potestatem visendi sui faciant,

---

^a *i.e.*, the pleasure derived from so much solicitude
becomes in itself a motive for living.

assailed even when no one is for laying hold on him, and not a moment must he have that is free from dread. Would any one endure to live such a life when, doing no harm to others and consequently fearless, he might exercise beneficently his privilege of power to the happiness of all ? For if any one thinks that a king can abide in safety where nothing is safe from the king, he is wrong ; for the price of security is an interchange of security. He has no need to rear on high his towering castles, or to wall about steep hills against ascent, or to cut away the sides of mountains, or to encircle himself with rows of walls and turrets ; through mercy a king will be assured of safety on an open plain. His one impregnable defence is the love of his countrymen.

And what is more glorious than to live a life which all men hope may last, and for which all voice their prayers when there is none to watch them ? to excite men's fears, not their hopes, if one's health gives way a little ? to have no one hold anything so precious that he would not gladly give it in exchange for his chieftain's safety ? Oh, surely a man so fortunate would owe it also to himself to live *a* ; to that end he has shown by constant evidences of his goodness, not that the state is his, but that he is the state's. Who would dare to devise any danger for such a man ? Who would not wish to shield him if he could, even from the chance of ill—him beneath whose sway justice, peace, chastity, security, and honour flourish, under whom the state abounds in wealth and a store of all good things ? Nor does it gaze upon its ruler with other emotion than, did they vouchsafe us the power of beholding them, we should gaze upon the immortal gods—with

413

intueamur venerantes colentesque. Quid autem?
9 non proximum illis locum tenet is, qui se ex deorum
natura gerit, beneficus ac largus et in melius potens?
Hoc adfectare, hoc imitari decet, maximum ita
haberi, ut optimus simul habeare.

1　20. A duabus causis punire princeps solet, si aut
se vindicat aut alium. Prius de ea parte disseram,
quae ipsum contingit; difficilius est enim moderari,
2 ubi dolori debetur ultio, quam ubi exemplo. Supervacuum est hoc loco admonere, ne facile credat, ut
verum excutiat, ut innocentiae faveat et, ut appareat,
non minorem agi rem periclitantis quam iudicis sciat;
hoc enim ad iustitiam, non ad clementiam pertinet;
nunc illum hortamur, ut manifeste laesus animum
in potestate habeat et poenam, si tuto poterit, donet,
si minus, temperet longeque sit in suis quam in
3 alienis iniuriis exorabilior. Nam quemadmodum
non est magni animi, qui de alieno liberalis est, sed
ille, qui, quod alteri donat, sibi detrahit, ita clemen-
tem vocabo non in alieno dolore facilem, sed eum,
qui, cum suis stimulis exagitetur, non prosilit, qui
intellegit magni animi esse iniurias in summa potentia pati nec quicquam esse gloriosius principe
impune laeso.

1　21. Ultio duas praestare res solet: aut solacium

veneration and with worship. But tell me : he who
bears himself in a godlike manner, who is beneficent
and generous and uses his power for the better end
—does he not hold a place second only to the gods ?
It is well that this should be your aim, this your ideal :
to be considered the greatest man, only if at the
same time you are considered the best.

A prince usually inflicts punishment for one of
two reasons, to avenge either himself or another. I
shall first discuss the situation in which he is personally concerned ; for moderation is more difficult when
vengeance serves the end of anger rather than of
discipline. At this point it is needless to caution him
to be slow in believing, to ferret out the truth, to be-
friend innocence, and to remember that to prove
this is as much the business of the judge as of the man
under trial ; for all this concerns justice, not mercy.
What I now urge is that, although he has been
clearly injured, he should keep his feelings under
control, and, if he can in safety, should remit the
punishment ; if not, that he should modify it, and be
far more willing to forgive wrongs done to himself
than others. For just as the magnanimous man
is not he who makes free with what is another's,
but he who deprives himself of what he gives to
some one else, so I shall not call him merciful
who is peaceable when the smart is another's, but
him who, though the spur galls himself, does not
become restive, who understands that it is magnanimous to brook injuries even where authority is
supreme, and that there is nothing more glorious
than a prince who, though wronged, remains un-
avenged.

Vengeance accomplishes usually one of two pur-

adfert ei, qui accepit iniuriam, aut in reliquum securi-
tatem. Principis maior est fortuna, quam ut solacio
egeat, manifestiorque vis, quam ut alieno malo
opinionem sibi virium quaerat. Hoc dico, cum ab
inferioribus petitus violatusque est ; nam si, quos
pares aliquando habuit, infra se videt, satis vindicatus
est. Regem et servus occidit et serpens et sagitta ;
servavit quidem nemo nisi maior eo, quem servabat.
2 Uti itaque animose debet tanto munere deorum
dandi auferendique vitam potens. In iis praesertim,
quos scit aliquando sibi par fastigium[1] obtinuisse,
hoc arbitrium adeptus ultionem implevit perfecitque,
quantum verae poenae satis erat ; perdidit enim
vitam, qui debet, et, quisquis ex alto ad inimici pedes
abiectus alienam de capite regnoque sententiam
expectavit, in servatoris sui gloriam vivit plusque
eius nomini confert incolumis, quam si ex oculis
ablatus esset. Adsiduum enim spectaculum alienae
3 virtutis est ; in triumpho cito transisset. Si vero
regnum quoque suum tuto relinqui apud eum potuit
reponique eo, unde deciderat, ingenti incremento
surgit laus eius, qui contentus fuit ex rege victo
nihil praeter gloriam sumere. Hoc est etiam ex
victoria sua triumphare testarique nihil se, quod

---

[1] ⟨par⟩ fastigium *Pincianus* : fastigio MSS.

poses : if a person has been injured, it gives him either a compensation or immunity for the future. But a prince's fortune is too exalted for him to feel the need of compensation, and his power is too evident to lead him to seek a reputation for power by injury to another. That, I say, is so, when he has been assailed and outraged by his inferiors ; for in the case of foes whom he once counted his equals, he has vengeance enough if he sees them beneath his heel. A slave, a snake, or an arrow may slay even a king ; but no one has saved a life who was not greater than the one whom he saved. Consequently he who has the power to give and to take away life ought to use this great gift of the gods in a noble spirit. If he attains this mastery over those who, as he knows, once occupied a pinnacle that matched his own, upon such especially he has already sated his revenge and accomplished all that genuine punishment required ; for that man has lost his life who owes it to another, and whosoever, having been cast down from high estate at his enemy's feet, has awaited the verdict of another upon his life and throne, lives on to the glory of his preserver, and by being saved confers more upon the other's name than if he had been removed from the eyes of men. For he is a lasting spectacle of another's prowess ; in a triumph he would have passed quickly out of sight. If, however, it has been possible in safety to leave also his throne in his possession, and to restore him to the height from which he fell, the praise of him who was content to take from a conquered king nothing but his glory will rise in increasing greatness. This is to triumph even over his own victory, and to attest that he found among

417

4 dignum esset victore, apud victos invenisse. Cum civibus et ignotis atque humilibus eo moderatius agendum est, quo minoris est adflixisse eos. Quibusdam libenter parcas, a quibusdam te vindicare fastidias et non aliter quam ab animalibus parvis sed obterentem inquinantibus reducenda manus est; at in iis, qui in ore civitatis servati punitique erunt, occasione notae clementiae utendum est.

1   22. Transeamus ad alienas iniurias, in quibus vindicandis haec tria lex secuta est, quae princeps quoque sequi debet: aut ut eum, quem punit, emendet, aut ut poena eius ceteros meliores reddat, aut ut sublatis malis securiores ceteri vivant. Ipsos facilius emendabis minore poena; diligentius enim vivit, cui aliquid integri superest. Nemo dignitati perditae parcit; impunitatis genus est iam non 2 habere poenae locum. Civitatis autem mores magis corrigit parcitas animadversionum; facit enim consuetudinem peccandi multitudo peccantium, et minus gravis nota est, quam turba damnationum levat, et severitas, quod maximum remedium habet, 3 adsiduitate amittit auctoritatem. Constituit bonos mores civitati princeps et vitia eluit, si patiens eorum est, non tamquam probet, sed tamquam invitus et cum magno tormento ad castigandum veniat. Verecundiam peccandi facit ipsa clementia

the vanquished nothing that was worthy of the victor. To his fellow-countrymen, to the obscure, and to the lowly he should show the greater moderation, as he has the less to gain by crushing them. Some men we should be glad to spare, on some we should scorn to be avenged, and we should recoil from them as from the tiny insects which defile the hand that crushes them; but in the case of those whose names will be upon the lips of the community, whether they are spared or punished, the opportunity for a notable clemency should be made use of.

Let us pass now to the injuries done to others, in the punishment of which these three aims, which the law has had in view, should be kept in view also by the prince: either to reform the man that is punished, or by punishing him to make the rest better, or by removing bad men to let the rest live in greater security. You will more easily reform the culprits themselves by the lighter form of punishment; for he will live more guardedly who has something left to lose. No one is sparing of a ruined reputation; it brings a sort of exemption from punishment to have no room left for punishment. The morals of the state, moreover, are better mended by the sparing use of punitive measures; for sin becomes familiar from the multitude of those who sin, and the official stigma is less weighty if its force is weakened by the very number that it condemns, and severity, which provides the best corrective, loses its potency by repeated application. Good morals are established in the state and vice is wiped out if a prince is patient with vice, not as if he approved of it, but as if unwillingly and with great pain he had resort to chastisement. The very mercifulness

419

regentis; gravior multo poena videtur, quae a miti
viro constituitur.

1 23. Praeterea videbis ea saepe committi, quae
saepe vindicantur. Pater tuus plures intra quin-
quennium culleo insuit, quam omnibus saeculis
insutos accepimus. Multo minus audebant liberi
nefas ultimum admittere, quam diu sine lege crimen
fuit. Summa enim prudentia altissimi viri et rerum
naturae peritissimi maluerunt velut incredibile scelus
et ultra audaciam positum praeterire quam, dum
vindicant, ostendere posse fieri; itaque parricidae
cum lege coeperunt, et illis facinus poena monstravit;
pessimo vero loco pietas fuit, postquam saepius
2 culleos vidimus quam cruces. In qua civitate raro
homines puniuntur, in ea consensus fit innocentiae
et indulgetur velut publico bono. Putet se innocentem esse civitas, erit; magis irascetur a communi
frugalitate desciscentibus, si paucos esse eos viderit.
Periculosum est, mihi crede, ostendere civitati,
quanto plures mali sint.

1 24. Dicta est aliquando a senatu sententia, ut
servos a liberis cultus distingueret; deinde apparuit,
quantum periculum immineret, si servi nostri nume-
rare nos coepissent. Idem scito metuendum esse,
si nulli ignoscitur; cito apparebit, pars civitatis
deterior quanto praegravet. Non minus principi

---

^a *i.e.*, Claudius, Nero's adoptive father; not a cruel, but
an antiquarian, emperor.
^b *i.e.*, punished more parricides; *cf.* i. 15. 7.

of the ruler makes men shrink from doing wrong; the punishment which a kindly man decrees seems all the more severe.

You will notice, besides, that the sins repeatedly punished are the sins repeatedly committed. Your father[a] within five years had more men sewed up in the sack[b] than, by all accounts, there had been victims of the sack throughout all time. Children ventured much less often to incur the supreme sin so long as the crime lay outside the pale of the law. For by supreme wisdom the men of the highest distinction and of the deepest insight into the ways of nature chose rather to ignore the outrage as one incredible and passing the bounds of boldness, than by punishing it to point out the possibility of its being done; and so the crime of parricide began with the law against it, and punishment showed children the way to the deed; filial piety was truly at its lowest ebb after the sack became a more common sight than the cross. In that state in which men are rarely punished a sympathy for uprightness is formed, and encouragement is given to this virtue as to a common good. Let a state think itself blameless, and it will be so; its anger against those who depart from the general sobriety will be greater if it sees that they are few. Believe me, it is dangerous to show a state in how great a majority evil men are.

A proposal was once made in the senate to distinguish slaves from free men by their dress; it then became apparent how great would be the impending danger if our slaves should begin to count our number. Be sure that we have a like danger to fear if no man's guilt is pardoned; it will soon become apparent how greatly the worse element of the state preponderates.

turpia sunt multa supplicia quam medico multa
2 funera ; remissius imperanti melius paretur. Natura
contumax est humanus animus et in contrarium
atque arduum nitens sequiturque facilius quam
ducitur ; et ut generosi ac nobiles equi melius facili
freno reguntur, ita clementiam voluntaria innocentia
impetu suo sequitur, et dignam putat civitas, quam
servet sibi. Plus itaque hac via proficitur.

1   25. Crudelitas minime humanum malum est in-
dignumque tam miti animo ; ferina ista rabies est
sanguine gaudere ac vulneribus et abiecto homine
in silvestre animal transire. Quid enim interest,
oro te, Alexander, leoni Lysimachum obicias an ipse
laceres dentibus tuis ? Tuum illud os est, tua illa
feritas. O quam cuperes tibi potius ungues esse,
tibi rictum illum edendorum hominum capacem !
Non exigimus a te, ut manus ista, exitium familiarium
certissimum, ulli salutaris sit, ut iste animus ferox,
insatiabile gentium malum, citra sanguinem caedemque satietur ; clementia iam vocatur, ad occi-
dendum amicum cum[1] carnifex inter homines
2 eligitur. Hoc est, quare vel maxime abominanda sit
saevitia, quod excedit fines primum solitos, deinde
humanos, nova supplicia conquirit, ingenium advocat
ut[2] instrumenta excogitet per quae varietur atque

---

[1] cum *added by Baehrens.*
[2] ut *added by Gertz.*

---

[a] *i.e.,* " mercy."
[b] One of Alexander's generals ; *cf. De Ira*, iii. 17. 2.
422

Numerous executions are not less discreditable to a prince than are numerous funerals to a physician; the more indulgent the ruler, the better he is obeyed. Man's spirit is by nature refractory, it struggles against opposition and difficulty, and is more ready to follow than to be led; and as well-bred and high-spirited horses are better managed by a loose rein, so a voluntary uprightness follows upon mercy under its own impulse, and the state accounts it *a* worthy to be maintained for the state's own sake. By this course, therefore, more good is accomplished.

Cruelty is an evil thing befitting least of all a man, and is unworthy of his spirit that is so kindly; for one to take delight in blood and wounds and, throwing off the man, to change into a creature of the woods, is the madness of a wild beast. For what difference does it make, I beg of you, Alexander, whether you throw Lysimachus *b* to a lion, or yourself tear him to pieces with your teeth? That lion's maw is yours, and yours its savagery. How pleased you would have been had its claws been yours instead, and yours those gaping jaws, big enough to swallow men! We do not require of you that that hand of yours, the surest destruction of familiar friends, should save the life of any man, that your savage spirit, the insatiate curse of nations, should sate itself with anything short of blood and slaughter; we call it now a mercy if to kill a friend the butcher is chosen among mankind. The reason why brutality is most of all abhorred is this: because it transgresses first all ordinary, and then all human, bounds, searches out new kinds of torture, calls ingenuity into play to invent devices by which suffering may be varied and prolonged, and takes

extendatur dolor, delectatur malis hominum ; tunc
illi dirus animi morbus ad insaniam pervenit ultimam,
cum crudelitas versa est in voluptatem et iam
3 occidere hominem iuvat. Matura talem virum a
tergo sequitur aversio, odia, venena, gladii ; tam
multis periculis petitur, quam multorum ipse periculum est, privatisque non numquam consiliis, alias
vero consternatione publica circumvenitur. Levis
enim et privata pernicies non totas urbes movet ;
quod late furere coepit et omnes appetit, undique
4 configitur. Serpentes parvulae fallunt nec publice
conquiruntur ; ubi aliqua solitam mensuram transit
et in monstrum excrevit, ubi fontes sputu inficit et,
si adflavit, deurit obteritque, quacumque incessit,
ballistis petitur. Possunt verba dare et evadere
5 pusilla mala, ingentibus obviam itur. Sic unus aeger
ne domum quidem perturbat ; at ubi crebris mortibus
pestilentiam esse apparuit, conclamatio civitatis ac
fuga est, et dis ipsis manus intentantur. Sub uno
aliquo tecto flamma apparuit : familia vicinique
aquam ingerunt ; at incendium vastum et multas
iam domos depastum parte urbis obruitur.
1 26. Crudelitatem privatorum quoque serviles
manus sub certo crucis periculo ultae sunt ; tyrannorum gentes populique et, quorum erat malum,

---

delight in the afflictions of mankind; then indeed
the dread disease of that man's *a* mind has reached
the farthest limit of insanity, when cruelty has
changed into pleasure and to kill a human being
now becomes a joy. Hot upon the heels of such a
man follow loathing, hatred, poison, and the sword;
he is assailed by as many perils as there are many men
to whom he is himself a peril, and he is beset sometimes by the plots of individuals, at times, indeed,
by an uprising of the community. For whole cities
are not roused by the trivial destruction of single
individuals; but that which begins to rage widespread and aims at all becomes the mark of every
weapon. Tiny snakes pass unnoticed and no
organized hunt is made for them; but when one
exceeds the usual size and grows into a monster,
when it poisons springs with its venom, with its
breath scorches and destroys, then, wherever it
advances, it is attacked with engines of war. Petty
evils may elude us and escape, but we go out against
the great ones. So, too, one sick person causes no
confusion even in his own household; but when
repeated deaths show that a plague prevails, there
is a general outcry and flight of the community,
and threatening hands are lifted toward the gods
themselves. If a fire is discovered beneath some
single roof, the family and the neighbours pour on
water; but a widespread conflagration that has now
consumed many homes is put down only by the
destruction of half the city.

The cruelty even of men in private station has
been avenged by the hands of slaves despite their
certain risk of crucifixion; nations and peoples have
set to work to extirpate the cruelty of tyrants, when

et ei, quibus inminebat, exscindere adgressi sunt.
Aliquando sua praesidia in ipsos consurrexerunt
perfidiamque et impietatem et feritatem et, quidquid
ab illis didicerant, in ipsos exercuerunt. Quid enim
potest quisquam ab eo sperare, quem malum esse
docuit ? Non diu nequitia apparet nec, quantum
2 iubetur, peccat. Sed puta esse tutam crudelitatem,
quale eius regnum est ? Non aliud quam captarum
urbium forma et terribiles facies publici metus.
Omnia maesta, trepida, confusa ; voluptates ipsae
timentur ; non convivia securi ineunt, in quibus
lingua sollicite etiam ebriis custodienda est, non
spectacula, ex quibus materia criminis ac periculi
quaeritur. Apparentur licet magna impensa et
regiis opibus et artificum exquisitis nominibus, quem
tamen ludi in carcere iuvent ?

3   Quod istud, di boni, malum est occidere, saevire,
delectari sono catenarum et civium capita decidere,
quocumque ventum est, multum sanguinis fundere,
aspectu suo terrere ac fugare ? Quae alia vita
esset, si leones ursique regnarent, si serpentibus
in nos ac noxiosissimo cuique animali daretur po-
4 testas ? Illa rationis expertia et a nobis immanitatis
crimine damnata abstinent suis, et tuta est etiam
inter feras similitudo ; horum ne a necessariis quidem
sibi rabies temperat, sed externa suaque in aequo

some were suffering from it and others felt its menace. At times the tyrants' own guards have risen up against them, and have practised upon their persons the treachery and disloyalty and brutality and all else that they themselves had taught them. For what can any one expect from him whom he himself has taught to be bad? Wickedness is not obsequious long, nor guilty of crime only to the extent that it is bid. But suppose that cruel rule is safe, what sort of a kingdom has it? Nothing but the bare outlines of captured cities and the terror-stricken countenances of widespread fear. Everywhere is sorrow, panic, and disorder; even pleasures give rise to fear; men are not safe when they go to the festal board, for there the tongue even of the drunkard must guard itself with care, nor to the public shows where the material is sought for accusation and ruin. Provided though they are at huge expense, in regal opulence, and with artists of the choicest reputation, yet whom would games delight in prison?

Ye gods! what curse is this—to kill, to rage, to take delight in the clank of chains and in cutting off the heads of fellow-countrymen, to spill streams of blood wherever one may go, and by one's appearance to terrify and repel? What else would living be if lions and bears held sway, if serpents and all the creatures that are most destructive were given supremacy over us? These, devoid of reason and doomed to death by us on the plea of their ferocity, yet spare their kind, and even among wild beasts likeness forms a safeguard; but tyrants do not withhold their fury even from their kin, strangers and friends are treated just alike, and the more they

427

habet, quo plus se exercitat, eo incitatior.[1] A
singulorum deinde caedibus in exitia gentium serpit,
et inicere tectis ignem, aratrum vetustis urbibus
inducere potentiam putat ; et unum occidi iubere aut
alterum parum imperatorium credit ; nisi eodem
tempore grex miserorum sub ictu stetit, crudelitatem
suam in ordinem coactam putat.

5   Felicitas illa multis salutem dare et ad vitam ab
ipsa morte revocare et mereri clementia civicam.
Nullum ornamentum principis fastigio dignius pul-
chriusque est quam illa corona ob cives servatos, non
hostilia arma detracta victis, non currus barbarorum
sanguine cruenti, non parta bello spolia.   Haec
divina potentia est gregatim ac publice servare ;
multos quidem occidere et indiscretos incendii ac
ruinae potentia est.

[1] ⟨eo incitat⟩ior *supplied by Gertz.*

---

[a] A chaplet of oak leaves, with which the soldier who
had saved the life of a fellow-Roman in battle was
honoured. The distinction was bestowed on Augustus
as the saviour of citizens and was frequently assumed by
later emperors.

indulge their fury, the more violent it becomes.
Then from the murder of one and again another it
creeps on to the wiping out of nations, and to hurl
the firebrand on the roofs of houses and to drive
the plough over ancient cities are considered a sign
of power, and to order the killing of one or two is
believed to be too small a show of royal might;
unless at one time a herd of poor wretches stands
beneath the blade, rage counts its cruelty forced
under control.

True happiness consists in giving safety to many,
in calling back to life from the very verge of death,
and in earning the civic crown [a] by showing mercy.
No decoration is more worthy of the eminence of a
prince or more beautiful than that crown bestowed
for saving the lives of fellow-citizens; not trophies
torn from a vanquished enemy, nor chariots stained
with barbarian blood, nor spoils acquired in war.
To save life by crowds and universally, this is a
godlike use of power; but to kill in multitudes
and without distinction is the power of conflagration
and of ruin.

AD NERONEM CAESAREM
DE CLEMENTIA

LIBER II

1 1. Ut de clementia scriberem, Nero Caesar, una me vox tua maxime compulit, quam ego non sine admiratione et, cum diceretur, audisse memini et deinde aliis narrasse, vocem generosam, magni animi, magnae lenitatis, quae non composita nec alienis auribus data subito erupit et bonitatem tuam cum fortuna tua litigantem in medium adduxit. 2 Animadversurus in latrones duos Burrus praefectus tuus, vir egregius et tibi principi natus, exigebat a te, scriberes, in quos et ex qua causa animadverti velles ; hoc saepe dilatum ut aliquando fieret, instabat. Invitus invito cum chartam protulisset traderetque, exclamasti : " Vellem litteras nescirem ! " O dignam vocem, quam audirent omnes gentes, quae Romanum imperium incolunt quaeque iuxta iacent dubiae libertatis quaeque se contra viribus aut animis attollunt ! O vocem in con-

TO THE EMPEROR NERO

ON MERCY

BOOK II

I HAVE been especially induced to write on mercy
by a single utterance of yours, Nero Caesar, which
I remember, when it was made, I heard not without
admiration and afterwards repeated to others—a
noble, high-minded utterance, showing great gentleness, which unpremeditated and not intended for
others' ears suddenly burst from you, and brought
into the open your kind-heartedness chafing against
your lot. Burrus, your prefect, a rare man, born to
serve a prince like you, was about to execute two
brigands, and was bringing pressure upon you to
record their names and the reasons why you wished
their execution ; this, often deferred, he was insist-
ing should at last be done. He was reluctant, you
were reluctant, and, when he had produced the paper
and was handing it to you, you exclaimed, " Would
that I had not learned to write." What an utterance !
All nations should have heard it—those who dwell
within the Roman empire, and those on its borders
who are scarcely assured of their liberty, and those
who through strength or courage rise up against it.
What an utterance ! It should have been spoken

431

SENECA

tionem omnium mortalium mittendam, in cuius
verba principes regesque iurarent ! O vocem publica
generis humani innocentia dignam, cui redderetur
4 antiquum illud saeculum ! Nunc profecto con-
sentire decebat ad aequum bonumque expulsa alieni
cupidine, ex qua omne animi malum oritur, pietatem
integritatemque cum fide ac modestia resurgere et
vitia diuturno abusa regno dare tandem felici ac
puro saeculo locum.
1   2. Futurum hoc, Caesar, ex magna parte sperare
et confidere libet. Tradetur ista animi tui man-
suetudo diffundeturque paulatim per omne imperii
corpus, et cuncta in similitudinem tuam formabuntur.
A capite bona valetudo : inde omnia vegeta sunt
atque erecta aut languore demissa, prout animus
eorum vivit aut marcet. Erunt cives, erunt socii
digni hac bonitate, et in totum orbem recti mores
2 revertentur ; parcetur ubique manibus tuis. Diutius
me morari hic patere, non ut blandum auribus tuis
(nec enim hic mihi mos est ; maluerim veris offendere
quam placere adulando) ; quid ergo est ? Praeter
id, quod bene factis dictisque tuis quam familiarissi-
mum esse te cupio, ut, quod nunc natura et impetus
est, fiat iudicium, illud mecum considero multas
voces magnas, sed detestabiles, in vitam humanam
pervenisse celebresque vulgo ferri, ut illam :
" Oderint, dum metuant," cui Graecus versus similis

ᵃ The Golden Age—Shelley's
          The world's golden dawn
     Earliest and most benign.
ᵇ *Cf.* i. 12. 4.
ᶜ
          Ἐμοῦ θανόντος γαῖα μιχθήτω πυρί·
          οὐδὲν μέλει μοι· τἀμὰ γὰρ καλῶς ἔχει.
     (Nauck, *Trag. Graec. Fragm., Adesp.*, 513.)

before a gathering of all mankind, that unto it princes and kings might pledge allegiance. What an utterance! Worthy of the universal innocence of mankind, in favour whereof that long past age *a* should be renewed. Now assuredly it were fitting that men, thrusting out covetousness from which springs every evil of the heart, should conspire for righteousness and goodness, that piety and uprightness along with honour and temperance should rise again, and that vice, having misused its long reign, should at length give place to an age of happiness and purity.

We are pleased to hope and trust, Caesar, that in large measure this will happen. That kindness of your heart will be recounted, will be diffused little by little throughout the whole body of the empire, and all things will be moulded into your likeness. It is from the head that comes the health of the body; it is through it that all the parts are lively and alert or languid and drooping according as their animating spirit has life or withers. There will be citizens, there will be allies worthy of this goodness, and uprightness will return to the whole world; your hands will everywhere be spared. Permit me to linger longer on this point, but not merely to please your ears; for that is not my way—I would rather offend with the truth than please by flattery. What then is my reason? Besides wishing you to be as familiar as possible with your own good deeds and words in order that what is now a natural impulse may become a principle, I reflect upon this, that many striking but odious sayings have made their entry into human life and are bandied about as famous; as for example, "Let them hate if only they fear," *b* and the Greek verse *c* similar to it, in

est, qui se mortuo terram misceri ignibus iubet, et
3 alia huius notae. Ac nescio quomodo ingenia in[1]
immani et invisa materia secundiore ore expresserunt
sensus vehementes et concitatos; nullam adhuc
vocem audii ex bono lenique animosam. Quid ergo
est ? Ut raro, invitus et cum magna cunctatione,
ita aliquando scribas necesse est istud, quod tibi in
odium litteras adduxit, sed, sicut facis, cum magna
cunctatione, cum multis dilationibus.

1 3. Et ne forte decipiat nos speciosum clementiae
nomen aliquando et in contrarium abducat, videamus,
quid sit clementia qualisque sit et quos fines habeat.

Clementia est temperantia animi in potestate
ulciscendi vel lenitas superioris adversus inferiorem
in constituendis poenis. Plura proponere tutius
est, ne una finitio parum rem comprehendat et, ut
ita dicam, formula excidat; itaque dici potest et
inclinatio animi ad lenitatem in poena exigenda.
2 Illa finitio contradictiones inveniet, quamvis maxime
ad verum accedat, si dixerimus clementiam esse
moderationem aliquid ex merita ac debita poena
remittentem : reclamabitur nullam virtutem cuiquam minus debito facere. Atqui hoc omnes
intellegunt clementiam esse, quae se flectit citra id,
quod merito constitui posset.

1 4. Huic contrariam imperiti putant severitatem;

---

[1] in *added by Madvig*: ingenia inmania et invisa materia
secundiori expresserunt *OT corrected by Lipsius.*

---

[a] Here, apparently "pity," which is shown below to be
a fault, not a virtue.

[b] A praetor's statement of the issue between contestants
in a suit was called a *formula.* This was transmitted to
the *iudex*, who after hearing the evidence decided whether
the statement was true or false. Hence to lose a suit was
formulā cadere or *excidere.*

which a man would have the earth convulsed with
flame when once he is dead, and others of this type.
And somehow or other gifted men when dealing with
a cruel and hateful theme have moulded violent and
passionate thoughts into more felicitous phrase; never
before have I heard from good and gentle lips an
utterance that was full of spirit. What then is the
conclusion? Though it be seldom, against your will,
and after great reluctance, yet there are times when
you must write the sort of thing that made you hate
all writing, but you must do it, as you now do, after
great reluctance, after much procrastination.

And in order that we may not perchance be
deceived at times by the plausible name of mercy
and led into an opposite quality,[a] let us see what
mercy is, what is its nature, and what its limitations.

Mercy means restraining the mind from vengeance
when it has the power to take it, or the leniency of
a superior towards an inferior in fixing punishment.
In the fear that one definition may not be comprehensive enough, and, so to speak, the case[b] be
lost, it is safer to offer several; and so mercy may
also be termed the inclination of the mind towards
leniency in exacting punishment. The following
definition will encounter objections, however closely
it approaches the truth; if we shall say that mercy
is the moderation which remits something from the
punishment that is deserved and due, it will be
objected that no virtue gives to any man less than
his due. Everybody, however, understands that
the fact of the case is that mercy consists in
stopping short of what might have been deservedly
imposed.

The ill-informed think that its opposite is strict-

sed nulla virtus virtuti contraria est. Quid ergo
opponitur clementiae ? Crudelitas, quae nihil aliud
est quam atrocitas animi in exigendis poenis. " Sed
quidam non exigunt poenas, crudeles tamen sunt,
tamquam qui ignotos homines et obvios non in
compendium, sed occidendi causa occidunt nec inter-
ficere contenti saeviunt, ut Busiris ille et Procrustes
et piratae, qui captos verberant et in ignem vivos
2 imponunt." Haec crudelitas quidem ; sed quia nec
ultionem sequitur (non enim laesa est) nec peccato
alicui irascitur (nullum enim antecessit crimen),
extra finitionem nostram cadit ; finitio enim continebat in poenis exigendis intemperantiam animi.
Possumus dicere non esse hanc crudelitatem, sed
feritatem, cui voluptati saevitia est ; possumus
insaniam vocare : nam varia sunt genera eius et
nullum certius, quam quod in caedes hominum et
3 lancinationes pervenit. Illos ergo crudeles vocabo,
qui puniendi causam habent, modum non habent,
sicut in Phalari, quem aiunt non quidem in homines
innocentes, sed super humanum ac probabilem
modum saevisse. Possumus effugere cavillationem
et ita finire, ut sit crudelitas inclinatio animi ad
asperiora. Hanc clementia repellit longe iussam
stare a se ; cum severitate illi convenit.
4 Ad rem pertinet quaerere hoc loco, quid sit
misericordia ; plerique enim ut virtutem eam
laudant et bonum hominem vocant misericordem.
Et haec vitium animi est. Utraque circa severitatem
circaque clementiam posita sunt, quae vitare debemus ; per speciem enim severitatis in crudelitatem

ness ; but no virtue is the opposite of a virtue. What then is set over against mercy ? It is cruelty, which is nothing else than harshness of mind in exacting punishment. "But," you say, "there are some who do not exact punishment, and yet are cruel, such as those who kill the strangers they meet, not for the sake of gain, but for the sake of killing, and, not content with killing, they torture, as the notorious Busiris and Procrustes, and the pirates who lash their captives and commit them to the flames alive." This indeed is cruelty ; but because it does not result from vengeance—for no injury was suffered— and no sin stirs its wrath—for no crime preceded it— it falls outside of our definition ; for by the definition the mental excess was limited to the exaction of punishment. That which finds pleasure in torture we may say is not cruelty, but savagery—we may even call it madness ; for there are various kinds of madness, and none is more unmistakable than that which reaches the point of murdering and mutilating men. Those, then, that I shall call cruel are those who have a reason for punishing, but do not have moderation in it, like Phalaris, who, they say, tortured men, even though they were not innocent, in a manner that was inhuman and incredible. Avoiding sophistry we may define cruelty to be the inclination of the mind toward the side of harshness. This quality mercy repels and bids it stand afar from her ; with strictness she is in harmony.

At this point it is pertinent to ask what pity is. For many commend it as a virtue, and call a pitiful man good. But this too is a mental defect. We ought to avoid both, closely related as they are to strictness and to mercy. For under the guise of

incidimus,[1] per speciem clementiae in misericordiam.
In hoc leviore periculo erratur, sed par error est a
1 vero recedentium. 5. Ergo quemadmodum religio
deos colit, superstitio violat, ita clementiam man-
suetudinemque omnes boni viri praestabunt, misericordiam autem vitabunt; est enim vitium pusilli
animi ad speciem alienorum malorum succidentis.
Itaque pessimo cuique familiarissima est; anus et
mulierculae sunt, quae lacrimis nocentissimorum
moventur, quae, si liceret, carcerem effringerent.
Misericordia non causam, sed fortunam spectat;
clementia rationi accedit.

2 Scio male audire apud imperitos sectam Stoicorum
tamquam duram nimis et minime principibus regi-
busque bonum daturam consilium; obicitur illi,
quod sapientem negat misereri, negat ignoscere.
Haec, si per se ponantur, invisa sunt; videntur
enim nullam relinquere spem humanis erroribus,
3 sed omnia delicta ad poenam deducere. Quod si
est, quidnam haec scientia, quae dediscere humanitatem iubet portumque adversus fortunam certissimum mutuo auxilio cludit? Sed nulla secta
benignior leniorque est, nulla amantior hominum
et communis boni attentior, ut propositum sit usui
esse et auxilio nec sibi tantum, sed universis sin-
4 gulisque consulere. Misericordia est aegritudo animi
ob alienarum miseriarum speciem aut tristitia ex
alienis malis contracta, quae accidere immerentibus

---

[1] per . . . incidimus *supplied by Gertz.*

strictness we fall into cruelty, under the guise of mercy into pity. In the latter case a lighter risk is involved, it is true, but the error is equal in both, since in both we fall short of what is right. Consequently, just as religion does honour to the gods, while superstition wrongs them, so good men will all display mercy and gentleness, but pity they will avoid ; for it is the failing of a weak nature that succumbs to the sight of others' ills. And so it is most often seen in the poorest types of persons ; there are old women and wretched females who are moved by the tears of the worst criminals, who, if they could, would break open their prison. Pity regards the plight, not the cause of it ; mercy is combined with reason.

I am aware that among the ill-informed the Stoic school is unpopular on the ground that it is excessively harsh and not at all likely to give good counsel to princes and kings ; the criticism is made that it does not permit a wise man to be pitiful, does not permit him to pardon. Such doctrine, if stated in the abstract, is hateful ; for, seemingly, no hope is left to human error, but all failures are brought to punishment. And if this is so, what kind of a theory is it that bids us unlearn the lesson of humanity, and closes the surest refuge against ill-fortune, the haven of mutual help ? But the fact is, no school is more kindly and gentle, none more full of love to man and more concerned for the common good, so that it is its avowed object to be of service and assistance, and to regard not merely self-interest, but the interest of each and all. Pity is the sorrow of the mind brought about by the sight of the distress of others, or sadness caused by the ills of others which

credit ; aegritudo autem in sapientem virum non
cadit ; serena eius mens est, nec quicquam incidere
potest, quod illam obducat. Nihilque aeque hominem quam magnus animus decet ; non potest
5 autem magnus esse idem ac maestus. Maeror con-
tundit mentes, abicit, contrahit ; hoc sapienti ne
in suis quidem accidet calamitatibus, sed omnem
fortunae iram reverberabit et ante se franget ;
eandem semper faciem servabit, placidam, inconcussam, quod facere non posset, si tristitiam reciperet.

1 6. Adice, quod sapiens et providet et in expedito
consilium habet ; numquam autem liquidum sin-
cerumque ex turbido venit. Tristitia inhabilis est
ad dispiciendas res, utilia excogitanda, periculosa
vitanda, aequa aestimanda ; ergo non miseretur,
2 quia id sine miseria animi non fit. Cetera omnia,
quae, qui miserentur, volo facere, libens et altus
animo faciet ; succurret alienis lacrimis, non accedet ;
dabit manum naufrago, exuli hospitium, egenti
stipem, non hanc contumeliosam, quam pars maior
horum, qui misericordes videri volunt, abicit et
fastidit, quos adiuvat, contingique ab iis timet, sed
ut homo homini ex communi dabit ; donabit lacrimis
maternis filium et catenas solvi iubebit et ludo
eximet et cadaver etiam noxium sepeliet, sed faciet
3 ista tranquilla mente, vultu suo. Ergo non misere-
bitur sapiens, sed succurret, sed proderit, in com-

it believes come undeservedly. But no sorrow befalls the wise man; his mind is serene, and nothing can happen to becloud it. Nothing, too, so much befits a man as superiority of mind; but the mind cannot at the same time be superior and sad. Sorrow blunts its powers, dissipates and hampers them; this will not happen to a wise man even in the case of personal calamity, but he will beat back all the rage of fortune and crush it first; he will maintain always the same calm, unshaken appearance, and he could not do this if he were accessible to sadness.

Consider, further, that the wise man uses foresight, and keeps in readiness a plan of action; but what comes from a troubled source is never clear and pure. Sorrow is not adapted to the discernment of fact, to the discovery of expedients, to the avoidance of dangers, or the weighing of justice; he, consequently, will not suffer pity, because there cannot be pity without mental suffering. All else which I would have those who feel pity do, he will do gladly and with a lofty spirit; he will bring relief to another's tears, but will not add his own; to the shipwrecked man he will give a hand, to the exile shelter, to the needy alms; he will not do as most of those who wish to be thought pitiful do—fling insultingly their alms, and scorn those whom they help, and shrink from contact with them—but he will give as a man to his fellow-man out of the common store; he will grant to a mother's tears the life of her son, the captive's chains he will order to be broken, he will release the gladiator from his training, he will bury the carcass even of a criminal, but he will do these things with unruffled mind, and a countenance under control. The wise man, therefore, will not pity, but will succour,

mune auxilium natus ac bonum publicum, ex quo dabit cuique partem. Etiam ad calamitosos pro portione improbandosque et emendandos bonitatem suam permittet; adflictis vero et forte laborantibus multo libentius subveniet. Quotiens poterit, fortunae intercedet; ubi enim opibus potius utetur aut viribus, quam ad restituenda, quae casus impulit? Vultum quidem non deiciet nec animum ob crus alicuius aridum aut pannosam maciem et innixam baculo senectutem; ceterum omnibus dignis proderit et deorum more calamitosos propitius respiciet.

4 Misericordia vicina est miseriae; habet enim aliquid trahitque ex ea. Imbecillos oculos esse scias, qui ad alienam lippitudinem et ipsi subfunduntur, tam mehercules quam morbum esse, non hilaritatem, semper adridere ridentibus et ad omnium oscitationem ipsum quoque os diducere; misericordia vitium est animorum nimis miseria paventium, quam si quis a sapiente exigit, prope est, ut lamentationem exigat et in alienis funeribus gemitus.

1 7. "At quare non ignoscet?" Agedum constituamus nunc quoque, quid sit venia, et sciemus dari illam a sapiente non debere. Venia est poenae meritae remissio. Hanc sapiens quare non debeat dare, reddunt rationem diutius, quibus hoc propositum est; ego ut breviter tamquam in alieno

will benefit, and since he is born to be of help to all and to serve the common good, he will give to each his share thereof. He will extend a due measure of his goodness even to the unfortunates who deserve to be censured and disciplined; but much more gladly will he come to the rescue of the distressed and those struggling with mishap. Whenever he can, he will parry Fortune's stroke; for in what way will he make better use of his resources or his strength than in restoring what chance has overthrown? And, too, he will not avert his countenance or his sympathy from any one because he has a withered leg, or is emaciated and in rags, and is old and leans upon a staff; but all the worthy he will aid, and will, like a god, look graciously upon the unfortunate.

Pity is akin to wretchedness; for it is partly composed of it and partly derived from it. One knows that his eyes are weak if they too are suffused at the sight of another's blear eyes, just as always to laugh when other people laugh is, in faith, not merriment, but a disease, and for one to stretch his jaws too when everybody else yawns is a disease. Pity is a weakness of the mind that is over-much perturbed by suffering, and if any one requires it from a wise man, that is very much like requiring him to wail and moan at the funerals of strangers

"But," you ask, "why will he not pardon?" Come then, let us now also decide what pardon is, and we shall perceive that the wise man ought not to grant it. Pardon is the remission of a deserved punishment. Why a wise man ought not to give this is explained more at length by those who make a point of the doctrine; I, to speak briefly as if giving

iudicio dicam : " Ei ignoscitur, qui puniri debuit ;
sapiens autem nihil facit, quod non debet, nihil
praetermittit, quod debet ; itaque poenam, quam

2 exigere debet, non donat. Sed illud, quod ex venia
consequi vis, honestiore tibi via tribuet ; parcet
enim sapiens, consulet et corriget ; idem faciet,
quod, si ignosceret, nec ignoscet, quoniam, qui
ignoscit, fatetur aliquid se, quod fieri debuit, omisisse.
Aliquem verbis tantum admonebit, poena non
adficiet aetatem eius emendabilem intuens ; aliquem invidia criminis manifeste laborantem iubebit
incolumem esse, quia deceptus est, quia per vinum
lapsus ; hostes dimittet salvos, aliquando etiam
laudatos, si honestis causis pro fide, pro foedere,

3 pro libertate in bellum acciti sunt. Haec omnia
non veniae, sed clementi   opera sunt. Clementia
liberum arbitrium habet ; non sub formula, sed ex
aequo et bono iudicat ; et absolvere illi licet et,
quanti vult, taxare litem. Nihil ex his facit, tamquam iusto minus fecerit, sed tamquam id, quod
constituit, iustissimum sit. Ignoscere autem est,
quem iudices puniendum, non punire ; venia debitae
poenae remissio est. Clementia hoc primum praestat, ut, quos dimittit, nihil aliud illos pati debuisse
pronuntiet ; plenior est quam venia, honestior est.

another's opinion, explain it thus : " Pardon is given to a man who ought to be punished ; but a wise man does nothing which he ought not to do, omits to do nothing which he ought to do ; therefore he does not remit a punishment which he ought to exact. But in a more honourable way he will bestow upon you that which you wish to obtain by pardon ; for the wise man will show mercy, be considerate, and rectify; he will do the same that he would do if he pardoned, and yet he will not pardon, since he who pardons admits that he has omitted to do something which he ought to have done. To one man he will give merely a reproof in words, and he will not inflict punishment if he sees that the other's age will permit reformation ; another who is clearly suffering from the odium of crime he will order to go free, because he was misled, because wine made him fall ; he will let his enemies go unharmed, sometimes even with praise if they were stirred to fight by honourable motives—to maintain their loyalty, a treaty, or their liberty. These are all the operations of mercy, not of forgiveness. Mercy has freedom in decision ; it sentences not by the letter of the law, but in accordance with what is fair and good ; it may acquit and it may assess the damages at any value it pleases. It does none of these things as if it were doing less than is just, but as if the justest thing were that which it has resolved upon. But to pardon is to fail to punish one whom you judge worthy of punishment ; pardon is the remission of punishment that is due. Mercy is superior primarily in this, that it declares that those who are let off did not deserve any different treatment ; it is more complete than pardon, more creditable. In my opinion the dispute

4 De verbo, ut mea fert opinio, controversia est, de
re quidem convenit. Sapiens multa remittet, multos
parum sani, sed sanabilis ingenii servabit. Agricolas
bonos imitabitur, qui non tantum rectas procerasque
arbores colunt ; illis quoque, quas aliqua depravavit
causa, adminicula, quibus derigantur, applicant ;
alias circumcidunt, ne proceritatem rami premant,
quasdam infirmas vitio loci nutriunt, quibusdam
5 aliena umbra laborantibus caelum aperiunt. Videbit,
quod ingenium qua ratione tractandum sit, quo modo
in rectum prava flectantur." . . .

---

^a The rest of the essay is lost. It had apparently three
books corresponding to the three divisions of the subject
indicated in i. 3. 1.

is about words, but concerning the fact there is
agreement. The wise man will remit many punishments, he will save many whose character though
unsound can yet be freed from unsoundness. He
will be like the good husbandman who tends, not
merely the trees that are straight and tall, but also
applies props to those that for some reason have
grown crooked in order that they may be straightened;
others he will trim, in order that their branching
may not hamper their height; some that are weak
because set in poor soil he will fertilize; to some
suffering from the shade of the others he will open
up the sky. So the wise man will see what method
of treatment a given character should have, how
the crooked may be made straight." . . .*

SENECA

Hildebertus Cenomanensis ep. I. 3 (CLXXI. 145 Mign.) :
De clementia quoque compendiosa principibus capitula
Seneca evigilavit, in quibus ideo brevitatem dilexit non
obscuram, ut magnis occupatos legere non taederet. Ea
igitur pro te et ad te suscepta suscipe atque recordare,
quae dudum didiceris ex te et per te. Pauca ea sunt :

Clementiae est aliquid ultrici detrahere sententiae.
Quisquis nihil reatus impunitum relinquit, delinquit.
Culpa est totam persequi culpam. Immisericordem
profitetur, cui quicquid licet, libet.

Item : Gloriosa virtus est in principe citra punire
quam liceat. Virtus est ad vindictam necessitate
trahi, non voluntate venire. Magnum quid et
divinum sapit offensus clemens.

Item : Bonus princeps neminem sine poena punit,
neminem sine dolore proscribit. Bonus princeps ita
crimen insequitur, ut quem punit, hominem re-
miniscatur.

Item : Bonus princeps sibi dominatur, populo
servit, nullius sanguinem contemnit : inimici est,
sed eius, qui amicus fieri potest ; nocentis est, sed
hominis. Cuiuscumque sit, quia non potuit dare,
crimen putat auferre. Ideo quotiens funditur,
confunditur.

ON MERCY : FRAGMENTS

*Extracts from the treatise " On Mercy " preserved
in a letter by Hildebert of Tours*

It is the part of mercy to cause some abatement of
a sentence that aims at revenge.   He who does not
remit the punishment of wrong-doing is a wrong-doer.
It is a fault to punish a fault in full.   He shows himself
merciless whose might is his delight.

It is a shining virtue for a prince to punish less
than he might.   It is a virtue to be forced by necessity to take vengeance, not to visit it voluntarily.
The merciful man when injured savours of something
great and godlike.

A good prince punishes no one without being
punished, proscribes no one without suffering.   A
good prince follows up crime, yet keeps in mind the
man whom he is punishing.

A good prince masters himself, serves his people,
esteems lightly the life-blood of no man ; if it is an
enemy's, yet it is of one who may become a friend ; if
it is a criminal's, yet it is a human being's ; whose-
ever it may be, because he could not give it, he
considers it a crime to take it away.   Therefore its
effusion is ever his confusion.

INDEX OF NAMES

(The references are to the pages of the English translation.)

INDEX OF NAMES

INDEX OF NAMES

INDEX OF NAMES

INDEX OF NAMES

INDEX OF NAMES

Printed in Great Britain by R. & R. CLARK, LIMITED, *Edinburgh*

THE LOEB CLASSICAL LIBRARY

VOLUMES ALREADY PUBLISHED

LATIN AUTHORS

AMMIANUS MARCELLINUS. J. C. Rolfe. 3 Vols.

APULEIUS: THE GOLDEN ASS (METAMORPHOSES). W. Adlington (1566). Revised by S. Gaselee.

ST. AUGUSTINE: CITY OF GOD. 7 Vols. Vol. I. G. E. McCracken. Vol. II. W. M. Green. Vol. III. D. Wiesen. Vol. IV. P. Levine. Vol. V. E. M. Sanford and W. M. Green. Vol. VI. W. C. Greene.

ST. AUGUSTINE, CONFESSIONS OF. W. Watts (1631). 2 Vols

ST. AUGUSTINE: SELECT LETTERS. J. H. Baxter.

AUSONIUS. H. G. Evelyn White. 2 Vols.

BEDE. J. E. King. 2 Vols.

BOETHIUS: TRACTS AND DE CONSOLATIONE PHILOSOPHIAE. Rev. H. F. Stewart and E. K. Rand.

CAESAR: ALEXANDRIAN, AFRICAN AND SPANISH WARS. A. G. Way.

CAESAR: CIVIL WARS. A. G. Peskett.

CAESAR: GALLIC WAR. H. J. Edwards.

CATO AND VARRO: DE RE RUSTICA. H. B. Ash and W. D. Hooper.

CATULLUS. F. W. Cornish; TIBULLUS. J. B. Postgate; and PERVIGILIUM VENERIS. J. W. Mackail.

CELSUS: DE MEDICINA. W. G. Spencer. 3 Vols.

CICERO: BRUTUS AND ORATOR. G. L. Hendrickson and H. M. Hubbell.

CICERO: DE FINIBUS. H. Rackham.

CICERO: DE INVENTIONE, etc. H. M. Hubbell.

CICERO: DE NATURA DEORUM AND ACADEMICA. H. Rackham.

CICERO: DE OFFICIIS. Walter Miller.

CICERO: DE ORATORE, etc. 2 Vols. Vol. I: DE ORATORE. Books I and II. E. W. Sutton and H. Rackham. Vol. II: DE ORATORE, Book III; DE FATO; PARADOXA STOICORUM; DE PARTITIONE ORATORIA. H. Rackham.

CICERO: DE REPUBLICA, DE LEGIBUS, SOMNIUM SCIPIONIS. Clinton W. Keyes.

CICERO : DE SENECTUTE, DE AMICITIA, DE DIVINATIONE. W. A. Falconer.

CICERO : IN CATILINAM, PRO MURENA, PRO SULLA, PRO FLACCO. Louis E. Lord.

CICERO : LETTERS TO ATTICUS. E. O. Winstedt. 3 Vols.

CICERO: LETTERS TO HIS FRIENDS. W. Glynn Williams. 3 Vols.

CICERO : PHILIPPICS. W. C. A. Ker.

CICERO : PRO ARCHIA, POST REDITUM, DE DOMO, DE HA-RUSPICUM RESPONSIS, PRO PLANCIO. N. H. Watts.

CICERO : PRO CAECINA, PRO LEGE MANILIA, PRO CLUENTIO, PRO RABIRIO. H. Grose Hodge.

CICERO : PRO CAELIO, DE PROVINCIIS CONSULARIBUS, PRO BALBO. R. Gardner.

CICERO : PRO MILONE, IN PISONEM, PRO SCAURO, PRO FONTEIO, PRO RABIRIO POSTUMO, PRO MARCELLO, PRO LIGARIO, PRO REGE DEIOTARO. N. H. Watts.

CICERO : PRO QUINCTIO, PRO ROSCIO AMERINO, PRO ROSCIO COMOEDO, CONTRA RULLUM. J. H. Freese.

CICERO : PRO SESTIO, IN VATINIUM. R. Gardner.

[CICERO] : RHETORICA AD HERENNIUM. H. Caplan.

CICERO : TUSCULAN DISPUTATIONS. J. E. King.

CICERO : VERRINE ORATIONS. L. H. G. Greenwood. 2 Vols.

CLAUDIAN. M. Platnauer. 2 Vols.

COLUMELLA : DE RE RUSTICA, DE ARBORIBUS. H. B. Ash, E. S. Forster, E. Heffner. 3 Vols.

CURTIUS, Q.: HISTORY OF ALEXANDER. J. C. Rolfe. 2 Vols.

FLORUS. E. S. Forster ; and CORNELIUS NEPOS. J. C. Rolfe.

FRONTINUS : STRATAGEMS AND AQUEDUCTS. C. E. Bennett and M. B. McElwain.

FRONTO : CORRESPONDENCE. C. R. Haines. 2 Vols.

GELLIUS. J. C. Rolfe. 3 Vols.

HORACE : ODES AND EPODES. C. E. Bennett.

HORACE : SATIRES, EPISTLES, ARS POETICA. H. R. Fairclough.

JEROME : SELECT LETTERS. F. A. Wright.

JUVENAL AND PERSIUS. G. G. Ramsay.

LIVY. B. O. Foster, F. G. Moore, Evan T. Sage, A. C. Schlesinger and R. M. Geer (General Index). 14 Vols.

LUCAN. J. D. Duff.

LUCRETIUS. W. H. D. Rouse.

MARTIAL. W. C. A. Ker. 2 Vols.

MINOR LATIN POETS : from PUBLILIUS SYRUS TO RUTILIUS NAMATIANUS, including GRATTIUS, CALPURNIUS SICULUS, NEMESIANUS, AVIANUS, with " Aetna," " Phoenix " and other poems. J. Wight Duff and Arnold M. Duff.

THE LOEB CLASSICAL LIBRARY

Ovid : The Art of Love and other Poems. J. H. Mozley.

Ovid : Fasti. Sir James G. Frazer.

Ovid : Heroides and Amores. Grant Showerman.

Ovid : Metamorphoses. F. J. Miller. 2 Vols.

Ovid : Tristia and Ex Ponto. A. L. Wheeler.

Petronius. M. Heseltine ; Seneca : Apocolocyntosis. W. H. D. Rouse.

Phaedrus and Babrius (Greek). B. E. Perry.

Plautus. Paul Nixon. 5 Vols.

Pliny : Letters, Panegyricus. B. Radice. 2 Vols.

Pliny : Natural History. 10 Vols. Vols. I-V and IX. H. Rackham. Vols. VI-VIII. W. H. S. Jones. Vol. X. D. E. Eichholz.

Propertius. H. E. Butler.

Prudentius. H. J. Thomson. 2 Vols.

Quintilian. H. E. Butler. 4 Vols.

Remains of Old Latin. E. H. Warmington. 4 Vols. Vol. I (Ennius and Caecilius). Vol. II (Livius, Naevius, Pacuvius, Accius). Vol. III (Lucilius, Laws of the XII Tables). Vol. IV (Archaic Inscriptions).

Sallust. J. C. Rolfe.

Scriptores Historiae Augustae. D. Magie. 3 Vols.

Seneca : Apocolocyntosis. Cf. Petronius.

Seneca : Epistulae Morales. R. M. Gummere. 3 Vols.

Seneca : Moral Essays. J. W. Basore. 3 Vols.

Seneca : Tragedies. F. J. Miller. 2 Vols.

Sidonius : Poems and Letters. W. B. Anderson. 2 Vols.

Silius Italicus. J. D. Duff. 2 Vols.

Statius. J. H. Mozley. 2 Vols.

Suetonius. J. C. Rolfe. 2 Vols.

Tacitus : Agricola and Germania. Maurice Hutton ; Dialogus. Sir Wm. Peterson.

Tacitus : Histories and Annals. C. H. Moore and J. Jackson. 4 Vols.

Terence. John Sargeaunt. 2 Vols.

Tertullian : Apologia and De Spectaculis. T. R. Glover : Minucius Felix. G. H. Rendall.

Valerius Flaccus. J. H. Mozley.

Varro : De Lingua Latina. R. G. Kent. 2 Vols.

Velleius Paterculus and Res Gestae Divi Augusti. F. W. Shipley.

Virgil. H. R. Fairclough. 2 Vols.

Vitruvius : De Architectura. F. Granger. 2 Vols.

THE LOEB CLASSICAL LIBRARY

4

THE LOEB CLASSICAL LIBRARY

ARISTOTLE: POETICS; LONGINUS ON THE SUBLIME. W. Hamilton Fyfe; DEMETRIUS ON STYLE. W. Rhys Roberts.

ARISTOTLE: POLITICS. H. Rackham.

ARISTOTLE: POSTERIOR ANALYTICS. H. Tredennick; TOPICS. E. S. Forster.

ARISTOTLE: PROBLEMS. W. S. Hett. 2 Vols.

ARISTOTLE: RHETORICA AD ALEXANDRUM. H. Rackham. (With PROBLEMS, Vol. II.)

ARISTOTLE: SOPHISTICAL REFUTATIONS. COMING-TO-BE AND PASSING-AWAY. E. S. Forster; ON THE COSMOS. D. J. Furley.

ARRIAN: HISTORY OF ALEXANDER AND INDICA. Rev. E. Iliffe Robson. 2 Vols.

ATHENAEUS: DEIPNOSOPHISTAE. C. B. Gulick. 7 Vols.

BABRIUS AND PHAEDRUS (Latin). B. E. Perry.

ST. BASIL: LETTERS. R. J. Deferrari. 4 Vols.

CALLIMACHUS: FRAGMENTS. C. A. Trypanis.

CALLIMACHUS: HYMNS AND EPIGRAMS, AND LYCOPHRON. A. W. Mair; ARATUS. G. R. Mair.

CLEMENT OF ALEXANDRIA. Rev. G. W. Butterworth.

COLLUTHUS. Cf. OPPIAN.

DAPHNIS AND CHLOE. Cf. LONGUS.

DEMOSTHENES I: OLYNTHIACS, PHILIPPICS AND MINOR ORATIONS: I-XVII AND XX. J. H. Vince.

DEMOSTHENES II: DE CORONA AND DE FALSA LEGATIONE, C. A. Vince and J. H. Vince.

DEMOSTHENES III: MEIDIAS, ANDROTION, ARISTOCRATES, TIMOCRATES, ARISTOGEITON. J. H. Vince.

DEMOSTHENES IV-VI: PRIVATE ORATIONS AND IN NEAERAM. A. T. Murray.

DEMOSTHENES VII: FUNERAL SPEECH, EROTIC ESSAY. EXORDIA AND LETTERS. N. W. and N. J. DeWitt.

DIO CASSIUS: ROMAN HISTORY. E. Cary. 9 Vols.

DIO CHRYSOSTOM. 5 Vols. Vols. I and II. J. W. Cohoon. Vol. III. J. W. Cohoon and H. Lamar Crosby. Vols. IV and V. H. Lamar Crosby.

DIODORUS SICULUS. 12 Vols. Vols. I-VI. C. H. Oldfather. Vol. VII. C. L. Sherman. Vol. VIII. C. B. Welles. Vols. IX and X. Russel M. Geer. Vols. XI and XII. F. R. Walton. General Index. Russel M. Geer.

DIOGENES LAERTIUS. R. D. Hicks. 2 Vols.

DIONYSIUS OF HALICARNASSUS: ROMAN ANTIQUITIES. Spelman's translation revised by E. Cary. 7 Vols.

EPICTETUS. W. A. Oldfather. 2 Vols.

EURIPIDES. A. S. Way. 4 Vols. Verse trans.

EUSEBIUS: ECCLESIASTICAL HISTORY. Kirsopp Lake and J. E. L. Oulton. 2 Vols.

GALEN: ON THE NATURAL FACULTIES. A. J. Brock.

THE GREEK ANTHOLOGY. W. R. Paton. 5 Vols.

THE GREEK BUCOLIC POETS (THEOCRITUS, BION, MOSCHUS). J. M. Edmonds.

GREEK ELEGY AND IAMBUS WITH THE ANACREONTEA. J. M. Edmonds. 2 Vols.

GREEK MATHEMATICAL WORKS. Ivor Thomas. 2 Vols.

HERODES. *Cf.* THEOPHRASTUS: CHARACTERS.

HERODIAN: C. R. Whittaker. 2 Vols. Vol. I.

HERODOTUS. A. D. Godley. 4 Vols.

HESIOD AND THE HOMERIC HYMNS. H. G. Evelyn White.

HIPPOCRATES AND THE FRAGMENTS OF HERACLEITUS. W. H. S. Jones and E. T. Withington. 4 Vols.

HOMER: ILIAD. A. T. Murray. 2 Vols.

HOMER: ODYSSEY. A. T. Murray. 2 Vols.

ISAEUS. E. S. Forster.

ISOCRATES. George Norlin and LaRue Van Hook. 3 Vols.

[ST. JOHN DAMASCENE]: BARLAAM AND IOASAPH. Rev. G. R. Woodward, Harold Mattingly and D. M. Lang.

JOSEPHUS. 9 Vols. Vols. I-IV. H. St. J. Thackeray. Vol. V. H. St. J. Thackeray and Ralph Marcus. Vols. VI and VII. Ralph Marcus. Vol. VIII. Ralph Marcus and Allen Wikgren. Vol. IX. L. H. Feldman.

JULIAN. Wilmer Cave Wright. 3 Vols.

LIBANIUS: SELECTED WORKS. A. F. Norman. 3 Vols. Vol. I.

LONGUS: DAPHNIS AND CHLOE. Thornley's translation revised by J. M. Edmonds; and PARTHENIUS. S. Gaselee.

LUCIAN. 8 Vols. Vols. I-V. A. M. Harmon. Vol. VI. K. Kilburn. Vols. VII and VIII. M. D. Macleod.

LYCOPHRON. *Cf.* CALLIMACHUS.

LYRA GRAECA. J. M. Edmonds. 3 Vols.

LYSIAS. W. R. M. Lamb.

MANETHO. W. G. Waddell; PTOLEMY: TETRABIBLOS. F. E. Robbins.

MARCUS AURELIUS. C. R. Haines.

MENANDER. F. G. Allinson.

MINOR ATTIC ORATORS. 2 Vols. K. J. Maidment and J. O. Burtt.

NONNOS: DIONYSIACA. W. H. D. Rouse. 3 Vols.

OPPIAN, COLLUTHUS, TRYPHIODORUS. A. W. Mair.

PAPYRI. NON-LITERARY SELECTIONS. A. S. Hunt and C. C.

Edgar. 2 Vols. LITERARY SELECTIONS (Poetry). D. L. Page.

PARTHENIUS. *Cf.* LONGUS.

PAUSANIAS : DESCRIPTION OF GREECE. W. H. S. Jones. 5 Vols. and Companion Vol. arranged by R. E. Wycherley.

PHILO. 10 Vols. Vols. I-V. F. H. Colson and Rev. G. H. Whitaker. Vols. VI-X. F. H. Colson. General Index. Rev. J. W. Earp.
Two Supplementary Vols. Translation only from an Armenian Text. Ralph Marcus.

PHILOSTRATUS : THE LIFE OF APOLLONIUS OF TYANA. F. C. Conybeare. 2 Vols.

PHILOSTRATUS : IMAGINES ; CALLISTRATUS : DESCRIPTIONS. A. Fairbanks.

PHILOSTRATUS AND EUNAPIUS : LIVES OF THE SOPHISTS. Wilmer Cave Wright.

PINDAR. Sir J. E. Sandys.

PLATO : CHARMIDES, ALCIBIADES, HIPPARCHUS, THE LOVERS, THEAGES, MINOS AND EPINOMIS. W. R. M. Lamb.

PLATO : CRATYLUS, PARMENIDES, GREATER HIPPIAS, LESSER HIPPIAS. H. N. Fowler.

PLATO : EUTHYPHRO, APOLOGY, CRITO, PHAEDO, PHAEDRUS. H. N. Fowler.

PLATO : LACHES, PROTAGORAS, MENO, EUTHYDEMUS. W. R. M. Lamb.

PLATO : LAWS. Rev. R. G. Bury. 2 Vols.

PLATO : LYSIS, SYMPOSIUM, GORGIAS. W. R. M. Lamb.

PLATO : REPUBLIC. Paul Shorey. 2 Vols.

PLATO : STATESMAN, PHILEBUS. H. N. Fowler : ION. W. R. M. Lamb.

PLATO : THEAETETUS AND SOPHIST. H. N. Fowler.

PLATO : TIMAEUS, CRITIAS, CLITOPHO, MENEXENUS, EPISTULAE. Rev. R. G. Bury.

PLOTINUS. A. H. Armstrong. 6 Vols. Vols. I-III.

PLUTARCH : MORALIA. 16 Vols. Vols. I-V. F. C. Babbitt. Vol. VI. W. C. Helmbold. Vol. VII. P. H. De Lacy and B. Einarson. Vol. VIII. P. A. Clement, H. B. Hoffleit. Vol. IX. E. L. Minar, Jr., F. H. Sandbach, W. C. Helmbold. Vol. X. H. N. Fowler. Vol. XI. L. Pearson, F. H. Sandbach. Vol. XII. H. Cherniss, W. C. Helmbold. Vol. XIV. P. H. De Lacy and B. Einarson. Vol. XV. F. H. Sandbach.

PLUTARCH : THE PARALLEL LIVES. B. Perrin. 11 Vols.

POLYBIUS. W. R. Paton. 6 Vols.

THE LOEB CLASSICAL LIBRARY

Procopius: History of the Wars. H. B. Dewing. 7 Vols.
Ptolemy: Tetrabiblos. *Cf.* Manetho.
Quintus Smyrnaeus. A. S. Way. Verse trans.
Sextus Empiricus. Rev. R. G. Bury. 4 Vols.
Sophocles. F. Storr. 2 Vols. Verse trans.
Strabo: Geography. Horace L. Jones. 8 Vols.
Theophrastus: Characters. J. M. Edmonds; Herodes, etc. A. D. Knox.
Theophrastus: Enquiry into Plants. Sir Arthur Hort. 2 Vols.
Thucydides. C. F. Smith. 4 Vols.
Tryphiodorus. *Cf.* Oppian.
Xenophon: Anabasis. C. L. Brownson.
Xenophon: Cyropaedia. Walter Miller. 2 Vols.
Xenophon: Hellenica. C. L. Brownson.
Xenophon: Memorabilia and Oeconomicus. E. C. Marchant. Symposium and Apology. O. J. Todd.
Xenophon: Scripta Minora. E. C. Marchant and G. W. Bowersock.

VOLUMES IN PREPARATION

GREEK AUTHORS

Aristides: Orations. C. A. Behr.
Musaeus: Hero and Leander. T. Gelzer and C. H. Whitman.
Theophrastus: De Causis Plantarum. G. K. K. Link and B. Einarson.

LATIN AUTHORS

Asconius: Commentaries on Cicero's Orations. G. W. Bowersock.
Benedict: The Rule. P. Meyvaert.
Justin-Trogus. R. Moss.
Manilius. G. P. Goold.

DESCRIPTIVE PROSPECTUS ON APPLICATION

CAMBRIDGE, MASS.   LONDON
HARVARD UNIV. PRESS   WILLIAM HEINEMANN LTD

8